WHEN
COURTS &
CONGRESS
COLLIDE ❧

WHEN COURTS & CONGRESS COLLIDE

The Struggle for Control of America's Judicial System ❧

CHARLES GARDNER GEYH

THE UNIVERSITY OF MICHIGAN PRESS
Ann Arbor

Copyright © by the University of Michigan 2006
All rights reserved
Published in the United States of America by
The University of Michigan Press
Manufactured in the United States of America
⊛ Printed on acid-free paper

2009   2008   2007   2006   4   3   2

No part of this publication may be reproduced, stored
in a retrieval system, or transmitted in any form
or by any means, electronic, mechanical, or otherwise,
without the written permission of the publisher.

A CIP catalog record for this book is available from the British Library.

Library of Congress Cataloging-in-Publication Data

Geyh, Charles Gardner.
    When courts and congress collide : the struggle for control of
America's judicial system / Charles Gardner Geyh.
        p.   cm.
    Includes index.
    ISBN-13: 978-0-472-09922-1 (cloth : alk. paper)
    ISBN-10: 0-472-09922-1 (cloth : alk. paper)
        1. Judicial power—United States.   2. Legislative power—United States.
I. Title.

KF5130.G49   2006
347.73′12—dc22   2005031392

To my family of origin—

Patricia Keeney Geyh,
Gardner Asahel Keeney (1898–1982), *and*
Prudence Martin Keeney (1901–91)

*—for their unqualified love and support,
from Milwaukee to Minong and back*

Contents ~

Acknowledgments ❧

THIS IS MY FIRST BOOK. That is probably why I have found myself struggling with the temptation to acknowledge those who have contributed not just to the development of this monograph but to the development of me, from J. D. Salinger and JFK to the nuns at Alverno College Elementary School and my childhood hamster, Stubby. I am pleased to report, however, that after grappling through several drafts, I have emerged, if not triumphant, then at least with my worst excesses in check.

First and foremost, I thank my spouse, Emily Field Van Tassel. I know that authors often acknowledge their partners at times like these, but I *really* need to acknowledge mine. Emily has published a body of work that is quite familiar to students of federal court history generally and judicial impeachments and resignations in particular. As originally conceived, the present book was to be a jointly authored project, and chapter 1 is indeed derived in significant part from my section of an article written by the two of us. Issues of schedule and timing ultimately conspired against our following through on plans to write the book together, but her impact on the project remains profound. I rely heavily on her scholarship throughout the chapter on impeachment, and more broadly, she has influenced the direction and scope of the work through innumerable conversations and manuscript edits. The expression of thanks that I offer here grossly understates the extent of my dependence on her support and guidance throughout the life of this project, to say nothing of my admiration and love.

A number of intrepid scholars have given generously of their time to endure and comment on drafts culminating in one or more chapters of this book, including Professors Pat Baude, Barry Friedman, Luis Fuentes-Rohwer, Mike Gerhardt, Howard Gillman, Roger Hartley, Bill Henderson, Dawn Johnsen, Mitch Pickerill, Judith Resnik, Lauren Robel, Bill Ross, Alan Tarr, Carol Tobias, and Elisabeth Zoller. It is customary to add that I take responsibility for any errors that remain, and so I do (although it seems only fair that if I followed their advice, then I should be permitted to blame them for the resulting mistakes). Thanks also go to Professors Jeannine Bell, Jim Pfander, and David Williams, for their help with my book proposal, and to Professors Fred Aman, Neal Devins, Mark Graber, and Gene Shreve and attorney David Lee, for their counsel and support. This project would not have come to fruition without Jim Reische, my editor at the University of Michigan Press, whose guidance proved indispensible and whose sense of humor made him a joy to work with.

Discussions of seemingly modest consequence at the time sometimes prove pivotal in retrospect: I would thus like to acknowledge Professor Jim Wilson, for his thoughts on constitutional conventions during the formative stages of this project, and Professor Neil Kinkopf, for his coffee, company, and conversation on constitutional norms, which served as an intellectual Club Med amid the squalor of my temporary environs. Finally, I cannot say enough about my friend and mentor Professor Steve Burbank, who was instrumental to my joining the professoriate, who deserves credit for much of whatever success I have enjoyed in this profession, and who has given tirelessly of his time to critique my work, including a draft of this book.

On a related front, I would like to thank a number of institutions for hosting conferences or programs where I developed some of the ideas expressed in this book: the American Judicature Society, the Brennan Center for Justice, the Indiana University School of Law at Bloomington, the Indiana University School of Law at Indianapolis, the Indianapolis Law Club, and the University of Pennsylvania Law School. I would also like to acknowledge the *Chicago-Kent Law Review,* the *Indiana Law Journal,* the *New York University Law*

Review, and Sage Publications, for their permission to republish, in modified form, work that I first published with them.

Assembling the primary source materials for this book required my research assistants—Matt Bruno, Philip Adam Davis, Robert Downey, Joe Ferino, Dave Giampetroni, Aleka Jones, Ryan O'Conner, Aaron Raff, Chris Rasmussen, Mickey Weber, and Barbara Zwecker—to inhale the dust of ancient records, overcome the nausea of revolving microfilm, and weather the boredom of countless hours in windowless rooms. They have my eternal gratitude, although if I were them, I would just as soon swap the gratitude for better pay and working conditions. Thanks likewise go to Patricia Gray, for her superb technical, administrative, and secretarial support, and to Lara Gose, for service above and beyond the call as my administrative assistant and in-house editor.

Throughout the gestation of this manuscript, I have worked with the American Bar Association on a variety of projects (relating to judicial independence, accountability, and conduct) that have informed the views developed here. I would like to express my deepest affection for and appreciation to Ned Madeira, who chaired two ABA commissions I was privileged to serve as reporter, in the course of which we taught each other everything we knew about judicial independence. Thanks likewise go to past ABA president A. P. Carlton, for his leadership and support of this project, and to the ABA staff—Seth Andersen, Denise Cardman, and especially Eileen Gallagher. Finally, I would like to tip my hat (if I ever wore one) to a great scholar, administrator, and friend, Dr. Luke Bierman (director of the Institute for Emerging Issues at North Carolina State and former director of the ABA Justice Center), for his years of thoughtful advice and assistance.

My perspective on the relationship between judges and legislators has been influenced to no small extent by, well, judges and legislators. I owe much to the insights and intellectual energy of Senator Joe Biden, with whom I developed a law school course on courts and Congress (at Widener University in the early 1990s) that created an early forum to explore the issues in play here. Thanks likewise go to former congressman Bob Kastenmeier, whose House Judiciary Committee's Subcommittee on Courts I served as counsel before joining the academy, whose National Commission on Judicial Discipline and

Removal I served as consultant after he left office, and whose approach to congressional oversight of the federal courts gave me my first exposure to the dynamic equilibrium—between judicial independence and accountability—that I describe and defend here. I am also indebted to Judge Bob Katzmann, for leading the way with his own pathbreaking scholarship and for lending his aid to this project, and to current professor and former judge, congressman, and White House counsel Ab Mikva, whose support was instrumental to the publication of this book and whose professional life experience—relayed via an incomparable capacity for storytelling—has considerably deepened my understanding of several events discussed in this work.

This project was generously supported with a sabbatical leave from Indiana University and by annual summer research grants from the IU School of Law. As long as I am on the subject of IU, I would like to thank my wonderful colleagues and administrators at the law school (many of whom I have already acknowledged by name), for their optimism, encouragement, and unparalleled collegiality.

Finally, I extend special thanks to my teenage daughters, Sarah Van Tassel and Hallie Geyh, without whom I would have finished this book years ago. It is better to have an incomplete manuscript than an incomplete life. I will not allude to my love and affection for them in a public place, knowing that if I did, they would gently remind me that I am a "freak" and a "loser." But I note for the record that the absence of such an allusion here is attributable solely to my fear of abuse.

Introduction ∾

This book explores the nature and extent of the federal judiciary's independence from and accountability to the United States Congress. It seeks to demonstrate that the considerable independence federal judges enjoy is attributable less to constitutional structure than to the emergence and entrenchment of institutional norms that shield the federal judiciary from congressional encroachments that could diminish the capacity of judges to follow the "rule of law" without fear or favor. As elaborated in the chapters that follow, the customary independence that these norms foster is in constructive tension with a countervailing impulse to render the judiciary acquiescent to congressional will and has given rise to a state of dynamic equilibrium in the relationship between the legislative and judicial branches of government. However, the ascendance of postlegal realist thinking, which posits that independent judges disregard the law and implement their political predilections, challenges core assumptions underlying the perceived need for an independent judiciary and puts long-standing independence norms in a state of flux, portending an uncertain future for judicial independence and the dynamic equilibrium.

AMERICANS TAKE THEIR SYSTEM of justice for granted much of the time. The aging maxims "Ours is a government of laws and not men," "All men are equal before the law," and "No man is above the law" spill from the speeches of pundits and politicians like a waterfall in the background of our collective consciousness—accepted, omnipresent, and usually ignored. By comparison with nations that have endured a history of puppet courts, judicial assassinations, and "telephone justice," the U.S. judicial system has been remarkably stable and downright boring. The mechanisms that allow for its successful operation have been upstaged by its very success. And so, as long as it seems to work, we do not worry very much about why.

This tendency toward complacency obscures the complex alchemy responsible for creating and preserving a justice system grounded in the rule of law. Such a system depends, for its success, on its judges remaining outside the control of those who would benefit if the law was disregarded and yet within the control of those who would ensure that the judges not disregard the law for the benefit of themselves or others. To complicate matters further, the line that separates those who would improperly control the courts to evade the law from those who would properly control them to uphold it blurs considerably when opinions differ and emotions flare over which case outcomes follow the law and which disregard it. It is then that complacency periodically yields to anger—at judges, whom critics accuse of usurping political power, and at the critics themselves, whom court defenders accuse of threatening the judiciary's independent judgment.

Bouts of court-directed animus have come and gone at generational intervals since the founding of the nation. The first occurred at the turn of the nineteenth century: when Thomas Jefferson succeeded John Adams as president, the Jeffersonian Republican Congress dedicated itself to undoing damage they perceived the outgoing Federalists as causing in the federal courts. A generation later, President Andrew Jackson, his supporters in Congress, and several southern states locked horns with the Marshall Court over the supremacy of the Supreme Court's authority to impose its interpretation of the U.S. Constitution on the state and federal governments. Another generation after that, a Radical Republican Congress squared off against the Supreme Court in the aftermath of the Civil War, over a number of issues pivotal to the Reconstruction agenda. Roughly twenty-five years later, near the turn of the twentieth century, congressional Populists and Progressives advocated a variety of means to restrain the courts from invalidating legislative reforms at the state and federal levels. During the 1930s, an exasperated Franklin Roosevelt invited Congress to pack the Supreme Court with additional justices, to thwart the Court's conservative majority, which had struck down several New Deal programs. The passage of another generation saw members of the Warren Court targeted for impeachment, all or in part because of their liberal-leaning decisions in civil rights and civil liberties cases.

Yet another generation has passed since the Warren Court receded into the history books, and the next round of court bashing and curbing is upon us. At the center of the latest cycle, as with each of its predecessors, is the U.S. Congress. And like earlier periods of public disaffection with the courts, the most recent period began with a series of cases decided by the Supreme Court and lower courts. Conservatives have attacked the Supreme Court for decisions that decriminalized homosexual sodomy, upheld affirmative action, and perpetuated abortion rights. They have likewise excoriated lower court decisions that forbade reciting the Pledge of Allegiance in public schools, invalidated popular voter initiatives, (temporarily) suspended California's gubernatorial recall election, and ordered a state to remove a display of the Ten Commandments from its supreme court lobby. Meanwhile, liberals have attacked the U.S. Supreme Court for its decisions in *Bush v. Gore* (which resolved the 2000 presidential election in favor of George W. Bush) and in other cases that diminished congressional power to regulate commerce, protect civil rights, or secure state compliance with federal law.

Two examples suffice to capture how vituperative recent criticism has been. From the political right of center, former federal judge and Supreme Court nominee Robert Bork has branded the "arrogantly authoritarian" Supreme Court "a band of outlaws" for its "promotion of anarchy and license in the moral order."[1] From the political left of center, legal commentator and former district attorney Vincent Bugliosi has dubbed the majority of the Court that decided *Bush v. Gore* the "felonious five," "transparent shills for the right wing of the Republican Party," and "judicial sociopaths" who "belong behind bars" for their "treasonous" behavior.[2]

Public anger over these recent decisions has given rise to any number of proposals for Congress to control the federal courts. In 1997, the Republican House majority whip proposed to "go after" liberal judicial activists in a "big way" by targeting them for impeachment.[3]

Six years later, the chairman of the Constitution Party National Committee called for the impeachment of the six-member majority of the Supreme Court that decided the homosexual sodomy case.[4] On the other side of the political aisle, the Oregon Democratic Party initiated a campaign in 2001 to impeach the Supreme Court majority that decided *Bush v. Gore.*[5]

In 2003, House Republicans began a campaign to strip the federal courts of jurisdiction to hear cases on such subjects as the Pledge of Allegiance and gay marriage.[6] In a related vein, some speculated that anger over recent decisions of the U.S. Court of Appeals for the Ninth Circuit (concerning, among other issues, the Pledge of Allegiance and the California recall election) would intensify political pressure to split the Ninth Circuit in two.[7] Later that same year, a Republican congressman introduced an appropriations bill amendment (which passed the House of Representatives) that refused to fund executive branch enforcement of judicial orders in the Pledge of Allegiance and Ten Commandments cases.[8] At about the same time, Republican legislators formed a thirteen-member task force called the House Working Group on Judicial Accountability. As described in one press account, the group will subject judges who "legislate from the bench" to "exposure, public pressure and denunciation" and may call them before Congress "to explain themselves."[9]

Court control is not a club for conservatives only. In 2001, Larry Kramer, then a chaired professor of law at the New York University School of Law and soon to be the dean at Stanford, published an op-ed in the *New York Times* in which he complained that the Supreme Court's "five conservative justices have steadily usurped the power to govern." He suggested that legitimate remedial powers available to the political branches included defiance, court packing, jurisdiction stripping, and control of the judiciary's budget, and he concluded with the plea "We need to hear from our political leaders."[10] Kramer later developed his thinking more fully in a book on the broader subject of judicial review.[11]

Despite their shrill indignation and earnest calls to recapture renegade judges, many court bashers all but concede that their sound and fury is likely to culminate in nothing. Kramer, amid pleas for Congress to rein in a dangerously conservative Supreme Court, complained of "the complacency of the citizenry in the face of such outrageous conduct,"[12] which he attributed to "the general assumption that not much can be done."[13] At roughly the same time, a conservative congressman digressed from his call for congressional action against the courts long enough to concede that Congress "for so long has been lax in standing up for the Constitution"[14] and "has given up its responsibility in [overseeing] judges and their performances on the bench."[15]

These critics have a point. No judge has ever been impeached and removed for making unpopular or outrageous decisions. There are no modern examples of Congress "packing" or abolishing a court in response to a particular case or line of cases; no evidence that Congress has ever held the judiciary's budget hostage, manipulated the judiciary's administration, or withheld a pay increase in retaliation for a court decision; and no recent episode in which Congress has deprived the federal courts of all jurisdiction to hear a particular type of case. Whereas threats to diminish and control judges are commonplace, making good on those threats is not.

One significant deviation from this tradition of congressional comity and deference has been in the area of judicial appointments, which has been intensely partisan and politicized since the Washington administration. In the last century or so, the Senate's diffused partisan wrangling over isolated nominations gradually developed into a more focused effort to control the courts' future decision making by rejecting nominees whose political ideology would likely lead them to make judicial decisions unacceptable to the Senate majority. In the past generation, that effort has moved to the front burner of American politics.

In the 1980s, President Ronald Reagan's commitment to peopling the federal courts with ideological conservatives was opposed by Senate Democrats and liberal interest groups. The conflict culminated in a pitched battle over the 1987 nomination of Robert Bork to the Supreme Court. The Democrats prevailed, but Republicans neither forgave nor forgot, and when they gained control of the Senate during Bill Clinton's presidency, they embarked on a campaign to thwart the nomination of "liberal judicial activists" to the lower federal courts, primarily by means of tactical delay. When George W. Bush became president, Senate Democrats sought to block the confirmation of ideological conservatives with strategic delays of their own, coupled with aggressive resort to filibusters and other procedural devices, making clear that the shoe was back on the other foot and had acquired cleats. Shortly before this book went to press, President Bush nominated Judge Samuel Alito to fill the vacancy created by the retirement of Justice Sandra Day O'Connor. The nomination of Alito—a darling of the political right and a demon of the political left—all but ensured a fight over nominee ideology the likes of which the nation has not seen since Bork.

So, on the one hand, Congress has been disinclined to control judicial decision making by means of impeachment or manipulation of the judiciary's budget, structure, jurisdiction, or removal. Yet, on the other hand, it has been quite willing to manipulate judicial decision making by means of the appointments process. What can explain these dual, seemingly contradictory developments?

Judicial Independence, Judicial Accountability, and Their Relationship to Constitutional Law ᴏᴠ

Each of the various means at Congress's disposal for curbing the courts derives from a power enumerated in the Constitution—to establish inferior courts, adjust the Supreme Court's jurisdiction, tax and spend, impeach and remove, or advise and consent to judicial nominations. A logical starting point in a discussion of the judiciary's independence from and accountability to Congress thus begins with a review of conventional constitutional law—that is, constitutional text and structure and court-generated doctrine.

Speeches on the American judiciary are typically larded with references to "judicial independence," but one should not take this phrase too literally. Dictionaries tell us that *independence* means "the absence of dependence"—complete autonomy and insusceptibility to external guidance, influence, or control. Federal judges, however, are neither completely autonomous nor insusceptible to external influence. They are dependent on Congress for their annual budget, subject matter jurisdiction, structure, size, and administrative and rule-making authority, and they are dependent on the executive branch for their security and for the enforcement of court orders. If judges engage in behavior (on or off the bench) that the political branches characterize as criminal, they may be prosecuted and imprisoned; if they make politically unacceptable decisions, the president and Senate may decline to appoint them to higher judicial office; if they commit "high crimes and misdemeanors," they may be impeached and removed from office; if they make decisions with which higher courts disagree, their decisions may be reversed; and if they engage in behavior that judicial councils regard as misconduct, they may be disciplined.[16]

Some scholars have dismissed judicial independence as a fiction because judges are not literally independent.[17] But saying that judicial independence does not exist because judges are not literally independent is a bit like saying that guinea pigs do not exist because they are not literally pigs. In other words, the prefatory term *judicial* contextualizes the term *independence* in important ways that qualify its meaning. For federal judges, judicial independence must be defined and qualified with at least some reference to the U.S. Constitution, Article III of which gives federal judges three guarantees: first, they are afforded tenure "during good behaviour"; second, they are assured a "compensation, which shall not be diminished"; and third, they alone are authorized to exercise "the judicial power."[18] Federal judges are thereby rendered autonomous in the limited sense that they have an enforceable monopoly over "the judicial power" and are insulated from two discrete forms of influence or control—threats to their tenure and salary. And while the phrase *judicial independence* appears nowhere in the text of the Constitution, there can be no doubt that those who drafted the document sought to render federal judges "independent," albeit in this qualified sense of the term.[19]

When judicial independence is redefined in qualified (rather than absolute) terms, the various ways in which judicial behavior is constrained do not undermine judicial independence but simply define its limits. Thus, the independence that judges are afforded by Article III is circumscribed by various forms of accountability to the political branches, to other judges, to their oaths of office, and ultimately to their own consciences. In this sense, the judiciary's independence must be defined with reference to judicial accountability, which Stephen Burbank rightly characterizes as "different sides of the same coin."[20]

The preceding discussion begs the critical question of why judicial independence is qualified by accountability rather than defined in literal or absolute terms. If judicial independence is "one of the crown jewels of our system of government" (to borrow a phrase from Chief Justice Rehnquist),[21] it would seem, superficially at least, that the bigger the jewel, the better. Likening judicial independence to a crown jewel, however, misleadingly implies that it is an end in itself, to be admired for its own intrinsic beauty. A more apt metaphor would be an industrial diamond that is employed in the service of other objectives. Most thoughtful scholars thus characterize judicial independence as an instrumental value that serves to insulate judges from the influence of pressure from the public or political branches, so that judges can fairly and impartially follow the facts, follow the law, preserve due process, or maintain the separation of powers by keeping the political branches in check through the exercise of judicial review. Reduced to its essence, then, judicial independence is instrumental in helping judges bracket out extraneous influences and uphold the "rule of law."[22] That being the case, the importance of qualifying judicial independence with accountability becomes obvious: we want judges who are independent enough of external influences to uphold the law but who are not so independent that they feel free to disregard the law altogether.

In short, we want judges who are independent and accountable, but not in the absolute sense of those terms. Rather, absolute independence and absolute accountability are at opposite ends of a continuum in which the middle ground is occupied by varying combinations of each. The trick is to determine which combination is optimal, with court-curbing proponents champing at the bit for greater accountability and opponents pushing to conserve independence. There is not a complete absence of consensus. For example, few would argue that when a judge has taken a bribe, Congress would be impinging unjustifiably on judicial independence if it held that judge individually accountable by initiating impeachment proceedings. But when a judge or a court makes a decision that is unpopular or outrageous, disagreement ends as to what Congress can or should do to ameliorate the problem.

An unhappy Congress could conceivably seek to constrain rogue judges individually or collectively, which highlights two discrete forms of independence. Thinking about judicial independence with reference to judges as individuals highlights the role independence plays in judicial decision making. It is said that if we want judges to decide cases on the basis of facts as they find them and law as they construe it to be written, we must insulate them from external influences that could corrupt their integrity or impartiality—hence the need for "decisional" or "decision-making" independence. On the other hand, thinking about judicial independence in terms of judges collectively, as a branch, shifts our focus toward the role of the judiciary in a representative democracy where the powers of government are separated. The argument goes that if the judiciary is to maintain its structural separation from the legislative and executive branches and to keep the other branches in check through the exercise of judicial review, it must be able to preserve its institutional integrity and resist encroachments—hence the need for "institutional" or "branch" independence.

The constitutional structure imposes some limits on Congress's capacity to restrict decisional and institutional independence. By guaranteeing judges tenure during good behavior and a salary that may not be diminished, Article III enables them to decide cases fairly and impartially, without fear that they will have their pay docked by an angry Congress, be denied reappointment by an angry president, or lose their next election to an angry electorate. The judicial power clause provides at least some foundation for institutional independence. By delegating "the judicial power" to the Supreme Court and inferior courts alone, the Constitution grants the federal courts collectively an exclusive reservoir of power and a measure of constitutional separation from the political branches, equipping the judiciary as an institution with a means to defend its autonomy from encroachment.

Conventional wisdom consigns branch independence to a "murky area" with "less claim in history"—that is, "a matter of considerably less importance than decisional independence."[23] Whatever autonomy the judiciary may possess by virtue of its monopoly on judicial power is diminished by Congress's constitutional authority to alter the Supreme Court's jurisdiction, to appropriate funds for court operations, and to establish and (by negative implication) disestablish the lower courts—authority that logically subsumes the lesser included powers to control court size, structure, administration, and procedure.[24] One pair of scholars thus characterize the federal system as one in which we have "independent judges" and a "dependent judiciary."[25]

If we limit ourselves to a discussion of constitutional structure, it may be true to say that the federal judiciary is guaranteed little in the way of institutional independence, but by the same token, individual judges are assured equally little in the way of decisional independence. Yes, a judge enjoys tenure during "good behaviour," but Congress decides when good behavior degenerates into impeachable high crimes and misdemeanors and whether a judicial office that it previously established is still necessary. Thus, having made one unpopular decision, a judge could find herself removed from office by impeachment or her office eliminated by legislative enactment. Yes, Congress may not diminish a judge's compensation, but it still retains control over pay raises and the budgetary resources a judge needs to do her job. Again, after making one unpopular decision, a judge could be deprived of clerks, secretaries, chambers, or office supplies and left with a salary that is never again adjusted for inflation.

The problem with structural arguments aimed at exposing the limits of institutional and decisional independence is that they are largely hypothetical. We can always speculate on the boundaries of congressional power to hold the judiciary collectively accountable by slashing its budget, stripping its jurisdiction, or obliterating its courts. We can likewise speculate on whether Congress could hold unpopular judges individually accountable by impeachment, abolition of their judgeships, or surgical strikes against their nonremunerative resources. However, we are forced to speculate only, because—as noted earlier—such manipulations occur so rarely. When it comes to exercising power to control judicial decision making, Congress has, with the important exception of judicial appointments, traditionally struck the independence-accountability balance in a way that favors the independence side of the continuum. This returns us to the question of why.

Judicial Independence, Judicial Accountability, and Their Relationship to Institutional Norms ∾

We can attribute some measure of the judiciary's autonomy to constitutional structure, but, as just noted, that is a partial explanation at best. We can attribute an additional measure of the judiciary's independence to congressional noninterference born of neglect or indifference, but that does not explain the relative constancy of noninterference over time despite periods of intense disaffection with the courts.

A more complete explanation lies in the emergence and entrenchment of customs, conventions, or norms that have guided Congress in its regulation of the federal judiciary. These customs, conventions, or norms have created for the judiciary a zone of autonomy that Congress respects in the exercise of its constitutional powers over courts and judges—a zone I refer to as "customary independence." Customary independence is derived from time-honored interpretations of constitutional and policy limits on congressional power as Congress has defined them, together with closely related notions of interbranch comity that courts and Congress have traditionally respected as a permanent or semipermanent fixture of government in a system of separated powers. Over the course of our history, Congress has slowly come to accept the role of an independent judiciary in American government. In that time, it experimented with a variety of means to control court decision making, eventually jettisoning them as antithetical to judicial independence.

What, then, explains the emergence of judicial appointments as the battlefield of choice for control of the courts, given the rejection of alternate sites? As customary independence became increasingly entrenched toward the end of the nineteenth century and as Congress gradually rejected other means at its disposal to curb the courts, the appointments process—which had always been highly politicized and comparatively unrestrained—emerged as the one remaining viable mechanism that would allow Congress to influence judicial decision making. Given the contemporaneous emergence of legal realism and its appreciation for the influence that judges' backgrounds and ideologies have on their decision making, the ascendance of the appointments process as the preferred forum for control of the federal courts became a logical development, if not a virtual inevitability.

Before launching into a study of the customs, conventions, or norms that have emerged to govern the relationship between Congress and the courts, it may be helpful to define or at least describe "norms," "customs," and "conventions," so that we know them when we see them. Generally stated, norms are "shared prescriptions or proscriptions for behavior" that "tell people what to do or not to do."[26] In the context of intragovernmental relations, Michael Gerhardt defines institutional norms as "informal agreements or arrangements that have developed over time for governing or constraining the discretion of principal actors."[27] In this book, I am concerned with two related but discrete sets of institutional agreements or arrangements: the first tells the courts what they are and are not permitted to do and so establishes the extent of their independence from Congress; the second regulates the process by which Congress develops and revises the norms that govern the courts.[28]

It is one thing to theorize about institutional norms as informal arrangements or agreements and quite another to spot them in the field. Norms tend to emerge gradually, from indistinct origins, over the course of complex social interactions within a group. They are rarely born like babies on specified dates and times, with readily identifiable features. Moreover, they can recede, mutate, disappear, or reemerge with equally intricate subtlety. Some sociologists therefore counsel "curbing historical discussions concerning the emergence of some particular norm . . . which are . . . likely to be as futile as those concerning the origin of language, or of a folk-joke."[29]

Without minimizing the difficulty of the task, there are reasons to be more optimistic about tracing the historical development of institutional norms that regulate the relationship between courts and Congress. First, the "informal" agreements or arrangements that constitute the institutional norms at issue here are elucidated by the men and women who made them, in published records of congressional debates, hearings, and reports. While one cannot always count on members of Congress saying what they mean, the fact remains that we have a transcript, which is more than we can say for those unfortunate souls dedicated to tracing the origins of a "folk-joke." Second, many of the institutional norms at issue here have been formalized in constitutions, statutes, and judicial decisions, which add to the information base. Such laws may formalize norms imperfectly from the start and fail to keep pace with them later, but they can still reveal important insights into the priorities of the founders, legislators, and judges who made them.

Studies of custom and convention in intergovernmental relations suggest some useful ways to go about detecting and describing institutional norms of the sort at issue here. In an article on interbranch custom in separation of powers adjudication, Michael Glennon explores when one branch's informal acquiescence, over time, to the established practices of another will authorize the actions of the latter. Glennon develops a useful list of six factors that contribute to the establishment of "customs" that regulate the relationship between the branches of the federal government: (1) consistency—the similarity of the unrelated events that purportedly constitute a custom; (2) numerosity—the number of times a custom has been followed; (3) duration—the length of time during which a custom has been respected; (4) density—how frequently the custom has been followed relative to its duration; (5) continuity—the regularity with which the custom is followed; and (6) normalcy—the extent to which the custom cuts across different Congresses, so as to exist independently of the personalities or political agendas of particular decision makers.[30] Although all six attributes contribute to the finding of a custom, Glennon argues that among them, only consistency is indispensable.[31]

Of interest here are particular kinds of interbranch customs: those that can explain the way judicial independence and accountability mechanisms are employed. Insofar as Congress's ultimate authority to regulate the judiciary and thereby influence its relative independence and accountability derives from the Constitution, we need to account for the role that constitutional understandings play in the development of these institutional norms or customs. James Wilson seeks to integrate this constitutional dimension into institutional customs in an article on "constitutional conventions" (a concept Wilson borrows from the British system), which he describes as "judicially unenforceable rules that combine with judicial doctrine and public opinion to regulate political behavior."[32]

The combined thinking of Gerhardt, Glennon, and Wilson provides a useful point of departure for developing the concept of customary independence. At bottom, we are looking for a series of factually comparable but otherwise unrelated historical events spanning a significant period of time, giving rise to recurring constitutional questions that relate to the independence and accountability of the judiciary and that different Congresses have resolved in similar ways, with reference to common norms, customs, or conventions.

Customary Independence and Its Relationship to Existing Literature on the Courts and Congress ~

To date, no serious attempt has been made to understand judicial independence with reference to institutional norms.[33] Political scientists have studied institutional norms, but not as they relate to judicial independence, and academic lawyers have studied judicial independence, but not as it relates to institutional norms. Political and legal scholars have, however, pursued related projects that bear note here, insofar as this book straddles the two disciplines and seeks to build on the foundations of each.

Political Science Scholarship

With exceptions, political scientists have not focused very much attention on judicial independence and accountability per se.[34] They have, however, devoted considerable time to the study of judicial behavior, with respect to which they have tended to gravitate toward one of two camps that think about judicial independence in different ways.

Attitudinalists. Jeffrey Segal and Harold Spaeth described and developed the "attitudinal" model of judicial decision making in their enormously influential work *The Supreme Court and the Attitudinal Model.*[35] In the words of Segal and Spaeth, attitudinalists maintain that "justices make decisions by considering the facts of the case in light of their ideological attitudes and values."[36] Emerging out of the legal realist and behavioralist schools, attitudinalists are deeply skeptical of claims that other considerations—such as the law or institutional pressures from within or without the judicial branch—can help to explain, in any meaningful way, the decisions judges make.

For attitudinalists, judicial independence undermines, rather than promotes, the rule of law, by enabling judges to flout the law and implement their political predilections without fear of reprisal.[37] I take issue with this point in the last chapter of this book. There is, however, an extent to which our respective projects are complementary: insofar as judges disregard the law in favor of their political proclivities (or at least insofar as judges' interpretations of the law are influenced by their political ideologies in cases where the law remains sufficiently ambiguous to accommodate conflicting views, which is how I prefer to characterize it), one must logically infer the existence of an interbranch arrangement or relationship that tolerates "independent" decision making of this kind, given that Congress has the constitutional authority to curb the courts if it were so inclined.[38] While we may disagree as to whether the customary independence Congress affords the courts is integral to preserving the rule of law or simply liberates judges to follow their ideological fancy, its existence adds explanatory force to both arguments, by developing a theoretical and empirical explanation for why the judiciary is insulated from the political branches more than is technically required by the letter of the Constitution.

Neoinstitutionalists. The second political science camp devoted to the study of judicial behavior includes a diverse array of approaches that share the common conviction that judicial decision making is more complicated than the attitudinalists make it out to be—that the political, legal, social, and cultural institutions of which judges are a part contribute to the way they think about the cases they decide. This camp traces its roots back to more traditional, "old" institutional scholarship that emerged out of the legal realist movement but predated the rise of the attitudinal school. In the introduction to a superb collection of essays, Howard Gillman and Cornell Clayton credit Thomas Koebe for unpacking the neoinstitutionalists into three subgroups.

(1) *Rational choice theorists.* This group includes Lee Epstein and Jack Knight among its leading proponents. Epstein and Knight accept the attitudinalists' premise that judges "may be primarily seekers of legal policy." They take issue, however, with the notion that judges "make choices based merely on their own political prefer-

ences"; rather, they argue that "justices are strategic actors who realize that their ability to achieve their goals (primarily policy goals) depends on a consideration of the preferences of other actors," such as Congress.[39]

(2) *Historical interpretivists.* Cornell Clayton, Howard Gillman, and Rogers Smith are among the more prominent proponents of an approach that evaluates judicial decision making with reference to "historical accounts of institutional development."[40] In their view, the norms (including, but not limited to, legal norms) that judges bring to bear in deciding cases are influenced by the institutional setting in which they find themselves; as the setting changes over time, so can the norms that motivate judicial behavior.[41] Unlike their rational choice counterparts, historical interpretivists argue that the institutions of which political actors are a part do not merely constrain the ways in which those actors implement their preferences but contribute to the formation and development of norms that shape those preferences in the first place—as a consequence of which historical interpretivists find that the forces motivating the choices judges make are more complex and varied than either attitudinalists or rational choice scholars suggest.

(3) *Social institutionalists.* This third group broadens the study of institutions further still by theorizing that "the conduct of individuals within particular institutions must be understood within the contextual web of attachments, obligations and affective bonds" created by "such broad social and cultural structures as class, race, gender and religion."[42] Presumably included within this group are devotees of the critical legal studies movement launched in the late 1970s by Roberto Unger, Duncan Kennedy, and others who hypothecate that predominantly white, male, elite judges exploit the fiction of the law's rationality and evenhandedness to perpetuate the domination of their race, gender, and class.

Unlike attitudinalists, then, the new institutionalists do not view the independence of Supreme Court justices as unfettered but accept that judicial behavior is constrained by a variety of institutional influences, ranging from a strategic need to account for the preferences of Congress and other political actors, to respect for institutional norms (including the rule of law), to the conscious or subconscious tethers of race, gender, and class. Although this book does not dwell on judicial decision making (with the partial exception of chapter 5), its approach is very much in keeping with that of the neoinstitutionalists in general and the historical interpretivists in particular, in that it evaluates the constraints on the judiciary's independence with reference to the emergence of interbranch institutional norms over time.

That said, most political science scholarship to date has focused on the Supreme Court to the virtual exclusion of the circuit and district courts—a gap this work seeks to shrink. Relative to the Supreme Court, the lower federal courts are less visible, more vulnerable to additional forms of congressional control, and more subject to the orders and administrative oversight of higher courts, which renders the independence and accountability of district and circuit judges distinct from that of their Supreme Court counterparts.

Legal Scholarship

In contrast to political scientists, academic lawyers have devoted considerably more attention to the subject of judicial independence as such.[43] With some exceptions, they have fixated (perhaps unsurprisingly) on the law, specifically on the text of the Constitution and on judicial and theoretical analyses of that text, in search of lines that delineate the outer boundaries of congressional authority to control the courts.[44] This painstaking search through constitutional text, foundational documents, judicial decisions, and constitutional theory, in an effort to find the floor beneath which Congress may not go without violating Article III, has yielded a range of conclusions, some more definitive than others. The extent of scholarly fascination with judicial doctrine in particular, however, has tended to obscure its limited scope. Congressional regulation of judges and courts typically implicates constitutional questions best characterized as political or quasi-political, because the discretion courts have afforded Congress to answer such questions is vast and sometimes exclusive. The questions at issue are not subconstitutional; rather, they are questions that courts defer to Congress and do not themselves address with an accumulated body of doctrine.

When, for example, the constitutional questions at issue concern the definition of impeachable "high crimes and misdemeanors" or the grounds on which the Senate may legitimately withhold its "consent" to a judicial nominee, Congress is, for all practical purposes, the interpreter of first and final resort.[45] When it comes to implementing the constitutional framework by enacting legislation establishing and regulating the lower federal courts, the judiciary retains an interpretive role, but Congress is afforded what has rightly been characterized as "broad discretion to structure the federal courts as it sees fit."[46] This "broad discretion" that the Constitution delegates to Congress makes questions concerning court size, jurisdiction, administration, and structure functionally quasi-political in nature. Although the Supreme Court will rule on the constitutionality of the congressional actions in question (as it will not with questions explicitly denominated "political"), it has repeatedly and emphatically deferred to Congress's plenary power to regulate lower court operations.[47] Accordingly, quasi-constitutional questions—such as whether it would be consistent with the principle of an independent judiciary in a federal system of separated, independent and interdependent powers to establish or disestablish courts, to "pack" the Supreme Court, or to give the judiciary powers of self-administration—are ones that Congress must answer without much help from court-generated doctrine.

A Dynamic Equilibrium ❧

The foregoing paragraph details some of the constitutional questions that the following chapters are dedicated to exploring, not through the interpretative lens of judicial decisions, but through the practices, proceedings, actions, and inactions of Congress. Viewing judicial independence and accountability through the eyes of Congress remains a largely untried exercise that is well worth the effort, given the profound influence that the legislative branch of government has exerted on the very nature of the judicial branch. Chapter 1 examines preliminary understandings of judicial independence and accountability from the perspective of those who drafted, ratified, and implemented the U.S. Constitution. Chapter 2 explores the emergence and entrenchment of customary independence over time, in the course of congressional oversight of court structure, jurisdiction, and administration. Chapter 3 does the same with respect to judicial impeachment. Chapter 4 details the different dynamic at work in Senate confirmation and rejection of judicial nominees.

The independence norms that Congress has come to respect in its oversight of the courts did not arise in a vacuum, and while it is illuminating to focus on the part Congress has played in the care and feeding of those norms, it would be a mistake to neglect the corresponding role of the courts in that process. As discussed in chapter 5, Congress may possess the power to render the judiciary subservient, but having concluded that doing so would be inappropriate, it has stayed its hand most of the time. Perpetuation of norms that guard against "inappropriate" or "improper" congressional intrusions upon the judiciary's autonomy has been aided by the courts' timely sensitivity and deference to Congress and the political process, which has made such intrusions largely unnecessary.

The federal courts routinely decide cases that incense discrete segments of the public, and they occasionally decide cases that rub the majority the wrong way. Rarely, however, have they so alienated themselves from Congress or the people as to compromise their institutional legitimacy. To paraphrase Lincoln, the judiciary can anger some of the people all of the time and all of the people some of the time but cannot anger all of the people all of the time without jeopardizing the independence norms that the courts themselves are acutely desirous of preserving. Thus, federal judges have avoided doing so, to some extent because the appointments process is increasingly calculated to yield judges who gravitate toward the ideological mean (as argued in chapter 4) and to some extent because judges have devised coping strategies to avert unnecessary confrontations (as argued in chapter 5).

The courts' deference to Congress is not static. Over the course of the twentieth century, independence norms became ever more deeply entrenched as Congress embarked on a long-term project to create a self-governing judicial branch—by establishing an elaborate intermediate appellate structure, creating an administrative infrastructure, delegating rule-making authority to the courts, and providing the judiciary with the means to study its operations, educate its officers and staff, and impose discipline. As court jurisdiction, caseload, and workforce have expanded throughout this period, the increasingly autonomous judicial branch has become more emboldened to challenge proposed legislation that would add to its docket burdens. Recently, the U.S. chief justice and the Judicial Conference of the United States have gone further still by publicly questioning the constitutionality of legislative proposals to which they are averse, thereby implying, at least, that if Congress enacts the legislation over their objections as lobbyists, they will later invalidate it as judges.[48] And, as noted earlier, in a series of recent decisions, the Supreme Court has begun to limit congressional power in significant ways for the first time since the Roosevelt administration.

Ultimately, the long-term relationship between Congress and the courts has been one of dynamic equilibrium, as described in chapter 6: an equilibrium fostered by respect for institutional norms has been infused with a dynamism supplied by cycles of court-directed disaffection that periodically put those norms to the test. To date, independence norms have passed these tests, adapting to meet changing needs and emerging from each challenge strengthened and revitalized. But norms can change; developments nearly a century in the making give rise to the possibility that independence norms may soon be tested as never before.

The legal realist movement of the 1920s and 1930s challenged the then conventional view that judges decided cases by divining the law from fixed and absolute principles. Legal realists posited instead that judicial decision making was influenced by any number of considerations, including, but not limited to, the law. By the latter third of the century, legal realism had given way to darker scholarly visions of judges as elites who peddle myths about equality before the law as a means to placate the underclass and perpetuate its subjugation or as juristic libertines whose decisions disregard the law and serve only to satisfy the judges' political desires. For its part, the general public has not been oblivious to these emerging schools of thought, as evidenced by recent polling data reflecting the widespread belief that judges are fairly characterized as "political" decision makers.[49]

Against this backdrop, the recent events described in this introduction may reflect more than just another cycle of ineffectual, court-directed hostility. If the public and its elected representatives come to embrace the view that judges generally are less committed to upholding the law than to implementing their personal public policy preferences and are thus little more than renegade legislators, the argument for insulating the judiciary's decision-making independence from political control all but disappears. It would be premature to claim that this day has already arrived: surveys reveal that the public continues to have confidence in its courts and believes that judges are fair, impartial, and dedicated to the law.[50] But Americans have been steeping in a culture of legal realism for long enough that it may well have begun to color the way they and their representatives in Congress think the judiciary should be governed. That factor gives rise to the possibility that the latest campaign to curb the courts may be different from its predecessors. When Congress's emerging interest in asserting greater control over the courts is coupled with the courts' emerging interest in asserting greater control over Congress, the potential for a more sustained confrontation becomes manifest.

Suffice it to say that we live in interesting times. Those desirous of disrupting the dynamic equilibrium that has moderated the relationship between the legislative and judicial branches of government, in favor of asserting greater political branch control over the federal judiciary, are in the right place at the right time to make their move, but they must overcome a constitutional understanding that has, with only occasional interruptions, governed the courts since the founding of the United States. Conversely, those desirous of conserving that equilibrium (and I count myself among them) have two centuries of inertia on their side but must be willing and able to defend the status quo against the assault of an opponent that is gaining in strength and credibility.

CHAPTER ONE

The Origins of American Judicial Independence and Accountability ℘

THERE IS AN INESCAPABLE LOGIC to beginning the story of American judicial independence at the beginning, with the founding of the nation. The "original intent" of those who conceived, drafted, ratified, or implemented the Constitution, however, does not tell us too terribly much about what judicial independence means today. When it came to providing for a judicial branch, the founders of the United States not only painted with an unusually broad brush but left their work in dire need of additional coats, which they assigned Congress to apply. This book is dedicated to demonstrating that our current conception of the judiciary's independence from Congress is the product of a developmental process two centuries in the making. That process began with the framers of the Constitution, who set a tone solicitous of the judiciary's autonomy, but who left so many details to political branch resolution as to require that the contours of the judiciary's independence be developed by subsequent generations. The net effect of describing a system of government in such general terms, with so many questions left unresolved, was to create an opportunity, if not the necessity, for conventions or customs to fill the void. Given their clear, if undeveloped, commitment to judicial independence, the founders created a constitutional climate hospitable to the subsequent development of independence norms, chronicled in later chapters of this book.

Judicial Independence Prior to the Constitutional Convention ∾

The dependence of colonial courts on the English monarch was among the flash points that sparked the Declaration of Independence. English judges had been granted tenure during "good behavior" in the 1701 Act of Settlement, as a means of protecting them against at-will discharge of the crown.[1] Colonial judges, in contrast, were made to serve at the pleasure of the king, an arrangement that, in the words of one scholar, was "met with stiff resistance from colonial legislatures and pamphleteers."[2] In Massachusetts, the English governor insisted that colonial judges remain dependent on the crown—rather than on the Massachusetts legislature for their salaries—prompting the outcry that it would be "unconstitutional for the judges to be independent of the people and dependent on the crown."[3] Such conflicts over tenure and salary ultimately gave rise to a grievance in the Declaration of Independence—that the king "has made Judges dependent on his Will alone, for the tenure of their offices, and the amount and pay-ment of their salaries."[4]

On a related front, judicial independence issues were implicated, at least indirectly, by the monarch's repeated rejection of laws enacted by state legislatures to reauthorize judicial systems in North Carolina, Pennsylvania, and Virginia.[5] These episodes brought the administra-tion of justice in the affected states to a grinding halt[6] and precipi-tated an additional grievance in the Declaration of Independence—that the king "has obstructed the Administration of Justice, by refusing his Assent to Laws for establishing Judiciary powers."[7]

One conceivable lesson that the colonists could have learned from these recurrent battles over control of the state judicial systems is that the integrity of the judicial branch and the separate power it exercises can and will be undermined unless the judiciary is afforded a measure of institutional independence. In 1776, John Adams made just such a point in a pamphlet on the Virginia Constitution, when he declared that "the judicial power ought to be distinct from both the legislative and executive, and independent upon both, that so it may be a check upon both."[8]

This view, however, did not immediately win the day. "Despite John Adams's warnings," writes Gordon Wood, "most of the early constitution-makers had little sense that judicial independence meant independence from the people."[9] In other words, the perceived "problem," as articulated in the Declaration of Independence, was not judicial dependence per se but judicial dependence on the monarch. Accordingly, the perceived "solution" to judicial dependence on the executive was not judicial independence but judicial dependence on the legislature or the electorate.

Many of the early state constitutions thus imposed judicial term limits or subjected judges to reselection, while those constitutions that established tenure during "good behavior" often gave the general assembly control over judicial salaries or subjected judges to removal upon a simple address of the legislature.[10] Wood concludes:

> These constitutional provisions giving control of the courts and judicial tenure to the legislatures actually represented the culmination of what the colonial assemblies had been struggling for in their eighteenth-century contests with the Crown. The Revolutionaries had no intention of curtailing legislative interference in the court structure and in judicial functions, and in fact they meant to increase it. As Jefferson said to Pendleton in 1776, in relation to the legislature the judge must "be a mere machine."[11]

Against this backdrop, support for judicial dependence on the legislature becomes understandable, but it remains difficult to reconcile such support with the widespread commitment to constitutional separation of legislative, judicial, and executive power. That the judiciary could be wholly dependent on the legislature and still be expected to exercise judicial power in ways that justified separating legislative from judicial power in the first place underscores how supremely trusting the fledgling states were of their legislatures and how little they had actually thought about separation of powers as it applied to the judicial branch. Julius Goebel has observed, "For all the anxieties to make explicit the fundamentals proper to a constitution, the judicial generally came off with little more than an honorable mention because these anxieties were everywhere spent upon making less of the executive and more of the legislative branch."[12]

Despite their good intentions, concluded Goebel, the framers of the state constitutions failed to recognize that "provisions for salary and tenure designed to assure the independence of judges were insufficient safeguards for the independence of the judicial function itself."[13] In the years following the Declaration of Independence, a series of events deflated support for judicial dependence on the legislature and the electorate and created momentum for greater judicial independence. In 1784, a New York court effectively struck down state legislation as contrary to the law of nations, prompting an unsuccessful attempt to remove the opinion writer.[14] In 1786, a comparable exercise of judicial review by the Rhode Island Superior Court culminated in a successful effort by the legislature to remove the judges who decided the case.[15]

These and like events catalyzed considerable support for two discrete forms of judicial independence by the eve of the Constitutional Convention: (1) the decision-making independence of individual judges to resist political branch interference with their rulings in isolated cases and (2) the institutional independence of the judicial branch to resist political branch encroachments on judicial power. On the one hand, in a speech at the Pennsylvania ratification convention in 1787, James Wilson made the case for the former species of independence, arguing that Article III tenure and salary protections were needed to give federal judges the independence state judges lacked, to enforce individual rights impartially.

> [I]t has often been a matter of surprise, and frequently complained of even in Pennsylvania, that the independence of the judges is not properly secured. The servile dependence of the judges, in some of the states that have neglected to make proper provision on this subject, endangers the liberty and property of the citizen; and I apprehend that, whenever it has happened that appointment has been for a less period than during good behaviour, this object has not been sufficiently secured.[16]

Thomas Jefferson, on the other hand, had become troubled by the judiciary's incapacity as an institution to resist legislative encroachments on the judicial power. His 1776 pronouncement that the judiciary should be "a mere machine" for the legislature was eclipsed eight years later by the concern (albeit a fleeting one, in a career marked more by hostility to than support for judicial independence) that his state judiciary now lacked the independence needed to exercise judicial power without legislative branch interference.

> [Under the Virginia Constitution, t]he judiciary . . . members were left dependant on the legislative, for their subsistence in office, and some of them for their continuance in it. If therefore the legislature assumes . . . judiciary powers, no opposition is likely to be made; nor, if made, can it be effectual; because in that case they may put their proceedings into the form of an act of assembly, which will render them obligatory on the other branches. They have accordingly, in many instances, decided rights which should have been left to judiciary controversy.[17]

In sum, events leading up to the Constitutional Convention created a perceived need for judges to be independent individually as decision makers and collectively as a separate branch of government. The distinction between these two forms of independence was, however, conflated to a considerable extent, because the one sustained threat to state judicial independence during this period—manipulation of judicial tenure and salary—simultaneously undermined decision making and structural independence. With all eyes focused on threats to tenure and salary, comparatively little attention was paid to other ways in which the legislature could compromise the integrity of the judicial branch, such as by manipulating the courts' duties or nonremunerative resources. To the extent such issues arose among the states, judicial review provided an apparent remedy: judges otherwise secure in their stations could simply invalidate unconstitutional encroachments on their institutional autonomy.

Thus, for example, in January 1788, the Virginia legislature enacted a statute that established district courts by imposing on "the judges of the high court of appeals" the duty to "attend the [district] courts, allotting among themselves the districts they shall respectively attend."[18] In a "Respectful Remonstrance of the Court of Appeals," the Virginia High Court of Appeals declared the act unconstitutional.

At the outset, the court observed, "The propriety and necessity of the independence of the judges is evident in reason and the nature of their office."[19] Judges must be dependent on neither the government nor the people, the court continued: "And this applies more forcibly, to exclude a dependence on the legislature; a branch, of whom, in cases of impeachment, is itself a party."[20] The act in question, by imposing on the judges duties that, "though not changed as to their subjects, are yet more than doubled, without any increase of salary,"[21] was nothing short of "an attack upon the independency of the judges."[22]

> For vain would be the precautions of the Founders of our government to secure liberty, if the legislature, though restrained from changing the tenure of judicial offices, are at liberty to compel a resignation . . . by making it a part of the official duty to become hewers of wood, and drawers of water: Or, if, in case of a contrary disposition . . . , by lessening the duties, render offices, almost, sinecures: the independence of the judiciary is, in either case, equally annihilated.[23]

Accordingly, the Virginia court concluded that "the constitution and the act are in opposition and cannot exist together" and that "the former must control the operation of the latter."[24]

In the contemporaneous debate over ratification of the U.S. Constitution in Virginia, Patrick Henry alluded to the preceding remonstrance[25] in support of his argument that an independent judiciary was needed to exercise judicial review and that judicial review was needed to preserve an independent judiciary.

> Yes, sir, our judges opposed the acts of the legislature. We have this landmark to guide us. They had fortitude to declare that they were the judiciary, and would oppose unconstitutional acts. Are you sure that your federal judiciary will act thus? Is that judiciary as well constructed, and as independent of the other branches, as our state judiciary? Where are your landmarks in this government? I will be bold to say you cannot find any in it.[26]

The landmark that Henry sought for federal court exercise of judicial review was later supplied in *Marbury v. Madison*.[27] Before federal judicial review could enable otherwise independent judges to resist encroachments on their institutional independence, however, a second landmark was also needed—one in support of the proposition that legislative encroachments on the judicial branch, akin to those deemed contrary to the Virginia Constitution in the preceding remonstrance, would likewise be declared invalid under the U.S. Constitution. As discussed shortly, delegates to the Constitutional Convention may have unwittingly obscured this second landmark by delegating to Congress more regulatory authority over the courts than was consistent with the delegates' expectation that the judiciary would possess the means to rebuff assaults on its institutional integrity.

Judicial Independence at the Constitutional Convention ∽

In the years leading up to the Constitutional Convention, threats to judicial independence—in its institutional and decision-making forms—had been largely confined to issues of judicial tenure and salary. It is therefore unsurprising that efforts relating to the protection of judicial independence were focused on insulating judicial tenure and salary from political branch manipulation. Accordingly, the ninth resolution of the Virginia delegation to the Constitutional Convention proposed that federal judges "hold their offices during good behavior" and receive a "compensation for their services, in which no increase or diminution shall be made so as to affect the persons actually in office at the time."[28]

The Good Behavior Clause

The good behavior clause remained essentially intact throughout the Constitutional Convention and was directly challenged only once. On August 27, 1787, John Dickinson moved to follow the good behavior clause with a proviso that judges "may be removed by the Executive on the application [by] the Senate and House of Representatives."[29] The motion met with overwhelming opposition, despite the prevalence of comparable restrictions on judicial tenure in many state constitutions established just a decade earlier.[30] James Madison's notes reported Gouverneur Morris as arguing that it was "a contradiction in terms to say that the Judges should hold their offices during good behavior, and yet be removable without a trial," leading Morris to conclude that it would be "fundamentally wrong to subject Judges to so arbitrary an authority."[31] James Wilson agreed, saying, "The Judges would be in a bad situation if made to depend on every gust of faction which might prevail in the two branches of our Gov[ernmen]t";[32] Edmund Randolph likewise objected on the grounds that the amendment would "weaken[] too much the independence of the Judges."[33] Dickinson's motion was overwhelmingly defeated by a vote of seven delegations to one.

The Compensation Clause

The compensation clause, as proposed by the Virginia delegation, was modified at the Constitutional Convention to permit periodic increases in judicial salaries. The original resolution forbade upward as well as downward adjustments. The debate on the modification underscored the tension between two competing aims: to insulate judicial salary from legislative manipulation and to permit the legislature to increase judicial pay to ensure that judges receive salaries commensurate with their status as members of an independent branch of government.

On July 18, 1787, Gouverneur Morris moved to permit periodic increases in judicial salaries, on the grounds that "the value of money" might change during a judge's tenure, as might "the style of living" and the volume of judicial business, all of which could make upward adjustment of judicial salaries necessary.[34] James Madison opposed the amendment, on the grounds that "[w]henever an increase is wished by the Judges, or may be in agitation in the legislature, an undue complaisance in the former may be felt towards the latter" and that "it will be improper even so far to permit a dependence."[35] Madison, unmoved by the concern that judicial salaries would need to be adjusted for inflation, suggested that a simple solution would be to establish compensation "by taking for a standard wheat or some other thing of permanent value."[36] Morris's motion carried, but on August 27, Madison moved to have the bar on increases in judicial salaries reinstated. Charles Pinckney opposed Madison's motion, arguing, "The importance of the Judiciary will require men of the first talents:

large salaries will therefore be necessary, larger than the U.S. can allow in the first instance."[37] Granted, incoming judges could be appointed at higher salaries; nevertheless, Pinckney "did not think it would have a good effect or a good appearance, for new Judges to come in with higher salaries than the old ones."[38] Madison's motion was defeated.

The Judicial Power Clause

In addition to the good behavior and compensation clauses, the ninth resolution of the Virginia delegation began by providing that "a national judiciary be established," language that would be amended over the course of the Constitutional Convention to state that "[t]he judicial Power of the United States, shall be vested in one supreme Court, and in such inferior Courts as the Congress may from time to time ordain and establish."[39] The judicial power clause, as finally approved, did not establish the lower federal courts but merely authorized Congress to establish them. Contemporary acceptance of Congress's authority to regulate the lower federal courts' practice, procedure, and administration derives from its power to constitute (or not to constitute) the federal courts. This power, when taken in combination with the last clause of Article I, section 8 of the U.S. Constitution, which authorizes Congress to "make all laws which shall be necessary and proper for carrying into execution the foregoing powers," is understood to give Congress the authority to regulate the operations of whatever lower courts it sees fit to create.[40] The framers of the Constitution decided to authorize Congress to establish the lower federal courts rather than to have the Constitution establish them directly, dramatically limiting the scope of the judiciary's guaranteed institutional autonomy. Even so, this limitation appears not to have been an intended consequence so much as a side effect of a decision aimed at reducing tension in the relationship between state and federal power.

As introduced, the Virginia delegation's ninth resolution provided "that a national judiciary be established," without any mention of the Supreme Court or the lower courts.[41] On June 4, 1787, when the resolution was initially considered, the first clause was amended (and later approved as amended) to state that the delegation "[r]esolved that a National Judiciary be established, to consist of one supreme tribunal, and of one or more inferior tribunals."[42] Early in the proceedings on June 5, the phrase "one or more" was deleted,[43] so that the resolution, as it stood, provided for the establishment of a supreme court and an unspecified number of inferior courts.[44] Later that day, John Rutledge moved for reconsideration of the clause establishing inferior tribunals. According to Madison's notes, Rutledge argued that "the State Tribunals might and ought to be left in all cases to decide in the first instance" and that establishing lower federal courts would make "an unnecessary encroachment on the jurisdiction [of the States]."[45] Madison objected, arguing that "[a]n effective Judiciary establishment commensurate to the legislative authority, was essential,"[46] but Rutledge prevailed (on a close vote), and the phrase was deleted.

James Wilson and James Madison then moved to add a clause to the resolution, providing "that the National Legislature be empowered to institute inferior tribunals." According to Madison's notes, "[t]hey observed that there was a distinction between establishing such tribunals absolutely, and giving a discretion to the Legislature to establish or not establish them," and they "repeated the necessity of some such provision." Pierce Butler protested that "[t]he people will not bear such innovations" and that "[t]he states will revolt at such encroachments," but the motion carried by an overwhelming margin.

The issue of whether to grant Congress the power to establish inferior tribunals was revisited on July 18. Steadfast opponents argued that federal trial courts were unnecessary and would interfere with the operation of state courts.[47] Equally steadfast proponents argued that federal trial courts posed no threat to state courts and were essential to the administration of national laws.[48] Only the ambivalent delegate Roger Sherman alluded to the provision as a delegation of power to Congress, and he did so for the limited purpose of expressing his "wish[] [that Congress] make use of the State Tribunals whenever it could be done."[49]

In short, the decision to make the creation of the lower federal courts a matter of congressional prerogative rather than constitutional mandate was the product of a political compromise designed to deflect the Antifederalist fear that a national judiciary would usurp the role of the state courts. Little, if any, attention appears to have been given to the impact of that decision on the relationship between

Congress and the federal courts, on the limits of Congress's regulatory authority over the judiciary, or on the extent to which that regulatory authority could be exploited to constrain judicial independence. Rather, concern over the judiciary's dependence on Congress was confined largely to insulating judicial tenure and salary from political branch control. The delegates apparently gave no thought to the judiciary's dependence on Congress for nonremunerative resources, such as building, clerical, and circuit-riding expenses, which Congress could manipulate to the same effect as salaries. Nor did they appear to consider the possibility that congressional control over court structure, size, practice, procedure, or administration might be exploited to compromise the judiciary's institutional integrity.

This oversight is, to some extent, understandable. As previously discussed, threats to judicial independence in the years leading up to the Constitutional Convention were limited largely to legislative manipulation of judicial tenure and salary. With respect to manipulation of the judiciary's nonremunerative resources, it must be remembered that the monies appropriated to the lower courts, over and above judicial salaries, were relatively meager in the early years of the federal judiciary, and the possibility that such limited resources would or could be manipulated may not have been anticipated.[50] Other threats—to the extent they arose—could presumably be rebuffed through judicial review. James Madison's notes reflect that Elbridge Gerry prevailed on just such a point in opposing Madison's proposed "council of revision," which would have established a council comprised of judges and others empowered to veto proposed legislation: "Mr. Gerry doubts whether the Judiciary ought to form a part of [the council of revision], as they will have a sufficient check agst. encroachments on their own department by their exposition of the laws, which involved a power of deciding on their Constitutionality."[51]

The delegates never focused on the possibility that the courts' authority to invalidate congressional encroachments on the judicial branch might be impaired by delegating to Congress the decision of whether to establish inferior courts, because that was the product of a compromise struck with Antifederalists for an unrelated purpose. To the extent that the delegates nevertheless operated on the unstated assumption that the judicial power clause authorized Congress not only to establish the federal courts but also to regulate their operation, the delegates do not appear to have thought that such a power would undermine the judiciary as a coequal branch of government. To the contrary, the Constitutional Convention was rife with discussion of the delegates' intention to establish three separate, structurally independent departments of government. Madison's notes of his own words at the convention are illustrative: "If it be a fundamental principle of free Govt. that the Legislative, Executive & Judiciary power should be separately exercised; it is equally so that they be independently exercised."[52]

The extent of the delegates' resolve to preserve the independent institutional identity of the judicial branch was manifested in their repeated rejection of the previously mentioned proposal for a council of revision. Despite several attempts by James Madison and others to win acceptance for a council of revision, the proposal was defeated, in part because it was feared that having judges play a formal role in enacting laws they would later interpret might compromise the structural independence and separation of the judicial branch.[53] The perceived coequality of the three branches was further underscored when the Committee of Detail revised the first clause of Article III to vest "the judicial power" in the Supreme Court and whatever lower courts Congress established.[54] By conforming Article III to parallel language in Article II (vesting "the executive power" in the president) and Article I (vesting "all legislative powers" in Congress), the delegates highlighted the parity they sought to establish among the branches.

I am not suggesting that the delegates perceived the judiciary to be "coequal" in the sense of being as powerful or as critical to the day-to-day operation of government as the other branches—such a conclusion is belied by the judiciary's rank in the constitutional hierarchy as the branch relegated to the third article. Nor do I suggest that the delegates devoted as much reflection and energy to crafting the language establishing the third branch as they devoted to the other two. To the contrary, available evidence supports the following conclusion from Julius Goebel:

> [T]o some delegates, provision for a national judiciary was a matter of theoretical compulsion rather than of practical necessity. In

other words, it was received more in deference to the maxim of separation than in response to clearly formulated ideas about the role of a national judicial system and its indispensability.[55]

The delegates were committed to an independent judicial branch, but theirs was a commitment in concept only. Unhappy experiences with judicial dependence on the crown prior to the Revolution had given way to equally unhappy experiences with judicial dependence on the legislatures afterward, leaving the delegates desirous of decision-making and structural judicial independence as a theoretical matter, but with precious little practical experience to guide them. In the absence of an established judicial independence culture, it was inevitable that the delegates would fix the tenure and salary problems they had recently encountered in their respective states and otherwise devote minimal attention to addressing speculative threats to independence, threats for which they had little or no precedent.

Contemporary commentators sometimes argue that the authority that Article III delegates to Congress for establishing inferior courts and regulating the jurisdiction and (implicitly) the size of the Supreme Court indicates that the framers of the Constitution intended to give the judiciary no structural independence over and above that afforded by life tenure, a fixed salary, and the exclusive right to exercise "judicial power."[56] Such an argument views eighteenth-century developments through a twenty-first-century lens. All evidence suggests that the Constitutional Convention delegates were committed to a structurally independent judicial branch. Their failure to protect the judiciary's structural independence by additional means may be a function more of their lack of experience, foresight, and time than of their lack of commitment to structural independence in principle.

Judicial Accountability and the Impeachment Clauses

Whereas the delegates to the Constitutional Convention may have devoted little intellectual energy to exploring the subtleties of judicial independence and its relationship to congressional power, they paid even less attention to judicial accountability. To the extent that they discussed it at all, they did so in the context of drafting the impeachment clauses. Even then, their focus was on the president and on whether subjecting him to impeachment and removal at the hands of Congress (they considered and rejected lodging the impeachment power with the Supreme Court and the state legislatures) was unnecessary (given that the president was already subject to "removal" in periodic elections) or undesirable (insofar as it would create a dependency of the second branch on the first).

Apart from sporadic acknowledgment that judges would be subject to impeachment procedures,[57] Madison's notes of the convention debates make meaningful reference to judicial impeachment only once—and even then as a foil for distinguishing presidential impeachment. On July 20, 1787, Rufus King argued that judges, but not presidents, should be subject to removal by impeachment.

> It had been said that the Judiciary would be impeachable. But it should have been remembered at the same time that the Judiciary hold their places not for a limited time, but during good behaviour. It is necessary therefore that a forum should be established for trying misbehaviour. Was the Executive to hold his place during good behaviour?—The Executive was to hold his place for a limited term like the members of the Legislature. Like them . . . he would periodically be tried for his behaviour by his electors, who would continue or discontinue him in trust according to the manner in which he had discharged it. Like them therefore, he ought to be subject to no intermediate trial, by impeachment. He ought not to be impeachable unless he hold his office during good behavior.[58]

Implicit in King's observation is the hint of an underlying consensus on the need for judicial—as distinguished from presidential—impeachment.

As to the behaviors for which a judge could be held accountable in the impeachment process, relevant discussion of impeachable offenses occurred almost exclusively in the context of debates on presidential impeachment. One somewhat elliptical exception occurred when Charles Pinckney proposed the creation of a council of state to be comprised of specified officers, including the chief justice, each of whom, Pinckney asserted, "shall be liable to impeachment & removal from office for neglect of duty malversation, or corruption."[59] Otherwise, on July 20, the convention approved a preliminary proposal subjecting the president to removal by impeachment for "mal-practice or neglect of duty."[60] Edmund Randolph argued that an impeachment mechanism was necessary to remedy the president's "great opportunitys of abusing his power."[61] Gouverneur Morris opined, "the Executive ought . . . to be impeachable for treachery; Corrupting his electors, and incapacity were other causes of impeachment."[62] Gunning Bedford worried that "an impeachment would reach misfeasance only, not incapacity," and he urged the inclusion of some means to remove a president for senility and insanity.[63]

Toward the end of the convention, it was proposed that impeachable offenses be limited to treason and bribery.[64] On September 8, George Mason moved to add "maladministration" to the list, arguing that "[a]ttempts to subvert the Constitution may not be Treason" but should be impeachable.[65] James Madison opposed Mason's motion, arguing that so vague a standard for impeachment would "be equivalent to a tenure during pleasure of the Senate."[66] As a compromise, Mason amended his motion without further explanation, substituting language that subjected civil officers to impeachment for "other high crimes & misdemeanors."[67]

The implication would seem to be that the phrase "high crimes & misdemeanors" was understood to reach "attempts to subvert the constitution" but did not reach so far as to establish "tenure during pleasure of the Senate." In a number of respects, the drafters of the Constitution put a "uniquely American stamp"[68] on the impeachment process they devised, but "high crimes & misdemeanors" had English antecedents that imbued the phrase with a preexisting meaning, as Michael Gerhardt explains.

> [I]n the English experience prior to the drafting and ratification of the Constitution, impeachment was considered a political proceeding, and impeachable offenses were political crimes. For instance, Raoul Berger found that the English practice treated "[h]igh crimes and misdemeanors as *political* crimes against the state." . . . In England, the critical element of injury in an impeachable offense was injury to the state. The eminent legal his-

torian, Blackstone, traced this peculiarity to the English law of treason, which distinguished "high" treason, which was disloyalty against some superior, from "petit" treason, which was disloyalty to an equal or inferior. According to Arthur Bestor, "[t]his element of injury to the commonwealth—that is, to the state and its constitution—was historically the criterion for distinguishing a 'high' crime or misdemeanor from an ordinary one."[69]

On September 14, the convention fended off one final attempt to expand Congress's impeachment power over the president. John Rutledge and Gouverneur Morris moved "that persons impeached be suspended from their office until they be tried and acquitted." Madison objected:

> The President is made too dependent already on the Legislature, by the power of one branch to try him in consequence of an impeachment by the other. This intermediate suspension, will put him in the power of one branch only. They can at any moment, in order to make way for the functions of another who will be more favorable to their views, vote a temporary removal of the existing magistrate.[70]

Madison's objection won the day, and the motion was defeated.

Although the Constitutional Convention fixated on presidential, not judicial, impeachment, the provisions they devised were unitary and applicable to both executive and judicial branch officials. The convention's efforts to limit the impeachment power so as to protect the president from becoming overly dependent on Congress thus served equally (if serendipitously) to benefit the judiciary's independence.

Judicial Independence in the Ratification Debates ◊

The ratification debates reinforce, amplify, and in some cases qualify the "original understanding" of Article III. The Federalist Papers underscore the influence of Montesquieu, Adams, and other likeminded theorists on the framers of the judiciary article. In these papers, Alexander Hamilton refers to the independence of the judiciary as a means to resist encroachments by Congress and the president and thereby keep the political branches in check. He makes the point first in defense of the good behavior clause.

> If, then, the courts of justice are to be considered as the bulwarks of a limited Constitution against legislative encroachments, this consideration will afford a strong argument for the permanent tenure of judicial offices, since nothing will contribute so much as this to that independent spirit in the judges which must be essential to the faithful performance of so arduous a duty.[71]

He then makes the point in defense of the compensation clause.

> Next to the permanency in office, nothing can contribute more to the independence of judges than a fixed provision for their support. . . . [A] power over a man's subsistence amounts to a power over his will. And we can never hope to see realized in practice the complete separation of the judicial from the legislative power, in any system which leaves the former dependent for pecuniary resources on the occasional grants of the latter.[72]

With respect to the good behavior clause, prominent Antifederalists agreed that life tenure was a necessary and appropriate means to ensure judicial independence.[73] The compensation clause likewise drew only occasional fire. Of greater concern to the Antifederalists was the fact that the Constitution did not counterbalance judicial independence with a more powerful institutional check that would ensure judicial accountability.

> [J]udges under this system will be independent in the strict sense of the word. . . . [T]here is no power above them that can control their decisions, or correct their errors. There is no authority that can remove them from office for any errors or want of capacity, or lower their salaries, and in many cases their power is superior to that of the legislature.[74]

In the minds of these Antifederalists, an insufficiently accountable federal judiciary would, through the exercise of judicial review, usurp the role of Congress. The best known of the Antifederalists, writing under the pen name "Brutus," argued, "If . . . the legislature pass any laws, inconsistent with the sense the judges put upon the constitution, they will declare it void; and therefore in this respect their power is superior to that of the legislature."[75] Moreover, Brutus concluded, impeachment is unavailable to remedy such judicial excesses, because judges are "removable only for crimes," and "errors in judgment" are not crimes in the absence of "wicked and corrupt motives."[76]

Alexander Hamilton responded to this charge in the Federalist Papers. First, Hamilton agreed that the federal courts would possess the power to void unconstitutional acts of Congress.

> The complete independence of the courts of justice is peculiarly essential in a limited Constitution. By a limited Constitution, I understand one which contains certain specified exceptions to the legislative authority. . . . Limitations of this kind can be preserved in practice no other way than through the medium of courts of justice, whose duty it must be to declare all acts contrary to the manifest tenor of the Constitution void.[77]

Second, Hamilton argued that this power posed no real threat to Congress. "[T]he supposed danger of judiciary encroachments on the legislative authority . . . is in reality a phantom," he declared. Conceding that "[p]articular misconstructions and contraventions of the will of the legislature may now and then happen," Hamilton was nevertheless confident that "they can never be so extensive as to amount to an inconvenience," given the "comparative weakness" of the judicial branch (an allusion to its lack of control over sword or purse) and the availability of impeachment.

> There never can be danger that the judges, by a series of deliberate usurpations on the authority of the legislature, would hazard the united resentment of the body intrusted with it, while this body was possessed of the means of punishing their presumption by degrading them from their stations.[78]

At first blush, Brutus and Hamilton appear to disagree as to whether impeachment and removal would be available to remedy bad judicial decision making. A closer look, however, reveals that their interpretations are in accord. Hamilton and Brutus agreed that judicial "errors in judgment" (Brutus's phrase) or "misconstructions and contraventions of the legislature" (Hamilton's phrase) are not high crimes and misdemeanors, subject to impeachment—although Brutus may have wished it were otherwise. These men were likewise in accord that a "series of deliberate usurpations on the authority of the legislature" (Hamilton's phrase), which would clearly imply the presence of "wicked or corrupt motives" (Brutus's phrase), would subject judges to impeachment. In short, the Federalist Papers and the Antifederalist Papers reinforce the view, apparently shared at the Constitutional Convention, that impeachment and removal were available to remedy crimes politically defined—including abuse of judicial decision-making power[79]—but would not reach simple errors in judgment in isolated cases.[80]

The ratification debates thus reflect an appreciation for the tension and balance the Constitution created between accountability and independence. Like the Constitutional Convention debates, however, discussions of the perceived need for judicial accountability to counterbalance life tenure, nonreducible salaries, and judicial review began and ended with the impeachment mechanism. Noticeable by its absence from the debates over judicial accountability is any meaningful discussion of Congress's general powers to organize the judicial branch.

Most explications of the clause authorizing Congress to establish the lower courts characterized it not as a means to regulate court operations but as a means to adjust the size of the lower court system in response to changing circumstances the framers could not anticipate and to avoid cluttering the Constitution with details.[81] There was, however, some sporadic recognition that Congress's power to establish the courts subsumed a power to regulate them. One prominent Antifederalist, writing as "the Federal Farmer," saw "some good things" in Article III, one being that "[t]he inferior federal courts are left by the constitution to be instituted and regulated altogether as the legislature shall judge best."[82] James Monroe made a similar point in the course of the Virginia ratification debates.

> It will therefore be the duty of Congress to organize this branch, by the establishment of such subordinate courts, . . . in such manner as shall be found necessary to support the authority of the gov-

ernment. . . . What mode may be best calculated to accomplish this end, belongs to that body to determine.[83]

This occasional recognition that the congressional power to establish the courts may have subsumed the power to regulate them did not, however, give rise to the perception that the power was a tool for promoting judicial accountability or confining judicial independence. At most, it was seen as a power to serve the greater good of the national government by enabling Congress to contour the size, shape, and operation of the judicial branch to meet the changing needs of the nation. As a consequence, the contemporary view that such regulatory authority engenders a dependence of the judicial branch on the legislative branch[84] was lost on the framers of the Constitution. Edmund Pendleton was therefore able to opine that "the power of that Judiciary must be coextensive with the legislative power" and to credit the good behavior and compensation clauses for "secur[ing] an important point—the independency of the judges," while adding, without apparent irony, that "Congress must be the judges" of whether to establish inferior courts and "may find reasons to change and vary them as experience shall dictate."[85] For Pendleton, the operating assumption was that tenure during good behavior and a salary that could not be diminished were all that was necessary to preserve judicial independence; the possibility that Congress could undermine the independence of the judicial branch by exploiting its power to "change and vary" court structure and nonremunerative resources appears not to have occurred to him.

In short, a study of the Constitutional Convention and the ratification debates reveals that the founders of the United States shared an aspiration for the judiciary to be one of three "coequal" branches of government, in the sense of being equally separate, equally independent, and equally capable of resisting encroachments from the other two branches. Tenure and salary protections alone were perceived to be the necessary and sufficient means to guarantee independence for both the individual judges and the judicial branch. The founders' theory was that individual judges insulated by tenure and salary protections would resist unauthorized political branch incursions upon the structural independence of the judicial branch, through the exercise of judicial review. In the founders' minds, since the Constitution provided for a structurally independent judicial branch, any incursions on that independence would necessarily be unauthorized. By delegating to Congress the power to establish inferior courts, however, the framers of the Constitution may have inadvertently authorized Congress to undermine the judiciary's structural independence, by empowering Congress to manipulate court structure, practice, procedure, jurisdiction, administration, and nonremunerative resources.

The explanation for this inadvertent oversight is at least threefold. First, threats to judicial independence in the years leading up to the Constitutional Convention and the ratification debates had been limited largely to threats against tenure and salary. Other threats to the judiciary's institutional integrity had been insufficiently frequent to prompt vigilance in guarding against more speculative political branch encroachments. Second, authorizing Congress to establish inferior courts (or not) was the product of a compromise in a disagreement over intersystem, not interbranch, relations. As a result, when the fight between those who wanted federal trial courts and those who wanted only state trial courts was settled by deferring the issue for congressional resolution, the extent to which that compromise authorized the legislative branch to impose its will on the judicial branch escaped notice.

Third, the founders' conceptual commitment to an independent judicial branch was a reaction to bad prior experiences with dependent judiciaries rather than the outgrowth of a preexisting culture of judicial independence. As a consequence, the delegates lacked the experience and enthusiasm needed to devote as much attention to establishing the third branch of government as they had given the first two. Indeed, the compromise to postpone deliberation over the fate of the inferior courts by delegating the task to Congress without regard to the implications for the balance of power between the legislative and judicial branches underscores the founders' comparatively tepid interest in plumbing the depths of the subject.

Judicial Independence and the Judiciary of 1789 ∽

When the Constitutional Convention delegates authorized Congress to establish inferior courts, there is no indication that they did so with the intention of creating a new mechanism for Congress to hold the courts accountable for their behavior or to circumscribe their independence. The notion that Congress's power to establish the courts subsumed the power to make the third branch of government dependent on the first was so unfamiliar that some feared the opposite was true—that the Constitution had left Congress without power to structure and oversee the courts in any meaningful way. Samuel Osgood, who would later serve as the first postmaster general, raised this concern in a letter written in the aftermath of the ratification.

> The Arrangement of the Judicial should be left perfectly free for the Legislature, for otherwise however inconvenient the Manner of administering Justice may be found, there can be no legal Remedy other than by an Appeal to those who can alter the Constitution itself. There was a Necessity of drawing some Kind of a Line between the General & the State Judiciarys. The Line being drawn, the Powers of arranging the general Judiciary ought to have been vested solely in the Legislature. But they are not; Rights are vested in the Judiciary which may affect the Happiness of the People extremely & it is not in the Power of the Legislature or the Judiciary to alter them.[86]

When the First Federal Congress convened to draft and enact the Judiciary Act of 1789, attitudes had not changed. Those supporting the act construed their authority to establish inferior courts not as a discretionary power over the life or death of the federal judiciary, to be suspended above it like the sword of Damocles, but as a duty to implement the constitutional framework. Debates over the bill in the House (Senate debates were not transcribed) reflect the surprisingly widespread view that the Constitution left Congress with no choice but to establish inferior courts—though two years earlier, the founders had rejected a proposal directing Congress to establish inferior courts, in favor of the "Madisonian compromise," which was explicitly designed to give Congress the latitude not to establish inferior courts at all.

Many members of Congress focused on the pronouncement of Article III, Section 1, that the judicial power "shall" (not "may") be vested in the Supreme Court and in whatever inferior courts Congress may establish. Congress thus had no choice but to vest federal judicial power, the argument went, and could only vest it in Article III courts. Vesting judicial power in the Supreme Court alone was not an option, since Article III, Section 2, clearly contemplated that the Supreme Court would exercise appellate jurisdiction. If the Supreme Court were to decide appeals, those appeals had to come from somewhere, and since many of the state trial courts lacked Article III powers and protections, Congress lacked the authority to vest judicial power there. Accordingly, the argument concluded, Congress had no choice but to establish inferior federal courts.[87] Even some opponents of federal trial courts grudgingly conceded what they perceived to be an ineluctable constitutional mandate to create them. Representative Aedanus Burke professed to have "turned himself about to find some way to extricate himself from this measure," but "which ever way he turned, the constitution still stared him in the face, and he confessed he saw no way to avoid the evil."[88]

In an exhaustive study of the issue, Michael Collins argues that contrary to the accepted wisdom that Article III gives Congress the discretion to create inferior federal courts or not, the dominant view at the time was that the Constitution compelled their creation.[89] Collins acknowledges that such a view is difficult to reconcile with the terms of the "Madisonian compromise" at the Constitutional Convention. But he argues persuasively that the terms of the compromise were less than completely understood by Convention delegates and were unfamiliar to participants in the ratification debates.[90]

The First Congress was not united in the view that Article III compelled it to establish inferior courts. Apart from those in the minority who argued that the state courts could and should be utilized in lieu of federal courts,[91] there were those who argued for establishing inferior courts not because the Constitution deprived them of discretion to do otherwise but because doing so was necessary to implement policies underlying the constitutional structure.[92] The overriding point remains, however, that Congress's power to establish inferior courts was not viewed as a mechanism for engendering judicial branch dependence or accountability. It was, rather, the foundation for a constitutional duty to establish a separate and independent judicial branch that would stand up to antagonistic state interests and impartially uphold the constitutional order. Representative John Vining's impassioned speech on the floor of the House is illustrative.

> I conceive that the institution of general and independent tribunals, are essential to the fair and impartial administration of the laws of the United States. . . . The gentleman has told us, that the people do not like courts—that they have been opposed and prevented by violence—nay, by insurrection in Massachusetts: Surely this operates as a powerful reason to prove that there should be a general, independent, and energetic judicature—otherwise, if either the State Judges should be so inclined, or a few sons of faction choose to assemble, they could ever frustrate the objects of Justice.[93]

Prior to the 1789 act, discussions of independent judges and an independent judicial branch were coterminous: tenure and salary protection provided for independent judges, who would possess the fortitude to preserve the independence of the judicial branch through the exercise of judicial review. Precious little discussion was devoted to elaborating on the founders' conception of the independent judicial branch they sought to create, separate and distinct from the independent judges who would constitute it. Indeed, the framers consciously declined to sweat the details that might have provided us with a picture of the independent judiciary as a branch as they visualized it. The size of the Supreme Court, where it would sit and how often, the scope of its appellate jurisdiction, whether there would be inferior trial courts or intermediate courts and, if so, how many there would be, where they would sit, and what their jurisdiction would be—these were all questions that the framers left to Congress for a later day.

It was not until that later day arrived, in 1789, that a more detailed conception of the judiciary as a unified branch began to emerge. In the 1789 act, a trilevel court structure was instituted, with district courts, regional circuit courts, and a Supreme Court.[94] To overcome the concern that federal court litigation would force state citizens to litigate in distant and unfamiliar federal forums,[95] Congress drew federal judicial district boundaries along state lines and located a federal district court in each state.[96]

That solved one problem but left another: a centrally located Supreme Court might rapidly lose touch with the geographically dispersed district courts and the communities they served. As Massachusetts Supreme Court justice David Sewall worried in a letter to Representative George Thatcher, "to have [the Supreme Court] Stationary, at the place where Congress reside (6 or 700 mile) so far distant from the Extremes of the union such a fixation will not be Satisfactory."[97] To unify the court system, Congress lit upon the idea of assigning the three regional circuit courts to hear cases semiannually in each judicial district within their respective circuits and of staffing the circuit courts with the local district judge and two justices of the Supreme Court. In a letter to Vice President John Adams, Massachusetts Supreme Court justice Nathaniel Sargeant offered a justification for such an approach.

> [N]othing in my view of things tends more to Strengthen Government in [the] extream Parts, than sometimes to have a court come among them—perhaps [the] want of this may be one reason among many, why large & extensive Governments have not been so quiet & happy as smaller ones.[98]

Precedent for judicial circuit riding could be found in several state court systems, which in turn borrowed the practice from the English courts at Westminster.[99] Sir Matthew Hale's *The History of the Common Law of England,* which Julius Goebel characterized as "a basic text for those commencing the study of law" in the mid- to late eighteenth century,[100] touted the virtues of the English corollary to circuit riding in terms that underscore the impact of the practice on administrative unification of the courts.

> [B]y this Means their Judgments and their Administrations of Common Justice carry a Consonancy, Congruity and Uniformity

one to another, whereby both the Laws and the Administrations thereof are preserved from that Confusion and Disparity that would unavoidably ensue, if the Administration was by several incommunicating Hands.[101]

It would be more than a hundred years before the centralized, bureaucratized, independent judicial branch as we know it today would begin to emerge—with the establishment of circuit courts of appeals in 1891, the Conference of Senior Circuit Judges in 1922, a workable process for court-promulgated rules of procedure in 1934, and the Administrative Office of the United States Courts in 1939 (as described in chapter 2). Even so, it would be an overstatement to suggest, as some have, that as of 1789, the drafters of the Judiciary Act had no shared concept of the judiciary as a branch independent of the courts that constituted it.[102] They regarded themselves as duty-bound to establish the Supreme Court and the inferior courts but were troubled by the notion of a stationary, geographically isolated Supreme Court exercising appellate review over a sprawling contingent of judges scattered across the United States. To facilitate the development of a cohesive judicial branch in the teeth of geographical dispersion, they introduced circuit riding as a means to guarantee systematic interaction among the justices of the Supreme Court, district court judges, and citizens of the several states. In the words of Representative Fisher Ames, these provisions for the establishment of the courts ought to be read together and "treated as a system."[103]

To say that the First Federal Congress manifested a rudimentary grasp of a cohesive judicial branch is not to suggest that the grasp was especially firm. Well before the Judiciary Act was passed, the circuit-riding solution was recognized as an imperfect one that would facilitate interaction among judges of the federal judiciary at the expense of considerable hardship to the circuit-riding justices. "[T]he middle circuit . . . is so extensive," wrote Judge Edward Shippen to Senator Robert Morris on July 13, 1789, "that it will be scarcely practicable for two Judges twice a year to perform it, and at the same time attend the Sitting of the Supreme Court at the Seat of Government."[104]

More generally, among the Judiciary Act's proponents, there was a widespread recognition that the act was an imperfect first pass at an enormously complicated subject that would need to be revisited early and often. Representative James Madison wrote:

> It is pregnant with difficulties, not only as relating to a part of the constitution which has been most criticized, but being in its own nature peculiarly complicated & embarrassing. . . . The most that can be said in its favor is that it is the first essay, and in practice will be surely an experiment. In this light, it is entitled to great indulgence.[105]

Representative Thomas FitzSimons was even less sanguine: "[W]e are in our house totally incompetent to such a business," he lamented, and "tho the one preparing in the Senate May be found defective it will possibly go down because we are incapable of producing a better."[106] Edmund Randolph, soon to be named the first attorney general, likewise questioned the competence of Congress to structure the courts in detail and argued that the judicial branch itself should be consulted before a permanent plan was implemented.

> The minute detail ought to be consigned to the judges. Every attempt towards it must be imperfect, and being so may become a topic of ridicule to technical men. I wish this idea had been thought worthy of attention; thus the bill would have been less criticized. I wish even now, that the judges of the supreme court were first to be called upon, before a definitive step shall be taken.[107]

Randolph's suggestion may have been impractical, in the sense that it would have been difficult to suspend passage of a bill pending consultation with judges who had not yet been nominated and whose offices would not exist until such time as a bill was passed. Nevertheless, his comments reflect an appreciation for the judiciary as an autonomous branch of government that ought to be delegated some measure of self-regulatory power.

Those who drafted and ratified the Constitution desired to establish an independent judicial branch but lacked the time, experience, or inclination to translate that desire into a detailed blueprint. So they assigned Congress to serve as architect, to complete and implement the governmental framework consistent with the framers' very general directives. In the Judiciary Act of 1789, Congress began the business of establishing the independent and cohesive judicial branch that—in its view—the Constitution demanded. The First Congress's conception of the judiciary as an independent branch may have been rudimentary but was nonetheless extant; Congress, like the founders, exhibited no awareness that its power to organize (or reorganize) the courts was in tension with the principle that the judicial branch should be independent of the political branches. It would not be long, however, before this tension became manifest. Once the Judiciary Act was passed and the courts were created, the judges would be consulted for their insights on judicial structure and practice, but the expectation of branch autonomy would receive several blows, with the most debilitating setback flowing from the partisan division of government that occurred after the end of the first decade, as discussed in the next chapter.

chapter TWO

Congressional Oversight of the Judicial Branch and the Emergence of Customary Independence ∾

ALTHOUGH IT IS CLEAR that the founders of the United States were committed to judicial independence in principle, it is equally clear that the Constitution—and the independent judiciary it established—were fragile innovations with uncertain futures. Judicial independence would survive only if the political branches responsible for its care and feeding took that responsibility seriously, because the Constitution gave Congress in particular (and the political branches generally) ample latitude to obliterate the judiciary's autonomy if it was so inclined. Although Congress has threatened the judiciary's independence on any number of occasions, it has rarely made good on those threats, for reasons that have a lot to do with the emergence of customary independence.

The study of court curbing (or attempted court curbing) in Congress should logically focus on those periods in time when calls for Congress to rein in the courts have been most persistent and shrill. There are at least five such periods preceding the one that confronts us today. These periods were marked by (1) court packing, unpacking, and impeachment when the Federalists lost power and Thomas Jefferson became president in the early nineteenth century; (2) altercations with the Marshall Court during the Jackson administration; (3)

Republican confrontations with the Supreme Court before, during, and after the Civil War; (4) Populist, Progressive, and New Deal criticism of the Supreme Court; and (5) the backlash against the Warren Court in the mid-twentieth century.

These cycles of court-directed animus have occurred at more or less regular intervals and thus provide a useful means to frame a discussion of proposals to constrain the courts and the judicial independence norms that have operated to stay Congress's hand. Concentrating on these high points in the history of court bashing has, however, at least two limitations. First, it tends to feature the Supreme Court to the relative exclusion of the lower courts, because it is the former whose decisions have usually grabbed national headlines and provoked nationwide anger. Second, such a fixation on examples of interbranch confrontation overlooks the periods of calm that separate them, periods when independence norms have tended to emerge and mature. To overcome these limitations, I will begin each section of this chapter by summarizing briefly one or two of these five well-documented spikes of court-directed hostility. These summaries will serve as bookends for lengthier discussions of the intervening periods and contemporaneous events that relate to lower court governance and contributed to the gradual emergence of independence norms.

As elaborated in this chapter, emerging independence norms exhibited themselves across these cycles in three distinct ways. First, there was a gradual decline in the acceptability of various means for Congress to retaliate against the judiciary for its decision making. Second, during most of the nineteenth century, there was increasing congressional reluctance to deviate sharply from the structure of the Judiciary Act of 1789, out of respect for the stability and autonomy of the judiciary as an institution. Third, in the twentieth century, there was a congressional movement toward promoting intrajudicial accountability via the establishment of a self-governing, independent judicial branch.

Spikes One and Two: Jeffersonian Anger, Jacksonian Defiance, and the Intervening Period of Calm ∾

The first two sustained waves of criticism directed at the federal courts were humdingers. Viewed in isolation, they represent two serious assaults on the judiciary's independence and institutional legitimacy, occurring in successive generations. In context, however, they might better be characterized as spasms of anger separated by a period of relative calm, during which an ethos of congressional respect for the autonomy of the slowly emerging judicial branch began to take root.

As discussed in chapter 1, those who drafted and ratified the Constitution were committed to an independent judiciary in principle but lacked the time or enthusiasm to complete the constitutional framework, leaving Congress to resolve such fundamental issues as whether the federal government would include a system of inferior courts. In 1789, the First Congress filled that gap by establishing two tiers of trial courts: district courts (one to a state) and three regional circuit courts (which, in addition to being trial courts, were authorized to hear appeals from some district court decisions). While district courts were staffed with separately appointed district judges, no additional judgeships were created to people the circuit courts. Rather, they were staffed by moonlighting district and Supreme Court judges. Thus, the six justices of the Supreme Court, in addition to hearing cases as the Supreme Court, were obligated to ride to each judicial district within a regional circuit twice a year and convene circuit courts (hence the term *circuit riding*).

Jeffersonian Anger

The election of Thomas Jefferson ushered in the first sustained wave of national anger directed at federal judges. Although reform of the judicial system had been sought for several years, it was the lame-duck president John Adams, with the aid of a lame-duck Federalist Congress, who—in the so-called Midnight Judges Act—created sixteen new federal judgeships (most of which were designated to staff redesigned circuit courts and relieve the Supreme Court of circuit-riding responsibilities) and packed them with Federalist partisans. That, in turn, catalyzed a drive by the incoming Jeffersonian Republicans to disestablish the courts the Federalists had created and then remove by impeachment objectionable Federalist judges whose offices had not been abolished. "[T]he only check upon the Judiciary system as it is now organized and filled," wrote Republican senator William Giles to Thomas Jefferson, "is the removal of all its executive officers indiscriminately."[1]

The Jeffersonian Republicans succeeded in repealing the judgeships the outgoing Federalists had created, despite profound uncertainty surrounding the constitutionality of circumventing the tenure
and salary protections of Article III by removing judges via abolition
of their offices. After all, the Constitution does say that federal judges
are entitled to remain in office "during good behavior," and the sixteen judges who lost their jobs when Congress repealed legislation
establishing their courts had not had time to misbehave.

The issue was briefed and argued in *Stuart v. Laird.* In *Marbury v.
Madison,*[2] decided less than a month earlier, the Supreme Court,
under Chief Justice John Marshall, had been willing to assert its
power of judicial review to strike down an inconsequential procedural
statute enacted years before by the now impotent Federalists. In *Stuart,* however, the Court was confronted with a constitutional challenge to the 1802 act recently passed by the powerful and antagonistic
Jeffersonians. The Marshall Court upheld the statute in a short, timid
opinion that failed even to acknowledge that the issue of the repeal's
constitutionality was before the Court.[3]

The 1802 repeal qualifies as an episode of court unpacking in
which the Supreme Court was intimidated into acquiescence. However, it may not be an especially good illustration of what Congress
can or will do to hold judges accountable for their behavior. The
repeal was motivated less by disaffection for the newly appointed
judges (*qua* judges) than by anger at the impudence of the outgoing
Federalist Congress and president for packing the courts in the first
place.

Unlike their initiative to obliterate the circuit courts, the Jeffersonian Republicans' campaign to impeach and remove Federalist
judges was more clearly directed at jurists whom members of Congress wished to rebuke for their behavior on the bench. The campaign
culminated in the ouster of district judge John Pickering and the
impeachment of Justice Samuel Chase. A more detailed discussion of
these cases is reserved for chapter 3. Suffice it to say here that Chase's
acquittal (he was impeached by the House but acquitted by the Senate) sucked the life out of the Jeffersonians' antijudiciary campaign
and set a precedent against removing judges for high-handed decision
making. Of the three primary manifestations of emerging judicial

independence norms within Congress described earlier, this would prove to be an initial encounter with the first—the gradual decline over time in the acceptability of Congress holding the judiciary accountable for its decisions by extrajudicial means.

Jacksonian Defiance

With the ascendancy of Jacksonian Democracy at the close of the 1820s came a new wave of antagonism directed at the courts. Jackson's unique brand of majoritarian democracy was very much in tension with an appointed judiciary that imposed limits on the will of the majority. Legislation was introduced in Congress to strip the U.S. Supreme Court of jurisdiction to hear appeals from the decisions of state courts, and a groundswell of support for elective judiciaries directly challenged the notion of an independent judiciary. Jacksonian Democrat Frederick Robinson made the point bluntly: "Judges should be made responsible to the people by periodical elections. The boast of an independent judiciary is always made to deceive you. We want no part of our government independent of the people."[4]

If disestablishment of courts and the impeachment of Pickering and Chase were the legacies of the first spike of judicial criticism, defiance of Supreme Court rulings was the legacy of the second. Indisputably, the high-water mark was Georgia's refusal to submit itself to the jurisdiction of the Supreme Court in a series of cases involving the Cherokee Indian tribe. "Georgia will never so far compromi[se] her sovereignty, as an independent state, as to become a party to the case sought to be made before the Supreme Court of the United States," declared a resolution of the Georgia legislature.[5] The resolution was directed to the governor, who subsequently executed a Cherokee prisoner in the teeth of a writ of error issued by the Supreme Court.

For his part, Jackson expressed the view that "[t]he opinion of the judges has no more authority over Congress than the opinion of Congress has over the judges and on that point the president is independent of both."[6] In response to another of the Cherokee Indian cases in which the Supreme Court invalidated a Georgia statute, Jackson is reported to have said, "John Marshall has made his decision, now let him enforce it."[7] Jackson's confrontational posture with the Court must be qualified, however. Apart from the likelihood that his statement concerning Chief Justice Marshall was apocryphal, no showdown with the Supreme Court ever materialized during Jackson's administration: Jackson rejected the extreme views of state sovereignty that animated Georgia's disregard for federal authority, and he never acted on his philosophical aversion to judicial supremacy over matters of constitutional interpretation.[8]

The Intervening Period of Calm

Although, as discussed in chapter 1, the drafters of the Constitution and those who enacted the very first Judiciary Act (in 1789) shared a rudimentary commitment to the establishment of an independent judicial branch, that commitment was thrown into a cocked hat by the events of 1801 and 1802, as the outgoing Federalists and incoming Jeffersonians packed and unpacked the courts for partisan political ends, with the courts helpless to control their own destiny. Indeed, as of 1808, events of the recent past had emboldened Senator William Giles—a cheerleader for the Jeffersonian Republicans—to dispute the very existence of the judiciary as a separate and independent branch of government, the founders' intentions to the contrary notwithstanding. "The theory of three distinct departments in government is, perhaps, not critically correct; although it is obvious that the framers of our Constitution proceeded upon this theory in its formation," Giles posited, further stating that an independent branch would have "powers to organize itself and to execute the peculiar functions assigned to it without aid," which "is not in the Constitutional character of our judicial Department."[9]

As the first great cycle of court-directed hostility receded into the past, court-related legislation in the early decades of the nineteenth century began to focus on enlarging the judicial workforce as the nation gradually expanded westward. The struggle to expand the federal courts westward during and between the first two spikes of court-directed animus bears emphasis here for three reasons. First and most generally, the debate over westward expansion of the courts reflects the extent to which Congress governed the courts with reference to its understanding of and appreciation for judicial independence and accountability. Second and more specifically, Congress's uneasy resolution of the westward expansion problem illuminates the emergence of what was described earlier as an important manifestation of judicial independence norms that would dominate Congress's regulation of the courts for the remainder of the nineteenth century—a preference for conserving the structure of the Judiciary Act of 1789, which was viewed as an implementation of the constitutional framers' vision for an independent judiciary. Third (and related to the second reason), the resolution illustrates how Congress preserved and furthered its institutional conservatism by relying on its own precedent to reject potentially destabilizing departures from the 1789 act.

As new states entered the Union, new judicial districts were created to service the new states, new district judges were added to staff the new judicial districts, new circuits were added to include the new states, and new Supreme Court justices were added to oversee the new circuits. Throughout the period, circuit riding—which the Judiciary Act of 1801 had abolished and which the Judiciary Act of 1802 restored—remained a conceptual linchpin of the federal courts as a "system."[10] Requiring Supreme Court justices to take their show on the road and preside over circuit courts in tandem with district judges would create points of contact (among the justices and judges themselves and between the justices or judges and the lay and legal communities) that—it was thought—would promote a competent, cohesive judiciary.[11] As inconvenient as interstate travel may have been when the nation was young and small, however, it quickly became insufferable with westward expansion. The 1789 act sidestepped an initial manifestation of the problem by excluding the territories of Kentucky and Maine from the three circuits that the justices of the Supreme Court were required to ride. The act instead conferred exclusive circuit court jurisdiction on the local district judges in those states.[12] Once Kentucky and Maine became coequal sovereign states, however, they began to press for inclusion in the circuit system. Relief was prompt in coming for Maine, by virtue of its geographic proximity to other New England states, but the same could not be said for Kentucky, which was later joined by Tennessee and Ohio as newly admitted western states excluded from the circuit system. Congress eventually capitulated in 1807, establishing a new circuit comprised of the three new western states and adding a seventh Supreme Court justice to staff it.[13]

Along the way, Congress made occasional attempts to ease circuit-riding burdens, if only slightly. In 1793, it reduced from two to one the number of Supreme Court justices who must preside at any given circuit court.[14] In 1802, at the same time it repealed the 1801 act and thereby restored circuit riding, Congress authorized circuit courts to be held with only one judge presiding, making it possible for district judges to hold circuit court without a Supreme Court justice in attendance.[15]

Between 1812 and 1821, Louisiana, Indiana, Mississippi, Illinois, Alabama, and Missouri joined the Union. "From the extent of the country, the number of the states, and the increasing mass of business constantly depending in the circuit courts," Representative William Plumer explained in 1823, "it was obviously impossible for seven judges to hold two courts annually in each of the twenty-seven judicial districts, into which the United States are now divided."[16] Accordingly, upon entering the Union, the six new western states were treated as Kentucky had been, by assigning them district judges with circuit court jurisdiction rather than including them in circuits staffed by Supreme Court justices. This did not sit well with the newly admitted western states. As Plumer explained in his floor statement on behalf of the House Judiciary Committee, "these States which, under the present arrangements, are deprived of the benefits of a circuit court, are desirous . . . that such alterations should be made in the existing system as would extend to them the advantages enjoyed by the states where such courts exist."[17]

To address the western expansion problem, Plumer presented three alternatives on behalf of the House Judiciary Committee, to which I refer throughout the remainder of this section: (1) establish two additional circuits that would include the new western states, and add two more Supreme Court justices to ride the two new circuits; (2) end circuit riding and establish a new system of circuit courts staffed by judges appointed to serve as circuit judges; or (3) confine Supreme Court justices' circuit riding to the eastern circuits, and establish two new circuit courts for the western states, staffed by circuit judges in lieu of Supreme Court justices.[18] Beginning in 1823, Congress repeatedly debated the relative merits of these three alternatives, to no concrete end until 1837, when the first alternative was adopted.[19] Understanding why the debate was so protracted and fruitless requires an appreciation for the emerging institutional conservatism of Congress when it came to restructuring the courts.

It is well to begin the discussion of Plumer's three alternatives with Senator Asher Robbins, whose comfort with sweeping reform embodied a minority view that helps to illuminate the majority's reticence. Robbins was unimpressed with the argument, attributed to Senator Martin Van Buren, "that it is dangerous to change the principle of a judiciary system established by law." With rhetorical flourish, Robbins asked, "when [was it] that it became dangerous to alter that law? Was it the day after the law was passed? [I]f not, and if it is dangerous now, at what intermediate time did it become dangerous?" As far as Robbins was concerned, it was "ridiculous, to suppose . . . that there was any danger at any time." Bringing his point to a dismissive close, Robbins concluded, "So much for the danger of amending a law, a thing we are in the daily habit of doing."[20]

For Robbins, amending the structure of the federal judiciary was no different than amending any other federal law—it was something Congress was "in the daily habit of doing." But his was not a widely shared view. The prevailing view was that legislation regulating the courts was different because it altered the structure of an independent branch of government, the long-standing stability of which legislators admired and were desirous of preserving. "[I]t may well excite astonishment," remarked House Judiciary Committee chairman Daniel Webster in 1826, that the system which "very able men [enacted in] 1789 has been found to fulfill, so far, so well, and for so long a time, the great purposes which it was designed to accomplish." Accordingly, he concluded, "[t]he general success of the general system, so far, may well inspire some degree of caution in the minds of those who are called on to alter or amend it."[21] Representative Thomas Crawford made the same point four years later, in prose that was floral, if not florid.

When, therefore a plan has been happily laid in our land, which, in its execution commands the public confidence, and so ensures obedience to its decrees, will prudence, will the careful watchfulness that belongs to our stations, allow us to leave the road we have found so smooth, and fragrant from the flowers that bloomed upon its sides, and to enter upon an unbeaten way that may lead us into miry and swampy grounds?[22]

General acceptance of the view that Congress should use special restraint in approaching the task of restructuring the courts is apparent from legislators' pervasive recourse to prior enactments in support of or opposition to proposed reforms. Such arguments inevitably strove to reconcile favored proposals with statutory precedent and to condemn disfavored proposals for departing from such precedent, thereby underscoring Congress's preference for cautious, incremental change when it came to governmental framework legislation of this kind. Thus, for example, in his defense of a proposal (akin to the first alternative presented by Plumer in 1823) to add two new circuits and three Supreme Court justices to service them, Representative James Buchanan argued that the plan simply expanded on past precedent, and he professed to be "greatly astonished" by the objection "that the principles contained in this bill were new." To the contrary, he argued:

So far have the committee been from recommending any new project, that, on the contrary, they have but proposed to extend to other portions of the Union, the benefits of a system, the wisdom of which has been already tested by the experience of all the Atlantic States. . . . [T]he question for the committee now to decide is, whether the country shall go on in this prosperous and happy judicial course, extending the present well-tried system to meet the wants of the People, or whether we shall commence a career of new and untried and hazarded experiments.[23]

By the same token, Senator Levi Woodbury opposed a similar proposal in the Senate on grounds that it was, well, unprecedented. He argued that unlike the Judiciary Act of 1801 and that of 1802, which added no justices to the Supreme Court, and unlike the Judiciary Act of 1807, which added only one, expanding the size of the Supreme

Court from seven to ten (as then proposed) would alter its quorum and enable the appointing authority to select judges to orchestrate the reversal of unpopular decisions. "But such could not be the effect or tendency of the addition in A.D. 1807," Woodbury concluded. "Where, then," he asked, "is the precedent?"[24]

Similarly, proponents of proposals to relieve Supreme Court justices of their circuit-riding duties by replacing them with a new tier of circuit court judges (the second alternative presented by Plumer) struggled to distinguish the adverse precedent set by the 1801 Midnight Judges Act, which created such a system, only to be repealed the next year. Senator Robbins acknowledged "a similar system, that was once adopted, and soon after laid aside," which had caused some to infer "that the system itself is unpopular." He argued, however, that "[t]he inference is incorrect"—that "the men who made that system, made it unpopular, and nothing else." He noted that the circuit courts had been created in 1801 by outgoing Federalists intent on court packing and on retaining control of the judicial power and that "the system was broken down" in 1802 in order "to wrest this power out of their hands." Although an "ostensible objection" to the 1801 act was to its creation of a new circuit court system, that system "could not be shown to be bad," Robbins opined; rather, it was simply "called by many bad names; . . . and the bad name raised a hue and a cry against it, and not the demerits of the system itself."[25]

As right as Robbins may have been with regard to history, opponents of proposals to reintroduce the circuit courts regarded the 1802 repeal as an adverse precedent so powerful as to stop the proposal dead in its tracks, without the need for further elaboration.[26] For Senator Martin Van Buren, among others, the significance of the precedent established by the 1802 repeal went beyond counseling against the reintroduction of a circuit court system with circuit court judges; rather, it counseled against any dramatic departure from precedent in regulating court structure.

If there be a case in which, more than any other, the hand of innovation should be watched with lynx-eyed jealousy, this is surely that case. A total change was made in 1801, but the measure met with a total overthrow in one short year. Strong as the feelings then produced were, time and experience have demonstrated the wisdom of the act of 1802, by which the system of 1789 was restored and improved.[27]

Moreover, the proposal to create permanent circuit courts would end circuit riding for Supreme Court justices, which, in the minds of many, was another time-honored practice Congress should not lightly jettison, in part because of its role in promoting judicial accountability. Representative Daniel Webster, for example, defended circuit riding on the grounds that having Supreme Court justices preside over trials would permit them to "see in practice the operation and effect of their own decisions," which would "prevent theory from running too far[,] inspire Courts with caution," and make each justice more "prominent, conspicuous, and responsible" than one who merely "give[s] a vote upon a bench, (especially if it be a numerous bench[])."[28]

The third alternative presented by Plumer in 1823—which, like the status quo, would have restricted Supreme Court circuit riding to the eastern circuits and conferred circuit court jurisdiction on inferior courts in the west—was also supported and opposed with reference to statutory precedent. Supporters, such as Woodbury, defended the differential treatment of eastern and western states in light of the Kentucky and Maine precedents. Woodbury stated:

> [I]f we trace down our judicial history, it will be seen that this part of our system, now the cause of so severe complaint, was afterwards introduced into all other places beside Maine and Kentucky, where the population and territory were similar, and retained not only during their District and Territorial condition, but, in many of them, long after they became sovereign and independent States.[29]

Conversely, Representative John Wright opposed such an approach, on the grounds that unequal treatment of western states "overlooked or changed" long-standing legislative precedent "from 1789 down, some of which may be regarded as a contemporaneous exposition of the Constitution, in relation to this subject."[30]

Widespread reliance on statutory precedent for and against court reform proposals reflects a congressional commitment to cautious, incremental reform, born of the desire to preserve the stability of the independent judicial branch and born also of a reverence for the 1789 act as "a contemporaneous exposition of the Constitution." This predisposition against significant change helps to explain the ultimate enactment of Plumer's first alternative—adding two new western circuit courts and two new additional Supreme Court justices to ride them. Proponents of this approach could legitimately claim that it offered nothing new but simply extended the existing circuit system to reach newly admitted states, just as Congress had done before, in 1807. This does not mean, however, that Congress embraced this option with open arms. To the contrary, the faults of the plan were all too obvious, particularly to legislators able to foresee the precedent it would set for the next round of western states admitted to the Union.

As many noted, the proposal would increase the size of the Supreme Court, not because there was any need for a larger Supreme Court, but because more justices were needed to ride the new circuits in the western states. Representative James Strong, among others, saw this as a case of the tail wagging the dog.

> The present court is admitted to be large enough for the business of the bench. Wherefore increase the number of justices? . . . What is this but changing the principle into the incident—thereby making the secondary duties of the old court the main object and excuse for creating the new court.[31]

There was no escaping the conclusion that increasing the size of the Supreme Court whenever the nation expanded westward, just so that more justices were available to try cases as circuit judges in the newly admitted states, merely deferred, rather than solved, the problem. "[T]he time is coming," warned Senator Robbins, "when this growing defect will call for another supply of Judges." He continued, "having begun with this plan, we must go on with it; and the Supreme Court will become so numerous that the sense of individual responsibility will be lost." Robbins conceded that such a pronouncement was overly apocalyptic, inasmuch as "[n]o man has said . . . that this plan of a Judiciary will do for any length of time" and inasmuch as "the advocates of the plan content themselves with saying that it will do for the present," but he warned that the precedent set by this temporary measure would still "operate as an impediment to" more meaningful reform in the future.[32] Senator John Berrien echoed Robbins's dissatisfaction: "Though the bill under consideration is defective in principle," he complained, "though it affords no remedy for the evils to which the existing system is liable," the "unanswerable argument of its advocates is, that it is the best which can be done."[33]

After three weeks of uninterrupted debate in early 1826, the House passed its variation of Plumer's first alternative, which would have added two new circuits and two new Supreme Court justices to ride them. The Senate passed the House bill with amendments altering the configuration of the western circuits and imposing a residency requirement on the justices assigned to them.[34] The House, piqued by the Senate's changes and by allegations that some senators had sought to bully the House into acquiescence, called for a joint conference of representatives from the House and Senate to resolve their differences.[35] The Senate, equally piqued at the House's pique, stood firm, refusing the House's request for a joint conference.[36]

The bill thereupon died an ignominious, if temporary, death. It was reintroduced in successive Congresses and finally won passage in 1837, after repeated urgings by Andrew Jackson. The implication that President Jackson's serial attacks on the Marshall Court during the second spike reflected a fundamental hostility to an independent federal judiciary is thus qualified, if not contradicted, by his ardent support for legislation to expand the federal court system.[37]

Felix Frankfurter and James Landis blame congressional indifference for this decade of legislative failures. But their conclusion is belied by their own observation that the three weeks of discussion the House devoted to the issue in 1826 was "one of the most distinguished debates dealing with judicial organization."[38] The better explanation may be that developing and sometimes conflicting notions of judicial independence and accountability had put Congress in a box that was difficult to escape.

Respect for the judiciary as a separate and independent branch of government counseled Congress against radical reform, in favor of incremental adjustments that adhered to legislative precedent and preserved the stability of the courts. There were, however, no good incremental alternatives. To jettison circuit riding and revamp the circuit system was not an incremental approach; it would require a radical reversal of legislative precedent, which many believed would diminish Supreme Court accountability. To preserve the circuit system but not expand it westward was politically unsalable to the western states that the legislation was intended to accommodate. Finally, extending the circuit system westward was impractical in that it required two moonlighting justices to traverse six states by boat and horse to conduct trials in every judicial district twice a year; it was also shortsighted, because Congress could not keep increasing the size of the Supreme Court to staff each new circuit without eventually compromising the Court's decision-making integrity.

Weeks of debate in 1826 enabled Congress to winnow the field of ineffective, incremental alternatives to the one least objectionable. No one, however, was deluded enough to suppose that simply adding to the growing pile of circuits and justices offered more than a short-term solution to the westward expansion problem. Support for the proposal was thus understandably tepid, which may be the best explanation for why it was so easily derailed by a junior-varsity round of intercameral name-calling. Most important for our purposes here, however, is the extent to which congressional concern for judicial autonomy dominated debates over proposals to restructure the courts and was consciously resolved by disturbing the status quo as little as possible.

Spike Three: Radical Republicans and Less than Radical Reform During the Civil War and Its Aftermath ∾

The death of John Marshall in 1835 and the end of the Jackson administration in 1837 led to a period of relative calm in the Supreme Court, but not elsewhere. The issue of slavery had become increasingly heated in the decades preceding the Court's 1856 decision in *Scott v. Sanford.* The Missouri Compromise of 1820, the Compromise of 1850, and the Kansas-Nebraska Act of 1854 marked the widening sectional divide of the nation on the slavery issue.[39]

Radical Republican Challenges to the Supreme Court

In the *Dred Scott* case, the Supreme Court held, first, that freed black slaves could not invoke the jurisdiction of the federal courts, because they were not citizens of the United States, and, second, that because the Constitution acknowledged and protected the right to own slaves as property, Congress lacked the power to prohibit slavery in the territories.[40] In so holding, the Court simultaneously appeared to manifest a proslavery bias and crippled congressional moderates in their efforts to preserve any semblance of détente between pro- and antislavery forces, thereby driving the nation inexorably into war.

Reaction to *Dred Scott* among those with abolitionist leanings was swift and severe. One journalist accused the "five slaveholders and two doughfaces on the bench" of "rush[ing] into politics voluntarily, and without other purpose than to subserve the cause of Slavery."[41] It was a decision "entitled to just so much moral weight as would be the judgment of a majority of those congregated in any Washington barroom," claimed the *New York Daily Tribune*,[42] which continued, "If epithets and denunciation could sink a judicial body, the Supreme Court of the United States would never be heard of again."[43]

The wounds created by *Dred Scott* had not healed by the time that Radical Republicans gained control of Congress after the Civil War and threatened to busy themselves by "annihilating" judges who interfered with their legislative agenda.[44] The Republican press applied the derisive brand "Dred Scott II and III" to Supreme Court decisions limiting Congress's virtual monopoly on national power during Reconstruction.[45] Whereas previous efforts to control the courts featured disestablishment, impeachment, and defiance, this latest wave arguably exploited Congress's power to control Supreme Court size and undeniably brought its power over the Court's jurisdiction into play. In 1866, with Democrat Andrew Johnson in the White House, the Republican Congress reduced the size of the Supreme Court to seven (after having increased it from nine to ten just three years earlier, when Lincoln was in power), thereby depriving Johnson of the opportunity to replace several retiring justices.[46] It then returned the Court's size to nine after Republican president Ulysses S. Grant took office, which enabled Grant to shift the decision-making majority of the Court in important cases concerning legal tender.

In 1867, newspaper editor William McCardle was arrested for writing articles critical of Reconstruction. McCardle filed a petition for writ of habeas corpus, challenging the constitutionality of the Military Reconstruction Act, which subjected civilians, such as McCardle, to trial before a military commission, when deemed necessary to suppress insurrection or disorder. McCardle's petition was denied by the Mississippi circuit court, whereupon he appealed to the U.S. Supreme Court, which brushed aside the government's objections and declared that it would hear the appeal. Congress reacted swiftly, enacting legislation to deprive the Supreme Court of jurisdiction to hear a pending case that would have presented the Court with an opportunity to limit congressional power to impose military rule in the nonreconstructed South. Congress made no bones about it; as one member of the House explained, the legislation was "aimed at striking at a branch of the jurisdiction of the Supreme Court, thereby sweeping the [McCardle case] from the docket."[47] Then, in *Ex parte McCardle,* a compliant Supreme Court acquiesced to Congress, dismissing the case for want of jurisdiction. "The provision of the Act of 1867, affirming the appellate jurisdiction of this court in cases of habeas corpus is expressly repealed," observed Chief Justice Salmon Chase, who continued, "It is hardly possible to imagine a plainer instance of positive exception."[48]

The legacy of this third spike of court-directed anger is far murkier than the preceding synopsis suggests. *McCardle* is sometimes cited for the general proposition that the Constitution gives Congress carte blanche to deprive the Supreme Court of jurisdiction to hear specific cases or categories of cases.[49] Barry Friedman argues persuasively, however, that these scholars have divorced *McCardle* from historical context and that the duress under which the Court decided that case renders its precedential value dubious.[50] Moreover, uncertainty surrounding the durability of *McCardle* has never been resolved, because Congress has rarely attempted to strip the Court of jurisdiction so blatantly in the years since,[51] which seems to corroborate the gradual ascendance of judicial independence norms that this chapter seeks to document.

With respect to the implication that the Republican Congress packed and unpacked the Supreme Court, the legacy is murkier still. From 1789 to 1866, the Supreme Court's size remained firmly soldered to the number of regional circuits Congress created. Thus, when Congress added a tenth circuit and a tenth justice in 1863,[52] it may have had nothing to do with court packing and everything to do with Congress's long-standing respect for preserving the court system's traditional structure.

In 1866, however, when Congress reduced the number of circuits from ten to nine and decreased the size of the Supreme Court from ten to seven, the specter of court unpacking appears. Even so, opinions differ as to whether court unpacking actually occurred in this case. Frankfurter and Landis say it did. They argue that the move was designed by an overwhelmingly Republican Congress to deprive Democratic president Andrew Johnson of the opportunity to make appointments that could influence the balance of power on the Supreme Court.[53] Charles Fairman concludes that unpacking did not occur. He maintains that the reduction was made at the behest of Chief Justice Salmon Chase, who hoped to trade a drop in Supreme Court workforce for an increase in the remaining justices' salaries.[54]

The essential point for our purposes here is that speculation as to the motivations underlying the 1866 reduction is so open because the legislative record is so spare. Senator Lyman Trumbull introduced the measure on the Senate floor as an amendment to legislation, originating in the House, on configuration of the circuits.[55] The Senate approved the amendment, with literally no explanation for the reduction and no debate of its merits.[56] When the Senate amendment was considered once the bill returned to the House, Representative John Wentworth inquired as to whether the amendment would eliminate a vacancy on the Court for which a nomination was then pending. Representative James Wilson replied in the affirmative, adding, "I know that a number of the members of the Supreme Court think it will be a vast improvement."[57] That is about it. The House accepted the amendment, and President Johnson signed the legislation into law.

Unlike nearly every other piece of legislation discussed in this chapter, deliberation preceding adoption of the 1866 amendment to reduce the size of the Supreme Court from ten to seven was so truncated that no conclusive inferences can be drawn as to Congress's underlying motivations. Although Trumbull must have had his reasons, he proposed the amendment to his colleagues for adoption *sans* rationale, and given the paucity of discussion, it is altogether likely that they obligingly approved the amendment as proposed—*sans* rationale. The 1866 Supreme Court reduction may thus be better characterized as an example of "sneak" legislation akin to that enacted in 1875, granting the district courts jurisdiction to hear all questions arising under federal law (legislation likewise insinuated into a court improvements bill as an unexplained, undebated, eleventh-hour amendment) than as an example of court-packing legislation akin to the Midnight Judges Act.[58] The paucity of debate or disagreement thus belies the inference that the 1866 measure was widely understood as part of a partisan campaign to unpack the Supreme Court. In the year following the measure's passage, an article in the *American Law Review* observed, "There seems to have been no serious opposition to the law, which was in no sense a political measure, however much political feelings may have aided its passage."[59]

When the Supreme Court's size was again increased to nine in 1869,[60] it was as part of a court reform package (discussed at greater length later in this chapter) enacted after a protracted gestation that restored the traditional parity between the size of the Court and the number of regional circuits—making the move at least as easy to explain as a product of convention as one of court packing. If court packing was Congress's dominant motivation, Congress took great pains to conceal it behind alternating veneers of silence and professed commitment to incremental, apolitical court improvement. Given the Reconstruction Republicans' penchant for threatening the Supreme Court with annihilation whenever it suited their mood, it is curious that they would feel constrained to conceal their court-packing motives. Either court packing was not their dominant motivation, or congressional Republicans recognized that their plans to engage in court packing ran counter to norms against such a practice and so needed to be obscured. The unparalleled chutzpah of the Reconstruction Congress makes it conceivable that Reconstruction legislators did indeed pack and unpack the courts. If they did engage in such activity, however, it may be better characterized either as an exception to an emerging rule against court packing or as a tacit acknowledgment that such a rule had already emerged and needed to be quietly sidestepped. This emerging norm in opposition to court packing follows naturally from Congress's continuing reluctance to restructure the judicial branch in potentially disruptive ways, as discussed in the next section of this chapter.

The Less than Radical Reform of the Lower Federal Courts during the Civil War and Its Aftermath

Accounts of the relationship between the political branches and the courts during Reconstruction dwell on the Republican Congress's attempts to dominate and suppress the Supreme Court, which gave rise to the third cycle of confrontations between the courts and the political branches. Congressional antipathy toward the Supreme Court notwithstanding, the Republican Congress turned to the courts for implementation of the Reconstruction agenda. Congress greatly expanded federal court jurisdiction and thereby added to the docket of the Supreme Court, which had increased from 310 cases pending in 1860 to 636 cases pending in 1870.[61]

In other words, notwithstanding its occasional bullying of the Supreme Court, the Reconstruction-era Congress had a vested interest in preserving and promoting a strong, stable, and expanded federal judiciary that would enforce the statutes that Congress enacted in the teeth of regional resistance. Ironically, then, the high-profile episodes of court bashing that dominate contemporary discussions of courts-Congress relations during Reconstruction did nothing to destabilize established norms respecting the institutional independence of the federal judiciary. Nowhere is that more evident than in the debates on the 1869 expansion of the federal courts, which manifest Congress's support for a larger, stronger judiciary and Congress's continued opposition to extreme reforms that could disrupt the judiciary as an institution.

In the 1850s and again in the 1860s, respectively, Senator Stephen Douglas and Senate Judiciary Committee chair Lyman Trumbull sponsored legislation that would have reintroduced intermediate courts of appeals, proposals that Frankfurter and Landis rightly characterize as "premature," given Congress's entrenched preference for incremental change.[62] In 1869, Trumbull took a different tack, introducing legislation that, when finally enacted, established nine circuit judgeships, added one justice to the Supreme Court, and reduced the circuit-riding responsibilities of Supreme Court justices to one tour of duty every two years.[63] When originally introduced, the bill raced through Congress—being introduced in the Senate on January 18,[64] approved by the Senate Judiciary Committee on February 3,[65] passed by the Senate on February 23, and passed by the House on March 3 (the last day of the Fortieth Congress)—only to be inadvertently pocket vetoed by President Johnson.[66]

Trumbull reintroduced his bill at the beginning of the next Congress. "[T]he Supreme Court of the United States is overloaded with business," and "[t]he district courts throughout the United States are also overloaded," Trumbull declared.[67] The problem was perceived to be especially acute in the South, where efforts to enforce Reconstruction legislation hinged on the availability of judicial machinery to enforce recently adopted laws.[68] By creating nine permanent circuit judgeships, Trumbull explained, the bill would reduce (though not eliminate) the circuit court duties of Supreme Court justices and district judges alike, thus enabling each to devote more time to their primary responsibilities.[69] Trumbull effectively conceded that the bill was incremental in its approach and left much to be done.

> [T]here are many other provisions in regard to the judicial system which it would be desirable to enact into a law, but it was thought . . . that the simpler we could make this bill the better, and we could supply the other defects afterward. It leaves the judicial system of the United States just as we found it.[70]

In an earlier round of debates on the measure, Senator William Stewart echoed the same pragmatic sentiments: "This system appears to be about the only one we can get. If we spend all our time in discussing different methods we shall agree upon nothing."[71]

The Senate's inability to pursue more significant reform may be attributable to a tension between "two things" that, in Senator Eugene Casserly's view, "seem[ed] to be conceded." The first was "that in the remarkable growth of the country for the last twenty years an accession to the judicial force of the Union is required." Casserly identified the second by saying, "I think it will also be conceded that such accession should be made at the expense of as little disturbance as possible of the existing system."[72] Given the dual desire to increase the judicial workforce without changing the existing court structure, adding more judges may have been the only viable option. But why was the Senate so reluctant to disturb the existing system? There are several, related answers.

First, some legislators regarded the long-standing judicial structure with even greater reverence than had their counterparts in the 1820s and 1830s. They did not want to change it because, as Casserly argued, "it is a system under which the country has grown up and under which its jurisprudence has been formed."[73] In the House, Representative Michael Kerr worried that any significant changes to the structure of the courts could jeopardize their independence.

> [A]ny changes to be made in [our judicial] system . . . should be made with very great deliberation and with the utmost degree of caution, to the end that hasty legislation upon this grave and important subject shall not be indulged in. If there is one institution in our country which more than any other should challenge the vigilant and affectionate solicitude of every citizen for its integrity and protection, it is our Federal judiciary. In that department, if its absolute purity and independence be properly maintained, is the surest anchorage of our system of Government against the encroachments of the other departments. In it is the highest safety of the citizen against the invasions of power upon the rights of property and the liberties of the people. We should look with distrust upon any proposition materially to change it.[74]

Second, many legislators noted that any significant restructuring of the courts would effectively be permanent, so that any mistakes Congress made would, for all practical purposes, be irreversible. For some, the point was simply that if Congress made any changes that authorized the appointment of additional federal judges, life tenure would preclude—or at least ought to preclude—Congress from abolishing those positions any time soon.[75] A lively exchange occurred between Senator Trumbull, a sponsor of the 1869 legislation, and Senator George Edmunds, who favored an amendment that would double the size of the Supreme Court. The issue was whose scheme would be easier to fix "if you find it does not work."[76] Trumbull argued that Congress could later abolish the circuit court offices that he proposed (echoes of the 1802 repeal of judgeships created by the Judiciary Act of 1801) but could not eliminate the Supreme Court justices that Edmunds would add. Edmunds replied that "you can diminish the number of judges on your Supreme bench any day you please by the operation of nature," to which Trumbull inquired, "Do they die daily?" Undaunted, Edmunds retorted:

> They do die daily, almost. . . . It is much better to diminish the number of judges by letting them die daily, or as often as they get an opportunity, . . . than it is to undertake to create a legislative revolution, and fly in the face of the substance and spirit of the Constitution by legislating bodily out of existence nine men whom you have appointed and who the Constitution declares shall hold their offices during good behavior.[77]

For others, however, retooling court structure was by its very nature a semipermanent undertaking. "In amending the judiciary system of the United States," observed Senator George Williams, "it is necessary . . . to proceed with great deliberation, for the reason that whenever we do agree to any amendment the system which that amendment establishes is fastened upon the country and is entirely beyond our reach."[78] Senator Roscoe Conkling made a similar point: "This bill becoming a law, during the lifetime of men now living no great change is likely to occur in the judicial system and the judicial staff of the United States. Therefore it is, in the present and in the future, a subject of very grave importance."[79] Again, Senator Edmunds urged,

> we ought not make haste to adopt this new method, this new system, but rather, if there be a difference of opinion upon it, take time to reflect, so that a system which when adopted under our Constitution is a final one, at least for many years, may be thoroughly considered before it is put into operation.[80]

Third, against this backdrop of persistent resistance to fundamental change, the biggest hurdle that the 1869 legislation had to overcome was the objection that it did indeed effect a significant alteration in court structure, notwithstanding Senator Trumbull's representation that it "leaves the judicial system of the United States just as we found it."[81] Although the act did not eliminate (but only reduced) the Supreme Court justices' circuit-riding duties to biannual events, some objected to the bill on the grounds that it constituted circuit riding's death knell.[82] Circuit riding, they argued, remained critically important. Said Edmunds:

> We have found ever since the Government was founded that the administration of national justice . . . has been serenely and successfully carried on, on the whole, by a system which carried to the remotest corners of the Union the highest judges of the land to try causes at *nisi prius,* to mingle with the people, to hear witnesses, to see the jurors, to charge grand juries, and to dignify and make holy . . . justice at the very doors of the people; and then bringing from the people . . . that practical knowledge, that practical experience, that knowledge of men and things, which is just as essential to the decision of causes in the last resort as it is to the trial of causes at *nisi prius.*[83]

Without circuit riding, argued Senator Charles Buckalew, the justices of the Supreme Court "will become a court of error . . . separated altogether from the people of the country with no travel imposed upon them." He warned, "They will not be brought in contact with the great mass of the community, as they now are."[84] Williams was more hyperbolic, arguing that the Court would become "a fossilized institution" and that "the judges will know nothing about the business of the circuits,"[85] adding that the Court would be "a kind of Star Chamber that never sees or knows of the people."[86]

Trumbull defended the bill against these objections by acknowledging widespread congressional support for circuit riding; by arguing that he, too, was a great friend of the tradition; and by underscoring that the proposed legislation preserved circuit riding to the maximum extent practicable.[87] Senator Roscoe Conkling, however, saw the bill's preservation of circuit riding as a problem. He noted that under existing law, the justices were supposed to be riding circuit regularly but were not doing so. To the contrary, he asserted, "as a rule the judges of the Supreme Court do not devote as much time to *nisi prius* sitting in truth as they would be obliged to do in order substantially and fairly to comply" with the diminished circuit-riding duties provided for in Trumbull's bill.[88] Given that the bill would thus saddle Supreme Court justices with more circuit duty than before, Conkling asked, "Where is the relief . . . that the Supreme Court is to have under this bill?"[89]

Conkling's argument opened the door for Senators Edmunds and Williams to revisit an amendment to double the size of the Supreme Court to eighteen justices, of whom only nine would serve on the Supreme Court at any given time, with the remainder riding circuit.[90] Trumbull opposed the amendment on the grounds that the Supreme Court would declare it unconstitutional. "The Constitution establishes the Supreme Court, and you provide how many judges shall constitute it," he opined, "but you have no right to say that half of those judges shall take no part in the adjudications of that court." If the Court struck the law down, "you would have eighteen judges of your Supreme Court of the United States," Trumbull continued, inquiring rhetorically, "Does anybody want such a court as that?"[91]

Senator Casserly shared Trumbull's view that the amendment raised some "constitutional questions of a very grave character." His core concern, however, was not that the nation would wind up with too many justices if the Court declared the law unconstitutional but that it was irresponsible for Congress to "vex posterity" by provoking a constitutional crisis that tested the limits of its power over the Court. "[I]n so delicate a matter as the construction of the highest tribunal in the country," he asked rhetorically, is it "the part of wise men to leave a fundamental question of constitutional power to be a trouble and an obstruction to the members of that court and to the validity of its decisions for all time?"[92]

The 1869 debates evidence a nuanced interplay of concerns. There appears to have been almost unanimous agreement that the courts had fallen behind in their work and were in immediate need of assistance. The judiciary that Congress sought to reform in 1869 had many more judges among its ranks, many more cases on its dockets, many more states within its geographical scope, and many more matters within its jurisdictional reach than the judiciary that Congress had established in 1789, yet Congress was clearly hesitant to make significant changes. The legislators were acutely aware of the fact that they were legislating in the long shadow of the Judiciary Act of 1789, which had implemented the constitutional structure of the judicial branch eighty years before and which remained essentially intact in the interim. They were thus understandably reluctant to entertain proposals that would alter the judicial system in fundamental ways, for two reasons: (1) because of their reverence for the long-standing structure that the 1789 act established and (2) because the 1789 act served as a powerful precedent for the proposition that any structural changes they made—for worse as well as better—would likewise be long-standing.

Nowhere was the tension between tradition and exigency more evident than in Congress's uneasy resolution of the circuit-riding problem. In 1789, one could debate the potential for circuit riding to unify the judiciary and keep the justices in touch with local laws, legal communities, and citizens when there were only three circuits spanning thirteen geographically compressed states to traverse annually. But it is difficult to imagine that many in Congress were fatuous enough to suppose that these objectives could still be achieved eighty years later by having the justices sit once every other year in three times as many circuits spanning three times as many states covering half a continent. Indeed, proponents of circuit riding spoke of its virtues in such sweeping and abstract terms as to betray an awareness that its value was largely symbolic—a conclusion bolstered by the fact that the act of 1869 preserved circuit riding only in vestigial form. Were Congress truly committed to a functional circuit-riding system, it presumably would have taken more seriously proposals to enlarge the stable of circuit-riding justices. It did not because whatever good might have resulted from reenergizing the circuit-riding process would have come at the price of provoking a constitutional crisis with the Supreme Court over the limits of congressional power to restructure the separate and independent judicial branch and dictate its responsibilities. That was a price Congress was unwilling to pay.

By 1869, few labored under the delusion that the circuit courts were still being staffed to any significant extent by peripatetic Supreme Court justices, but there was no denying that circuit riding retained symbolic significance. As a symbol, circuit riding remained a subtle but important means to preserve the appearance of judicial accountability: the judges of the nation's highest court may have been appointed for life and may have been isolated in Washington most of the time, but every now and again they had to come down from their perch and face the people. Whatever its perceived value, Congress was not so committed to circuit riding that it was prepared to jeopardize the structural integrity of the courts and brave a constitutional showdown to make it work, but neither was it prepared to jettison circuit riding altogether merely as a means to achieve docket relief for the Supreme Court.

Spike Four: Populist, Progressive, and New Deal Disaffection with the Courts, and the Contemporaneous Emergence of an Independent, Self-Regulating Judiciary ∾

Populist, Progressive, and New Deal Disaffection with the Courts

The Populist period at the end of the nineteenth century and the Progressive era in the early twentieth century ushered in another wave of resentment directed at the courts. As Progressive reformers sought to address social ills through legislation, they came into conflict with state courts and a national Supreme Court that read the due process clause of the Fifth and Fourteenth Amendments to the U.S. Constitution as imposing distinct limits on the power of state and federal legislatures to regulate business and industry—typified by the Supreme Court's decision in *Lochner v. New York.*[93] Senator George Norris declared that federal judges on the trial and appellate levels were "not responsive to the pulsations of humanity [because] the security of a life position and a life salary makes them forget too often the toiling masses who are struggling for an existence."[94] Accordingly, as one scholar observed,

> the Populist-Progressives during the early decades of the century
> sought to infuse federal judicial institutions with elements of pop-

ular democracy, to alter the substance of judicial decisions, to change the selection of federal judges, and to circumscribe their power and the jurisdiction of their courts.[95]

Although the various attempts to end life tenure and control or manipulate the courts are too numerous to discuss each in detail, three are worthy of separate mention because of their apparent success: Congress's abolition of the unpopular Commerce Court in 1913; its enactment of the Norris-LaGuardia Act in 1932, which stripped the federal courts of jurisdiction to issue injunctions in labor disputes; and Franklin Delano Roosevelt's intimidation of the Supreme Court by means of his proposed court-packing plan.

Abolition of the Commerce Court

In 1910, Congress created the Commerce Court, comprised of Article III judges with circuit court jurisdiction, to hear appeals from decisions of the Interstate Commerce Commission (ICC) concerning railroad rates. It was thought that a single, specialized appellate court would be better able than the regional circuit courts to decide ICC appeals expeditiously, wisely, and without risk of intercircuit conflicts.[96] In the inaugural year of its nasty, brutish, and short existence, the Commerce Court succeeded in alienating just about everyone with an interest in its business: Congress and consumers were put off by the extent to which the Commerce Court overturned decisions of the popular ICC,[97] shippers lost interest when the Supreme Court declared that the Commerce Court lacked jurisdiction to hear their appeals from "negative" ICC orders dismissing rate-making petitions,[98] and the railroads preferred the ICC devil they knew to the Commerce Court they did not.[99]

Seemingly alone among the Commerce Court's true supporters was President William Howard Taft, who had lobbied for the court's creation and vetoed legislation providing for its abolition on the grounds that he could not find "a single reason why the court should be abolished except that those who propose to abolish it object to certain of its decisions," which he likened to "a recall of the judiciary" that he "utterly opposed."[100] By 1913, however, Taft was out of the White House. Congress again passed legislation to kill the Commerce

Court and pushed the judgeships (specifically created to staff the court) to the brink of obliteration, with the House voting for their elimination and the Senate declining to do so by a margin of twenty-five to twenty-three.[101] The Senate's position prevailed in the joint conference, and the legislation President Woodrow Wilson ultimately signed abolished the court but reassigned its judges to the regional circuits.[102] These events appear to signal a return to the ashes of the 1802 repeal of the Midnight Judges Act, ashes from which Congress had more or less steadily risen over the course of the intervening century. Indeed, when measured in terms of the relative threat to judicial independence, the more recent episode would seem to be even more troubling, insofar as it involved the obliteration of a tribunal in retaliation for its decisions.

The Norris-LaGuardia Act

In the first third of the twentieth century, federal courts issued a bevy of orders enjoining strikes by organized labor as a violation of the antitrust laws. Congress disapproved of this trend, and enacted the Norris-LaGuardia Act in 1932, which deprived the federal courts of authority to issue injunctions in labor disputes. Baldly put, Congress disagreed with decisions that federal judges made, and so stripped the courts of jurisdiction to make the offending decisions.

Roosevelt's Court-Packing Plan

Attacks on the Supreme Court accelerated after Franklin Roosevelt took office, when the Court continued in its laissez-faire role by striking down New Deal legislation, greatly frustrating the president.[103] On the disingenuous pretext that many federal judges were old and falling behind in their work, Roosevelt settled on a proposal originally developed in 1913 by then attorney general James McReynolds, who, a quarter of a century later, as an aging Supreme Court justice who often voted against New Deal legislation, would be hoisted on the petard of his own invention. Roosevelt proposed that whenever a federal judge remained on the bench past the age of seventy, the president be authorized to make an additional appointment, which would have enabled him to nominate six new Supreme Court justices. While legislation to implement the plan was pending in Congress, Justice

Owen Roberts, who had been one of the Court's five-member majority that invalidated New Deal legislation, switched sides and therefore systematically upheld such legislation. Pressure to pack the Court promptly subsided, the Court subsequently approved (among other New Deal enactments) the Norris-LaGuardia Act, and Robert's change of heart was dubbed the "switch in time that saved nine."

Populist, Progressive, and New Deal Disaffection with the Courts Reconsidered

In his superb study of the Populist and Progressive periods, William Ross documents the myriad attacks on the courts, which he describes as "a muted fury."[104] Despite widespread frustration with the courts for invalidating Populist, Progressive, and New Deal legislation, Ross finds a contrasting and even more widespread appreciation for the central role that the judiciary played in enforcing rights created by legislation that the courts upheld. Thus, proposals to end life tenure, curb judicial review, and so on were often given rhetorical support but were otherwise pursued less than enthusiastically by leading Populists and Progressives, were actively opposed by conservatives, and ultimately went nowhere.

This protracted period of disenchantment with the courts qualifies as the fourth cycle in the historical pattern of court-directed criticism chronicled in this chapter. By characterizing these episodes of heightened court criticism as "cycles," however, I do not mean to imply that each has crashed inexorably on the shore like a wave identical to its predecessors. To the contrary, although the level of criticism across the cycles may have been comparably shrill, the political branches' response to such criticism has diminished over time. The first cycle—the Jeffersonian Republican purge of the Federalist judiciary—featured a wholesale, partisan manipulation of congressional power to create and destroy inferior courts, coupled with an equally partisan and partially successful effort to impeach and remove Federalist judges. The impact of the second cycle was less extreme: some states did indeed defy the Supreme Court's constitutional authority, and President Jackson threatened to follow suit, but those threats never materialized. The third cycle was earmarked by the extraordinary anger of a Reconstruction Congress that ultimately came to comparatively little: Congress did deprive the Court of jurisdiction in *McCardle,* but in doing so, it made a backhanded concession to judicial supremacy by opting to circumscribe the Court's authority, rather than defy it as states had done in the second cycle; Congress also increased and decreased the size of the Supreme Court, but it either did not do so for partisan political purposes or felt constrained to conceal its true motives. At first blush, the fourth cycle was more productive, having featured a series of proposals to curb the courts, at least three of which appeared to succeed; the destruction of the Commerce Court; a retrenchment of the courts' remedial powers in labor disputes; and a court-packing plan that intimidated the Supreme Court into acquiescence to the New Deal agenda. When scrutinized more closely, however, these three developments reveal themselves to be significantly less independence-threatening than they initially appear, thereby rendering the fourth spike less destructive to customary independence than the third.

Abolition of the Commerce Court reconsidered.   Although Congress held its nose, followed the president's lead, and established the Commerce Court in 1910, it bears emphasis that its creation met with intense opposition and tepid support. Frankfurter and Landis go so far as to conclude that "[t]he fate of this proposal would have been doubtful" had it been voted on as a freestanding bill and that it won passage solely by virtue of its attachment as a rider to a larger piece of legislation "to which all parties were committed."[105] Indeed, Representative William Adamson later explained that "[t]he creation of this Commerce Court was a great mistake . . . caused by the absence of our colleagues at a baseball game," because the presence of those absent legislators on the House floor would have broken a tie vote on an amendment to delete the Commerce Court proposal from the legislative package to which it was affixed.[106]

To the extent that the Commerce Court's decisions contributed to its fate, it was because those decisions made prescient the objections of those opposed to creation of the court in the first place, rather than because those decisions caused a fickle Congress to annihilate a tribunal that it had welcomed into existence just three years earlier. Congress acted to repeal the Commerce Court in 1912, and as noted earlier, President Taft vetoed that legislation. In the next year, Congress tried again. Representative William Adamson took offense at Taft's veto message and "emphatically . . . dissent[ed] from any statement . . . that the only argument urged against this court is that some of the decisions of the judges are wrong."[107] To support his point, Adamson republished his original remarks in opposition to creation of the Commerce Court. Among his earlier arguments were his claims (1) that there were "so few cases in the past as to create no necessity for the court"; (2) that the special expertise of the court is overstated because "[i]t is not insisted by anybody that circuit judges will know any more while sitting in Commerce Court than when presiding on circuit"; and (3) that if judges are appointed with an eye to their special expertise, they "will be men who know more about . . . consolidation of railroads, destruction of competition, and disregard of public right, through long training as corporation lawyers," adding, "If anybody doubts this, let him wait and see."[108]

In the minds of Commerce Court critics, experience with the court in operation validated Adamson's arguments. As to the court's inconsequential docket, Adamson noted that "[d]ecisions of the Supreme Court"—such as those depriving the Commerce Court of jurisdiction to hear appeals from "negative" ICC orders—"have clarified the situation" and have thus ensured that "business of that character will be much less in the future than in the past."[109] Skepticism of the Commerce Court's special expertise and capacity to eliminate intercircuit conflicts was heightened by Supreme Court reversals in ten of its first twelve cases on appeal from the Commerce Court, which prompted Representative Thetus Sims to observe derisively, "they have had uniformity of decision, I am ready to admit, but it is uniformity of error."[110] As to the prediction that the Commerce Court would be biased in favor of the railroads, the suspicion appeared to be confirmed by a 1911 ICC report finding that "[o]ut of 27 cases passed upon by the Commerce Court, preliminary restraining orders or final decrees have been issued in favor of the railroads in all but seven cases, and of these only three are of any magnitude."[111] These developments—occurring as they did against the backdrop of an ongoing impeachment investigation of Commerce Court judge Robert Archbald on corruption charges—served to validate preexisting congressional concern that the court was, by its very nature, less than impartial. By 1913, Taft was gone from the White House, Congress acted to abolish the Commerce Court a second time, and President Wilson signed the bill into law.

Although one could argue that Congress unpacked the Commerce Court in much the same way as the Jeffersonian Republicans unpacked the circuit courts in 1802, there are three significant differences. First, there was more to the explanation for eliminating the Commerce Court than the political reality that the balance of decision-making power in Congress had shifted. Unlike the circuit courts of 1801, which never heard a case, the Commerce Court confirmed preexisting suspicions and sealed its fate by its performance on the job. While one could argue that this difference simply makes the abolition of the Commerce Court all the more threatening to judicial independence, such a conclusion needs to be qualified. The court was, in some sense, abolished because its decisions were unpopular, but the reasons offered to abolish the court (with its decisions being introduced as evidence) were that the court was unnecessary, that it lacked the special expertise that was its raison d'être, and that a specialized tribunal designed to second-guess the ICC would possess an inherent antiregulatory bias—reasons that linked abolition directly to improving judicial administration and that arguably removed it altogether from the definitional scope of court unpacking.

A second difference is that unlike its perception of the circuit courts of 1801, Congress never really conceptualized the Commerce Court as integral to the Article III judiciary. Historian George Dix argues persuasively that Congress instead thought of it as a sort of ICC adjunct that could be regulated out of existence without regard to the congressional ethic of restraint that the federal judiciary generally had come to enjoy over the course of the preceding century.[112] Insofar as abolition of the Commerce Court politicized federal court disestablishment in ways unprecedented since 1802, it did so not because Congress abandoned well-developed norms against politicizing federal court structure and size but because those norms were deemed less than fully applicable to this new, hybrid tribunal.

Third and most important, despite the hybrid status of the Commerce Court itself, Congress recognized that the court was constituted of Article III judges, and unlike its 1802 predecessor, the 1913 Congress resisted the temptation to decommission the judges when it closed down the court. In the House, momentum to abolish the judgeships along with the court was considerable. "If the creation of these judgeships was a mistake, their continuance now will be equally a mistake,"[113] declared Representative Melville Kelly, who quoted Thomas Jefferson for the proposition that "[t]he judiciary is a subtle corps of sappers and miners, constantly working underground to undermine the foundations of our confederated fabric," who "consider themselves secure" after "[h]aving found from experience that impeachment is an impracticable thing, a mere scarecrow."[114]

With the exception of this oblique reference, the relationship between the push to abolish judgeships in 1913 and 1802 went unappreciated in the House, which voted to expel the judges along with the Commerce Court. The Senate debates, however, were a different matter. Senator Hoke Smith, like Kelly in the House, favored eliminating the excess judges caused by abolition of the Commerce Court and saw no constitutional impediment to doing so: "Congress was given the power to say what inferior courts we should have, how many judges should be upon them, . . . decreasing the number if Congress saw fit."[115] Senator William Borah disagreed, suggesting that if Smith were right, legislators searching for an easy way to remove judges could bypass impeachment and simply abolish the judges' stations. Smith denied that a legislator could "vote simply for the abolition of a particular circuit or of a particular district because his object was in that way simply to remove a judge," because "[s]uch conduct would be highly improper" and "would be violative of the spirit of the Constitution." In the end, however, Smith stuck by his guns that Congress had the power to eliminate judgeships at will. "Exactly," Borah retorted, explaining:

> Then we come back to the proposition . . . that the country will be glad to know, in view of this urgent propaganda for the recall of judges, that they need not wait for the slow process of impeachment or recall, but that they can call upon their Senators and Representatives to eliminate any man from the bench that they want off the bench. They can simply abolish his circuit, get him out, and re-create the circuit.[116]

The debate then took a turn for the historical. For the framers of the Constitution, observed Senator Thomas Walsh, "independence of the judges was something which all parties at that time deemed of the very first consequence." This led Walsh to conclude that "the legality of . . . this method of getting rid of obnoxious judges, is open to the most serious doubt on constitutional grounds."[117] In defense of abolishing the judgeships, Senator Smith pointed to the 1802 repeal of the Midnight Judges Act as precedent, noting that "Congress proceeded to abolish . . . those inferior courts that had been established, and with their abolition went out of office the men who had filled them, . . . [s]o . . . it is clear that power is with Congress."[118] Senator John Shields, however, regarded the 1802 act as an exception to a different rule of considerably longer standing: "with . . . [the 1802 act] exception, for more than 100 years until this Act was introduced and passed by the House, it was never attempted to substitute a statute for the mode pointed out by the Constitution of removing judges by impeachment."[119] Walsh agreed, adopting as his own Justice Joseph Story's analysis of the 1802 act.

> The act may be asserted, without fear of contradiction, to have been against the opinion of a great majority of the ablest lawyers at the time; and probably now, when the passions of the day have subsided, few lawyers will be found to maintain the constitutionality of the act. No one can doubt the perfect authority of Congress to remodel their courts, or to confer or withdraw their jurisdiction at their pleasure, but the question is, whether they can deprive judges of the tenure of their office and their salaries after they have once become constitutionally vested in them.[120]

The Senate voted against elimination of the judgeships, and the House concurred. The Commerce Court was abolished. Its judges were assigned to the circuit courts of appeals, and the norm against court unpacking was respected.

The Norris-LaGuardia Act reconsidered. The Sherman Antitrust Act of 1890 forbade combinations in restraint of trade. The federal courts wasted no time in characterizing strikes by labor unions as a violation of the Sherman Act, and in 1895 the Supreme Court held that the federal courts were authorized to prevent strikes by means of injunctions and restraining orders. Thereafter, court injunctions in labor disputes proliferated like rabbits: 28 injunctions were issued in the 1880s; 122 in the 1890s, and 328 in the first decade of the twentieth century.[121] Congress was not happy; it favored a laissez-faire approach to labor disputes that was at odds with the interventionist tack the federal courts had taken. To remedy the problem, Congress enacted the Clayton Antitrust Act of 1914, which seemed calculated to exempt labor unions from antitrust restrictions. Section 6 of that Act declared:

> Nothing in the antitrust laws shall be construed to forbid the existence and operation of labor . . . organizations instituted for the purpose of mutual help . . . or to forbid or restrain individual members from such organizations from lawfully carrying out the legitimate objectives thereof; nor shall such organizations or members thereof, be held or construed to be illegal combinations or conspiracies in restraint of trade under the antitrust laws.[122]

In 1921, however, the Supreme Court interpreted the Clayton Act's exemption for labor unions narrowly, holding that it did not apply when unions "depart[ed] from . . . normal and legitimate objects."[123] And so, between 1920 and 1930, the number of injunctions issued against unions increased unabated to 921.[124] When Congress returned to the drawing board and emerged in 1932 with the Norris-LaGuardia Act, it left no room for doubt: Section 1 deprived the federal courts of "jurisdiction to issue any restraining order or temporary or permanent injunction in a case involving or growing out of a labor dispute."

Although the Norris-LaGuardia Act technically deprived the federal courts of "jurisdiction" to enjoin strikes in labor disputes, it was not a classic jurisdiction-stripping measure. In a true jurisdiction-strip, Congress seeks to avoid disfavored judicial interpretation and application of laws that are beyond Congress's power to control directly, by depriving the courts of jurisdictional authority to declare what the law is. Thus, a "classic" jurisdiction-stripping measure was that enacted in response to the McCardle case, where Congress barred the Supreme Court from hearing an appeal that would have given the Court an opportunity to declare a piece of Reconstruction legislation unconstitutional. More recent bills to deprive the courts of jurisdiction to hear cases challenging prayer in public schools, abortion restrictions, the Pledge of Allegiance, and public displays of the Ten Commandments fall into the same category: each would deny the courts an opportunity to assess the constitutionality of government actions which, if invalidated, would be beyond the power of Congress to fix, save by the impractical means of a constitutional amendment.

The Norris-LaGuardia Act was different in two respects. First, it had more to do with restricting the courts' remedial powers than curbing their subject matter jurisdiction. Second, and more important, the Act did not deprive the courts of authority to uphold laws that were otherwise beyond Congress's power to control. Congress was well within its commerce clause authority to immunize labor unions from antitrust liability, as it attempted to do in the Clayton Act. When the courts interpreted the Clayton Act in a way that Congress had not intended, Congress decided to override that interpretation by restricting the courts' remedial powers as an alternative way to ensure that antitrust laws were rendered inapplicable to unions in labor disputes. In this respect, the Norris-LaGuardia Act is more akin to a garden-variety legislative override of an unwelcome judicial interpretation of a statute (which Congress does regularly), than a true jurisdiction-strip that end-runs the judiciary's authority to declare what the law is (which legislators often propose but Congress rarely enacts). That may help to explain why the Norris-LaGuardia Act stands as an isolated success story amid a contemporaneous series of failed proposals to curb the courts by means of curtailing their subject matter jurisdiction—proposals discussed later in this chapter.[125]

Roosevelt's court-packing plan reconsidered.   I do not dispute the possibility that the threat of the court-packing plan may have influenced Justice Roberts's epiphany to embrace the New Deal (even though many have argued the contrary), which in turn made implementation of the plan unnecessary. But it is misleading to suggest that the plan would have been enacted had it not been for Roberts's change in vote. The claim that Roberts's "switch in time" saved the president a humiliating defeat in Congress may be less memorable but more accurate. Despite Roosevelt's popularity and the Supreme Court's unpopularity, the court-packing plan lacked majority public approval,[126] had the support of surprisingly few Court critics,[127] and received a tepid welcome in Congress. William Ross's explanation for the demise of the court-packing plan resonates nicely with the theme of this book.

> [The court-packing plan] ultimately failed because it contravened the respect for the judiciary so deeply engrained in the American character. . . . Roosevelt's calm and frequently repeated assertion that "the people are with me" underestimated the profound esteem that "the people" accord to the Supreme Court as long as its decisions do not diverge too radically from popular opinion. As an Idaho farmer wrote to Roosevelt, the Supreme Court "is a judicial body . . . and is not a plow horse for or with anyone."[128]

The incompatibility of the plan with what were by then well-established norms against court packing specifically and against precipitous, independence-threatening court reform generally was recognized at the time by scholars who testified before Congress in opposition to the plan. Professor Erwin Griswold began his testimony with the "dull but instructive subject of precedents" and, after surveying the history of congressional adjustments to the size of the Supreme Court, concluded:

> At their most they do not hold a candle to the present proposal. No one of them added more than two judges, and only once have as many as two places been added to the Court. And it cannot be shown that the dominant purpose in increasing the size of the Court was ever the desire to influence or control the results of its decisions.[129]

Even more striking was the extraordinary testimony of Raymond Moley, *Newsweek* editor and professor of public law at Columbia University.

> [A] deliberate attempt by one branch of Government to weaken another branch has very few parallels in our history. And none of them is creditable. . . . That way has always been open to the purposes of any dominant Executive and congressional majority. But the very fact that it has not been employed, except in one or two cases of which we are not very proud, has established an inhibition

upon the use of this method—an inhibition based upon custom and tradition. In other words, a custom has been established that fundamental changes should not be so attained—a custom of the Constitution, or a doctrine of political stare decisis, if you will, which is as binding upon public officials as a written provision of the Constitution itself. . . . The maintenance of the custom of the Constitution is essential to the preservation of a stable Government under which people are able to plan their lives and direct their actions. It is true that the custom of the Constitution changes, but it changes slowly and its existence is an indispensable element in a democratic government.[130]

In the years since the abandonment of Roosevelt's plan, there has been no concerted effort of comparable stature to pack or unpack the Supreme Court or the lower courts. Some scholars, however, remain of the view that a subtler form of court packing "has thrived."[131] John De Figueiredo and Emerson Tiller have developed this argument in a study of periodic legislation creating additional federal judgeships.[132] They found, first, that Congress generally enlarges the size of the federal judiciary only when the White House and both chambers of Congress are controlled by the same political party. Second, they found that while Congress "takes caseload burdens into account in deciding on the number of new judgeships," it frequently deviates from the Judicial Conference's recommendations as to the number of judgeships to be created and the circuits to which those judgeships are to be assigned. From these findings, De Figueiredo and Tiller conclude that "installing like-minded judges" enables Congress to "enjoy the benefits of having a judiciary in place that will ensure that the 'right' policies are achieved in court, thereby relieving the legislature of costly intervention."

De Figueiredo and Tiller's findings warrant qualification. As to the first finding, it should be noted that when Congress passes new judgeships legislation, it is almost invariably preceded by a Judicial Conference request for additional judges.[133] Deborah Barrow, Gary Zuk, and Gerard Gryski underscore the relevance of the Judicial Conference to the growth of the federal judiciary in the twentieth century when they characterize the conference as the "initiator or agenda setter for enlargement of the third branch," whose role as "'expert' on judgeship needs and judicial administration in general" has "translated into political influence."[134] Put another way, as necessary as unified government may usually be to the passage of new judgeships legislation, it remains insufficient absent a nonpartisan showing of need.

As to the second finding, De Figueiredo and Tiller's study elicits no information relevant to understanding why Congress deviates from Judicial Conference recommendations. If, as the authors assume, Congress packs the courts to ensure favorable decision-making majorities, Congress would presumably target its infusion of unnecessary judgeships at circuits that have made decisions unpopular with the congressional majority or that are dominated disproportionately by judges appointed by a president from the opposing party. Not only are such assumptions unproven, but they are contradicted by available anecdotal evidence, which suggests that patronage, rather than court packing, is the driving force behind congressional deviations from Judicial Conference recommendations. Thus, for example, when the 1990 judgeships bill was pending, L. Ralph Mecham, director of the Administrative Office of the United States Courts, accused the Democrat-controlled Senate of departing from Judicial Conference recommendations in order to placate influential Republicans, by giving "[v]irtually every Republican on the Senate Judiciary Committee. . . an extra judgeship for his state."[135] To the extent that accretions to court size are attributable to patronage, the practice may be partisan and political, but it is not court packing as I have defined it, because it is not employed as a means of court control.

De Figueiredo and Tiller's conclusions should likewise be qualified. These scholars present no convincing evidence that Congress manipulates court structure by creating unnecessary judgeships for the purpose of "ensur[ing] that the right results are achieved in court." They do, however, persuasively demonstrate that Congress manipulates the timing of needed judgeships legislation to ensure that "the nominating president and the confirming Senate . . . appoint judges who will have political preferences consistent with those of the enacting Congress." This is a means of court control, to be sure, but it is probably better characterized as a political manipulation of judicial appointments than of court structure. When Congress changes court structure by increasing the size of the federal judiciary, there is typically a good government need for it to do so, and insofar as some of the judgeships it creates are unnecessary, the explanation may have nothing to do with a desire to control court decision making. The decision to delay needed judgeships legislation, however, can often be explained only in terms of the congressional majority's desire to wait for a like-minded president to install ideologically compatible judges. This is neither court packing nor court unpacking but, rather, a delay imposed in the service of manipulating the appointments process. This distinction between manipulation of structure and appointment is critical to this study, because of the fundamental differences in the institutional norms applicable to each. As detailed in this chapter, independence norms have established and preserved an atmosphere of restraint when it comes to the governance of court structure. Judicial appointments, in contrast, are subject to a different set of norms that, as described in chapter 4, are less sensitive to judicial independence concerns and more focused on promoting prospective accountability of judges to the political branches.

The Contemporaneous Emergence of an Independent, Self-Regulating Judiciary

As previously discussed, the periods of calm separating the first three spikes of court-directed anger serve to contextualize and qualify those spikes, enabling us to recharacterize the independence-threatening actions of the political branches during those episodes as exceptions to an emerging rule of political branch respect for the judiciary's autonomy. A similar point can be made in regard to the fourth spike. The Populist, Progressive, and New Deal assaults on the federal courts spanned over forty years, from the 1890s to the 1930s—the longest period of sustained and intense frustration with the federal courts in our history. Yet during that same period, the modern, independent, self-regulating judiciary was established by Congress and approving presidents in a remarkable series of legislative measures. As discussed shortly, Congress passed legislation in 1891 creating intermediate courts of appeals, which enabled the federal courts to hold themselves more systematically accountable to each other for their decisions. In 1922, Congress authorized the judiciary to govern itself through the establishment of the Conference of Senior Circuit Judges, later renamed the Judicial Conference of the United States. In 1934, Congress revitalized the judiciary's power to promulgate its own procedural rules. And in 1939, Congress transferred budgetary control of the courts from the Department of Justice to the judiciary itself and created the Administrative Office of United States Courts to facilitate judicial self-administration.

This movement toward a self-regulating judiciary marks the third great manifestation of independence norms described at the beginning of this chapter. Why was Congress driven to expand judicial autonomy amid a period of intense disaffection with the courts? As explained shortly, although Congress sometimes acted despite such criticism, the movement toward a self-regulating judiciary is often better understood as a reaction to it.

Creating circuit courts of appeals. Congress painted itself into a corner during the first three-quarters of the nineteenth century. In that time, Congress had come around to the view that it could best respect the structural integrity and independence of the judiciary by resisting proposals to amend the Judiciary Act of 1789 in significant ways. This was all fine and well, as long as incremental reforms, such as simply increasing the number of judges, as was done in 1869, were adequate to enable the judiciary to manage its expanding docket. But the 1869 legislation did no better at easing the workload of the Supreme Court than its critics predicted.[136] In 1882, Senator David Davis noted that the 636 cases pending before the Supreme Court in 1870 had very nearly doubled, to 1,202, by 1880.[137] The push to reestablish intermediate courts of appeals resumed in earnest.

A decade of travail culminated in 1891 with the passage of the Evarts Act, which created an intermediate appellate court in each regional circuit and was named after its Senate sponsor, William Evarts. The Evarts Act has been ably described elsewhere and does not warrant detailed recapitulation here.[138] What does bear a second look, however, are the circumstances enabling the controversial legislation to pass after eight decades of failure. One obvious impetus for the reform, emphasized by Frankfurter and Landis, was that the docket of the Supreme Court had reached a crisis point.[139] Yet this is only a partial explanation, because the rhetoric of caseload crisis, invoked time and again throughout the century, had not previously budged Congress from its long-standing disinclination to make significant change.

Three related developments help to explain why Congress finally abandoned a century-long strategy of incremental reform. First, significant segments of Congress, particularly southern legislators, nonplused by Reconstruction, had become openly hostile to federal judges and what they perceived to be runaway judicial power and independence. Second, in a development closely related to the first, proponents of the court of appeals proposal won over court critics by characterizing it as a means to promote the accountability of megalomaniacal trial judges. Third, friends of the courts recast their debt of respect to the framers of the judiciary, from one that emphasized the duty to minimize departures from the system the founders established, to one that emphasized the importance of providing for a judiciary that achieved the objectives the founders envisioned.

Notwithstanding widespread hostility toward the Supreme Court during the Jacksonian era and Reconstruction, the debates that took place in the 1820s and 1860s concerning lower court reform were typified by excessive reverence for the judiciary generally. By the 1880s, however, that had changed. Southern legislators spewed venom at lower court Reconstruction judges, and Populist sentiments in opposition to a seemingly aristocratic judiciary began to take hold and give rise to the fourth spike.

Some thought federal judges were too political or partisan. The act of 1869 had established new circuit judgeships, at least in part for the explicit purpose of enforcing Reconstruction laws in the South. As far as many southern legislators were concerned, the results had been disastrous. Senator John Morgan of Alabama complained. "We have nine circuit judges in the United States. . . . [S]ome of [them] were appointed in times of high political excitement and seem to feel that it is a part of their judicial duty to respond on all occasions where opportunity is afforded to the sentiment which led to their appointment."[140] To make matters worse, Morgan continued, "more of the district judges have been appointed in consideration of their extreme party bias than of the circuit judges"[141] and have committed acts "which an American ought to blush to be compelled to recite."[142]

Others expressed the related concern that federal judges were too high-handed. Florida senator Williston Call opined that "[t]he public opinion of the country regards some of the judges . . . as men capable of any prostitution of judicial power,"[143] who "would not hesitate to convict innocent men for their own purposes."[144] Because the federal judiciary "has generally been on the side of tyranny and against the liberties of the people," he urged the passage of an amendment that would automatically stay trial court judgments in all criminal cases pending appeal.[145] Senator Benjamin Jonas pointed to an 1860 case in which the Supreme Court first authorized federal courts to grant writs of mandamus against state tribunals. "[W]e can well doubt whether this latent power would have been allowed to slumber for seventy years if it had been generally believed to exist,"[146] he observed accusingly. Alabama senator John Morgan later concluded: "the Federal tribunals have usurped all the judicial power that now belongs to the States and that has heretofore been exercised by them. The march in that direction is so rapid that it amounts to a crusade against the tribunals of the [s]tates."[147]

For still others, the problem was that federal judges were lazy or incompetent. "State judges . . . open court in the morning at 9 o'clock, some of them at 8, hold court until 12 or 1, meet again at 2, and hold court again until 6, and then have a night session,"[148] observed Senator George Vest, while "[a] Federal judge would think his life was in danger if he did such work as that."[149] In considering a proposal to convert the circuit courts to courts of appeals, Senator Matthew Butler of South Carolina conditioned his support on the adoption of an amendment that would require the judges to rotate among the courts, claiming that the South Carolina circuit judge was "utterly unfit,"—more specifically, "worthless[] and infamous."[150] Accordingly, Butler would not consent to giving this judge's court "additional power unless there is a prospect of getting rid of him and having his presence certainly not more than once in nine years."[151] James Ingalls of Kansas did not support Butler's amendment but agreed that the alleged acts of the circuit judge in question were "a much greater disgrace to justice and to liberty than has ever before been perpetrated on this continent."[152] Benjamin Jonas of Louisiana concurred, "There are incompetent judges on the bench in [the

South] and who will remain on the bench if this bill passes, and who will form part of the court of appeals."[153]

The independence that came with life tenure was a common thread that wove these perceived problems together. "The life tenure of office in federal judges is abhorrent to the people,"[154] argued George Vest, citing as evidence the fact that all of the western states had "taken the power of appointing judges away from the governors of the states and vested it in the people."[155] "[W]hen you put a man into an office with life tenure, and . . . put him on a sort of pedestal above the rest of the people,"[156] Vest later observed, "he then thinks that leisure is the first element of his new position." Vest maintained: "You may take the hardest-working lawyer in this country and make a Federal judge of him and he will quit. . . . He will immediately become a *dilettante*."[157] Senator Call noted that "a court holding power by life tenure"[158] is "separated from the sympathies and feelings which animate the great body of the country"[159] and that "take their color and tone from the political party in control of the Government."[160] Senator Morgan went a step further: "when you put [a judge] in for a life position and nobody to scrutinize his acts,"[161] he argued, "how can we expect a man of that sort not to drift off in the line of his convictions or his friendships or his enmities?"[162]

Perhaps the most telling indication of mounting hostility toward the federal courts was the increasing frequency with which members of Congress introduced constitutional amendments to end life tenure for federal judges. During the first century of the Republic, only about twenty amendments limiting the terms of federal judges were introduced. In contrast, between 1889 and 1929, such amendments were introduced at the rate of approximately one per year.[163] Many additional resolutions, such as those calling for the popular election of federal judges, were likewise introduced.[164]

For those legislators who saw federal judges as high-handed, lazy, and overly politicized, the argument that we needed to relieve overworked federal judges by creating a new tier of appellate courts staffed with even more federal judges was greeted with an understandable lack of enthusiasm. Skeptical legislators looked more smilingly on proposals to restrict the courts' subject-matter jurisdiction. The sentiments expressed by Florida senator Charles Jones are illustrative.

Why has the number of cases increased so greatly in the Federal courts, while in the state courts . . . no such increase is perceptible? . . . [I]t is because the courts of the United States have been by degrees usurping powers that the framers of the Constitution never intended they should exercise. . . .

And now instead of attempting to cut down on that jurisdiction, instead of beginning at the right end and bringing back this authority to the confines that originally bounded it, we are asked to pervert the entire scheme of the fathers of the Constitution and undertake to establish nine appellate courts instead of one.[165]

With rare exception, however, states' rights advocates who sought to limit the subject-matter jurisdiction of the federal courts suffered one humiliating defeat after another throughout the latter half of the nineteenth century. In the aftermath of the Civil War, Congress enacted a plethora of statutes that expanded the jurisdiction of the federal courts, including the National Bank Acts of the 1860s, the Bankruptcy Act of 1867, and the Federal Enforcement Act of 1870.[166] Adoption of the Fourteenth Amendment likewise flooded the federal courts with new cases and claims.[167] And in the 1877 decision of *Ex parte Schollenberger,* the Supreme Court construed the federal removal statute to permit corporations sued in state court to remove their cases to a federal forum, which effectively expanded the scope of the federal judiciary's diversity of citizenship jurisdiction.[168]

The high-water mark, however, was the Removal Act of 1875.[169] Prior to 1875, federal trial courts were granted only ad hoc jurisdiction to hear cases rising under particular federal laws. In one of the last gasps of the Reconstruction era, a relatively innocuous bill that the House passed to clarify the circumstances under which federal courts could hear diversity cases removed from state courts was quietly amended in the Senate to give the lower federal courts original jurisdiction over all questions arising under federal law. The amendment was passed by the Senate and, following a joint conference, accepted by both chambers without any meaningful explanation, discussion, or dissent—leading one pair of commentators to suspect it of being "sneak legislation."[170]

As an increase in the congestion of the federal court docket ensued, and states' rights proponents attempted to capitalize on the increase by introducing proposals to curtail subject-matter jurisdiction, they rarely came closer to this goal than close.[171] A bill to overturn *Schollenberger* and limit the scope of the federal courts' removal jurisdiction passed the House in three consecutive Congresses but failed each time in the Senate. Opponents of the measure, many from the Northeast, were unshakable in their view that only independent federal judges could be trusted to act impartially in interstate commercial disputes. Massachusetts representative George Robinson explained:

> Capital is needed to restore the waste places of the South and build up the undeveloped west; it must flow largely from the old states of the east and from foreign lands. But it will not be risked in the perils of sectional bitterness, narrow prejudices, or local indifference to integrity and honor. I say then, let us stand by the national courts; let us preserve their power.[172]

Legislators who supported a strong federal judiciary may have defeated proposals to strip the courts of jurisdiction, but those disgruntled with federal judges remained a force with which to reckon. The passage of the Evarts Act may have ultimately turned on its proponents' ability to position the establishment of an intermediate court of appeals as a means not only to relieve docket congestion but also to promote the accountability of rogue trial judges.[173]

Under the proposal finally adopted, new courts of appeals were to be established in each of the nine circuits. Judges comprising each circuit's three-member court of appeals were to be drawn from the ranks of the circuit's district judges, its two circuit judges (one newly established, the other previously established by the act of 1869), and circuit-riding justices. Although the proposal sat uneasily with such legislators as South Carolina senator Matthew Butler, who was loath to promote despised trial judges to the courts of appeals, his objection was deflected by Senator Augustus Garland, who professed to "sympathize, from [his] heart,"[174] with Butler's concern, but who noted, "If the Senator from South Carolina will reflect that we get an additional force upon such a judge there to hold him in check or to review or examine his acts, he will see that with that addition he has a safeguard which he did not have before."[175]

The notion that courts of appeals would serve to restrain bad fed-

eral judges struck a responsive chord among some of the same legislators who favored restricting the federal courts' subject-matter jurisdiction. Alabama senator James Pugh believed that "a large portion of
jurisdiction conferred upon Federal courts . . . can be safely restored
to and made exclusive in the State courts, and thereby relieve the
existing pressure."[176] He expressed regret at "[t]he failure to secure
this desirable reformation in the bill before the Senate."[177] He nevertheless favored establishing intermediate courts of appeals. In
response to fellow Alabama senator John Morgan's complaints about
their home state's district judge, John Bruce, Pugh commented that if
"Bruce and those like him are members of the new court of
appeals,"[178] then "they would have to obtain the concurrence of two
circuit judges . . . before they could secure affirmance of their judgments."[179] Pugh warned, "If there is no court of appeals, Judge Bruce
. . . can laugh at your criticisms and criminations in the Senate or elsewhere, and indulge himself at his own will and pleasure, without
restraint or interruption in the scope of his own jurisdiction."[180]

In the House, David Culberson of Texas—who had thrice led the
losing charge to restrict the federal courts' removal jurisdiction—was
likewise a convert to the court of appeals proposal.

> If this measure can be enacted into law an end will be put sum-
> marily to the judicial despotism exercised by circuit and district
> judges in many localities. . . . I have a supreme desire to witness
> during my time in Congress the overthrow of the kingly power of
> district and circuit judges.
>
> It is a fact established by actual examination that one judge
> alone presides in eight-ninths of all the cases tried in the circuit
> and district courts of the United States, and in more than half of
> them he is the final arbiter.[181]

Consistent with the views of Representative Culberson, the House
Judiciary Committee report cataloged the advantages of the bill and
listed as second (behind "[t]o unload the docket of the Supreme
Court") the fact that it "destroys the 'judicial despotism' of the present system by creating an intermediate appellate court, with power to
revise the final judgments of the district courts."[182]

Throughout the first three-quarters of the nineteenth century, a sticking point to establishing courts of appeals had been a fundamental resistance to significant change, born of a deep respect for the stability and independence of the judicial branch and the structure that the framers of the Constitution and the 1789 Judiciary Act had implemented. Indeed, reluctance to abandon the familiar remained a weight in the balance of the Evarts Act of 1891. The House bill would have combined circuit and district courts, added eighteen new circuit judges to staff the courts of appeals, eliminated all direct review to the Supreme Court from the trial courts, and ended Supreme Court circuit riding.[183] Frankfurter and Landis credit Senator Evarts for making enactment of the legislation possible by amending the House bill in ways that "satisfied traditionalists."[184] Evarts kept the district and circuit courts as they were, cut in half the proposed infusion of new circuit judges, preserved direct review to the Supreme Court in limited instances, and let sleeping circuit-riding lie.[185]

Notwithstanding these modest genuflections to preexisting court structure, the fact remained that the 1891 Evarts Act transformed the judiciary in fundamental ways that had theretofore been politically unviable. Ever-escalating caseloads and the reinvention of the court of appeals proposal as a means to keep increasingly unpopular federal trial judges in check partially explained congressional willingness to abandon a long-standing preference for incremental reform. In addition, however, there was a subtle but significant transformation in the role that Congress perceived itself playing in court reform.

During the first eighty years of the century, the prevailing sentiment among congressional leaders had been that Congress had a duty to preserve and protect the judicial system by respecting the structure that the founders had established—a duty best discharged by changing court structure as little as possible. In the waning years of the nineteenth century, legislators remained no less committed to protecting the judiciary and paying homage to the founders, but they began to interpret that commitment differently. Legislators now argued that the nation had outgrown the system implemented by the Judiciary Act of 1789 and that Congress's responsibility to preserve the well-being of the judicial branch could best be fulfilled by adopting reforms enabling the courts to serve the ends that the founders intended.

In the House, David Culberson—who served as a leading spokesman in the successful effort to win House acquiescence to the Senate version of the bill—made his case on the House floor.

> As the business and population of the country increase, litigation embraced within and covered by the judicial power of the United States correspondingly increases, and it is the unquestioned duty of Congress to provide the necessary courts and judicial force to meet the increased demands of the country upon the judiciary.
>
> The framers of the Constitution did not construct it for their day and time, but for all time.
>
> They foresaw the coming greatness and grandeur of the United States and looked onward to the time when this Government would outstrip all other nations in empire, in wealth, and popula-tion.
>
> The authority vested in Congress to make exceptions to and regulate the appellate jurisdiction of the Supreme Court was granted for the purpose of enabling the Congress to adapt the appellate jurisdiction of the court to the varying demands of the business, trade and commerce of the country, and to protect and shield that great tribunal from the conditions which exist to-day.[186]

While Culberson argued that Congress had not only the constitu-tional power but a constitutional duty to implement comprehensive reform in the Senate, Evarts took pains to explain why such reform showed no disrespect to the authors of the first Judiciary Act.

> The encomium upon the famous statute drawn by Chief-Justice Ellsworth is recognized by every lawyer and by every judge. The only thing that has happened to that statute has not been in the nature of man nor in the wisdom of jurisprudence nor in the credit of a judicial establishment; it has been the growth of the United States. . . . [Y]ou can not alter the fact that what was wise and what was sufficient, what was noble and generous and main-tained its supremacy for the great growth of this nation has now outlived that purpose.[187]

The 1891 act, then, was groundbreaking for two different reasons. First, it represented a significant change in Congress's attitude toward court reform. The long-standing disinclination to alter the judicial system in significant ways was suppressed in favor of a new desire to perfect a constitutional structure that Congress was duty-bound to implement—a sentiment harkening back to that animating the Judiciary Act of 1789.

Second, it was the first congressional enactment consciously designed to rein in the perceived excesses of federal trial courts, and it was the first step in the direction of making the judiciary more accountable to itself since the Judiciary Act of 1789. In 1805, Congress tried and failed to remove the high-handed Samuel Chase by impeachment. In the 1880s, Congress had repeatedly tried and failed to strip the courts of subject-matter jurisdiction. With increasing frequency toward the end of the century, legislators had tried and failed to end life tenure by constitutional amendment. Unlike this string of legislative failures, however, which sought to hold judges more accountable to Congress or the people, the 1891 act succeeded in making judges more accountable to each other through improved judicial review.

Authorizing the Conference of Senior Circuit Judges. The Evarts Act marked the beginning of a subtle but profound transformation of Congress's conceptualization of an independent but accountable judiciary. This would be the third great manifestation of emerging independence norms in Congress: the gradual establishment of an independent, self-governing judicial branch, beginning in 1891 and continuing throughout the twentieth century. Curtailing judicial despotism was one of the goals (albeit a secondary one) of that legislation. Unlike contemporaneous proposals with similar aims that sought to promote judicial accountability by weakening the judicial institution (e.g., ending life tenure, constraining judicial review, or narrowing subject-matter jurisdiction), the Evarts Act undertook to hold the courts accountable to themselves by strengthening the judiciary's structural framework.

As the twentieth century arrived, the Evarts Act did little to quiet the criticism of Populists and Progressives, who remained incensed both by the law's delay stemming from deficiencies in judicial practice, procedure, and administration and by the insolence of office as reflected in court decisions that flouted the popular will by invalidating legislation regulating business and industry. Although the latter weighed more heavily on the Populist and Progressive mind, conservative reformers, such as Roscoe Pound and William Howard Taft, strove to redefine the problem as beginning and ending with practice, procedure, and administration.

In 1906, Roscoe Pound delivered an address to the American Bar Association in which he isolated four "causes of popular dissatisfaction with the administration of justice":[188] (1) those common to all legal systems, (2) those attributable to the "peculiarities" of the Anglo-American legal system, (3) those relating to the American judiciary's organization and procedure, and (4) those relating to a transitory "environment" typified by public apathy and ignorance, commercialization of the legal profession, and politicization of the courts, among other things.[189] In Pound's view, the third cause alone merited attention.

> Reviewing the several causes for dissatisfaction with the administration of justice which have been touched upon, it will have been observed that some inhere in all law and are the penalty we pay for uniformity; that some inhere in our political institutions and are the penalty we pay for local self-government and independence from bureaucratic control; and some inhere in the circumstances of an age of transition and are the penalty we pay for freedom of thought and universal education. But too much of the current dissatisfaction has a just origin in our judicial organization and procedure. The causes that lie here must be heeded. Our administration of justice is not decadent. It is simply behind the times.[190]

By acknowledging "more than the normal amount of dissatisfaction with the present-day administration of justice"[191] and urging that its causes be heeded, Pound was no apologist for the status quo. At the same time, by characterizing antiquated court organization and procedure as the only legitimate cause of dissatisfaction, Pound simultaneously deflected Populist-Progressive attacks on the substance of the courts' decisions as the price we pay for our system of justice and redirected reform efforts toward empowering the judiciary to solve its own problems through improved self-administration.[192] In that regard, Pound's critique and the objectives of the Evarts Act shared common ground.

Consistent with Pound's outlook, in 1921, William Howard Taft—then chief justice—proposed that Congress establish the Conference of Senior Circuit Judges, to address the perception that some federal judges were underutilized (or "lazy," in the vernacular of court critics). Comprised of the senior-most circuit judges from each federal circuit and chaired by the chief justice, the judges of the conference would assemble once a year in Washington, D.C., where they would "report as to the condition of the dockets in their circuits . . . and submit recommendations as to the needs thereof and advise as to the improvement or expedition of the administration of justice in the courts."[193] The conference was directed to make a "comprehensive survey of the conditions of business in the courts" and to "prepare plans and schedules for the assignment and transfer of judges to or from circuits or districts where the state of the docket . . . indicates the need therefore."[194]

Given the seeming innocuousness of Taft's conference plan, opposition was surprisingly shrill. Some legislators, such as Representative Ewin Davis of Tennessee, felt that the proposal did not go far enough. He sought to include in the legislation a requirement that the judges specify the precise number of days and hours each was in court. He argued that "while many of our Federal judges render faithful, conscientious service and work a sufficient period of time, yet many of them do not,"[195] and maintained that he did not want the latter to "be given an assistant in order that they may loaf still further on the job."[196] Representative Thomas Walsh successfully countered the Davis amendment, explaining that it was not intended that "a judge shall work by a stop watch"[197] and that "[t]his proposal was made by the chief justice of the United States,"[198] for which reason "it would hardly seem necessary for the Congress to lay down any narrow restricted limits within which this conference should operate."[199]

More serious was the objection that making court administrators of federal judges was poor policy at best and unconstitutional at worst. Representative Clarence Lea of California objected that the proposal "assigns to the judges legislative and political functions,"[200] which "places the judiciary of the country in a self-seeking position"[201] that could "easily deteriorate into a publicity-seeking propaganda effort."[202] Senator John Shields was even more dubious: "The power given the Chief Justice to call conferences of the circuit judges, adopt plans, and ultimately himself assign judges is a dangerous innovation of doubtful constitutionality."[203] Shields's constitutional objections were twofold. First, he argued that the chief justice has "no right to interfere in any manner or to control the proceedings of [district] courts by moral or other influence"[204] and that to do so would "enter [a] wedge with regard to the independence of the judiciary";[205] second, he maintained that the "bill confers upon the Chief Justice executive power"[206] by granting him "administrative or other powers nonjudicial in their character [that] can not be conferred upon the judges of courts."[207]

In hearings before the Senate Judiciary Committee, the chief justice himself responded to Shields's first objection by agreeing with the latter's observation that "trial courts ought to be just as independent as the higher courts," but he added that "the mere fact of the ascertainment and determination of how much business is in one district and how much in another is not a limitation of the independence of a judge."[208] As to the second objection, Senator Albert Cummins inquired of Shields how it was that under existing law, the Constitution authorized judges to appoint their clerks—a seemingly executive function.[209] Shields obligingly opined, "our constitutions, both Federal and State, do not follow that strict division of power."[210] As to the appointment of clerks by federal judges, Shields continued, "It is executive but it is constitutional." This admission supplied Cummins with all the support he needed to conclude that the quasi-executive responsibilities imposed on federal judges by the pending legislation would likewise pass constitutional muster.[211]

Throughout the nineteenth century, as the judiciary expanded westward with the nation, federal trial judges enjoyed the functional independence that came with geographical isolation, the lack of an effective means of appellate review, and the absence of an administrative hierarchy. The prodigious reproductive powers of the pioneers, together with technological improvements in communications and transportation, gradually eliminated the autonomy born of isolation. At the same time, the newly established courts of appeals and the

Conference of Senior Circuit Judges circumscribed district court decision making and administrative autonomy, respectively. In other words, in 1891 and again in 1922, Congress, with the cooperation of the courts, elected to trade a measure of the judiciary's functional independence for a measure of intrajudicial accountability. In the process, a more truly independent, self-regulating judicial branch was born.

Opposition to this emerging notion of a self-regulating judiciary becomes more understandable when one appreciates the significance of the break it made from the past. Given Congress's perennial preference for proceeding incrementally when it came to issues of court structure and operation, qualms provoked by morphing the judiciary from a scattered array of autonomous judges into an organized, administrative hierarchy are surprising only when viewed through a twenty-first-century lens that has come to accept the development as a defining feature of an independent judicial branch, rather than as an independence-constraining imposition on the autonomy of individual judges.

Enacting the Rules Enabling Act of 1934. The Rules Enabling Act, which authorized the federal courts to devise their own rules of procedure, does not fit as squarely within the judicial independence and accountability story line as do other reforms detailed in this section, for two reasons. First, the act was not intended primarily to promote an independent judiciary. Rather, passage of the act was fueled by dissatisfaction with the hodgepodge of procedural rules in the federal system and by the perception that the federal judiciary was better able than Congress to supply the time, interest, and expertise needed to promulgate procedural rules intelligently. Second, one cannot characterize as a "new" development congressional delegation of rule making to the courts. Congress had previously conferred rule-making authority on the Supreme Court in 1792 and had strengthened that authority in 1842. The Supreme Court declined to exercise that authority, however, which Congress effectively withdrew in 1872, before restoring it with passage of the Rules Enabling Act. Establishing a more independent judiciary was not, strictly speaking, a primary goal. Rather, members of Congress took pains to emphasize that they were simply making an efficient delegation of authority from Congress to courts, in which congressional authority to second-guess judicial rule making was carefully preserved.

Even so, the Rules Enabling Act bears notice for two reasons. First, the act is another in a series of congressional efforts beginning in the late nineteenth century to make the judiciary a more self-regulating branch of government, which served to enhance its institutional autonomy and its intrabranch accountability. It may not have been the first time that Congress undertook to give the courts rule-making authority, but it was the first time it worked.

Second, although judicial independence may not have occupied a position of prominence in legislative debates on the act, it was not altogether absent. Thus, for example, one early minority Senate Judiciary Committee report, which supported the bill in the teeth of a majority vote against it, characterized the legislation as "a belated recognition of the true balance between the legislative and judicial departments; a tardy correction of a situation that would not be tolerated in the reverse."[212] Another early committee report made the related point that "the trouble with the procedure of the courts is due to the fact that coordination between these two departments of government has been destroyed by exclusive legislative control." Characterizing "the true balance" between courts and Congress in procedural rule making as one in which the judiciary has a cooperative, if not primary, role to play indicates at the very least that Congress adopted the Rules Enabling Act with the perceived need to respect the judiciary's autonomy in mind. Paradoxically, perhaps, judicial rule making would later give rise to a civil process that emphasized pretrial resolution of disputes, reduced the incidence of trials, and thereby diminished the opportunities for intrajudicial accountability via the appellate process envisioned by the Evarts Act—a "misunderstood consequence" that Stephen Yeazell has explored.[213]

Creating the Administrative Office of United States Courts. In 1937, even as it lobbied to pack the courts, the Roosevelt administration began an active campaign in support of legislation that would transfer financial control of the lower federal courts from the Department of Justice to an Administrative Office of United States Courts. Under the control of the chief justice and the Conference of Senior Circuit Judges (later renamed the Judicial Conference of the United States), the new administrative office would assume primary responsibility for the administration of the federal judiciary. Over the course of the preceding fifty years, the concept of a self-regulating judicial branch had been born, matured, and was now poised to win acceptance as a cornerstone of judicial independence. In his testimony before the Senate Judiciary Committee in 1938, Attorney General Homer Cummings observed: "The Constitution, of course, contemplates that the judiciary shall be an independent, coordinate branch of the Government, and yet, administratively, it is in large part connected with the Department of Justice. I think that system grew up as Topsy grew up. It 'just growed.'"[214]

As of 1922, advocates of the proposed Conference of Senior Circuit Judges had defended their proposal against the charge that any delegation of administrative (i.e., executive) powers to the judicial branch was a dangerous, if not unconstitutional, innovation. Now, just fifteen years later, administrative autonomy was being characterized as a defining feature of judicial independence, the long-standing absence of which could not be justified but could only be explained as a kind of historical accident. A colloquy between the members of the Senate Judiciary Committee and Attorney General Cummings at the Senate hearing on the bill reveals their shared objectives.

> SENATOR [JOSEPH] O'MAHONEY: The administrative office of the judiciary would be, in effect, the budget office for the whole judicial system, and would make its report direct to Congress, which thereupon would reject or approve the recommendations?
>
> ATTORNEY GENERAL CUMMINGS: Absolutely. They would have to justify their budget the same as the rest of them.
>
> SENATOR [CARL] HATCH: It takes it out of the hands of the Justice Department and places it in the hands of the administrative office.
>
> SENATOR O'MAHONEY: This is upon the theory that the courts are an independent branch of the Government, and should be.
>
> SENATOR [ROBERT] NORRIS: Yes.
>
> SENATOR O'MAHONEY: Subject only to the control of Congress as to the total amount that should be expended.[215]

During floor deliberations on the bill, Senator Henry Ashurst reiterated the view that "giving of [*sic*] the judiciary the right to arrange their own budget, is a great advance and a great reform, making the judiciary more nearly independent."[216] In the House, Representative Walter Chandler concurred with the position of "[s]everal of the Attorneys General of the United States, [who] have considered it 'anomalous and potentially threatening to the independence of the courts' for the chief litigant before them to have control of the financing of the courts."[217]

Clearly, then, the Administrative Office Act was advocated to enhance the judiciary's institutional independence. But just as clearly, it was advocated as a means to promote intrajudicial accountability as well. As far as Attorney General Cummings was concerned, the act was designed so that the courts "may not only be independent, but that there may be a concentration of responsibility, so that if the business of the judiciary gets behind . . . they won't have someone else to blame for it."[218] On the House floor, Representative Chandler explained, "Another purpose of the bill is to secure an improved supervision of the work of the Federal courts through an organization under judicial control." Chandler continued,

> This measure places the responsibility for judicial administration where it belongs—with the judiciary—and it will be an urge to the avoidance of the evil of judicial delays that the citizens of the country know that the courts have in their power the prompt and adequate disposition of pending cases.[219]

The Administrative Office Act is an important part of the independence and accountability story for two reasons. First, it represents another step toward the creation of a more independent judiciary increasingly accountable to itself. Second, it serves as counterpoint to the contemporaneous, seemingly thuggish efforts of the FDR White House to gain control of the Supreme Court by packing it with FDR loyalists. The Roosevelt administration may have been willing to run roughshod over the Supreme Court's customary independence when the survival of the New Deal hung in the balance, but it was nonetheless an active participant in the larger and more enduring movement to create an independent, self-regulating, corporate judiciary.

The Fifth Spike ∾

After devoting considerable attention to each of the previous four spikes of court-directed animus, my abbreviated treatment of the fifth and final spike preceding the current round of anticourt sentiment may strike readers as short shrift, and it is. But for the purposes of this chapter, it will suffice, because the developments that transpired during the Warren Court era simply followed the trajectory of independence norms firmly set during the preceding century and were, in that sense, quite anticlimactic.

Attacks on the Warren Court

In the 1950s and 1960s, the Warren Court's decisions invalidating racial segregation of public institutions, disallowing prayer in public schools, and affording criminal defendants a range of previously unrecognized procedural protections provoked sharp criticism in some quarters. The John Birch Society accused Chief Justice Earl Warren of "voting 92 percent in favor of Communists" and "sanction[ing] treason."[220] Congress received a torrent of letters calling for Warren's impeachment, a sentiment echoed on billboards across the country.[221] Warren was not the only target. Then congressman Gerald Ford called for the impeachment of Justice William O. Douglas, in part because of Douglas's leftward leanings. In so doing, Ford argued for a reinterpretation of the phrase "impeachable offense" to mean "whatever a majority of the House of Representatives considers [it] to be at a given moment in history."[222] Several members of Congress repeatedly introduced legislation to deprive the Supreme Court of jurisdiction to hear cases involving school prayer.[223] And the best-known effort to strip the Supreme Court's subject-matter jurisdiction—the so-called Jenner-Butler bill—would have deprived the Court of authority to hear a wide array of cases.[224]

These efforts to curb the Warren Court failed miserably. There were no impeachment votes. Norms against resort to the impeachment process as a remedy for unpopular decisions had become so engrained that, with the possible exception of Justice Douglas, cries of impeachment amounted to little more than expletives intended to display the depths of the speakers' dissatisfaction. A previous century of uninterrupted expansion of federal court jurisdiction, coupled with the persistent failure of states' rights advocates to recapture federal jurisdiction after it had been ceded, revealed a high degree of congressional respect for and reliance on the federal courts, respect and reliance that a few unpopular decisions simply could not erode. *McCardle* could still be cited for the proposition that Congress possessed the power to strip the federal courts of jurisdiction to hear unpopular cases, but it stood alone like the proverbial cheese, increasingly aged and malodorous.

The Triumph (sort of) of Independence Norms

As with previous spikes of disenchantment with the courts, contemporaneous and subsequent developments reconfirm Congress's continuing commitment to an independent judiciary in which accountability was best promoted via intrajudicial mechanisms. In 1966, for example, Congress established the Federal Judicial Center, to serve three purposes: to conduct research on the operation of the courts, to provide judicial education, and to study ways in which improved data processing might improve judicial administration.[225] As the movement toward promoting intrajudicial accountability through self-administration matured, the judiciary's need for research support became increasingly obvious. Russell Wheeler thus describes the creation of the Federal Judicial Center as the next step in the long-standing "contest for control over how courts should be structured and operated," a contest in which judicial self-governance again emerged victorious.[226]

A little over a decade later, Congress enacted the Judicial Councils Reform and Judicial Conduct and Disability Act of 1980, which established an administrative structure within the judicial branch, enabling judges to discipline themselves.[227] Some federal judges objected that the act was antithetical to judicial independence, because through it Congress subjected individual judges to an unjustifiable form of control by their brethren.[228] When viewed in the larger context of the movement toward the creation of a self-regulating judicial branch, however, the act is better understood as a congressional effort to promote judicial accountability by transferring disciplinary power to the courts, thereby enhancing the judiciary's independence as an institution and reducing the need for congressional intrusions via the impeachment process.[229]

All of this may imply that critics of the Warren Court suffered a defeat at the hands of judicial independence champions, who rebuffed petitions to impeach unpopular judges, killed bills to strip the courts of jurisdiction, and resumed their victorious crusade for the creation of an independent judicial branch. But that would be inaccurate. The perceived excesses of the Warren Court were among the campaign issues that swept Richard Nixon into office in 1968.[230] The retirement of Earl Warren in 1969 and the resignation of Justice Abe Fortas that same year enabled Nixon to appoint Chief Justice Warren Burger and Justice Harry Blackmun, thereby closing the book on the Warren Court and the attendant period of criticism. In short, while the opportunities to hold judges accountable for their decisions by means of the political branches' control of court size, jurisdiction, and impeachment had gradually diminished as respect for an independent judiciary took hold, the power to control courts via the appointments process proceeded along a fundamentally different track, a track that merits separate attention, in chapter 4.

CHAPTER THREE

The Decline and Fall of Impeachment as a Means to Control Judicial Decision Making ∾

CHAPTER 2 CHRONICLED the increasing influence that judicial independence norms had, over time, on Congress's exercise of legislative power. This chapter does the same with respect to congressional exercise of the impeachment power.

The framers of the U.S. Constitution did not focus much attention on the judiciary and its accountability to the political branches, but to the extent they thought about it at all, what they thought about was the impeachment process. Although some appeared to acknowledge that Congress's power to establish inferior courts enabled the first branch of government to limit the size, jurisdiction, and so the influence of the third branch, little if anything in the commentary of the time suggests that this power could, would, or should be used to control a judiciary run amok. In characterizing the judicial branch as "least dangerous," Alexander Hamilton understood that the judiciary's inability to tax and spend limited the extent of its power, but neither he nor his contemporaries went so far as to state or imply that Congress's power of the purse could be used to hold uppity judges answerable for their conduct. When it came to how Congress might control judicial misbehavior, the founders spoke neither of Congress's power to disestablish judicial offices nor of its power to control the judiciary's budget, but only of its power to impeach, as the sole means to promote accountability without unduly compromising independence. Hamilton explained in the Federalist Papers (no. 79):

> The precautions for [the judges'] responsibility are comprised in the article respecting impeachments. They are liable to be impeached for malconduct by the House of Representatives, and tried by the Senate; and, if convicted, may be dismissed from office, and disqualified for holding any other. This is the only provision on the point which is consistent with the necessary independence of judicial character, and the only one which we find in our own Constitution with respect to judges.

With impeachment perceived (initially at least) as the primary means by which to curb judicial misconduct, the question arose early and often as to the kinds of misbehavior for which judges could be impeached. The founding generation left a limited number of clues, detailed in chapter 1. The most obvious is the text of the impeachment clauses in the U.S. Constitution: in section 4 of Article II, judges, as a subset of "civil officers," are subject to impeachment for "treason, bribery, and other high crimes and misdemeanors." The meaning of "treason" and "bribery" in this context seems clear enough as long as we do not get down to close cases, but what about "high crimes and misdemeanors"? From the perspective of those who drafted the Constitution, "high crimes and misdemeanors" comprised a more precise impeachment standard than "maladministration," which they considered and rejected as overly broad and susceptible to excessive manipulation by the Senate. Although "high crimes and misdemeanors" might not appear to possess an intrinsic meaning any more narrow or plain than "maladministration," the drafters were not writing on a clean slate with only a dictionary to guide them. Impeachment was a process they imported from England, where impeachable conduct had been confined to political offenses against the state and characterized as "high crimes."[1] Not surprisingly, then, those who lobbied for ratification opined that "high crimes and misdemeanors" reached crimes of a political nature that undermined the public trust and included deliberate usurpations of judicial power.

What would qualify as a deliberate usurpation of power, however, remained to be determined.

Separate and distinct from the forms of misbehavior that are subject to impeachment is the question of severity. How serious must a political offense be to qualify as a "high misdemeanor"? Since Article III limited judicial tenure to service during "good behaviour," one possibility would be to set the threshold for an impeachable misdemeanor at any behavior that is less than good. There are, however, some behaviors—such as senility—that may be less than good but cannot easily be characterized as "misdemeanors," a term that implies bad motives or blameworthiness. That, in turn, suggests that there may be a gap between the floor of good behavior and the ceiling of an impeachable misdemeanor. The breadth of that gap, if one existed, was another aspect of the scope of impeachable offenses that would need to be explored.

The Constitution delegates the "sole powers of impeachment and removal to the House and Senate, respectively." The task of unpacking and applying the impeachment clauses therefore falls to Congress alone. Of particular interest here is whether and how independence norms emerged and developed through adherence to past practice in the context of Congress defining and qualifying the meaning of "high crimes and misdemeanors" for which judges may be impeached and removed.

At first glance, the task would seem to be comparatively easy—the impeachment process mimics a judicial process in ways that appear to incline impeachment proceedings toward precedent-guided decision making of a sort that would cultivate respect for past practices and the institutional norms they perpetuate. Until the latter half of the twentieth century, the House Judiciary Committee served as the equivalent of a police detective, investigating complaints of misconduct filed by members of Congress or the public and reporting the results to the House of Representatives. The House, in turn, has acted much like a grand jury, reviewing the information it receives and indicting (or impeaching) the respondent on a majority vote if it finds evidence sufficient to charge the judge with an impeachable offense. Committee investigations and House proceedings are summarized, recorded, and explicitly denominated as precedents on which members can and do rely in arguing for or against impeachment in later cases.[2] A judicial officer who is impeached by the House then proceeds to the Senate, which functions as both petit jury and judge, trying the case and convicting upon a two-thirds majority vote. At the fully transcribed trial before the Senate or, in more recent cases involving judges, a Senate committee, a delegation of House "managers" serves as prosecutor. Both the managers and the respondent's counsel make opening and closing arguments liberally sprinkled with references to past impeachments that liken the respondent's conduct to or distinguish it from that deemed to constitute a high crime or misdemeanor in prior cases. Thus, it would seem that the task of determining whether Congress has established precedent and followed it consistently over time, to the end of eschewing independence-threatening attempts to remove judges out of disagreement with their decisions, would be a relatively straightforward one.

There are, however, three tricky bits that make the business of divining congressional impeachment precedent more art than science. First, appearances can be deceiving. Although the impeachment process may look like a judicial one, it is commonly characterized as political—and fairly so, in at least three respects: (1) it is political in the originalist sense of the term, insofar as it is a remedy for "political" crimes against the body politic; (2) it is political in the sense of being a process subject to resolution by popular or political majorities, through their representatives in one of the political branches; and (3) it can be political in the sense of being openly partisan. In a process that is so inherently political, one might reasonably predict that the importance of precedent as an inhibition on deviations from past practice in impeachment proceedings would be significantly diminished relative to judicial proceedings. After all, the kinds of misbehavior that are perceived to abuse the public trust and so to constitute "political crimes" may be subject to significant change over time; the passions of temporary political majorities may inspire frequent departures from past practice in the imposition of impeachment standards; and the vagaries of partisan agendas may cause precedent to be grossly distorted, if not ignored. The net effect may be that the precedent is honored more in the breach than in the observance. At a minimum, this concern underscores the importance of discounting isolated explanations offered for decisions in a given proceeding and of focusing more on decision-making patterns over time.

Second, the Senate produces no document comparable to a judicial opinion and deliberates off the record. This poses no particular problem if the Senate simply convicts the judge of a high crime or misdemeanor for violating a particular article of impeachment clearly articulated by the House. But suppose the Senate acquits on a particular article after the respondent's counsel has argued, in the alternative, that the judge did not demean himself as alleged in the article; or that if he did, he was right to do so; or that even if he was wrong to do so, his was an honest mistake that did not rise to the level of an impeachable offense? What is the precedent that the Senate's acquittal sets? By itself, the outcome tells us little; if anything is to be made of it, the decision must be read in combination with other impeachments resolved before and after, to ascertain whether it contributes to results from which conclusions may fairly be drawn.

Third, it may be very difficult—some might say impossible—to generalize about congressional norms in the impeachment arena, when the House and Senate play very different roles and may head in different directions. If, for example, the House evaluates a judge's behavior and votes it impeachable by a resounding margin but the Senate finds to the contrary by a margin equally resounding, to what extent is it fair to attribute the precedent set by the Senate's verdict to Congress as a whole? On the one hand, it seems no less reasonable to say that "Congress" declined to remove the judge in this case than to say that "Congress" declined to enact a piece of legislation that the House approved but the Senate did not. On the other hand, the House is under no obligation to embrace the Senate precedent as its own in subsequent cases, giving rise to the question of whether it tends to do so anyway. One might suppose that the House would typically acquiesce to avoid wasting its time impeaching judges that the Senate will not remove, but if the evidence needed to impeach is substantially less than that required for removal or if impeachment is threatened not to effect a removal as much as to send a message to judges that the House is unhappy with their performance, one could just as easily speculate that the House would go its own way.

Despite these obstacles, this chapter is dedicated to demonstrating that independence norms—the emergence and entrenchment of which were chronicled in chapter 2's discussion of congressional control of court operations—have exerted a significant influence in the context of impeachment. Before beginning this demonstration, however, one caveat is in order. In a study of judicial independence and its relationship to judicial accountability in Congress, the impeachment process is germane only insofar as it has been brandished to constrain decisional or institutional independence to the potential detriment of the rule-of-law values that judicial independence is designed to further. The judge who is impeached and removed for selling her decisions to the highest bidder or making gifts of decisions to friends and family may be deprived of her "independence" to behave corruptly, but that is not the sort of independence that promotes the rule of law—it is quite the contrary. Decisional and institutional independence concerns are raised only when impeachment is used (1) to punish judicial error or high-handedness and thereby to hold judges directly accountable for their decision making or (2) to weaken judges collectively as a branch so as to control their decision making indirectly. Thus, the remainder of this chapter will focus on impeachment in those cases where it has been pursued as a means to curb judicial decision making and power.

Table 1 illustrates graphically the limited scope of the mission here. To assemble table 1, available records of impeachment inquiries were reviewed, and the accusations made against federal judges were tabulated and categorized by form of misconduct. Ten categories of alleged misconduct were generated: (1) bench demeanor—the judge was surly, rude, or drunk; (2) abuse of judicial power—the judge took erroneous, arbitrary, or oppressive action from the bench, unaccompanied by any implication that the judge was motivated by financial gain or favoritism toward specific individuals; (3) extrajudicial misbehavior—the judge engaged in criminal or other misconduct unrelated to his judicial performance per se but that reflected badly on the judicial office; (4) favoritism—the judge made rulings or took other nonadministrative action for the benefit of friends, family, or business associates; (5) nonperformance or incompetence—the judge was either unable, unwilling, or unavailable to do his job; (6) misuse of funds—the judge misappropriated government monies by converting funds for private use, filing fraudulent expense reports, and so on; (7) accepting or soliciting bribes or favors—the judge accepted or requested something of value from others interested in cases before the judge; (8) abuse of administrative power—the judge abused or misused his power over court staff or appointees for the personal benefit of the judge or the judge's friends, family, or business associates; (9) misuse of the office for financial advantage—the judge capitalized on the prestige and power of his office to enter into favorable business ventures with lawyers, litigants, or others; and (10) other—a grab bag of infrequently employed charges that have run the gamut, from disloyalty, moonlighting, insanity, and failure to reside within the judicial district, to omnibus claims of unfitness premised upon separately alleged accusations of specific misconduct.

Although it is possible for accusations in any of these ten categories to undermine a judge's independence if they are employed as a subterfuge to silence the jurist on account of her decisions, the second category, abuse of judicial power, is the one where independence and accountability will clash most frequently. Even there, only when an alleged abuse of power takes the form of an erroneous or high-handed case ruling is the judge's decisional independence challenged directly. Thus, for example, if a judge were to abuse her judicial power by ordering all lawyers who appeared before her in a given case to dress as their favorite Star Wars character, speak in iambic pentameter, and bind their briefs in vellum, calling her to task for the abuse would not be in tension with the judge's independence to make judicial decisions without fear or favor.

Table 1 reflects that Congress (or some subset thereof) has inquired into the conduct of at least seventy-eight judges over time. In many instances, a given judge was accused of several types of wrongdoing, so that in the final tally, seventy-four judges have been subjected to a total of 148 accusations of misconduct by type (with the accusations against four judges remaining unknown).[3] Thirty-two judges were accused of abusing or misusing judicial power, which is by far the most frequently alleged form of misconduct, with abuse of administrative power coming in a distant second, at nineteen. The rest of this chapter will focus on those thirty-two cases.

TABLE 1. Impeachment Inquiries and Outcomes, Federal Judges

	(1)	(2)	(3)	(4)	(5)	(6)	(7)	(8)	(9)	(10)	(11)
Impeached and removed											
1804 Pickering, John (D.NH)	X*	X								X$^{\|}$	
1862 Humphreys, West (W.D.TN)					X					X§	
1913 Archbald, Robert (M.D.PA)							X	X	X		
1936 Ritter, Halsted (S.D.FL)			X	X				X	X	X‡*	
1986 Claiborne, Harry (D.NV)			X							X*	
1989 Hastings, Alcee (S.D.FL)				X			X			X†*	
1989 Nixon, Walter (S.D.MS)							X			X†*	
Subtotal	1	1	2	2	1	0	3	2	2	6	0
Impeached and acquitted											
1805 Chase, Samuel (S.Ct.)	X	X									
1830 Peck, James (D.MO)		X									
1905 Swayne, Charles (N.D.FL)		X		X	X	X	X			X#	
1933 Louderback, Harold (N.D.CA)		X		X			X			X*	
Subtotal	1	3	0	2	1	1	2	0	0	2	0
Impeached and resigned											
1873 Delahay, Mark (D.KS)	X										
1926 English, George (E.D.IL)	X	X		X		X			X		
Subtotal	2	1	0	1	0	1	0	0	1	0	0

(continues)

House investigation and resigned, retired, or died

Year	Name	1	2	3	4	5	6	7	8	9
1818	Stephens, William (D.GA) (resigned)									X
1818	Tallmadge, Matthias (D.NY) (resigned)			X						
1859	Irwin, Thomas (W.D.PA) (resigned)		X				X	X		
1873	Sherman, Charles (N.D.OH) (resigned)					X				
1873	Busteed, Richard (S.D.AL) (resigned)			X					X#	
1873	Durell, Edward (E.D.LA) (resigned)	X					X			
1874	Story, William (W.D.AR) (resigned)	X			X					
1912	Hanford, Cornelius (D.WA) (resigned)	X*								
1914	Wright, Daniel (S.Ct. D.C.) (resigned)	X				X	X	X	X‡	
1921	Landis, Kenesaw (N.D.IL) (resigned)	X							X‡	
1929	Winslow, Francis (S.D.NY) (resigned)	X					X			
1933	Lowell, James (D.MA) (died)	X								
1938	Geiger, Ferdinand (E.D.WI) (retired)	X								
1939	Davis, John Warren (3rd Cir.) (resigned)	X						X		

TABLE 1.—Continued

	(1)	(2)	(3)	(4)	(5)	(6)	(7)	(8)	(9)	(10)	(11)
1939 Manton, Martin (S.D.NY) (resigned)							X				
1941 Nields, John (D.DE) (resigned)											X
1945 Johnson, Albert (M.D.PA) (resigned)							X				
1969 Fortas, Abe (S.Ct.) (resigned)									X		
1974 Kerner, Otto (7th Cir.) (resigned)							X				
1976 Fogel, Herbert (E.D.PA) (resigned)									X		
Subtotal	1	6	2	1	2	1	5	4	5	3	2
House investigation and remained											
1796 Turner, George (T.NW Territory)		X						X			
1802 Bruin, Peter (T.MS)	X*				X						
1804 Peters, Richard (D.PA)		X	X								
1808 Innis, Harry (D.KY)										X[||]	
1811 Toulmin, Harry (T.MS)		X									
1818 Van Ness, William (D.NY)		X			X						
1822 Tait, Charles (D.AL)	X			X				X			
1826 Smith, Joseph (T.FL)					X			X	X		
1829 Conkling, Alfred (N.D.NY)								X			

Year	Name										
1833	Johnson, Benjamin (T.AR)	X	X			X					
1837	Thruston, Buckner (Cir.Ct. D.C.)	X	X			X					
1839	Lawrence, P.K. (E.D.LA)	X		X					X		
1840	McLean, John (S.Ct.)			X						X	
1851–58	Watrous, John (D.TX)			X	X				X	X	
1855	Grier, R.C. (S.Ct.)	X			X			X			
1868	Field, Stephen (S.Ct.)			X						X	
1875–76	Humphreys, David (S.Ct. D.C.)										X
1875–76	Wylie, Andrew (S.Ct. D.C.)	X		X	X				X	X	X
1879	Blodgett, Henry (N.D.IL)						X		X		
1880	Boarman, Aleck (W.D.LA)			X			X			X	
1884	Locke, James (S.D.FL)			X					X	X	
1884	Axtell, S. B. (T.NM)					X					
1894	Jenkins, J.G. (E.D.WI)	X		X						X	
1895	Ricks, Augustus (N.D.OH)						X		X		
1908	Wilfley, Lebbeus (China)	X	X	X					X	X	
1913	Speer, Emory (S.D.GA)	X	X	X			X		X	X	
1914	Dayton, Alston (N.D.WV)		X	X	X		X		X	X	
1925	Baker, William (N.D.WV)	X*		X	X						
1927	Cooper, Frank (N.D.NY)	X		X					X		
1930	Anderson, Harry (W.D.TN)			X					X		
1930	Moscowitz, Grover (E.D.N.Y.)				X				X		
1934	Molyneaux, Joseph (D. MN)	X	X	X					X		X[11]
1935	Alschuler, Samuel (7th Cir.)	X		X					X	X	

(continues)

TABLE 1.—*Continued*

	(1)	(2)	(3)	(4)	(5)	(6)	(7)	(8)	(9)	(10)	(11)
1945 Watson, Albert (M.D.PA)								X			
1966 Murrah, Alfred (10th Cir.)							X				
1966 Bohanon, Luther (W.D.OK)							X				
1966 Chandler, Stephen (W.D.OK)					X						
1969 Douglas, William O. (S.Ct.)			X								
1976 Atkins v. U.S. Judge Plaintiffs		X									
1979 Battisti, Frank (N.D.OH)		X									
1981 Scott, Nauman (W.D.LA)		X									
1981 Justice, William W. (E.D.TX)		X									
1986 Johnson, Frank (11th Cir.)		X									
1986 Anderson, Lanier (11th Cir.)		X									
1986 Clark, Thomas (11th Cir.)		X									
Subtotal	8	21	6	9	7	5	3	13	6	2	2
Total	13	32	10	15	11	8	13	19	14	13	4

Note: Columns are

(1) Bench demeanor (incl. *drunkenness)

(2) Abuse of judicial power

(3) Extrajudicial misbehavior

(4) Favoritism/animus

(5) Nonperformance/incompetence

(6) Misuse of funds

(7) Accepted/solicited bribes or favors

(8) Abuse of administrative power

(9) Misuse of office for financial advantage

(10) Other: *Catchall; †perjury; ‡moonlighting; §disloyalty; ‖insanity; #residency

(11) Unknown

Impeachments ∾

Seven federal judges have been removed via the impeachment process, another four were impeached and acquitted, and two were impeached but resigned before their Senate trial, for a total of thirteen impeachments. Of the thirteen judges impeached, four—Judge John Pickering, Justice Samuel Chase, Judge James Peck, and Judge Charles Swayne—were charged with abusing their judicial power by making one or more egregiously wrong case rulings from the bench.* Theirs were not just any four cases, but the first four cases contested at trial, and only the first judge—John Pickering—was ultimately removed, with the latter three being acquitted. This section will discuss the thirteen impeachments with a focus on the first four, to the end of demonstrating a trajectory of sorts by which congressional efforts to remove judges because one or more of their decisions was stupid, outrageous, or oppressive have become decreasingly viable over time.

District Judge John Pickering

The charges against New Hampshire district judge John Pickering as embodied in the articles of impeachment (for which he was ultimately convicted) reveal none of the complexities that made his case as easy as it was impossible. Article 1 accused Judge Pickering of acting with the "intent to evade" an act of Congress, when he ordered the government to return a ship it had seized (the *Eliza*) to its owner before the owner had produced papers showing that relevant duties had been paid, as required by statute. Article 2 made a related allegation that "with intent to defeat the just claims of the United States," Judge Pickering released the *Eliza* without hearing the government's witnesses in support of forfeiture. Article 3 then charged him with "disregarding the authority of the laws and wickedly meaning and intending to injure the revenues of the United States" by declining to permit an appeal to which the government was entitled. Finally, article 4 charged him with being a "man of loose morals and intemperate habits," who on specified dates appeared on the bench in "a state of total intoxication"

---

*The impeachment of district judge George English would seem, superficially at least, to constitute a fifth such case, but is distinguishable for reasons discussed later in this chapter.

and "did then and there frequently, and in a most profane and inde-cent manner, invoke the name of the Supreme Being, to the evil example of all the good citizens of the United States."[4]

These articles of impeachment portray Pickering as a profane drunk who intentionally disregarded substantive and procedural law. For those in search of support for the proposition that a judge may be held accountable for his rulings via the impeachment process and removed if he abuses his decision-making power, it would seem, superficially at least, as though they need to look no further than the inaugural proceeding: three of the four articles on which Judge Pick-ering was convicted were based on allegations that he made erroneous rulings of procedural and substantive law in a single case, to which his accusers ascribed ill motives. One only has to scratch the surface of the Pickering impeachment lightly, however, to reveal that the expla-nation for his removal had less to do with a failure to watch his lan-guage, his liquor, or his law than with his Federalist Party affiliation and his insanity, which together obscure the precedential value of an impeachment ostensibly aimed at removing the judge for making patently erroneous rulings from the bench.

As to the relevance of his Federalist pedigree, Pickering's impeach-ment followed hard upon the Jeffersonian Republicans' ascension to power in 1802. After winning landslide electoral victories in the first two branches of government, Republicans were rankled by the Feder-alists' lingering domination of the third. They became positively apoplectic when the Federalists, on their way out the door in 1801, created sixteen new Article III judgeships and packed them with party loyalists. As detailed in chapter 2, no sooner had the Republicans assumed power than they repealed those judgeships and, in so doing, ended the tenure of their recently appointed Federalist occupants. Impeachment was the next logical step in the continuing campaign of judicial cleansing. "We want your offices for the purpose of giving them to men who will fill them better," Senator William Giles declared bluntly.[5] Congressman Roger Griswold confirmed that "Giles & Company are decidedly of the opinion that the Supreme Court should be swept away together with those created at the last Session, and this opinion they have openly declared in all compa-nies."[6] Against that backdrop, it is less surprising that Pickering's

impeachment process would be initiated by Jefferson himself in a letter accompanied by affidavits that supported the judge's removal.[7]

As one scholar has described the forfeiture case that led to Pickering's impeachment, "[t]he trial was destined to be, in fact, not the
case of United States v. *Eliza,* but the case of Republican surveyor,
collector, marshal, clerk and district attorney v. Federalist claimant,
attorney and judge."[8] That Pickering's subsequent impeachment was
part of the Republicans' campaign to oust Federalist judges was clear
enough to Federalist senator William Plumer, who, on the day after
the judge's removal, expressed the "wish" that "those in New England
who are boasting of the independence of our Judiciary would reflect
on what a slender tenure Judges hold their offices whose political sentiments are at variance with the dominant party."[9] Lest Plumer's
grumbling be dismissed as that of a delusional partisan, it is telling to
note that within two weeks of Pickering's removal, President Jefferson nominated a successor, the U.S. attorney in Pickering's district,
Republican John Sherburne, who had submitted an affidavit in support of the judge's removal. To replace Sherburne as U.S. attorney,
Jefferson named Republican Jonathan Steele, Pickering's court clerk,
who had likewise supplied an affidavit in support of the judge's
removal, and Richard Shannon, a justice of the peace who notarized
Steele's affidavit and authored one of his own, was offered the clerk's
position left vacant by Steele.[10] Shannon alone declined his reward,
with the explanation that he had been "a contributing agent in creating vacancies" and that "a due regard to my reputation forbids me to
profit by that achievement."[11]

That Pickering's removal was related more to his party affiliation
than to his orders in the *Eliza* case does nothing to undermine its
vitality as precedent for Congress targeting judges as a means to control their decision making. The use of Pickering's Federalist affiliation
as a proxy for a pattern of judicial decision making that the Republican Congress found unacceptable (with the *Eliza* case relegated to the
status of illustration or pretext) portends the emergence of a powerful
weapon for court control. Ultimately, however, more than partisanship was at work here; while the balance of power in the House was
lopsided enough, with sixty-nine Republicans and thirty-six Federalists,[12] the vote to impeach was an even more lopsided forty-five to

eight.[13] The explanation lay in the judge's mental health, which complicated his case to such an extent as to render its application as precedent in future impeachments all but impossible.

Writing in the Federalist Papers (no. 79), Alexander Hamilton acknowledged that "the want of a provision for removing the judges on account of inability has been a subject of complaint." He defended its absence with the observation that were the Constitution to include such a mechanism, "the result, except in the case of insanity, must for the most part be arbitrary; and insanity, without any formal or express provision, may be safely pronounced to be a virtual disqualification." As easy as it may be to pronounce insanity a "virtual disqualification" from judicial office, the absence of actual law to support the removal of incapacitated judges soon presented a difficult problem.

In the House, the decision to impeach Pickering was unencumbered by debate, save a brief and unsuccessful effort to postpone deliberation of the matter until the next session.[14] It bears notice, however, that each of the affidavits that Jefferson submitted to the House in support of impeachment and that formed the basis for the impeachment resolution refers—in one way, shape, or form—to the judge's decrepit mental condition.[15] At Pickering's impeachment trial, Edward St. Loe Livermore testified, "In the beginning of the year 1800, I heard it intimated that Judge Pickering was deranged in his mind—that his extravagant actions and conversation could be accounted for upon no other principle."[16] The so-called Midnight Judges Act was enacted the very next year and provided:

> in the case of the inability of the district judge . . . to perform the duties of his office, and satisfactory evidence thereof being shown to the circuit court, in and for such district, it shall be the duty of such circuit court . . . to direct one of the judges of said circuit court to perform the duties of such district . . . for and during the period the inability of the district judge shall continue.[17]

The Federalists thus established a means to address the Pickering problem in the Judiciary Act of 1801, which was in place for less than a year when (as discussed in chapter 2), the act was repealed by the incoming Republicans. The impact of these developments on Pickering himself, was described by Livermore at Pickering's trial.

The judge continued to grow worse, and, after the passing of the late judiciary act . . . Judge Smith was appointed to do the duties of the office, and New Hampshire was relieved from the embarrassment until the repeal of the act, since which time several distressing scenes have passed, in consequence of the duties again devolving upon the unfortunate Judge.[18]

Pickering's insanity was acknowledged by all, including the House managers' star witnesses. John Sherbourne attested that "several years of ill health have . . . had an unhappy influence on the powers of his mind." Jonathan Steele described Pickering's "helpless condition" and "usual incoherent conversation." Richard Shannon testified that for the previous three years, Pickering appeared "greatly deranged in his mind."[19]

The problem for the Republicans was that the judge could not have chosen to lose his mind, which made it hard to accuse him of an impeachable crime or misdemeanor for doing so. Worse still, conduct that might be impeachable if animated by bad motives becomes blameless if driven by mental illness. That fact may help to explain why the articles of impeachment breathe nary a word on the subject of Pickering's mental health. The blamelessness accorded mental illness likewise imbues Judge Pickering's defense, as presented by his son Jacob, with a perverse logic (reminiscent of Lewis Carroll's *Alice in Wonderland*).

[A]t the time when the crimes wherewith the said John stands charged . . . the said John was, and for more than two years before, and ever since has been, and now is, insane, his mind wholly deranged, and altogether incapable of transacting any kind of business which requires the exercise of judgment, or the faculties of reason; and, therefore, that the said John Pickering is incapable of corruption of judgment, no subject of impeachment, or amenable to any tribunal for his actions.[20]

To extricate congressional Republicans from this predicament, Richard Shannon obligingly furnished an addendum to his original affidavit, in which he speculated that the judge's derangement "has been much increased, if not altogether occasioned by habits of intemperance." To counter the implication that Pickering's volitional (and therefore potentially impeachable) drunkenness caused his insanity, New Hampshire senators Simeon Olcott and William Plumer testified on the judge's behalf. Olcott stated that he "never heard . . . (before said Shannon's testimony) that any person suspected [Pickering's mental state] to be the effect of intemperance."[21] Olcott concluded: "from every circumstance by which I can judge, [I] am convinced said testimony is altogether incorrect and erroneous."[22] Plumer, in turn, testified to his belief that Pickering's "insanity was the cause of his intemperance."[23]

So the Senate was faced with a judge whose insanity rendered him utterly unfit to remain on the bench (as evidenced by the highly erratic behavior described in the articles of impeachment) and yet utterly without the capacity to commit a crime or misdemeanor for which he could be removed. Confronted by the "virtual disqualification" of the judge's insanity, the Senate sought refuge in a "virtual constitution." As to the manner of their voting, Senator Samuel White proposed that they vote "upon each article separately, as is practiced in the House of Lords," in which the Senate would be called on to answer the question "Is John Pickering, district judge of the district of New Hampshire, guilty of high crimes and misdemeanors upon the charges contained in the __ article of impeachment, or not guilty?"[24] White's proposal was rejected by a vote of ten in favor to eighteen against, and in its stead, the Senate approved (by a vote of eighteen to nine) a motion by Senator Joseph Anderson that recast the question to read, "Is John Pickering, district judge of the district of New Hampshire, guilty as charged in the __ article of impeachment?" A frustrated Senator Jonathan Dayton explained why the form approved by the Senate omitted any reference to high crimes and misdemeanors.

> [The Senate was] simply to be allowed to vote, whether Judge Pickering was guilty as charged—that is, guilty of the facts charged in each article—aye or no. If voted guilty of the facts, the sentence was to follow, without any previous question whether those facts amounted to a high crime and misdemeanor. The latent reason of this course was . . . too obvious. There were numbers who were disposed to give sentence of removal against this unhappy judge, upon the grounds of the facts alleged and proved,

who could not, however, conscientiously vote that they amounted to high crimes and misdemeanors, especially when committed by a man proved at the very time to be insane, and to have been so ever since, even to the present moment.[25]

If Pickering were removed without first finding him guilty of high crimes or misdemeanors, Dayton complained, "a precedent [would be] established for removing a judge in a manner unauthorized" by the Constitution.[26]

Pickering was subsequently declared "guilty as charged" on each article of impeachment and removed from office. The significance of the verdict is difficult to divine. It seems clear that when faced with a patently incapacitated jurist, the Senate was prepared to do what it needed to do to remove him—even if it could not bring itself to characterize incapacity as a crime or misdemeanor. Beyond that, the case simply raised a series of unanswered questions. Will judges henceforth be impeached and removed if they make arbitrary rulings, if they are affiliated with a disfavored political party, if they come to work drunk, if they curse to excess? Preliminary answers on the first two questions, which are of particular interest here, would have to await the next action-packed impeachment episode. The wait would be a short one. In their documentary history of impeachment, Emily Van Tassel and Paul Finkelman observe:

> Although Pickering was removed, his manifest disability undercut the precedential value his removal had for establishing the validity of the Jeffersonian theory of impeachment. That would be tested in the next impeachment proceeding, against Federalist Supreme Court justice Samuel Chase in 1804–1805.[27]

Supreme Court Justice Samuel Chase

In his biography of John Marshall, Albert Beveridge remarks, "for a long time everybody had understood that the impeachment of Chase was only the first step in the execution of the Republican plan to replace with Republicans Marshall and the four Federalist Associate Justices."[28] If so, Justice Samuel Chase may have been selected to go first because he was the easiest target of the bunch. By most accounts,

Chase was a Federalist partisan and an arrogant, bombastic pain in the neck. One scholar describes him as "a man of violent opinions, overbearing manners, and fierce temper," who "made enemies rapidly and easily, and . . . was always a center of controversy, in law as in politics."[29] Another scholar echoes that Chase "became the conspicuous symbol of the judicial arrogance that Republicans found so infuriating and that extremists among them were disposed to attribute to federal judges as a group."[30] District judge Richard Peters, who sat with Justice Chase as circuit court judge, minced no words.

> Of all others, I liked the least to be coupled with him. I never sat with him without pain, as he was forever getting into some intemperate and unnecessary squabble. If I am to be immolated, let it be with some other victim or for my own sins.[31]

Peters escaped immolation but was nonetheless singed by the radiated heat of the Chase impeachment, having presided with Chase over the treason trial of John Fries in 1800, which gave rise to the first article of impeachment against Chase.[32] Fries admitted that he led a group of insurgents to liberate prisoners who had been arrested for obstructing the enforcement of federal tax laws, but he denied that his acts constituted treason. At the trial, Justice Chase presented the jury with his own legal definition of treason while denying counsel for Fries the opportunity to present theirs.

Nearly four years later, with the Federalists purged from the first two branches and the Republicans flush from their victory in the Pickering case, Virginia congressman John Randolph went to the floor of the House, made allusions to the Fries episode, and called for an impeachment inquiry into the conduct of Justice Chase.[33] The single lengthiest House debate in the entire Chase affair then transpired, with the point of contention being whether Randolph's general allegations were sufficient to warrant a formal impeachment investigation. Congressman Roger Griswold argued that Randolph's accusation amounted to "nothing more than that the judge refused liberty to the counsel to argue a point of law after it was decided," with respect to which "the judge may have erred, but [it] was an error of judgment for which he cannot be impeached." Congressman James Elliott added that calling for such an inquiry was tantamount to an accusation of wrongdoing that would operate as a "vote of censure on this judge." In Elliot's view, "the streams of justice should be preserved pure and unsullied," and the "Judicial department should attach to itself a degree of independence," for which reason Elliot could not support a formal investigation "without any facts being adduced to show that such an inquiry should be made."[34]

There was, however, no stopping the inquiry. "We are told by the gentleman from Vermont that this House has no right to pass censure on a judge, and that judges should be highly independent," Congressman Joseph Clay began, referring to the remarks of Elliot. "I am afraid," he continued, "that unless great care be taken the doctrine of judicial independence will be carried so far as to become dangerous to the liberties of the country." As far as Clay was concerned, "I consider this house as the Constitutional guardians of the morality of the Judiciary" so that "[w]henever even suspicion exists as to that morality, a committee of inquiry should be appointed" because "the pure administration of justice is surely more important than the reputation of any particular judge."[35] The resolution calling for an impeachment inquiry was later amended to add Judge Peters and, as amended, was approved on a vote of eighty-one to forty.[36]

Two months thereafter, the committee investigating Justice Chase and Judge Peters issued a report that read, in its entirety:

> That in consequence of the evidence collected by them, in virtue of the powers with which they have been invested by the House, and which is hereunto subjoined, they are of opinion,
>
> 1) That Samuel Chase, Esq., one of the associates [*sic*] justices of the Supreme Court of the United States, be impeached of high crimes and misdemeanors.
>
> 2) That Richard Peters, district judge of the district of Pennsylvania, has not so acted in his judiciary capacity so as to require the interposition of the Constitutional powers of this House.[37]

Appended to the committee report was a volume of written testimony relating to the Fries case and three other episodes that would later be incorporated into eight articles of impeachment. One of the new matters concerned James Callender, who, like Fries, had encountered Chase four years before. Also like Fries, Callender had taken on the

Federalist establishment, not by leading an insurrection, but by publishing material critical of President Adams. In regard to Callender's sedition trial, Chase was variously accused of refusing to excuse a biased juror, declining to admit relevant testimony, prescreening the questions defense counsel wished to ask a prospective witness, being rude to the lawyers, and manifesting an "indecent solicitude . . . for the conviction of the accused." Another newly cited episode likewise occurred in 1800, this one in Delaware; in this case, the justice was accused of attempting to coerce a grand jury and prosecutor into pursuing sedition charges against an unnamed local printer. The final new development related to another grand jury proceeding that had taken place in Baltimore in 1803, where Chase was accused of "pervert[ing] his official right and duty to address the grand jury . . . for the purpose of delivering . . . an intemperate and inflammatory political harangue."

The House formulated two resolutions that tracked the two recommendations of the committee. Debate on the resolution to impeach Justice Chase began with Congressman Elliott, who explained that he "opened the discussion with a view to preclude [himself] from taking part in the extensive debates which the subject can scarcely fail of producing hereafter."[38] After a careful analysis of the testimony published with the committee's report, Elliott concluded that an impeachable offense occurred only in the Callender case, where he found himself unable to "ascribe [Chase's] conduct to the passion of the moment, or to those ordinary prejudices which invariably constitute a part of the infirmities of human nature."[39]

That is where the "extensive debates" ended. The House agreed to impeach Chase on a vote of seventy-three to thirty-two, while Peters was exonerated unanimously. Whereas the earlier House debate on the resolution to investigate Justice Chase occupies nearly seventy pages in the *Annals of Congress,* the deliberation that preceded its vote to impeach him spans only six— all devoted to the remarks of a single legislator. Immediately after the vote was taken, Congressman Roger Griswold, a dissenting member of the investigating committee, offered an explanation for the deafening silence.

> I would . . . have undertaken on this occasion to enter minutely
> into the testimony, were I not of opinion that the sentiments of

the House are already formed. I have examined the depositions critically, and I am ready to say that they constitute no grounds for impeachment. But I have been lamentably convinced, by a mournful experience, that nothing which can be said in the case of impeachments will have any effect on this House. I shall therefore, say nothing.[40]

Congressman John Randolph, who chaired the committee that investigated Chase and previously served as a House manager in the Pickering trial, feebly rejoined that "if there had been no discussion, it was because there was an indisposition on either side to provoke it."[41] Either way, the decision to impeach Samuel Chase in March 1804 capped off a process so preordained and partisan that the participants felt an "indisposition" to preserve even the pretense of a deliberative process. Although the House revisited the matter in November and again in December to refine and approve specific articles of impeachment (and to add two new accusations in connection with the Callender case, incorporated into articles V and VI), the issue of whether to impeach was not revisited.[42]

Like the Pickering case, Chase's impeachment for arbitrary and oppressive decision making occurred in a highly partisan environment and after almost no debate. Unlike the Pickering case, however, the Chase impeachment was uncluttered by extraneous issues (e.g., the judge's sanity) that could obscure its meaning: if Chase were removed, it would be to punish him for making rulings from the bench that Congress deemed so wrong or high-handed as to constitute high crimes or misdemeanors. The implications of such a precedent for the independence of the judiciary were not lost on Chief Justice John Marshall, who, in a letter written to Justice Chase shortly before the impeachment trial began, lamented that "the present doctrine seems to be that a judge giving a legal opinion contrary to the opinion of the legislature is liable to impeachment."[43]

The Senate trial provided a forum to litigate when, if ever, a judge's bench rulings could give rise to an impeachable offense—an issue that went largely undebated on the House floor. The trial showcased three different positions on that issue, with a moderate view sandwiched between two extremes. At one extreme was the argument of Joseph Hopkinson, lead counsel for Justice Chase, who argued that "no judge can be impeached and removed from office for any act or offence for which he could not be indicted."[44] Hopkinson's point was premised on the view that impeachment should be reserved for truly serious offenses and that an offense not subject to indictment was too trivial to be impeachable.

> Look around you, sir, upon this awful tribunal of justice. . . . Was such a court created . . . to scan and punish paltry errors and indiscretions too insignificant to have a name in the penal code . . . ? This is indeed employing an elephant to remove an atom too minute for the grasp of an insect.[45]

If accepted, Hopkinson's argument would have provided judges with categorical immunity from impeachment for wrongheaded, outrageous, or high-handed decisions, insofar as no indictable crime was implicated by such conduct.

In opposition to Hopkinson, Congressman Joseph Nicholson, speaking on behalf of the House managers, noted first that he "might refer to English authorities of the highest respectability, to show that offices of the British government have been impeached for offences not indictable under any law whatever." He was, however, loath to take such a tack, because, he argued, "the constitution of the United States ought to be expounded on its own principles, and . . . foreign aid ought never to be called in."[46] Instead, Nicholson grounded his argument in the text of the Constitution, observing first that "the plain and correct inference to be drawn" from the good behavior clause was that "a judge is to hold office so long as he demeans himself well in it" and that "whenever he shall not demean himself well, he shall be removed."[47] Alternatively, Nicholson continued, even if "a judge were not made liable to removal from the very nature of the tenure by which he holds his office, we still insist that every judge conducting himself improperly in office" commits a "misdemeanor" under the impeachment clauses. In defense of this proposition, Nicholson contextualized the definition of "misdemeanor" as follows:

> In a state court, I would speak of a misdemeanor as an offence against a state law; in the courts of the United States, I would

speak of it as an offence against an act of Congress; but sir, as a member of the House of Representatives, acting as a manager of impeachment, before the highest court in the nation, appointed to try the highest officers of the government, when I speak of a misdemeanor, I mean an act of official misconduct, a violation of official duty, whether it be a proceeding against a positive law, or a proceeding unwarranted by law.[48]

As to Hopkinson's claim that an offense must be indictable to be impeachable, a winner's view of history renders Nicholson's counterargument compelling in light of the impeachments of Judges Archbald and Ritter, who would be removed over a century later on charges that did not constitute indictable crimes. Even by the standards of the time, however, Nicholson's contention on that point was consonant with the views expressed at the Constitutional Convention and in the ratification debates fifteen years earlier. Recall from chapter 1 that a majority of delegations to the Constitutional Convention appeared to agree that "attempts to subvert the constitution" were impeachable, while Hamilton, in the Federalist Papers, in his capacity as pitchman for the proposed Constitution, characterized "deliberate usurpations on the authority of the legislature" as subjecting judges to removal by impeachment. If, as Hamilton declared in the Federalist papers (no. 65), impeachment is an appropriate remedy for "the misconduct of public men" taking the form of an "abuse or violation of some public trust" that "may with peculiar propriety be denominated *political*," then impeachable offenses could not easily be confined to indictable crimes. Hopkinson's extreme view that impeachable offenses were limited to indictable crimes may not have enjoyed widespread support, but that is not to suggest a general acceptance of Nicholson's equally extreme alternative that impeachable misconduct arises in any "proceeding against a positive law" or "proceeding unwarranted by law." Utilizing impeachment and removal whenever Congress concluded that a judge had made a decision against or unwarranted by the law would be tantamount to "tenure during pleasure of the Senate," which Madison and his fellow founders had successfully opposed at the Constitutional Convention.[49]

Between the extremes offered by Hopkinson and Nicholson was a third definition of impeachable offenses, advanced by Justice Chase himself. The critical issue for Chase was one of motive: he contended that judicial conduct that is illegal, that reflects "ignorance or error in judgment," or that is otherwise "irregular or improper" rises to the level of an impeachable offense only if it has "flown from a depravity of heart, or any unworthy motive."[50] Thus, he concluded (speaking of himself in the third person) that if the Senate found that he "hath acted in his judicial character with willful injustice or partiality, he doth not wish any favor; but expects that the whole extent of the punishment permitted in the constitution will be inflicted upon him." If, however, the Senate found otherwise, Chase was "confident that this court will make allowances for the imperfections and frailties incidental to man."[51]

Chase's view appears in concert with that of the Antifederalist known as "Brutus," who, during the ratification debates, had opined that "errors in judgment" were not impeachable offenses unless accompanied by "wicked and corrupt motives." Chase's argument is also in accord with that of the Federalist Hamilton, who had distinguished between "[p]articular misconstructions and contraventions of the will of the legislature" that "may now and then happen" and "deliberate usurpations on the authority of the legislature" for which removal by impeachment was available. More fundamentally, Chase's definition of impeachable offenses would appear to be that adopted by the House of Representatives. With the lone exception of article V—the only article that received no Senate votes in favor of conviction—the articles of impeachment approved by the House charged Chase not simply with making rulings or statements that were contrary to law but with doing so "in a manner highly arbitrary, oppressive and unjust" (article I); "prompted by a similar spirit of persecution and injustice" (article II); "with intent to oppress" (articles III and VI); with "manifest injustice, partiality, and intemperance" (article IV); with the "intention to procure the prosecution" of a printer, thereby "degrading his high judicial functions" (article VII); and with "the low purpose of an electioneering partisan" (article VIII). Presumably, if the House was of the view that bad motives were unnecessary to establish an impeachable offense, it would not have imposed on its managers the burden of proving to the satisfaction of the Senate that the justice acted with such motives.

The respondent and his accuser thus appear to have been more or less in accord on the issue of when a judge was subject to removal by impeachment for his judicial decisions. Where the consensus collapsed was on the question of proof. Justice Chase and his counsel sparred at length with the House managers over whether the respondent's specific decisions were correct as a matter of law, but the issue of greater importance to future proceedings concerned the evidence needed to demonstrate bad motive if the decisions were in error.

On that point, the House managers were unified in the view that the error itself evidenced the evil underlying motive. John Randolph contended that "the criminal intent is to be inferred from the boldness of the innovation itself."[52] Peter Early argued that "criminal intent is apparent upon the face of the act," asking rhetorically, "Can it be that such outrages should be committed upon the most ordinary principles of law and justice, and yet the conduct of the judge not be influenced by corrupt motives?"[53] Manager George Campbell made the same point even more bluntly.

> The judge insists, if he was mistaken, it was an error of judgment. This cannot be presumed. Ignorance of the law is no excuse in any man; but in a character of such high legal standing and known abilities as that of the accused, it is totally inadmissible and not to be presumed. How could any judge with upright intentions commit so many errors or hit upon so many mistakes in the course of one trial? . . . . They must have been the result of design.[54]

If, as these managers contended, a base motive should be presumed once it was shown that the judge committed obvious or extreme errors, then judges could, in effect, be removed for errors alone, as Nicholson claimed.

Unsurprisingly, counsel for Justice Chase challenged the position taken by the House managers. Hopkinson belittled the view that "the common sense of the House is the standard of guilt, and their opinion of the error of the act conclusive evidence of corruption."[55] Philip Barton Key declared: "the truth is that no judge is liable for an error of judgment. I apprehend this is conceded by the article itself, which states a criminal intent." As to the evidence that Chase acted with "criminal intention," Key asserted, "it is said that the respondent is highly gifted with intellectual powers and must have known in this instance the law," to which Key responded, "I dislike the compliment; the best gifted mortals are frail, and a single erroneous decision may be made by any man." He then cited English precedent for the proposition that "an error in judgment has never of itself been considered an evidence of corruption in a judge," a proposition leading Key to conclude that "however gross the error of the judge, it cannot itself contain any foundation for presuming fraud."[56]

As a theoretical matter, usurpation or abuse of power may be no different than bribery or favoritism in its impact on the judicial function. In each case, the decision maker's independent and impartial judgment is corrupted in a case or series of cases by inappropriate external influence, be it love of money, friends, or power. In each case, the judge may fairly be characterized as committing "an abuse or violation of some public trust" and so an impeachable offense. As a matter of proof, however, these two cases are quite different. Bribery and favoritism can be established with reference to extrinsic evidence, in the form of the individual who solicited the bribe, the money that exchanged hands, or the friend or relative who benefited from the judicial conduct. In the case of abuse of judicial power, however, the critical element that distinguishes the offense from simple judicial error occurs entirely within the mind of the judge, who typically pleads intentions pure as the driven snow.

Given the absence of extrinsic evidence in such cases, the Chase impeachment presented about as strong an argument for removing a judge for abuse of power as one is likely to find. "Through the whole tenor of his judicial conduct runs the spirit of party," declared John Randolph, who regarded Chase as "a judge anxious only to enforce a particular law whereby he may recommend himself to power, or to his party."[57] Latter-day commentators on the Chase impeachment have reached similar conclusions.[58] If the partisan supermajority of the Senate would not take this opportunity to remove so strident an ideologue and political enemy, perhaps it never would.

Given the strength of the case against Chase, why did less than a majority of the Senate vote to convict him on five of the articles, and why was only a bare majority prepared to vote him guilty on the remaining three? Although partisan politics played a role, the nine Federalists who voted to acquit on every count were joined by at least six Republicans, and had the Republicans not broken ranks, Chase would have been removed.[59] Because Chase defended himself in the alternative and because the Senate offered no formal rationale for its acquittal, one cannot be certain why he was exonerated. It is possible some senators remained unconvinced that Chase committed judicial error; others may not have been sure his errors were ill-motivated; and still others may have felt that even ill-motivated errors did not constitute indictable (and hence impeachable) crimes.

Over and above these narrower issues, the Senate's deliberations could not help but be colored by the realization that a vote to convict would be a first step down the path of reviewing judicial decisions for the purpose of removing judges who—in the minds of the Senate supermajority—erred too openly. Such a course may have been regarded as problematic in two respects. First, it portended to destroy the decisional independence of the fledgling judiciary, which was a concern that Chase's counsel called to the Senate's attention in the opening moments of the trial.

> I consider the judiciary of our country most important among the branches of government, and its purity and independence the most interesting consequence to every man. Whilst it is honorably and fully protected from the influence of favour or fear from any quarter, the situation of a people can never be very uncomfortable or unsafe—But if a judge is forever to be exposed to prosecutions and impeachments for his official conduct on the mere suggestion of caprice, and to be condemned by the mere voice of prejudice, under the specious name of common sense, can he hold that firm and steady hand his high functions require—No—if his nerves are of iron they must tremble in so perilous a situation.[60]

Openly hostile to the judiciary's independence, Senator Giles and his cohort would have been unmoved by such concerns, but they may not have spoken for the moderate Republicans who joined with the Federalists to acquit Justice Chase. A second problem with the precedent that could have been set by Chase's conviction was that even among those indifferent to the judiciary's independence, the Chase affair had just burned a year of congressional time, and the prospect of employing so cumbersome a device to purge the world of an isolated, irritating jurist may well have struck some, to borrow Hopkinson's phrase, as "employing an elephant to remove an atom too minute for the grasp of an insect."

In his book on the impeachment of Justice Samuel Chase, Chief Justice William H. Rehnquist concludes:

> [T]he Chase acquittal has come to stand for the proposition that impeachment is not a proper weapon for Congress . . . to employ in these confrontations [between the courts and the political branches]. No matter how angry or frustrated either of the other branches may be by the action of the Supreme Court, removal of individual members of the Court because of their judicial philosophy is not permissible.[61]

The picture Rehnquist paints, while generally accurate, employs brushstrokes that alternate between the overly broad and the unduly narrow. The impeachment and trial of Chase was about more than his "judicial philosophy," but by itself did less than establish a congressional consensus that it was "not permissible" to impeach judges for offenses of the sort Chase was accused of committing. More precisely, the impeachment was about whether egregiously erroneous judicial rulings could by themselves constitute an impeachable abuse of power; and because so much about the Senate's verdict remained speculative, the precedential significance of the Chase impeachment would have to await the Peck and Swayne trials for clarification.

District Judge James Peck

In many ways, the 1830–31 impeachment and trial of Judge James Peck was a low-budget sequel to the Chase blockbuster of a generation earlier. Both focused exclusively on abuse of judicial power, although the Chase impeachment had concerned multiple rulings in several cases spanning four years, while Judge Peck's impeachment related to an isolated ruling in a single case. The Chase impeachment occurred at the height of the first great wave of court-directed hostility (as discussed in chapter 2), while the Peck impeachment took place at the apogee of the second, amid a period of Jacksonian antipathy toward unelected, life-tenured judges. In both instances, anticourt sentiments were strongest among members of the political party in control of the first two branches of government—Jeffersonian Republicans at the time of Chase's impeachment proceedings and Jacksonian Democrats at the time of Peck's. Finally, both judges were acquitted, Chase following a majority (but not the required supermajority) vote to convict on three of eight articles, Peck after a less suspenseful majority vote to acquit.

The ruling at issue in the Peck impeachment is easy enough to describe. Early Missouri settlers had claimed title to land granted them by the Spanish crown prior to the Louisiana Purchase. In 1825, Judge Peck issued a decision in which he invalidated one such claim for want of required documentation, which generated considerable community anger. Given local interest in this issue, Peck agreed to publish the decision in a local newspaper. Several days later, the losing attorney, Luke Lawless, criticized the decision in the same newspaper, under a pseudonym. Peck regarded the critique as dangerously misleading. After it was revealed that Lawless had written it, Peck held him in contempt of court, imprisoned him for a day, and suspended him from practicing in federal court for a year and a half.[62] Lawless claimed that Peck either usurped contempt power that was not within his authority to exercise or abused that power if its exercise was within his authority.

Impeachment resolutions were introduced in 1826 and 1828 but died in committee. In 1829, Congressman George McDuffie reintroduced the resolution he had submitted the previous year. This time, it found the receptive ear of newly appointed House Judiciary Committee chair James Buchanan, who brought the resolution to the House floor in 1830, accompanied by his committee's recommendation that Judge Peck be impeached.[63]

Unlike the briefer Pickering and Chase proceedings, the House vote to impeach Peck followed hours of debate across three days and included a personal statement from Judge Peck himself. Although the debate was not transcribed,[64] one notable development is reflected in the record. On April 23, Representative Edward Everett rose to remark that he "could not admit that Judge Peck's conduct had been free from blame" but that he "could not bring his mind to the conclusion that Judge Peck ought to be impeached" either. Everett declared he "had looked in vain in the evidence for proof of evil intent" and found only "proof of the general good intentions and mildness of the Judge." Everett thus proposed an amended resolution providing that "this House does not approve the conduct of James H. Peck . . . yet there is not sufficient evidence of evil intent, to authorize the House to impeach the said judge of high misdemeanors in office."[65] Everett accepted a friendly amendment from Tristam Burges to strike "this House does not approve the conduct" and substitute the gentler phrase "although the House might not, if called on, altogether approve the conduct."[66] Representative Storrs, however, opposed this kind of censure or public reprimand as "affording a mischievous precedent"; he "admitted that to have stricken the attorney from the rolls might not have subjected the judge to censure," but he argued that "the violation of . . . personal liberty"—that is, "the imprisonment of Mr. Lawless in the felon's room"—constituted an impeachable "usurpation of a jurisdiction which the judge did not possess." William Ellsworth concurred that he saw "nothing in the publication of Mr. Lawless which ought to have drawn down the punishment inflicted by this judge"; it was thus "an arbitrary proceeding" for which impeachment was warranted. The Everett amendment was rejected, and Peck was impeached on a vote of 123 to 49. Of 213 House seats, 139 were held by Democrats, of whom 19 voted against impeachment.[67]

In the Senate, the House managers and counsel for Judge Peck were in accord on the definition of an impeachable offense in cases of abuse or usurpation of power. The lone article of impeachment charged Peck with "unjustly, oppressively, and arbitrarily" imprisoning and suspending Lawless, with an "intention wrongfully and unjustly to oppress, imprison, and otherwise injure him" under the "color and pretense" that Lawless was answerable for contempt.[68] Ambrose Spencer, speaking on behalf of the House managers, opined,

> A judicial misdemeanor consists . . . in doing an illegal act *colore officii* with bad motives, or in doing an act within the competency of the court or judge in some cases, but unwarranted in a particular case from the facts existing in that case, with bad motives.[69]

In his opening statement, Peck's counsel Jonathan Meredith articulated the questions presented by the case in terms that track both the allegations in the article of impeachment and Spencer's analysis.

1st. Was a contempt committed?

2d. If so, had the court legal warrant to punish it, as it was punished?

And 3d. If not, was the respondent actuated by a sense of official obligation, or by the evil and malicious intention of which he is charged?[70]

In short, both sides agreed that a judge could be impeached and removed for judicial error if the error was a product of "bad" or "evil" motives. Just as in the Chase trial, however, the parties disagreed on the issue of proof. As in Chase, the House managers argued that the judicial error itself evinced the evil motive. Ambrose Spencer thus declared,

If the illegality of the proceedings of Judge Peck, in the case of Mr. Lawless has been made out; if that illegality had been shown to be great and flagrant; then I insist that of itself furnished very strong, if not controlling evidence of a bad mind and an evil intent.[71]

James Buchanan likewise declared:

It is from the criminal action that judges must infer the criminal intention. If a judge has cruelly and illegally imprisoned and punished an American citizen, the court before whom he is impeached will never set out to hunt after a good motive for this bad action.[72]

Peck's lawyers, however, insisted that more was required; otherwise, every judicial error would become an impeachable offense.

We see the opinions of inferior courts reversed every day. . . . But no one ever thought of impeaching an inferior court because it had mistaken the law: and yet, according to this argument they ought to be impeached in every such case; because an unlawful act, we are told, necessarily involves a criminal intention. I respectfully insist, therefore, that although you should differ with Judge Peck and his counsel with respect to the extent of his judicial powers, and think that he had not the power to punish the conduct of Mr. Lawless with contempt of court, it does not follow that he is guilty of the misdemeanor charged in the impeachment; because the inquiry still remains whether this was an honest mistake of judgment, or whether he acted with the guilty intention charged in the impeachment . . . I insist too that this guilty intention is not to be inferred from the alleged incorrectness of his judicial opinion, but must be satisfactorily proved by evidence in the cause.[73]

Despite Jacksonian-era disenchantment with life-tenured federal judges, both sides laid claim to having the interests of judicial independence at heart. For Buchanan, removing Peck would forestall more problematic assaults on judicial tenure. "If the power of impeachment presents no prospect to the people of removing an arbitrary and tyrannical judge," he declared, "they will soon begin to inquire whether the judicial office ought not to be limited to a term of years."[74] Peck's subsequent acquittal suggests, however, that the Senate was more persuaded by the closing remarks of the judge's counsel William Wirt.

The question before you, sir, is not that of Judge Peck alone. It is the question of the independence of the American judiciary. . . . Is this Court prepared to suspend the sword by a hair over the heads of our judges, and constrain them to the performance of their duties amidst fear and trembling from the terrors of an impeachment? Or will you not rather, by your decision, maintain them in that firm, enlightened and honest discharge of their duties, which has heretofore so preeminently distinguished them? . . . Sir, there is not a considerate man who has not long regarded a pure, firm, enlightened judiciary as the great sheet-anchor of our national constitution. Snap the cable that binds us to that, and farewell to our union and the yet dawning glories of our Republic.[75]

As to the meaning of the Peck acquittal, the judge's defenders did not dwell on whether his conduct was indictable, which eliminates one issue that cluttered the Chase impeachment. The clarity of the Peck precedent is still obscured by uncertainty over whether he was acquitted because the Senate remained unconvinced that the judge had erred in his use of the contempt power or unconvinced that his error was the product of evil motives. It bears noting, however, that those in the House who were unprepared to impeach him nevertheless appeared ready to acknowledge that his ruling was erroneous, a possibility that Peck's own counsel conceded in closing argument (albeit in the alternative). And in some ways, the "bad" motive underlying Peck's conduct was more readily demonstrable than the inherently abstract, ideological zeal that motivated Chase, because Peck had openly punished his critic and could thus be charged with personal animus. That a majority of the Senate was still unwilling to remove Peck supports a reasonable suspicion, if not a tentative conclusion, that the impeachment process could not be used to remove judges for abusing their decision-making power in isolated cases.

Judge Charles Swayne

Thirty years after the Peck impeachment, district judge West Humphreys would be impeached and removed in 1862, amid the third great cycle of anticourt sentiment described in chapter 2. Although thirteen southern federal judges resigned to join the Confederacy during the Civil War, Humphreys openly advocated secession, abandoned his post, and became a Confederate judge without bothering to resign his federal commission first. His case was the only uncontested removal by impeachment in U.S. history, the outcome of which Van Tassel and Finkelman rightly characterize as a "foregone conclusion."[76] In 1873, district judge Mark Delahay, impeached in the House for drunkenness on the bench, resigned before his trial in the Senate began. These cases add little of value to this study, although it is worth noting that they were the first two impeachments that could not be characterized as challenging the decisional independence of the affected judges and, perhaps not coincidentally, were also the first two impeachments that the respondents did not bother to contest at trial.

After Delahay, no judge would be impeached for over thirty years, until Charles Swayne was impeached and acquitted in 1904 and 1905, during the Populist-Progressive era, the fourth period of court-directed hostility discussed in chapter 2. In the immediate aftermath of the Peck acquittal, Congress enacted legislation that restricted the contempt power of federal judges—a statute Swayne would violate seventy years later (Swayne would also be charged with other, unrelated misconduct, irrelevant for purposes here). In 1901, a suit was filed before Judge Swayne to recover a tract of land in which Judge Swayne himself allegedly had an interest. The plaintiff's counsel asked Swayne to recuse himself, which he declined to do, with the explanation that he had no interest in the property himself; his wife had undertaken to acquire such an interest, Swayne asserted, but the transaction had never been completed. The lawyers then filed and publicized a second suit on the same matter in state court, where Swayne was summoned to appear. Swayne responded by holding the lawyers in contempt and sentencing them to fine, imprisonment, and suspension.

As in the Peck case, opinions differed over whether Swayne erred when he held the lawyers in contempt. But this time, there was no dispute that the sentence imposed violated the applicable contempt statute, which authorized Swayne to fine or—not and—imprison the offenders. A divided House Judiciary Committee recommended impeachment, with six members dissenting on the grounds that "the evidence did not justify impeachment."

On the House floor, impeachment proponents conceded that "no judge may be held responsible for a mistake of law," but they argued that Swayne's "animus and evil intent," as "manifest[ed] by his action and speech," rendered his contempt orders impeachable misbehavior.[77] As in prior impeachments, the action or error itself was the best evidence of bad motive. As Representative Wilber Palmer contended, "the action of Judge Swayne was, to say the least, arbitrary, unjust and unlawful," and "if an unlawful act is committed by a judge . . . the law presumes an evil intent."[78] To the extent that such evidence would be insufficient to convict, impeachment supporters were unfazed. "This House has no constitutional power to pass on the question of the guilt or innocence of the respondent," argued Representative Samuel Powers. He continued, "all we can do is to ascertain whether or not this cause is worthy of trial," which Powers argued would be the case if the House found "probable cause of guilt."[79]

On this latter point, impeachment opponents disagreed. In their dissent from the select committee's draft articles, Representatives Charles Littlefield and Richard Parker contended, "The House must establish the truth of these articles, by competent testimony, beyond reasonable doubt."[80] On the House floor, Littlefield elaborated on his position.

> I do not think that it is a question altogether of probable cause.
> . . . I can not vote for any specification or any charge unless, in my judgment, the Senate of the United States, upon the record as it stands before us, would be required . . . to find the charge sustained.[81]

Littlefield and Parker were, however (on this occasion, at least), in the distinct minority. The House impeached Judge Swayne by a vote of 198 to 61.

As in the Pickering, Chase, and Peck cases, the articles of impeachment relating to Swayne's rulings alleged that they were not just unlawful but "maliciously" and "knowingly" so, which Swayne's own counsel characterized as "impeachable offenses . . . properly charged under the rule which the Constitution prescribes."[82] As with earlier impeachments, the respondent insisted that "whatever mistake he made . . . was made without malice and in the belief that such a sentence could be properly imposed under the law,"[83] while the House managers urged the Senate to infer knowledge and malice from the unlawful decision itself and conceded that they could not prove it otherwise because "[i]t is not to be expected that a judge who intends to use his judicial power to gratify his malice, or ill will or to punish one he hates will declare the fact in advance or confess it after the sentence is pronounced."[84] Swayne's lawyers, like counsel for Chase and Peck, countered that specific evidence of malice was essential, for if the Senate simply presumed that judicial errors were motivated by malice and hence impeachable, judicial independence would be irreparably damaged.

> Unless you show his dishonesty or malice in his judicial action he is protected by that shield which the wisdom of our judicial system throws around the bench, for if a man may be questioned for his decision from the bench, even if he be wrong, if for a decision wrongfully given from the bench he may be punished, imprisoned, or removed, our judiciary has no protection.[85]

On all articles of impeachment, the Senate acquitted Swayne by a substantial majority vote. Despite the facts that Swayne had committed an error and that the error was self-serving in that it enabled the judge to impose an excessive punishment on the lawyers who had challenged him, the Senate concluded, by a considerable margin, that no impeachable offense had occurred.

When the Senate's resounding vote against Swayne's removal is paired with the House's even more resounding vote for his impeachment, it is tempting to infer an emerging schism between the chambers on the definition of an impeachable offense. Such an inference, however, may not be justified. In multiple impeachment proceedings spanning the previous century, respondents and House managers had agreed that ill-motivated judicial errors were impeachable offenses, which suggests a general consensus on that point. Their difference of view in Swayne's case may be more easily attributed to the House majority's perception that the extent of the error itself established probable cause to believe that Swayne's order was ill-motivated and so impeachable, while the Senate required more to demonstrate guilt. How much evidence the House needs to impeach and the Senate needs to convict is an issue that has arisen repeatedly in the course of House impeachment investigations and will be revisited later in this chapter.

In any event, the House could not have been oblivious to the trajectory of its track record in cases concerning the abuse of power. After a technical victory in the Pickering case, Chase, Peck, and now Swayne had all been acquitted by increasingly lopsided margins.[86] Peck would be the last judge impeached on the basis of his judicial decisions alone, and Swayne would be the last judge impeached, even in part, on allegations that he abused his power by making egregiously erroneous rulings of law in the context of a specific case.

The grounds for subsequent impeachments are varied. In 1913, Robert Archbald would be impeached and removed for abusing his position by entering into business relationships with prospective litigants. In 1926, district judge George English would resign before trial after his impeachment for misbehavior that ranged from misusing bankruptcy funds for private gain, abusing his administrative powers over admission to practice before the court, and exhibiting favoritism in his oversight of bankruptcy receivers, to being generally tyrannical. Two of the smaller (but juicier) pieces of fruit in the cornucopia of his alleged misconduct merit separate mention.

One episode leading to English's impeachment featured an allegation that English threatened journalists with imprisonment if they reported on English's conduct in disbarring a local lawyer from practicing in his court. The second concerned what Van Tassel and Finkelman fairly describe as a "startling claim that the judge sent the U.S. marshal to round up" a passel of local public officials and "herded them into his court for an imaginary case."[87] Both events concerned an abuse of judicial power, but of a sort that is quite different from that at issue in prior impeachments. Chase, Peck, and Swayne were impeached for making erroneous rulings of law or fact in specific cases that came before them, so the impeachments seemed clearly calculated to curb their decisional independence. English, in contrast, was being called to task for making random, arbitrary demands akin to those of the hypothetical judge, discussed earlier, who would direct counsel to dress in Star Wars regalia. Had Chase, Peck, or Swayne been convicted, future judges might have had reason to worry about whether their views of the law in any given case differed too markedly from those of congressional partisans; the English impeachment raised no comparable concerns.

In 1933, district judge Harold Louderback would be impeached and acquitted of charges that he exhibited favoritism in his appointment of bankruptcy receivers. In 1936, Halsted Ritter would be convicted on an omnibus charge of bringing his court into "scandal and disrepute," in light of other specific charges (for which he was acquitted) that he received a kickback for appointing a former law partner as a receiver and continued to practice law as a sitting judge.[88] In the 1980s, Judges Harry Claiborne, Alcee Hastings, and Walter Nixon would be removed following criminal prosecutions for tax evasion, bribery, and perjury, respectively.

Impeachment Investigations ∾

Impeachment investigations are within the exclusive bailiwick of the House. Whereas the Senate has had occasion to try only eleven judges and in those cases has deliberated their fate off the record, the House has investigated several times that number and, in the course of those investigations, has published most of the information from which precedents can be ascertained. As a consequence, in terms of sheer volume the House has had more to say than the Senate about the constitutional meaning of "high crimes and misdemeanors." Without diminishing the critical role that Senate verdicts have played in defining the contours of impeachable offenses, the struggle to rationalize those verdicts and integrate them into a coherent view of high crimes and misdemeanors has taken place (to the extent it *has* taken place) primarily in the House. Moreover, insofar as independence norms have dissuaded Congress from removing judges on account of their decisions, such norms will more frequently manifest themselves in the context of House decisions not to impeach particular judges. Although decisions not to proceed have occurred in the Senate (as we saw in the Chase, Peck, and Swayne acquittals), they have been far more common in the House, which has winnowed the field of at least seventy-eight inquiries into the conduct of federal judges down to those thirteen that, in the view of the House majority, constituted impeachable offenses.

Excluding Judge George English (for reasons discussed in the preceding section), there have been thirty-one judges with respect to whom the House has taken action of some kind in response to allegations that one or more of a judge's rulings in judicial proceedings were so egregiously wrong as to constitute an impeachable abuse of power. As reflected in table 2, of those thirty-one judges, the investigations of fourteen were concluded with a committee recommendation not to impeach, and five were referred to but never acted on by the committee. Another five ended in resignation, four in impeachment, one with a House vote not to impeach (after the committee was equally divided), one with the death of the judge, and one with a referral of the investigation to the courts of the territory where the judge held court.

A review of House impeachment activity reveals three distinct developments or trends. First, at a very early stage, the House adopted a view—born of concern for judicial independence—that judicial error was unimpeachable absent a bad motive. Second, for a

TABLE 2. Impeachment Investigations of Judges Alleged to Have Abused Their Judicial Power

		(1)	(2)	(3)	(4)	(5)	(6)
1796	Turner, George						X*
1804	Pickering, John	X					
1804	Peters, Richard			X			
1805	Chase, Samuel	X					
1811	Toulmin, Harry			X			
1818	Van Ness, William			X			
1830	Peck, James	X					
1840	McLean, John			X			
1851–58	Watrous, John				X		
1868	Field, Stephen			X			
1873	Durell, Edward		X				
1874	Story, William		X				
1879	Blodgett, Henry			X			
1894	Jenkins, J. G.			X			
1908	Wilfley, Lebbeus			X			
1911	Swayne, Charles	X					
1912	Hanford, Cornelius		X				
1913	Speer, Emory			X			
1914	Dayton, Alston			X			
1914	Wright, Daniel		X				
1926	English, George	X					
1927	Cooper, Frank			X			
1933	Lowell, James						X†
1934	Molyneaux, Joseph					X	
1939	Geiger, Ferdinand		X				
1976	Atkins v. U.S. Judge Plaintiffs					X	
1979	Battisti, Frank					X	
1981	Scott, Nauman					X	
1981	Justice, William W.					X	
1986	Johnson, Frank; Anderson, Lanier; and Clark, Thomas			X			
	Total	5	5	12	1	5	2

Note: Columns are
(1) Impeached
(2) Resigned
(3) Committee recommends against impeachment
(4) House rejects committee recommendation to impeach
(5) No committee action taken
(6) Other: *investigation discontinued; †judge died

significant stretch of time, the House was prepared to impeach upon a showing of something like "probable cause" that the judge had committed an impeachable offense, which enabled it to infer a judge's evil motive from the erroneous decision itself; eventually, though, the House began to insist on evidence sufficient to support a conviction before it was willing to proceed in such cases, which helps to explain the decreasing frequency with which the House impeached judges for abuse of judicial power. This second development traveled in tandem with a third: over time, the House became increasingly reluctant to address judicial error via the impeachment process, out of a dual desire to establish a more truly independent judiciary accountable to itself through appellate review (as discussed in chapter 2) and to reduce distractions from more pressing legislative business. With only one exception, the House stopped investigating judges on its own by the middle of the twentieth century and thereafter initiated impeachment proceedings only after the Department of Justice had concluded criminal prosecution, effectively confining impeachable offenses to criminal wrongdoing. Ultimately, House Judiciary Committee leaders announced that their respect for decisional independence and appellate review altogether foreclosed the House from impeaching judges on account of their decisions.

Early Understandings: Ill-Motivated Judicial Error as an Impeachable Offense

After Pickering in 1803–4 and Chase in 1804–5, the next judge to be investigated on charges that he abused his judicial power was Mississippi territorial judge Harry Toulmin in 1811, followed by New York district judge William Van Ness in 1818. Toulmin was accused of forbidding a criminal defendant to consult with his lawyer in one case and of ordering a jury to find a defendant guilty in another,[89] while with Van Ness, there had been "complaints against some [of his] decisions and orders."[90] Both judges were exonerated by House investigating committees in terms that reflected a solicitude for the integrity and independence of the judges involved, a concern that had been absent from the Pickering and Chase proceedings. The committee went out of its way to praise Toulmin for his "vigilant attention to the duties of his station, and an inflexible zeal for the preservation of the public peace."[91] As to Van Ness, the committee declared that "the respect which this committee entertains for the constitutional rights of a judge . . . forbids their questioning any judicial opinions."[92]

A hiatus of over twenty-five years separated the 1830 impeachment of James Peck from the next judge who would be investigated for allegedly abusing judicial power. The charges leveled against Texas district judge John Watrous in the 1850s were varied. One petition alleged that in a land-grant case, he manipulated the parties and misrepresented the law to create jurisdiction when none existed.[93] In support of this petition, Congressman Miles Taylor cited Pickering's conviction, for the proposition that "an improper ruling was a proper subject of impeachment where it was of a gross and palpable character."[94] Echoing arguments from the Chase and Peck trials, Representative Garnett Adrain retorted that "although Judge Watrous may have committed an error of judgment on some of these points of law, yet that does not furnish a sufficient ground of impeachment."[95] Rather, for Adrain, an impeachable offense arose only when errors "spring from prejudice or some corrupt intent, or from such ignorance of the law as renders the judge incompetent for the discharge of his official duties."[96] In response, Taylor qualified his position: "No sir, a mere error in judgment would not authorize an impeachment, but . . . if, on the other hand, it should be found that the improper rulings were the result of . . . any motive which was inconsistent with the faithful and honest discharge of the judicial function . . . then it is clear to my mind that the judge should be condemned and removed from office."[97]

Watrous would not be impeached, for reasons explored in the next subsection. For our purposes here, the House debate confirms the presence of a rough consensus: judges may be impeached for improper rulings, but only if they are ill-motivated. In 1879, this consensus view was reaffirmed by the House Judiciary Committee in its investigation of Illinois district judge Henry Blodgett, who had been charged (in part) with having "willfully employed the power and authority of said court to perpetuate acts of gross judicial oppression upon the rights of a private citizen," by granting a bankruptcy receiver's request to modify a building to the detriment of one of the building's tenants.[98] The committee's view was that "it may be conceded that Judge Blodgett acted in this instance in excess of his jurisdiction,"[99] which rendered him "amenable to criticism or censure," but that "it is impossible to see how he can be held liable to impeachment therefore, unless it can be shown that he did not act in good faith . . . but with such malice and corruption as to render his act in the premises an official misdemeanor."[100] The committee defended this standard in light of a practical need to insulate judges from threats to their tenure for their official acts, which likewise justified their immunity from civil and criminal liability.

> [I]f the law was such that a judge . . . should be held responsible in damages, or at the bar of criminal justice, for every mistake he might make . . . , if he should be required to stake his fortune or his liberty upon every exercise of his judgment on the bench . . . it would be impossible to find one who would be willing to assume the responsibilities of such a position at all.[101]

As of 1933, the precedent of prior proceedings remained intact. In calling for an impeachment inquiry into the conduct of Massachusetts district judge James Lowell, who declined to extradite an African American murder suspect to Virginia on the grounds that he would not receive a fair trial there, Virginia representative Howard Smith declared:

> I do not contend that a judge may be impeached on an honest difference of opinion as to the law or for an erroneous decision of a case where he acts in good faith, but I do aver and proclaim that a judge is impeachable who is either (1) so ignorant of the law that it amounts to flagrant incompetency; or (2) who knowing the law deliberately, willfully, and knowingly, in direct contravention of the Constitution and well-established precedent and authorities of the courts of last resort releases on the world a self-confessed murderer of the most vicious type.[102]

In the next year, when opposing an impeachment inquiry into the conduct of Minnesota district judge Joseph Molyneaux for issuing a temporary restraining order against the state commerce commission in a bank fraud investigation, Representative Blanton declared: "No judge has ever been impeached for exercising discretion or for want of good judgment. The gentleman first must show something that is of a criminal or dishonest nature."[103] In support of the impeachment, Representative Francis Shoemaker replied, "If the gentleman will permit me to proceed, I will bring plenty of that out," reflecting agreement as to the circumstances under which an abuse of judicial power would rise to the level of an impeachable offense.[104]

Sufficiency of the Evidence: Beyond Probable Cause

Neither the House nor Senate has established formal rules governing the sufficiency of the evidence required to impeach or convict. The absence of such rules creates an opportunity for legislators to argue for a lesser or greater burden of proof, depending on whether they support or oppose impeachment in any given case. Notwithstanding these vagaries inherent in so political a process, it would appear that the House has moved gradually, if unevenly, toward imposing on itself a more exacting burden of proof in cases involving abuse of judicial power.[105]

In the impeachment process, the House and Senate have different roles, which may lead the House to impeach on the strength of less evidence than the Senate requires to convict. Section 2 of Article I of the U.S. Constitution tells us that the House "shall have the sole power of impeachment," while Section 3 provides that the Senate "shall have the sole power to try all impeachments" and adds that the accused is "convicted" upon a two-thirds majority vote. In the Federalist Papers (no. 65), Alexander Hamilton acknowledged that the impeachment mechanism was borrowed from England, where "it is the province of the House of Commons to prefer the impeachment, and of the House of Lords to decide upon it." As to the House of Commons' responsibility in the impeachment process, a manual of the time explained that its "general course is to pass a resolution containing a criminal charge against the supposed delinquent."[106] Similarly, Hamilton wrote in the Federalist Papers (no. 66) that the House possessed the "right of accusing" as distinguished from the Senate's "right of judging." In other words, the House formally charges or accuses the judges; the Senate tries and convicts them. The parallel between the role of the House and Senate in the impeachment process and that of the grand and petit juries in the criminal justice process was alluded to at the outset of this chapter and is too obvious to ignore. If, however, the analogy is extended, it implies that judges should be subject to impeachment in the House upon a significantly lesser showing than would be required to convict them in the Senate, insofar as grand juries indict upon a showing of "probable cause" while petit juries may not convict absent proof "beyond a reasonable doubt."

Given general agreement that ill-motivated judicial error will constitute an impeachable abuse of decision-making power (as described in the foregoing section of this chapter), the failure of the House and Senate to agree by ever-widening margins in the Chase, Peck, and Swayne impeachments may be attributable to differing standards of proof or scrutiny. It should be recalled that Pickering and Chase were impeached by the House following little or no deliberation, while their Senate trials occupied weeks of time and volumes of testimony and argument. At the trial of Judge Peck, the judge's counsel, William Wirt, dismissing the relevance of the House managers' point that Peck had been impeached "by a large majority," observed that "their vote on an impeachment is nothing more than the finding of a bill by a grand jury."[107] The House deliberations in Swayne reflect that those who voted to impeach did so on the basis of evidence sufficient only to establish "probable cause," evidence they openly acknowledged was less than that required to convict. Indeed, across the Chase, Peck, and Swayne impeachments, the House managers sought—unsuccessfully, it would seem—to convince their Senate counterparts that an obviously erroneous decision by itself furnishes proof sufficient to establish the judge's underlying bad motive.

The consequences of impeaching judges on a relaxed standard of proof, in which the only evidence the House proffers to show an ill-motivated abuse of judicial power is the wrongful decision itself, are twofold. First, it puts the House through the time and expense of impeachment proceedings with no removals to show for its trouble. Second, it places the House in the position of impeaching (and so impugning the reputations of) more judges who will ultimately be exonerated in the Senate, to the dual detriment of those judges and the decisional independence of their colleagues, who may shy from hard decisions in the future to avoid a similar fate. These concerns dominated debate over the impeachment investigation of John Watrous in the 1850s.

As described earlier in this chapter, Texas district judge John Watrous was charged, in part, with abusing his decision-making power in a land-grant case. In February 1857, the House Judiciary Committee recommended that Watrous be impeached on this charge because "the conduct of Judge Watrous . . . can not be explained without supposing that he was actuated by other than upright and just motives,"[108] but the Thirty-Fifth Congress expired before the House could act.[109] In the next year, the committee was equally divided on the issue.[110] In explaining his committee vote against impeachment, Horace Clark wrote that he was "not satisfied to vote an impeachment upon the ascertainment of what is commonly termed probable causes" and that the House, "failing to discover in the evidence disclosed any fact inconsistent with judicial integrity on the part of Judge Watrous," should not impeach in this case.[111] On the house floor, he argued that "the case could not be sent to the Senate on proof short of what would be sufficient to convict."[112] James Stewart concurred, warning, "this is not only a very serious matter in regard to its consequences to the individual accused, but also in relation to . . . the independence of your Federal judiciary when involved, it may be, by the conflicting views and prejudices of States or individuals."[113] Stewart maintained, "we have no right to, and should not, send this case up to the Senate . . . merely upon the impression that it ought to be further examined." He concluded, "if we transmit it to the Senate, we should do so from the conviction upon our minds that he is guilty."[114]

Representative Henry Chapman disagreed with Clark and Stewart, arguing that "the trial of the case belonged to the Senate" and that "[i]f the House advanced one step beyond the ascertainment of probable cause it was plunged into the trial."[115] Representative Clement Vallandigham went even further, noting that while he was voting to impeach, "I have not in this case made up my mind definitely" on the issue of Watrous's guilt, "because I am not willing to usurp the province nor anticipate the judgment of the Senate."[116] In an apparent victory for Clark and Stewart's position, however, the House declined to impeach Watrous by a vote of 111 to 91.[117]

After Watrous, the House took a more exacting look at the evidence underlying alleged abuses of judicial power in a series of cases and declined to proceed when such evidence was inconclusive. Against that backdrop, the 1904 decision to impeach Swayne becomes an isolated exception to an emerging rule. In 1894, Wisconsin district judge J. G. Jenkins was investigated by the House Judiciary Committee on charges that he "oppressively" exercised his powers through injunctions issued in a railway bankruptcy. The committee found that Jenkins's orders were "not sustained either by reason or authority" and were "in violation of a constitutional provision, an abuse of judicial power, and without authority of law" but that "the testimony adduced before us fails to show any corrupt intent on the part of the judge." Thus, the committee recommended a resolution condemning his orders but not calling for his impeachment.[118]

The committee reached a similar conclusion in its 1908 investigation into the conduct of Lebbeus Wilfley, judge of the United States Court for China, who was charged with being too harsh with criminal defendants and their counsel. The House Judiciary Committee recommended against impeachment. Its subcommittee report observed that "[t]error to evil doers if purchased at the price of judicial fairness and overstrained legal authority is achieved at too great an expense" and that "[s]uch acts of legal oppression and of abuse of judicial discretion lie at the base of the charges." Despite the "peculiar and dangerous significance" of these charges, the subcommittee concluded, "In this case they are dismissed as falling short of impeachable offenses, by what we believe to be sound principles of legal construction."[119]

In 1913, Georgia district judge Emory Speer was charged with "despotism, tyranny, oppression, and maladministration" in the course of his judicial decision making.[120] The committee found that there were "a large number of official acts on the part of judge Speer which are themselves legal, yet, when taken together, develop into a system tending to approach a condition of tyranny and oppression" and that "the power of the court has been exercised in a despotic and autocratic manner."[121] Nevertheless, the committee was "persuaded that the competent legal evidence at hand is not sufficient to procure a conviction at the hands of the Senate." It therefore concluded: "the record presents a series of legal oppressions and shows an abuse of judicial discretion which, though falling short of impeachable offenses, demand condemnation and criticism."[122]

The Collapse of Impeachment as a Form of Judicial Review

Insofar as Congress makes judges answerable for their decisions via the impeachment process, it is in effect serving as an appellate court with a shillelagh. Just as the House gradually tired of wasting its time impeaching judges under a relaxed standard of scrutiny that did not result in Senate convictions, so it eventually abandoned its role as a court of final resort for review of judicial error. The House has never perceived itself as a surrogate appellate court. In 1818, the House Judiciary Committee saw no need to take further action against Judge William Van Ness for erroneous decision making, arguing that "laws . . . provide adequate remedies for any errors he may commit."[123] And in 1858, Representative Garnett Adrain led the successful effort to stop the impeachment of Judge Watrous with the argument "We are not a court of appeals."[124]

In 1933, when (as described earlier in this chapter) Virginia representative Howard Smith accused Massachusetts district judge James Lowell of abusing his judicial power by refusing to extradite a black defendant, resistance to employing impeachment as a substitute for appellate review took a new turn. Ever since the Chase proceedings more than 125 years earlier, when a member of the House called for the impeachment of a federal judge, the matter was routinely referred to a committee for investigation. On this occasion, however, Massachusetts representative Robert Luce objected:

> [P]icture to yourself what will be the course of events if we establish the precedent that because a lawyer, disappointed and chagrined by the judgment of a judge, feels that he ought to pursue the case, he may come to Congress with his contention. . . . How many hundreds and thousands of cases would be brought to Congress if you . . . laid down the principle that a disappointed litigant may have an appeal to the Congress.[125]

Representative Frederick Lehlbach thought it was the "correct practice" to refer the matter to the House Judiciary Committee, and Luce conceded that it was the "custom."[126] Representative Samuel Pettengill, however, thought it was "premature to take this up before the appellate court files its decision," and Luce concurred that "the Court of Appeals may decide the same way" as the committee.[127] Representative Ralph Lozier, however, countered that "a decision of the higher courts will not purge this judge of his wrongdoing."[128] Lozier's position won the day, and the matter was referred to the committee (shortly after which the judge—and consequently the investigation— died). The referral to committee was made, however, on a surprisingly close vote of 209 to 151,[129] signaling that the House may have begun to lose its appetite for impeachment inquiries into abuse of judicial power.

The next year, when Judge Molyneaux was accused of misconduct for an order he issued, the House abided by its "custom" of referring the matter to committee. But for the first time, the committee took the unprecedented step of taking no steps at all.[130] Resolutions to impeach Ohio district judge Frank Battisti in 1979, Texas district judge William Justice in 1981, and Louisiana district judge Nauman Scott, also in 1981—all on account of decisions they had made in particular cases—would likewise be referred to committee without further action being taken.[131]

The House's recent disinclination to investigate judicial misconduct has not been confined to cases regarding abuse of judicial decision-making power. Setting to one side Judges Claiborne, Nixon, and Hastings, whose impeachments in the 1980s were preceded by criminal prosecutions, the House Judiciary Committee has formally investigated the conduct of only one federal judge since 1945. "A major cause" of this development, in the view of one scholar, is a decision made by the Department of Justice in 1945 to discontinue its past practice of referring matters of judicial misconduct to the House, prior to criminal indictment.[132] This may well explain a decline in impeachment activity aimed at judges accused of indictable crimes, but it has no bearing on the complete cessation of all investigations into allegations that a judge made an incredibly stupid or oppressive ruling from the bench, which is, after all, not a criminal offense.[133]

As far as cases of abuse of judicial decision-making power are concerned, a better explanation for the House Judiciary Committee's inactivity may be found in a 1986 report issued by the chair of the committee's Subcommittee on Courts.[134] In that year, Georgia congressman Charles Hatcher delivered to the committee eighty-thousand petitions and letters (which later ballooned to more than one hundred thousand) demanding the impeachment of three judges on the U.S. Court of Appeals for the Eleventh Circuit. The judges had granted a new trial to three defendants in a capital murder case the previous year.

The report of subcommittee chairman Robert Kastenmeier concluded bluntly and broadly that "impeachment does not apply to judicial decision-making."[135] He characterized impeachment as "a draconian remedy" that should be "directed at serious wrongs against our system of government."[136] In Kastenmeier's view, impeachment culminating in removal "is not an appropriate or responsible response to the resolution of cases and controversies by federal judges." First, impeaching judges on account of their decisions would undermine judicial independence.

> Federal judges should not and cannot be impeached for judicial decisionmaking, even if a decision is an erroneous one. The conduct complained about—entering a judgment and order—is an act that judges are required to do under the Constitution. It would be a great irony if the protections found in the Judiciary's constitutional charter—Article III—did not shield judges in their decisionmaking role.[137]

Second, impeachment for judicial decision making should not be used as a kind of appellate review.

> A judicial decision (right or wrong), standing alone, cannot rise to the level of a "high crime or misdemeanor." If this was otherwise the impeachment remedy would become merely another avenue for judicial review: a sort of legislative referendum on the quality of judicial decision-making.[138]

In a letter transmitting the Kastenmeier report to Representative Hatcher, House Judiciary Committee chairman Peter Rodino indicated that he "concur[red] with the conclusions reached by Mr. Kastenmeier in his report."[139]

Absent from the Kastenmeier report was the distinction between unimpeachable simple error and impeachable ill-motivated error, a distinction that had dominated debate in earlier impeachment investigations. No judge had ever been removed on account of a judicial decision. No judge had been impeached because of a decision alone since 1830 or in part since 1904, and it had been over fifty years since the committee had investigated a charge that a federal judge should be impeached because he abused his decision-making power. Whatever the theoretical legitimacy of the distinction, it had lost all practical significance. As far as the House Judiciary Committee was concerned, judges could not be impeached for their decision making—period.

As the twentieth century wound down, Congress was putting the finishing touches on a century-long campaign to establish an independent judicial branch more accountable to itself and less accountable to Congress. That effort had begun in the late nineteenth century (as described in chapter 2) with the Evarts Act, which established the comprehensive structure of the circuit court of appeals, a structure calculated in part to control district court "despotism." It would continue throughout the twentieth century, with a series of enactments enhancing the judiciary's administrative autonomy. This series culminated with the Judicial Councils Reform and Judicial Conduct and Disability Act of 1980,[140] which authorized the circuit judicial councils to investigate allegations of judicial misconduct and impose discipline on their judges for misbehavior unrelated to the merits of their decisions. The Evarts Act and the discipline statute thus provided the judiciary with the means to hold its judges accountable for conduct related and unrelated to judicial decision making. In the context of this movement toward greater independence from Congress and enhanced intrajudicial accountability, impeaching judges for their decision making became increasingly anachronistic.

The Future of Impeachment Investigations into Judicial Decision Making

There is an extent to which the story told here, of a frustrated House episodically chasing but never catching rogue judges until the Kastenmeier report brings the tale to an end, is reminiscent of old Warner Brothers cartoons, in which Elmer Fudd ineffectually attempts to hunt down Bugs Bunny until the credits roll and Porky Pig stammers,

"That's all, folks!" The metaphor would seem to imply that the efforts of House and Fudd were a comic failure, but that assumes, perhaps incorrectly, that their sole objective was to see their respective quarries boiled in a stew pot. To the extent that Fudd was looking, instead, for ways to redirect his anger, to get in a little target practice, or to send an irritating rabbit running for cover, his was a great American success story. So, too, it may be shortsighted to evaluate the success of the House's efforts with sole reference to the number of judges removed by conviction in the Senate.

The House has managed to impeach just thirteen judges in over two hundred years, of whom only four were charged with abusing their case decision-making power and none were convicted for it (recall that Pickering's conviction was attributable primarily to his insanity). But House investigations have led to an additional twenty judges resigning or retiring, of whom five were charged with abusing their judicial decision-making power. Insofar as the House has persuaded five judges to resign or retire rather than face impeachment charges for flagrantly errant decision making, perhaps the success of its efforts needs to be reassessed. A closer look at these five resignation cases reveals, however, that in only the first can it fairly be argued that the judge was hounded from office because of his decisions. That case concerned Louisiana district judge Henry Durell.

In 1872, the losing Republican candidate in Louisiana's gubernatorial race had filed suit against the Democratic incumbent, charging him with fixing their recent election. Judge Durell responded by issuing an injunction that barred the governor from canvassing the election returns. When the injunction was disregarded, Durell ordered U.S. marshals to take control of the state capitol. Pennsylvania representative William Kelley introduced a resolution instructing the House Judiciary Committee to inquire into whether Durell had "usurped jurisdiction" for the purpose of "overthrowing or controlling the government of the state of Louisiana."[141] The committee later expanded its investigation to include other, unrelated charges of drunkenness, misappropriating funds, and appointing and protecting a corrupt bankruptcy assignee. Its report recommended that Durell be impeached for the episodes relating to his bankruptcy appointee and his orders in the Louisiana election case.

Durell then resigned, and the House tabled the matter, but not before the judge's supporters and critics took the opportunity to state their views. Although the bankruptcy issue was the first impeachable offense discussed in the committee report, the debate on the House floor dwelled on the judge's orders in the election case. Impeachment proponent Benjamin Butler took the familiar tack of arguing that Durell's order was "so gross an exercise of power that if the judge did not know he was exceeding his powers he ought to have known." Impeachment opponent Luke Poland was of the equally familiar view that "because the judge made an order he had no legal jurisdiction to make, it by no means follows he is amenable to impeachment, unless it can be established that that order was made corruptly or made with a knowledge on his part— with a belief that he was exceeding his legal jurisdiction."[142]

It is possible that Durell was spooked into resignation over the bankruptcy charges, but that seems unlikely, given how little was made of those charges in the floor debates. There is equally little reason to believe that Judge Durell resigned to escape removal by impeachment for his errant decision making in the Louisiana election case, because there is nothing to suggest that the Senate was any likelier to convict in Durell's case than it had been in the cases of Chase or Peck. It is more likely, perhaps, that the feeding frenzy in the House over Durell's orders in the election case led him to resign so as to avoid the humiliation and angst of possible impeachment and trial.

The next four resignations, however, are a different matter. In 1874, Arkansas district judge William Story resigned amid an inquiry into a range of allegations, including one that he granted bail to defendants convicted of capital crimes.[143] Clearly, however, the core charges against Story related not to his judicial decisions but to misappropriation of government funds. In June 1874, the committee forwarded the evidence it had gathered on Story to the attorney general and the secretary of the treasury, so that they might "restore to the Treasury of the United States any moneys wrongfully paid to any of the officers of said court." Story resigned the next month.[144]

In 1912, Washington district judge Cornelius Hanford was charged with "a long series of unlawful and corrupt decisions," in addition to "being an habitual drunkard," who was "morally and temperamentally unfit to hold a judicial position." The latter charges appear to have held primary sway with the House Judiciary Committee when it recommended that the House accept the resignation Hanford tendered to the committee. "Judge Hanford's usefulness as a federal judge is over," the committee declared, and there was no need to impeach him to prevent his holding future public office, because "his age and the circumstances disclosed by the testimony render such a contingency highly improbable."[145]

In 1914, Daniel Wright, associate justice of the D.C. Supreme Court, resigned amid a hailstorm of accusations. Although he was charged with "judicial misconduct in the trial of a writ of habeas corpus to an extent which provoked a reviewing court . . . to justly characterize the trial as a 'travesty of justice,'" that allegation was dwarfed by a wide range of others that would constitute more readily impeachable offenses—from accepting favors from lawyers and parties, moonlighting as a private practitioner in contravention of federal law, and wrongfully appropriating other people's money, to tampering with case records and abusing his administrative powers for the benefit of friends. He resigned before the House Judiciary Committee issued its report.

Finally, in 1938, Attorney General Homer Cummings wrote the chair of the House Judiciary Committee to report that Wisconsin district judge Ferdinand Geiger "arbitrarily and against the protests of government counsel" dismissed a grand jury after it had voted to return indictments against several automobile companies in an antitrust case. At the committee hearing, Representative John Robsion noted that "[i]f he acted in good faith on what he heard and knew was the law, he ought not to be punished," prompting Assistant Attorney General Robert Jackson to reply, "I am not asking that he be punished," adding that "there has been no charge filed here in the sense of an impeachment charge." Rather, the problem in this case and several others had been that Geiger would retaliate against the government by dismissing its case if it negotiated settlements or pleas with defendants outside of court. Jackson explained that the House Judiciary Committee was "in a position to approve or disapprove matters brought before it" and was "the only place where the Department of Justice can go when it runs up against a situation in a judicial district, such as we are up against there."[146] Given that the would-be complainant in this case was avowedly not seeking to have the judge impeached, Geiger's subsequent retirement could not be attributed to fear of impeachment and was more likely due to considerations of poor health, given that the judge died two months after he retired.

Although it seems unlikely that the investigation into Judge Geiger's conduct caused him to resign, his case does raise a separate issue worth pursuing a bit further. The committee was puzzled by the government's objectives: "If [punishment] is not the purpose," Representative Michener inquired, "what is your understanding and hope as to what the committee can or will do?" Jackson was candid: the government had been stymied in its efforts to work with Judge Geiger and wanted the committee to investigate his conduct "in its broad aspect," presumably in the hope that the investigation itself or a critical committee report might persuade Geiger to relent. The House Judiciary Committee would quit the business of investigating judicial misconduct just six years later, but the Department of Justice would not. The Geiger case raises the specter of the government using investigations into judicial conduct as a means to gain leverage over the targeted judge. In a powerful essay, Emily Field Van Tassel argues that the Department of Justice's unsupervised power to investigate judges before whom the department routinely appears as a litigant can be a potent weapon to curb decisional independence, if used as a subterfuge to frighten uncooperative judges into acquiescence or resignation.[147]

The relationship between the executive branch and the judiciary is outside the scope of this book. But to the extent that threats of criminal prosecution can chasten an unaccommodating judge, perhaps threats of impeachment can have the same effect. There is no way to be sure, because judges can hardly be expected to admit that threats of impeachment sapped them of the fortitude to decide cases as they thought the law required. But as Second Circuit judge John Walker testified before an American Bar Association Commission: "Judges are human, and thus, perhaps depending on the thickness of a particular judge's skin, are not invulnerable to the influence of political pressure. To rely on constitutional protections alone, I think, is not enough."[148] After Justice Samuel Chase was acquitted in 1805, he returned to the bench as a shadow of his former self, some say due to his impeachment ordeal. Almost two centuries later, after a highly publicized threat to impeach New York district judge Harold Baer over his decision to suppress evidence in a drug case, the judge reversed himself, some say because of political pressure.

Despite the fact that no judge has ever been removed for flagrantly erroneous decision making, legislators persist in their calls to impeach judges for making stupid decisions. Some may simply be venting anger on behalf of their constituents. Others, however, may be think- ing— more strategically—that a well publicized threat of impeach- ment will cause the judge to think twice before making another con- troversial decision.

Conclusion ☙

In what may be the best-known quotation from a legislator on the subject of judicial impeachment, Congressman Gerald Ford once declared that "an impeachable offense is whatever a majority of the House of Representatives considers it to be at any given moment in history."[149] As a matter of raw constitutional power, Ford's assertion is unassailable. The Supreme Court has ruled that issues relating to the impeachment process present nonjusticiable political questions, which means that Congress alone decides when good judicial behav- ior degenerates into an impeachable misdemeanor. If a majority of the House and two-thirds of the Senate agree that a judge has com- mitted an impeachable offense—whatever that offense may be—no court will second-guess them.

As a matter of constitutional authority, it is equally true to say that the scope of what constitutes an impeachable offense is subject to change with the times, given the inherently political character of the proceedings. Ford's claim is more problematic, however, if he is understood to say that the Constitution gives Congress the authority to define "high crimes and misdemeanors" in any way it pleases. The Supreme Court may have held that the Constitution grants Congress the sole authority to define impeachable offenses, but Congress has interpreted the Constitution for itself and has concluded that there are constraints on its authority to characterize various offenses as impeachable. Congress could impeach and remove a judge for simple decision-making errors, but it never has. It could infer a bad motive from the erroneous decision itself and remove a judge on that basis, but it never has. It could establish itself as an all-powerful forum for judicial review, but it never has. To be sure, part of the explanation for these limits is pragmatic and political: impeaching and removing judges can be more trouble than it is worth, and in a two-party system, it is difficult to convince a supermajority of the Senate that any given judge's decisions were so wrong as to warrant removal. But time and again, Congress has defined and defended the limits of its impeachment authority with reference to constitutional norms: to impeach judges for innocent error would undermine judges' Article III independence, to presume that egregious errors are ill-motivated would deny judicial independence adequate breathing room, and for Congress to review and correct judicial error would be to usurp a role the Constitution has delegated to an independent judicial branch that Congress itself has nurtured.

The triumph of independence norms notwithstanding, individual members of Congress continue to rattle the impeachment saber in the face of judges whom they accuse of "legislating from the bench" or of otherwise being judicial "activists" or "imperialists." Perhaps only here, the impeachment power exerts a modest residual influence on judicial decision making. In this day and age, no judge can realistically fear impeachment or removal on account of her decisions, but the political heat that accompanies a well-publicized threat of impeachment may still be sufficient to burn a thin-skinned judge and prompt him to recoil.

CHAPTER FOUR

Judicial Appointments and the Prospective Accountability of Judicial Nominees to the U.S. Senate ∾

THE PROCESS BY WHICH judges are appointed can have an obvious impact on judicial independence and accountability. If, as a condition precedent to appointment, we insist that nominees vow to decide particular cases in particular ways, their independence will clearly be constrained. At the same time, holding nominees' feet to the fire and extracting assurances that they will not deviate from the majoritarian mainstream provides a measure of prospective accountability by increasing the likelihood that the nominees are and will remain acceptable to the public. Thus, we have seen presidents and senators accuse each other of undermining the independence of would-be judges by subjecting nominees to ideological litmus tests, while each has replied that inquiring into nominees' judicial philosophy is an important means to ensure their present and future acceptability.

The preceding chapters have been devoted to chronicling the emergence of a custom of restraint that has impeded congressional resort to impeachment or manipulation of court structure, size, administration, or jurisdiction as means to hold judges accountable for their decisions. *Restraint,* however, is not a word that comes readily to mind in describing recent developments in the appointments arena. As recounted in the introduction, the appointments process has become a battleground in the struggle for the future of the courts, pitting Democrats against Republicans, the president against the Senate, and the political branches against the judiciary. Given the pervasiveness of customary independence in other contexts, what explains its absence from the appointments venue?

One explanation lies in the mechanics of congressional decision making. In the context of impeachment and legislation regulating court operations, a culture of decision-making restraint is facilitated by the need for bicameral agreement before laws curbing the courts are passed or before judges can be impeached and removed. In the Senate, cloture rules can prevent controversial legislation from becoming law unless it receives the 60 percent majority support needed to overcome a filibuster, while the Constitution conditions removal by impeachment upon the agreement of a two-thirds majority. Thus, congressional decisions to diminish the courts and remove judges must receive supermajority congressional support before they become precedent adverse to customary independence, while decisions not to curb the courts add to the culture of customary independence, notwithstanding the fact that some such decisions may have been supported only by a congressional minority. In the appointments context, however, only the Senate must act. Moreover, it is the "restrained" alternative of approving the president's nominee that must always have at least majority Senate support. Ideologically motivated rejections aimed at manipulating judicial decision making, in contrast, can be accomplished if a Senate minority wields a filibuster, a blue slip, or a hold or if a bare majority of the Senate Judiciary Committee declines to report the nominee for floor action.

A second explanation for the relative absence of independence norms from the appointments process lies in the perceived significance of the appointment power coupled with its interbranch character. The power to name those who occupy the offices of government is the power to shape how and by whom the nation is governed. The division of so critical a power between the president and the Senate all but invites a struggle for primacy between the occupants of the first and second branches and their respective political parties, in which concern for the impact of that struggle on the prospective independence of nominees to the third branch may get lost in the fray. Moreover, because the appointments clause is unitary and does not differentiate between the selection of executive and judicial branch officers, the perceived need to pay special deference to the future independence of judicial nominees may be further attenuated.

A third explanation arises out of the circumstances in which the appointments process developed. During the formative years of that process, Senate rejections of Supreme Court nominees were typically payback for past political transgressions of the nominees or their nominating presidents. These rejections raised no concerns for the judiciary's independence and hence created no opportunity to sensitize the Senate to such concerns in the context of confirmation proceedings. It was not until the end of the nineteenth century that the Senate began to exploit confirmation proceedings as a means to constrain the judiciary's future decision making, by which time the appointments process had already developed and matured as a partisan, political process unencumbered by independence norms. Similarly, until recently, Senate confrontations with the president over lower court appointments were common enough but typically arose when the power of individual senators to advise presidents on whom to nominate from their home states came into conflict with the president's power to disregard such advice. Although deeply partisan, these disputes over political patronage implicated judicial independence concerns indirectly, if at all; when, in the 1980s, the Senate began to manipulate the confirmation process as a means to control future lower court decision making, it could do so unconstrained by a tradition of restraint or sensitivity for the prospective independence of judicial nominees.

This chapter begins by exploring the issues on the minds of those who drafted and ratified the appointments clause, which reveals that the original intentions of the framers were both conflicted and underdeveloped. The most that can be said, perhaps, is that the framers envisioned a process in which the focus would be on the nominee's merit, qualifications, and character—a myopic vision, it turns out, that could not see so far as the Washington administration. Rather, as elaborated in this chapter, the confirmation process has been thoroughly partisan and political from its inception. Beginning in the late 1900s, however, the Senate's rejection of Supreme Court candidates shifted focus from punishing nominees or nominating presidents for past political missteps or weaknesses to thwarting the appointment of nominees whose political ideologies would likely lead them to make judicial decisions disfavored by the Senate majority. This new focus on ideology and judicial decision making gradually became a pervasive feature of confirmation battles and, in the waning years of the twentieth century, spilled over into the arena of lower court appointments. The Senate, by rejecting nominees who were likely to make politically unacceptable decisions as judges, had found a way to hold judges accountable (albeit prospectively) for their decision making, at a time when alternative methods—such as court packing, jurisdiction stripping, and impeachment—had fallen into disfavor and disuse. By providing the Senate with an outlet to curb judicial excesses before they occurred, politicization of the appointments process in the twentieth century has helped to relieve the pressure on Congress to employ more extreme means of court control that could threaten the long-standing independence norms described in preceding chapters. At the same time, as discussed in the last section of this chapter, politicization of the lower court appointments process has recently accelerated in ways that threaten to destabilize the long-standing dynamic equilibrium between courts and Congress.

One final preliminary matter deserves attention: contemporary confirmation proceedings have dwelled on the issue of nominee ideology, as will this chapter, for which reason it may be helpful to clarify the scope of the term *ideology* for our purposes here. One standard English dictionary defines ideology as "a closely organized system of beliefs, values and ideas forming the basis of a social, economic or political philosophy or program."[1] Of particular concern in confirmation proceedings is that a judge's social, economic, or political philosophy may influence her to decide cases in inappropriate ways—most notably, in ways inconsistent with the rule of law. Numerous questions have arisen over the course of Senate debates: How does one ascertain what a nominee's ideology is? To what extent and in what ways is a nominee's ideology likely to affect her legal philosophy and judicial decision making, and when are such influences appropriate? At what point does a nominee's ideology become too "extreme" to be acceptable? What questions may the Senate properly ask to ascertain a nominee's ideology? What questions may the nominee properly decline to answer?

These are important questions, animated by differing views on how the Senate should exercise its authority to check presidential appointments prerogatives and curb judicial decision-making excesses. Proffered answers lie along a continuum. At one extreme, ideology is nothing: the Senate should ignore it, be deferential to the president's choices, and limit itself to ensuring that nominees possess the capabilities and qualifications necessary to understand and follow the law. At the other extreme, ideology is everything: a judge's political philosophy trumps the rule of law and dictates her decision making, which pits the president's political party against the party opposing the president, in a bare-knuckle brawl for ideological control of the courts and the judicial decisions that appointees will make for the next generation.

The first extreme is, for all practical purposes, a phantom. Judicial officers are bound by the Constitution to take an oath in which they swear to support the Constitution and laws of the United States.[2] A nominee who is philosophically opposed to supporting the law thus lacks an essential qualification of judicial service; accordingly, the Senate properly rejects the nominee who is an avowed anarchist, even if the Senate's role is limited to checking basic qualifications and credentials. That being the case, it must be conceded that ideology inevitably matters, the only remaining issues being how much and under what circumstances.

The opposite extreme threatens the very foundation of an independent judiciary. It proceeds from the premise that independent judges are unaccountable judges who disregard the law and implement their political predilections, and it concludes that judicial decision making must therefore be controlled by, among other things, rejecting judicial nominees who will not commit to deciding cases in ways the Senate majority deems publicly acceptable. For reasons elaborated in chapter 6, I challenge the premise underlying this second extreme, which rests on an incomplete empirical foundation, and I reject its conclusion, which threatens to destabilize the dynamic equilibrium between courts and Congress that has conserved core constitutional values for two centuries.

Between these two unviable extremes, however, lies a spectrum of more moderate alternatives that call on the Senate to exercise a role in confirmation proceedings that ranges from passive to aggressive, in which the perceived relevance of the nominee's ideology varies from limited to critical. Some would limit the Senate's review to extracting assurances that the nominee is committed to following the law; others would permit the Senate to evaluate the nominee in light of answers to general questions about judicial philosophy; still others would go further, hinging Senate approval on the outcome of more focused inquiries into the impact of a judge's ideology on issues specific to subject matter, including cases the nominee previously decided or litigated; finally, some would go so far as to solicit the nominee's views on politically volatile issues in cases that are likely to come before the nominee as a judge or justice. Unpacking these alternatives and arguing for one that is optimal is beyond the scope of this work. For our purposes here, it is enough to say that across this spectrum, Senate inquiries into nominee ideology are calculated to ensure that those confirmed will be more likely to make decisions that the Senate majority finds compatible with its conception of the law. To that extent, confirmation proceedings serve to hold judges prospectively accountable for their decision making, albeit to varying degrees.

Origins of the Appointments Clause ∾

Section 2 of Article II of the U.S. Constitution provides, in the relevant part, that the president "shall nominate, and by and with the Advice and Consent of the Senate, shall appoint . . . Judges of the supreme Court, and all other Officers of the United States." Although the approach embodied in this clause ultimately emerged as the consensus choice of delegates to the Constitutional Convention, it was the battle-scarred victor in a war of attrition among wounded combatants. Not too long ago, the chief justice of a state supreme court grumbled, "there is no method of selecting . . . judges that is worth a damn."[3] He is, in some sense, a man two centuries behind his time, who could just as easily have been speaking in the summer of 1787 from the convention floor in Philadelphia. None of the states represented at the Constitutional Convention had any experience with selecting their judges by popular election, so the range of options discussed was limited to differing forms of appointment. Nevertheless, when all was said and done, the convention had given serious consideration to at least three major alternative selection methods (each with subvariations) and rejected them all—including the one that found its way into the Constitution.

Appointment by the legislature or a subset of the legislature.   Edmund Randolph's Virginia Plan was introduced on May 29, 1787, during the first week of the Constitutional Convention. It provided that the judiciary be "chosen by the National Legislature." The proposal was resoundingly rejected the next week. James Wilson opposed the idea by arguing: "experience sh[o]wed the impropriety of such [appointments] by numerous bodies. Intrigue, partiality and concealment were the necessary consequences."[4] In addition to "the danger of intrigue and partiality," argued James Madison, "many of the members were not judges of the requisite qualifications" and would be predisposed to appoint fellow legislators, despite the fact that "legislative talents . . . were very different from those of a judge."[5] A motion to strike the provision from the Virginia Plan was approved by a vote of nine delegations to two. On June 13, Madison offered the alternative of appointment by the Senate, which "as a less numerous & more select body, would be more competent judges, and which was sufficiently numerous to justify such a confidence in them." Madison's motion was approved without debate or objection.[6]

The issue was subsequently revisited. Several delegates, such as Luther Martin, spoke in favor of Madison's proposal, arguing that "being taken from all the States," the Senate would be "best informed of characters & most capable of making a fit choice."[7] Opposition, however, began to surface. If members of the Senate "can not get the man of the particular State to which they may respectively belong," Nathaniel Gorham argued, "they will be indifferent to the rest," they will "feel no personal responsibility," and they will "give full play to intrigue and cabal."[8] Madison later had second thoughts on the merits of his own motion and expressed the concern that because each state was equally represented in the Senate without regard to its population, "the Judges might be appointed by a minority of the people, [though] by a majority of the states, which could not be justified on any principle as their proceedings were to relate to the people, rather than to the States."[9] Edmund Randolph asserted that "appointments by the Legislatures have generally resulted from cabal, from personal regard, or some other consideration than a title derived from the proper qualifications" and that "the same inconveniences will proportionally prevail if the appointments be referred to either branch of the Legislature."[10]

Appointment by the president. William Paterson's so-called New Jersey Plan, which was introduced at the Constitutional Convention on June 15, provided that "a federal judiciary be established to consist of a supreme Tribunal the judges of which to be appointed by the Executive."[11] Those, such as James Wilson, who advocated vesting the appointment power in the president argued that "a principal reason for unity in the Executive was that officers might be appointed by a single, responsible person."[12] The proposal nonetheless met with a chilly reception. Oliver Ellsworth expressed general concern that "the Executive will be regarded by the people with a jealous eye" and that "every power for augmenting unnecessarily his influence will be disliked."[13] In Roger Sherman's view, "the Judges ought to be diffused" geographically, which would not occur if the decision was left in the hands of one person.[14] George Mason, who favored presidential appointment only if it were accompanied by the creation of an executive council to advise the president, concurred that the president, acting alone, was likely to "form local and personal attachments" within the state where he resided and that such attachments "would deprive equal merit elsewhere, of an equal chance of promotion."[15] Sherman also believed that it would be too easy for "candidates to intrigue" with a single man,[16] and Ellsworth echoed that the president would be too open "to caresses and intrigues."[17] Finally, Charles Pinckney thought, "the Executive will possess neither the requisite knowledge of characters nor confidence of the people for so high a trust," and Elbridge Gerry agreed.[18] A motion to give the president sole authority to appoint judicial and other officers was defeated on a vote of two delegations in favor to six opposed.[19]

Nomination by the president, with Senate approval or acquiescence.
After a motion to lodge the appointment power with the president
had been defeated, after a motion to delegate the power to both
houses of Congress had been beaten back, and while Madison's proposal to vest the power in the Senate was still being considered,
Nathaniel Gorham moved that "the Judges be [nominated and
appointed] by the Executive, by & with the advice & consent of the
2d branch."[20] Gorham noted that "this mode had been long [prac-
ticed]" in Massachusetts, where it "was found to answer perfectly
well."[21] A similar proposal had been floated earlier in the Constitutional Convention, by Alexander Hamilton, whose plan included
among the executive's powers the "nomination of all other officers
. . . subject to the approbation or rejection of the Senate."[22] Gorham's
motion failed on a tie vote following virtually no debate, after which
Madison (who had lost interest in his own proposal to vest appointment power in the Senate alone) sought to resurrect the Gorham plan
in revised form, with the provision that "the judges should be nominated by the Executive & such nomination should become an
appointment [if not] disagreed to within __ days by 2/3 of the 2d
branch."[23]

Oliver Ellsworth, who favored an appointments process in which
the Senate would nominate, subject to a presidential veto and a Senate override, objected to Madison's latest proposal on the grounds
that the "right to supercede [the president's] nomination will be ideal
only." He maintained that "A nomination under such circumstances
will be equivalent to an appointment."[24] Edmund Randolph and
Elbridge Gerry both argued that requiring a two-thirds Senate majority to block an appointment diminished the Senate's role too greatly,
in response to which Madison amended his motion "to let a majority
reject."[25] George Mason remained unmoved, arguing that while,
under Madison's amended proposal, "the appointment seemed to be
divided between the Executive and the Senate, the appointment was
substantially vested in the former alone," because "the false complaisance which usually prevails in such cases will prevent a disagreement
to the first nominations."[26] Madison's latest motion was rejected on a
vote of six delegations to three, and his previous proposal to vest

appointment power with the Senate alone (which had been approved without discussion on June 5) was approved a second time by a vote of six delegations to three.[27]

Several weeks after being beaten twice and left for dead, a variation of the hybrid approach previously advocated by Hamilton, Gorham, and Madison returned to the rumble, this time with friends. The convention had charged a Committee of Eleven to revisit and make recommendations on a range of unresolved, controversial questions, and the committee returned with a proposal that judges be nominated by the president with the advice and consent of the Senate. Gouverneur Morris was satisfied with the balance that the proposal struck: "[A]s the President was to nominate, there would be responsibility, and as the Senate was to concur, there would be security."[28] Wilson, who favored appointment by the president alone, was less sanguine, complaining that "there can be no good Executive without a responsible appointment of officers to execute" and that "[r]esponsibility is destroyed by such an agency of the Senate."[29] Elbridge Gerry, who favored appointment by the Senate alone, criticized as "chimerical" the claim that the president would feel a sense of responsibility for his nominations, because "the President can not know all characters and can therefore always plead ignorance."[30] In the weeks that separated the initial rejection of the proposal from its reconsideration, however, advocates of presidential nomination and Senate confirmation had changed some minds. The state delegations unanimously approved the Committee of Eleven's recommendation, which became the Constitution's Article II, Section 2, Clause 2.

The drafters of the Constitution were united in their desire to create a system for the appointment of judges in which the appointing authority had the capacity and commitment to identify and select the most qualified "characters" from around the country, without "cabal," "intrigue," or "partiality." Achieving consensus on who was best suited to serve that purpose, however, was far more elusive. That the Constitutional Convention ultimately threw its support behind presidential nomination coupled with Senate confirmation is understandable, at least from a strategic standpoint, because such an approach included something for everyone: presidential nomination appealed to those who preferred appointment by the president; Senate confirmation appeased those who favored appointment by the legislature; and those who supported a hybrid, power-sharing arrangement from the outset had gotten what they asked for. But agreement that the president and the Senate would both play roles in making judicial appointments did not resolve continued uncertainty as to what those roles would be.

This was a confederation of odd bedfellows, some of whom had been prepared to entrust the president but not the Senate with the appointment power while others were prepared to do the opposite. It is thus reasonable to suspect that the "original understanding" of the Senate's role in rendering advice and consent would vary depending on whether the delegate one asked envisioned a process that minimized Senate interference with presidential prerogatives or one that maximized the Senate's capacity to check presidential power. That the Constitutional Convention rejected every method of appointment it considered, including two variations of the system it eventually adopted, underscores the framers' collective uncertainty as to how—and how well—any given approach would work in practice.

For those inclined to view the glass as half full, Article II, Section 2, Clause 2 may have included something to please everyone. The ratification debates, however, revealed the inevitable corollary: for those less optimistic, the clause left no one unchafed. In the Federalist Papers, Madison summarized the rainbow of opposition to the appointments clause.

> In the eyes of one the junction of the Senate with the President in the responsible function of appointing to offices, instead of vesting this executive power in the Executive alone, is the vicious part of the organization. To another, the exclusion of the House of Representatives, whose numbers alone could be a due security against corruption and partiality in the exercise of such a power, is equally obnoxious. With another, the admission of the President into any share of a power which ever must be a dangerous engine in the hands of the executive magistrate, is an unpardonable violation of the maxims of republican jealousy.[31]

Outside of Massachusetts (where a comparable system had been in place), delegates to the state ratifying conventions were left to speculate as to whether the appointments clause would give the upper hand to the president or the Senate. Like blind men describing an elephant with reference to whichever piece they were holding, Luther Martin would tell the Maryland convention that the president's power to nominate made him "king in everything but name," while Richard Henry Lee would tell the people of Virginia that with the power to confirm the president's nominees, the Senate "will not in practice be found to be a body to advise, but to order and dictate in fact; and the president will be a mere *primus inter pares.*"[32]

In the Federalist Papers (no. 76), Hamilton defended the appointments clause in terms that minimized the Senate's role. For Hamilton, it was best to give the president, rather than the Senate, the power to make nominations, because "the sole and undivided responsibility of one man will naturally beget a livelier sense of duty and a more exact regard to reputation." As to the Senate, Hamilton opined that it was "not very probable" that the president's nominations "would often be overruled," because senators "could not assure themselves that the person they might wish would be brought by a second or by any subsequent nomination" and "could not even be certain, that a future nomination would present a candidate in any degree more acceptable to them." He thus relegated the Senate's role to one of a "powerful, though, in general, a silent operation." For the president, Hamilton speculated, "the possibility of rejection would be a strong motive for care in proposing." Therefore, the Senate's power to withhold its consent, though largely unused, "would be an excellent check upon a spirit of favoritism in the president, and would tend greatly to prevent the appointment of unfit characters from State prejudice, from family connection, from personal attachment, or from a view to popularity."

Courts and commentators exhibit an occasional tendency to regard the Federalist Papers as the primary, if not the final, word on questions of original intent. But Hamilton did not stop being Hamilton simply because he wrote under a pseudonym and contributed to a work that would later be regarded with a reverence rivaling Holy Scripture. He was an outspoken advocate for a strong federal government with a powerful chief executive, and his thoughts on the anticipated operation of the appointments clause in the Federalist Papers are consistent with that perspective. Hamilton's views, moreover, were at one end of an eclectic spectrum of original intentions, the coalescence of which made adoption of the appointments clause possible. Recall, for example, that in a preliminary vote at the Constitutional Convention, six delegations to three favored appointment by the Senate alone, while six delegations to two opposed appointment by the president alone; it seems unlikely that those same six delegations would all agree to the system ultimately adopted, barely a month later, if they—like Hamilton—thought it relegated the Senate to a "silent" role. Amplifying Hamilton's voice above the cacophonous din of competing points of view may therefore convey a false sense of consensus among those who wrote and ratified the Constitution as to what the Senate's role in the appointments process would or should be.

The debates at the Constitutional Convention and the ratifying conventions did not dwell on the relationship between the appointments process and judicial independence. Rather, the founders were concerned primarily about judicial character and qualifications: they wanted an appointments process that would produce judges selected on the basis of their "intrinsic merit" (to borrow Hamilton's phrase) rather than their political connections, family ties, or personal friendships. But the relationship between this goal and judicial independence is implicit: the appointing authority's unqualified, weak-kneed friends or cronies who won their jobs by pulling strings would be more easily manipulated by—and so dependent on—whomever selected them than would be judges picked simply because they are the best people for the job. The point was not lost on George Mason, who worried that granting the president too much control over the appointments process could give him "an influence over the Judiciary department itself."[33] Nor was it lost on Alexander Hamilton, who sought to allay Mason's concern with the observation that the specter of Senate rejection would render the president "both ashamed and afraid to bring forward for the most distinguished or lucrative stations, candidates . . . possessing the necessary insignificance and pliancy to render them the obsequious instruments of his pleasure."[34]

As far as accountability is concerned, the founders were plainly interested in holding would-be judges accountable to the president and the Senate for their character and credentials. Altogether absent from the debates of the day, however, is any suggestion that the president or Senate could, would, or should hold judicial candidates prospectively accountable for their decision making by evaluating candidates' judicial philosophy or political ideology and rejecting candidates whose philosophical or ideological bent would likely lead them to interpret the law in ways the political branches deemed unacceptable. Why?

One possible answer is that the founders spoke only of evaluating judicial candidates with reference to their "intrinsic merit" because they thought that inquiries into other matters would be irrelevant or inappropriate. They were openly opposed to the political branches bending future judges to their will by appointing unqualified family members or sycophants, and one might suspect that they would be just as opposed to the president or Senate achieving the same end through a process of ideological cleansing. Their general aversion to the influence of factions likewise suggests that they would disapprove of the appointments process degenerating into a partisan battle between the president and the Senate over the political ideology of judicial nominees. If, as some contemporary commentators argue, the framers intended for the Senate to supply only a "relatively minor check on the President's authority," limited to preventing him from appointing unqualified candidates, then it follows naturally that "ideology—at least ideology of the kind that is unrelated to a candidate's ability to fulfill his oath of office—simply ha[s] no place in the Senate's decision."[35]

Alternatively, it may be that the framers did not dwell on the role of political ideology in judicial decision making or selection because they could not foresee it. The term *ideology* was not even coined until some seven years after the Constitution was ratified.[36] Moreover, as some have argued, until the Constitution was up and running, it would have been difficult for the founding generation to appreciate the extent to which competing constitutional philosophies could influence interpretation of the document.[37] Even then, the limited jurisdictional reach of the federal courts in the early years furnished scant opportunity to anticipate the extent to which their decisions would later influence the sociopolitical course of the nation. Indeed, the postmodern view that law is subject to conflicting interpretations routinely influenced in fundamental ways by the political ideologies of its interpreters would not truly take root until the twentieth century. All agree that the framers wanted the president and the Senate to evaluate judicial nominees with reference to their "intrinsic merit." If their eighteenth-century minds shared the twenty-first-century mindset that a judge's ideology is pivotal to his decision making and that some ideologies are more faithful to the law than others, would they have thought that a nominee's ideology was germane to his merit? Those who argue that the Senate was originally intended to play an active role in checking presidential power would say yes.

There is still a third possibility, which is that the framers did not talk about the role of political ideology in the appointments process for no better reason than that they did not give the issue sufficient thought. They unanimously approved the appointments clause in the waning days of an exhausting Constitutional Convention, following a brief debate in which only one delegate spoke in its favor. While they might not have predicted the emergence of a two-party system, surely they could have anticipated the possibility that neither the president nor the Senate would passively acquiesce to the other's preferences and that both might seek to maximize their political influence over judicial appointments. They did, after all, create a system of checks and balances premised on the assumption that each of the three branches would struggle for supremacy and might wrest power from the others unless their respective ambitions could be made to counteract each other. Moreover, they were on notice that the ideology of the Supreme Court's justices could become a bone of political contention: in the Federalist Papers (no. 81), Hamilton quotes a critic's warning that "the power of construing the laws according to the SPIRIT of the Constitution will enable that court to mould them into whatever shape it may think proper." Just a little over a decade later, many of these same founders would—in the course of enacting and then repealing legislation providing for the appointment of sixteen new federal judges—wage a political war for partisan, if not ideological, control of the federal courts.[38] From this perspective, the notion that ideology might play a role in Senate confirmation proceedings was neither anathema nor inconceivable; it was simply one to which the framers did not devote much attention.

These three possibilities are not mutually exclusive. It may be that the founders would have been troubled by the advent of partisan Senate inquiries into the political ideology of judicial nominees; that they could not have foreseen the extent to which ideology would dominate public discourse on judicial decision making and selection in the future; and that, with additional deliberation and reflection, they could have anticipated that the appointments process might become quite politicized. The essential point for our purposes here, however, is that the originalist literature is sufficiently Delphic to permit widely varying interpretations. A clearer understanding of the Senate's role in the appointments process would therefore have to await Senate interpretation and implementation of its powers to render advice and consent on a case- by-case basis.

Appointment of Supreme Court Justices ∾

A review of the Senate's confirmation record reveals that Alexander Hamilton's powers of prognostication were not at their peak when he predicted that the Senate would play a "largely silent" role in the appointments process. To date, the Senate has barred the confirmation of 28 of 151 Supreme Court nominees. Of those 28, 12 were rejected by Senate vote,[39] 3 were defeated on a Senate vote to postpone,[40] 5 ended with no final Senate action,[41] and 8 withdrew their nominations in the face of Senate opposition.[42] A closer look at these cases reveals that the confirmation process has never been confined to an evaluation of the nominee's qualifications, character, or intrinsic merit. From its inception, the process has been exploited by Senate factions to gain partisan political advantage. Over time, however, the nature of these partisan objectives has changed, from an early period in which rejections typically punished the nominee or the nominating president for various political transgressions or weaknesses, to the modern period in which rejection campaigns have increasingly focused on the political ideology of the nominees, to the end of holding them prospectively accountable for their future decision making.

Throughout our history, presidents have taken an interest in the ideology of their judicial nominees and in its impact on the way those nominees are likely to decide critical issues as justices, but it was not until the end of the nineteenth century that the Senate began to reject nominees in light of such considerations.[43]

The Early Period (1789–1881)

Until 1929, the Senate deliberated the fate of judicial nominations in executive session and published records of little more than the final vote taken. As a consequence, the explanation for those votes can only be derived haphazardly from contemporaneous accounts in newspaper articles, personal correspondence, diary entries, and so on. Moreover, then as now, senators may conceal partisan motives for rejecting any given nomination behind seemingly apolitical objections. When different explanations—including, but not limited to, the nakedly partisan—were offered for Senate opposition to a particular nominee, the task of divining the "real" or "primary" motive can be difficult, if not impossible. In such situations, the most one can sometimes say is that partisanship played a role in the rejection. That said, partisanship played a significant role in every Senate rejection between 1789 and 1881, with the possible exception of George Williams, whose nomination in 1874 was withdrawn by President Grant in the wake of corruption charges. The partisan political motives underlying opposition to nominees during this early period fell loosely into one of three categories: (1) punishing nominees for past political transgressions, (2) thwarting weakened presidents of the opposing political party, and (3) rebuking presidents for failing to respect the wishes of key senators before making nominations.

Punishing Nominees for Past Political Transgressions

During the early period, the Senate rejected several nominees in retaliation for their views on discrete political issues that bore no particular relationship to the nominees' prospective performance on the bench.

John Rutledge. In July 1795, George Washington nominated John Rutledge to replace John Jay as chief justice of the Supreme Court.

After the nomination was made but before the nominee was notified, Rutledge made an inflammatory speech publicly condemning the so-called Jay Treaty. The Senate did not react well to the news of Rutledge's speech and ultimately rejected his nomination, by a vote of ten to fourteen. In a letter to George Washington, Timothy Pickering wrote: "Private information as well as publications of his recent conduct relative to the treaty, have fixed my opinion that the commission intended for him ought to be withheld."[44] In an effort to link the views Rutledge expressed on the treaty to his lack of fitness to serve on the Court, Edmund Randolph wrote Washington that "the conduct of the intended Chief Justice is so extraordinary, that Mr. Wolcott and Col. Pickering conceive it to be proof of the imputation of insanity."[45] Although others questioned the nominee's sanity as well, while still others criticized his indebtedness, Thomas Jefferson remained convinced that the Senate's action was purely partisan.

> [T]he rejection of Mr. Rutledge by the Senate is a bold thing, because they cannot pretend any objection to him but his disapprobation of the treaty. It is of course a declaration that they will recieve [*sic*] none but tories hereafter into any department of the government.[46]

Jefferson's lifelong nemesis John Adams unapologetically shared Jefferson's assessment.

> I hope that Chief Justices at least will learn from this to be cautious how they go to popular meetings at especially unlawful assemblies to Spout Reflections and excite opposition to the legal Acts of Constitutional authority.[47]

Alexander Wolcott. On February 4, 1811, James Madison nominated Alexander Wolcott to the Supreme Court—after Madison's first choice, Levi Lincoln, had been nominated and quickly confirmed, only to decline the appointment.[48] When he was U.S. collector of customs in Connecticut, Wolcott had supported the unpopular Embargo and Non-Intercourse Acts, which did not sit well with New England merchants.[49] A newspaper from Wolcott's home state opposed his nomination, with the explanation that "if Congress were of his opinion, *the merchants might all go to hell in their own way—and* that the non-intercourse law would be rigorously enforced . . . let the consequences to the merchants be what they might."[50] Other New England newspapers ostensibly opposed Wolcott's nomination on the grounds that he was unqualified, but they did so in terms so vituperative that one is left to suspect that more was at issue than Wolcott's credentials and character. "Even those most acquainted with modern degeneracy were astonished at this abominable nomination," screamed one editorial.[51] Another declared:

> [T]he more the man is known, the greater . . . will be our astonishment. Can the public have any confidence in his legal knowledge? Have his friends, of the law, of any party, ventured to hint a word in his favour in this particular?[52]

These seemingly merits-based objections were countered by Levi Lincoln, who attested that few men were "of larger mind, greater perception, discriminating powers, of more steadfast and uniform adherence to the principles of the Union" than Wolcott. Nonetheless, a week after he was nominated, Wolcott was resoundingly rejected, on a vote of nine in favor to twenty-four opposed. While the grounds for opposition to Wolcott were technically varied, it is reasonable to infer that the margin of his defeat was attributable at least in part to retribution for the unpopular positions he had taken as a customs official.[53]

Roger Taney. Justice Taney is among the better-known chief justices, whose otherwise impressive career as a jurist was overshadowed by his opinion in *Dred Scott v. Sanford*. Likewise overshadowed is his initial nomination in 1835 and de facto rejection on the last day of that year's congressional session, by a Senate vote of twenty-four to twenty-one to postpone action on the nomination. Charles Warren attributes Taney's initial defeat to Senate Whig retaliation for his implementation, as secretary of the treasury, of Andrew Jackson's antibank policies.

> Their wrath was unbounded, their denunciations of the nominee were violent in the extreme, and they thrust aside all consideration of his preeminent professional qualification, in their desire to punish him for his acts as an executive official.[54]

The nonpartisan explanation for the Senate's decision was that the nominee should not be confirmed while the circuit structure (and the size of the Supreme Court) remained in a state of flux. As discussed in chapter 2, in 1835, Congress was approaching the end of a decade-long debate on the structure of the federal courts, which would culminate in 1837 with the creation of two new federal circuits and two additional justices to ride them.[55] However, none of the proposals under consideration then would justify postponement of the Taney nomination, because none contemplated shrinking the size of the Supreme Court by attrition. Moreover, Taney was renominated by Andrew Jackson and confirmed the next year, before the circuit restructuring plan was enacted. What difference did a year make? In the midterm elections, the Whigs lost control of the Senate to the Jacksonian Democrats. "Having lost our majority in the Senate," wrote Daniel Webster at the time, "there was no hope of defeating the nomination."[56]

Ebenezer Hoar.   In 1870, the Senate rejected Ulysses S. Grant's nomination of his attorney general, Ebenezer Hoar, to the Supreme Court, by a vote of twenty-four to thirty-three. There was an ostensibly apolitical explanation for the rejection: despite Hoar's exceptional credentials,[57] he was a New Englander nominated to fill a southern seat on the Court.[58] As of 1870, Supreme Court justices were still technically required to ride the circuits they oversaw, making the nominee's proximity to and familiarity with his assigned circuit an arguably relevant qualification. But by 1870, circuit-riding obligations were honored largely in the breach; although there may have remained a political need to preserve regional parity on the Court, the substantive need was greatly diminished.[59] One national magazine thus regarded the issue as a red herring: "Anybody who cherishes the belief that this action was taken from any lofty motives would do well to look at the vote before putting this impression away as a settled thing."[60] Many suspected that the Senate rejected Hoar simply because he had been an irritating attorney general. Afterward, Senator Morgan commented, "Hoar is a fit man for the place and if he had had a little more experience in intercourse with senators, I think he would have fared better in the Senate."[61] More specifically, Hoar had incensed the Senate by marginalizing its role in filling ten circuit court judgeships created the previous year. Hoar's brother George explained in his autobiography:

> Judge Hoar [as attorney general] strenuously insisted that the Judges of the newly created Circuit Courts of the United States should be made up of the best lawyers, without Senatorial dictation. President Grant acted in accordance with his advice. . . . But leading and influential Senators, whose advice had been rejected, and who were compelled by the high character of the persons nominated to submit, and did not venture upon a controversy with the President, were intensely angry with the Attorney-General. The result was that when he was nominated by the President for the office of Associate Justice of the Supreme Court of the United States, he was rejected by the Senate. A few Senators avowed as a pretext for their action that there was no Judge on that Bench from the South, and that the appointee ought to reside in the Southern Circuit.[62]

Senator Simon Cameron's thoughts on Hoar's rejection are a fitting epitaph for the episode: "What could you expect for a man who had snubbed seventy senators?"[63]

Thwarting Weakened Presidents of the Opposing Political Party

At various times during the nineteenth century, the Senate rejected Supreme Court nominees in a display of political opposition, less toward the would-be judge than toward the president who named him. In some cases, the president had been weakened by circumstances unique to his presidency. In other cases, he was either a lame duck or otherwise late in his term when the vacancy occurred, and his political opponents wished to preserve the nomination for the president's successor.

John J. Crittenden. John Quincy Adams's 1828 nomination of John Crittenden to the Supreme Court was greeted enthusiastically by Chief Justice John Marshall, who wrote to Secretary of State Henry Clay that he knew Crittenden by reputation to be "sensible, honorable and a sound lawyer" and "did not know the man I could prefer to him."[64] Crittenden's relationship to Clay created a seemingly merits-related objection to his candidacy in the mind of one newspaper editor, who asserted that the nominee "admits himself to be a devoted partisan of Mr. Clay, and would, no doubt, become his supple tool," which "would form sufficient reason for a disapproval" of the nomination.[65] But the better explanation for Crittenden's fate was nakedly partisan: Adams was a defeated National Republican, and Andrew Jackson, a Democratic Republican and Adams's bitter rival, was poised to take office.[66] As Clay explained to the nominee, "the policy of the Jackson party will be to delay, and ultimately to postpone [the nomination] altogether."[67] Such a tactic was at that time unprecedented, and Crittenden's supporters argued that "the duty of the Senate to confirm or reject the nomination of the President, is as imperative as his duty to nominate."[68] Their efforts were unavailing: by a vote of twenty-three to seventeen, the Senate adopted its Judiciary Committee's resolution that "it is not expedient to act upon the nomination of John J. Crittenden . . . during the present session of Congress."[69]

John Spencer, Reuben Walworth, Edward King, and John Read. In 1844, the Senate rejected the nomination of John Spencer to the Supreme Court on a vote of twenty-one to twenty- six and effectively tabled those of Reuben Walworth, Edward King, and John Read. All were nominees of the uniquely unpopular president John Tyler, derisively nicknamed "His Accidency" in recognition of his becoming the first unelected president, upon the death of William Henry Harrison. Tyler had alienated Democrats earlier in his career by bolting their party for the Whigs, and after becoming president, he had so alienated the Whigs with his policies that they expelled him from their party.[70] There were isolated, merits-related objections to some of Tyler's nominees. As to Spencer, Henry Clay complained, "[D]oes any man believe him true or faithful or honest?"[71] Of Walworth, one detractor wrote, "he is recommended by many distinguished members of the Bar . . . merely because they are anxious to get rid of a querulous, disagreeable, unpopular Chancellor."[72] On the whole, however, contemporaneous accounts appear to concede that the nominees were well qualified for the position.[73] The defeats were commonly ascribed to partisan gamesmanship. A newspaper of the day attributed the Senate's delay tactics to "a desire to make political capital"; King's delay, in particular, was linked to "a nasty intrigue" calculated to replace King with Read, whose nomination was delayed by Tyler's detractors, who were intent on saving the nomination for the incoming Democratic president, James Polk. Historians have therefore concluded that the rejections are better attributed to the bitter animosity between Tyler and the Whigs than to any substantive shortcomings of the nominees themselves.[74]

Edward Bradford, William Micou, and George Badger.   Like John Tyler, Millard Fillmore was an unpopular president who encountered considerable difficulty in making Supreme Court appointments. Fillmore was another unelected president, who took office in 1850 upon the death of Zachary Taylor and lost his own party's nomination for a full term three years later. Fillmore nominated Edward Bradford in August 1852, George Badger in January 1853, and William Micou that same February, scarcely a week before the end of the president's term. Bradford's nomination was killed by Senate inaction and Badger's by a vote to postpone, while Micou's was simply left to languish. There is little in the historical record to suggest that the Senate had objections to any of these nominees over and above their connection to Fillmore. One newspaper's insights into the rejection (by postponement) of Badger's nomination may thus have applied with equal force to all three rejections.

> The rejection by the United States Senate of Mr. Badger's nomination for Judge of the Supreme Court, is one of the purely party operations which the country will not sustain. There was no possible objection to the Senator from North Carolina, except that he is a Whig. No man dared utter a word against his private character; no breath of suspicion has tarnished his fame as a jurist. . . . All considerations of justice and the public good have been sacrificed to partisan zeal.[75]

Jeremiah Black.   The Senate rejected James Buchanan's 1861 nomination of Jeremiah Black to the Supreme Court on a vote of twenty-five to twenty-six. Black had served as Buchanan's attorney general and secretary of state, and he was later characterized by Senator Shelby Collum as "one of the ablest lawyers of his day."[76] Although one newspaper sneered that "the whole history of Mr. Black's life is most eloquent of satires upon his proposed appointment," his illustrious career speaks for itself—he would later serve as impeachment counsel to President Andrew Johnson and then secretary of war William Belknap, before representing Samuel Tilden in the aftermath of his controversial loss to Rutherford B. Hayes in the presidential election of 1876. Perhaps a bit closer to the mark in explaining Black's rejection is the fact that as Buchanan's attorney general, Black had espoused the unpopular view that it would be unlawful for the national government to use military force to prevent the South from seceding, a view that did not endear him to Senate Republicans.[77] More obviously, however, at the time of Black's nomination, Buchanan was a lame-duck Democrat seeking to appoint a prominent Democratic partisan while the Republican president-elect Abraham Lincoln waited in the wings.[78] The New York Tribune thus explained:

> [T]he declining Democratic strength in the Senate, and Southern opposition to the appointment, do not afford much encouragement for his confirmation. That place belongs properly to the next Administration, and will be so treated, after the examples of Messrs. Crittenden and Badger, who were suspended by Democratic majorities when nominated for this Court by Mr. Adams and Mr. Fillmore until Gen. Jackson and Mr. Pierce came into office. Their own medicine, judiciously administered, will do them good.[79]

Henry Stanbery. In 1866, Andrew Johnson, soon to be impeached, nominated Henry Stanbery to the Supreme Court. Stanbery, who was "well-known as an eminent lawyer,"[80] fell victim to downsizing when Congress shrank the size of the Court from ten to seven while Stanbery's nomination was pending.[81] As discussed in chapter 2, opinions differ as to whether the Republican Congress was motivated by a desire either to deprive the Democrat Johnson of his opportunity to influence the composition of the Court or to assist Supreme Court justices who had petitioned Congress for higher salaries in exchange for a reduction in their number. Either way, however, Congress's willingness to eliminate a position on the Court for which a nomination was pending reflects its indifference, if not hostility, toward the unpopular Johnson's appointment prerogatives.

Rebuking Presidents for Failing to Respect the Wishes of Key Senators before Making Nominations

In still other examples from the 1800s, rejection was predicated on the president's failure to consult adequately with key senators before making nominations. Appointments are made subject to the advice as well as the consent of the Senate, and senators have sometimes guarded their advisory prerogatives jealously.

George Woodward. In 1845–46, New York senator Simon Cameron led a successful campaign to defeat President James Polk's nomination of New York lawyer George Woodward to the Supreme Court. One of Woodward's supporters effused: "Nobody ever attempted to touch his character—it is purity itself. . . . [I]n point of real ability and energy there are few men in the country equal to him."[82] His critics were not so gentle. One characterized him as "an obscure and unsound man," whose "professional attainments are few" and whose "views are narrow."[83] But Polk reported, in his diary, on a conversation in which Vice President George Dallas and Senators Daniel Dickinson and William Allen assured him that such "frivolous objection[s] . . . had been fully refuted."[84] Ultimately, the nominee appears to have been a victim of political intrigue. Woodward, a Democrat, had recently lost the New York Senate race to the (quasi-)Democratic Cameron, who had been vying with Woodward to fill the vacancy created by James Buchanan after he left the Senate to become Polk's secretary of state. Although Buchanan, a close friend of Cameron's, may have been hoping to reserve the slot on the Court for himself,[85] while Cameron may have been loath to see his defeated opponent elevated to so lofty a perch, both explained their opposition to the nomination in terms of the president's failure to seek their advice before the nomination was made.[86] Woodward was defeated on a vote of twenty to twenty-nine.

William Hornblower and Wheeler Peckham.   In 1893 and 1894, New York senator David Hill led successful campaigns to reject the Supreme Court nominations of William Hornblower and then Wheeler Peckham, whom President Grover Cleveland had nominated. Of Hornblower, the *American Law Review* gushed that "not a flaw was found in his character as a lawyer or a citizen,"[87] while Peckham was similarly characterized as "a lawyer of high standing and unblemished reputation."[88] Although there were isolated murmurings about Peckham's temperament[89] and Hornblower's youth,[90] the long and short of it was that Hill disapproved of the nominees, whom Cleveland had named to fill the "New York vacancy" on the Court without first seeking Hill's advice. Senator Hill's earlier efforts to secure an appointment to the state bench for a lawyer named Maynard had been thwarted by an investigation with which Hornblower and Peckham had been involved, and the *New York Times* reported, "It is generally understood that the sole ground for rejecting [the nominations] rests in the desire of the New York senators to 'get even' for the downfall of Maynard and to administer what they think is a rebuke to the president."[91] Senator and Judiciary Committee member George Hoar concurred that "Mr. Cleveland ought not to have made such an appointment without consulting Mr. Hill, who was a lawyer of eminence and knew the sentiment of the majority of the Democratic Party,"[92] and Hill's biographer summarized the episode with the observation that "[b]y exercising the prerogative of senatorial courtesy, Hill defeated the nomination."[93]

The Modern Period

To say that the appointments process has always been partisan and political is not to imply that the partisan political considerations that influence the appointments process have remained static over time. The foregoing review of rejected Supreme Court nominees reveals that throughout most of the nineteenth century, such issues as the nominee's allegiance to the Senate's pet political causes, the president's popularity within the Senate, presidential respect for the Senate's advisory role, and the timing of a vacancy within a presidential term dominated political explanations for Senate action. Beginning in the late nineteenth century, however, there began a subtle trend toward rejecting nominees who appeared likely to make judicial decisions that would be objectionable to the Senate and its constituencies.

Caleb Cushing. An important antecedent to the movement of the modern period was President Ulysses S. Grant's withdrawal of Caleb Cushing's nomination to the Supreme Court in 1874. Shortly after his nomination, Cushing was tarred as a Confederate sympathizer. The "smoking gun" in the campaign to discredit him was a letter he had written, before the outbreak of the Civil War, to introduce one of his clerks to Jefferson Davis. Critics claimed that the letter evidenced a close personal relationship between Cushing and Davis.[94] The case against Cushing was summarized by the *New York Times.*

> As a supporter of the Dred Scott decision, as an advocate of the slave power, as a Whig who became a Democrat, as a politician whose place was never fixed from one week to another, as a gentleman who strongly objected to hear the patriotic tunes of the North during the war, as a partisan of the cause which the Northern people detested—in all these capacities Mr. Cushing has distinguished himself.[95]

Cushing was not the first nominee whose political ideology contributed to his downfall. The same could be said of John Rutledge, Alexander Wolcott, Roger Taney, and Ebenezer Hoar. In those earlier cases, however, nominees were punished for past political transgressions without much regard to how, if at all, those transgressions would affect their future decision making as justices. Were Cushing challenged simply for being a southern sympathizer, his case would have been like theirs. What made opposition to Cushing different is that his past political ideology was explicitly linked to his future performance as a justice. The *New York Herald* wrote:

> That opposition all takes shape from the allegation that he is not in accord with the republican party upon the great measures of reconstruction and the constitutional amendments which authorized them, and the fear is expressed that it may not be safe to trust him as the head of the Supreme Court with these cardinal principles of the republican party.[96]

Cushing defenders responded to such charges in kind, by disputing the extent of his southern sympathies and arguing that, if appointed, he would uphold the Republican agenda. Senator Charles Sumner wrote:

> Now I know him well,—having seen him for the last ten years constantly, & I know his position on questions in which I am deeply interested. I trust him absolutely &, believe, if the occasion had occurred, he would have vindicated our ideas judicially far better than any probable nominee of Grant.[97]

For the first time, then, the Senate arguably sought to hold a nominee prospectively accountable for the decisions he would make as a justice, and in so doing, it directly employed the confirmation process to control the Court's future decision making. One must be careful not to make too much of the Cushing episode: his was an extreme case arising at an extreme time, when the fragility of the Union was at the forefront of the public's mind and when a Radical Republican Congress was uniquely intolerant of judicial interference with its political agenda; moreover, Grant withdrew Cushing's nomination before the Senate could act.[98] The episode was, nonetheless, a harbinger of things to come.

Stanley Matthews.   In 1881, President Rutherford B. Hayes nominated former U.S. senator Stanley Matthews to the Supreme Court. Like those of Roger Taney, Matthews's confirmation troubles are sometimes overlooked because he was later renominated (by James Garfield) and confirmed. Matthews's initial nomination was attacked for various reasons, including his enforcement of the Fugitive Slave Law as a U.S. attorney in the 1850s and his lack of knowledge and judgment as a senator.[99] But the "most telling accusation" against him, in the view of one historian, was that he had been closely allied with corporate interests, including the railroads, and had been working indirectly for Jay Gould at the time of his nomination. As this commentator reported:

> The Senate Judiciary Committee received bitter protests against "Mr. Corporation Standby" Matthews from eight hundred firms

represented in the New York Board of Trade and Transportation, from thirty thousand farmers of the Pennsylvania State Grange, and from the membership of the National Anti-Monopoly League, all depicting grave dangers to the country that would follow Justice Matthews's elevation to the Supreme Court.[100]

Henry Abraham adds: "The Senate exploded in anger, its Committee on the Judiciary flatly refusing to report the nomination out for floor action. It was perhaps the first clear instance of concerted, patent opposition to a nominee on grounds of economic affiliation."[101] Matthews, therefore, was the first nomination that the Senate formally blocked at least in part on the grounds that the nominee's political ideology would lead him to make unacceptable judicial decisions.

Louis Brandeis, Harlan Stone, and Charles Evans Hughes. If we bracket out the Senate's rejections of Hornblower and Peckham in 1893 and 1894 as products of an essentially private power struggle between President Grover Cleveland and Senator David Hill,[102] the next confirmation battle of consequence after Matthews was that of Louis Brandeis. Like Matthews, the core of the opposition to the Brandeis nomination was obfuscated by a range of proffered justifications, some more defensible than others.[103] Some accused Brandeis of being dishonest and untrustworthy, which may well have been anti-Semitic code or an attack on Brandeis's record of representing both corporate clients and progressive causes.[104] Joseph Harris concludes, however, that "[t]he opposition to Brandeis was due chiefly to the fact that his opponents regarded him as a dangerous radical" who was "unfit to sit on the Supreme Court, which they regarded as the bulwark of conservatism."[105] Brandeis was confirmed, but the shift toward greater emphasis on ideology in confirmation proceedings—a shift that began with Matthews—continued unabated.

After conservatives failed in their effort to block the nomination of a liberal in Brandeis, it was the liberals' turn to challenge conservative nominees. In 1925, they sought to derail the nomination of Harlan Fiske Stone, who, notwithstanding impeccable credentials as an able attorney and the dean of the Columbia Law School, was opposed because of his ties to corporate America. Stone was eventually confirmed by a lopsided vote of seventy-one to six.[106] Five years later, liberals challenged Herbert Hoover's nomination of Charles Evans Hughes to replace William Howard Taft as chief justice. Hughes was attacked for his economic views, which Senator Robert La Follette regarded as a highly relevant consideration given the "usurpation of power" precipitated by recent decisions of the Supreme Court invalidating governmental regulation of business. Hughes, like Stone, was ultimately confirmed by a vote of sixty-two to twenty-six.[107]

John J. Parker. The next appointments conflagration enveloped circuit judge John J. Parker, whom Herbert Hoover nominated to the Supreme Court in 1930. In the year before, the Senate had changed its rules and made public the proceedings of its deliberations on judicial nominees, which intensified the public spotlight on confirmation proceedings. With Parker, the Senate reprised its role as spoiler of a nomination in which the nominee's past behavior called into question the political acceptability of the judicial decisions he would make in the future. As with the nominations of Matthews and Brandeis, opposition to the Parker nomination was cluttered with ancillary explanations; Senator Henry Ashurst, for example, thought the nominee unfit because he had "neither great character nor great courage, nor great learning."[108] The focus, however, was indisputably on ideology. The NAACP opposed Parker's appointment in light of racist remarks he had made as a Republican gubernatorial candidate ten years earlier—remarks that, in the NAACP's view, displayed "open, shameless flouting of the fourteenth and fifteenth amendments to the Federal Constitution."[109] Organized labor opposed Parker's nomination on the basis of an injunction he had issued in a case as a district judge, upholding a so-called yellow-dog antiunion contract.[110] A newspaper editorial complained that "the presence of Judge Parker on the bench would increase, rather than lessen, the top heavily conservative bias of the Supreme Court."[111] Senator George Norris defended the relevance of Senate inquiries into such matters.

> So we are down to this one thing. When we are passing on a judge,
> therefore, we not only ought to know whether he is a good lawyer,

not only whether he is honest—and I admit that this nominee possesses both of those qualifications—but we ought to know how he approaches these great questions of human liberty.[112]

Parker was rejected on a vote of thirty-nine to forty-one. Leading the defense of Parker had been Senator Simeon Fess, who argued for confirmation on the grounds that ideological attacks against Parker and the conservative Supreme Court were another manifestation of "legislative proposals" that had been advanced from the earliest days of the nation "to curb the power of the Supreme Court."[113] Fess noted that previous court-curbing proposals "all failed of favorable action" and so should the effort to reject the Parker nomination, which Fess regarded as a direct assault on the independence of the Court.[114]

Senator William Borah, in contrast, was among the leading opponents of the Parker nomination. Borah was a champion of judicial independence earlier in his career, when he successfully led the campaign (discussed in chapter 2) to retain the judges of the Commerce Court after that court itself was dissolved. For Borah, however, the confirmation process was governed by a body of congressional precedent entirely distinct from that applicable to other forms of court curbing. In Borah's view, there was ample precedent for the Senate rejecting nominees on the grounds that they had previously taken action contrary to the Constitution, and that was the precedent of relevance in Parker's case.[115]

Abe Fortas. It would be almost forty years until the Senate's next series of rejections. In the interim, however, political interest in judicial appointments continued to escalate. In 1939, with the testimony of Felix Frankfurter, the Senate Judiciary Committee began "the practice—if still not the tradition—of questioning nominees," which became a regular feature of the confirmation process by the 1950s.[116] In 1949, as a further reflection of intensifying political interest in confirmation proceedings, the Senate implicitly acknowledged the applicability of the filibuster to confirmation debates by rendering such debates subject to a cloture rule (enabling the Senate to end debate on a confirmation if a supermajority of the Senate agreed).[117] In 1968, the Senate made its first use of the filibuster, to block President Lyndon Johnson's nomination of Justice Abe Fortas to be chief justice.[118] Chief Justice Earl Warren had indicated his intention to resign once his replacement was appointed; Lyndon Johnson nominated Fortas to take Warren's slot as chief justice (and Judge Homer Thornberry to fill the seat Fortas would vacate on becoming chief). But Senate resistance was intense, and Johnson withdrew the nomination in the wake of a filibuster. There are several possible explanations for the Senate's reaction to the Fortas nomination. For one, Johnson was a weakened Democratic president in the final year of his presidency, with a possible Republican successor; also, as a sitting justice, Fortas continued to serve as a political advisor to Johnson, which some regarded as improper; in addition, Fortas was accused of accepting exorbitant speaking fees.[119]

In the minds of contemporary scholars, however, these explanations are overshadowed by the fact that Fortas became a lightning rod for a backlash against the Warren Court. Fortas's withdrawal followed hearings before the Senate Judiciary Committee in which the nominee was questioned at length on decisions he had made in cases concerning the constitutional rights of criminal defendants. Professor Henry Abraham attributes the defeat of the Fortas nomination to "accumulated hostility to the Warren Court." Professor Michael Gerhardt reaches a similar conclusion, noting that Fortas's withdrawal was "compelled by some Republican and southern Democratic senators in retaliation against the liberalism of the Warren Court."[120] In sum, although the explanation for the Senate's objections to Fortas is clouded by a mix of issues, the movement toward greater emphasis on the nominee's ideology—a movement begun with Matthews and continued with Brandeis, Stone, Hughes, and Parker—had gained momentum with Fortas.

Clement Haynesworth and Harold Carswell.   After President Richard Nixon took office, the Supreme Court nominee's ideology remained on the Senate's front burner in its rejections of Fourth Circuit judge Clement Haynesworth and Florida judge Harold Carswell in 1968 and 1969. There is ample evidence for the unsurprising proposition that presidents have tended to pick Supreme Court nominees whose views on key issues appear compatible with their own. Nixon went further, however, by making a campaign pledge to dismantle the Warren Court by appointing "strict constructionists" who would further his "law-and-order" agenda. This served to heighten the political profile of his nominees' judicial philosophy and political ideology.[121] Haynesworth's confirmation, like that of Fortas, presented a mixed bag of issues: allegations of conflict of interest surfaced alongside objections to the nominee's ideology in light of his earlier stands on civil rights and labor, and Haynesworth was rejected by a vote of forty-five to fifty-five.[122]

Nixon was convinced that the Senate's rejection of Haynesworth had been driven by an "anti-southern, anti-conservative, and anti-strict constructionist prejudice,"[123] and as if to spite the Senate, he nominated another southern conservative, Harold Carswell. At bottom, Carswell was simply unqualified to serve on the Supreme Court,[124] which, like the ethical problems that confronted Haynesworth and Fortas, provided a nonpartisan justification for rejection. Even so, Carswell had left a very long and public paper trail revealing him to be a white supremacist, which contributed to his Senate downfall.[125] Although a dispassionate observer might conclude that Senate rejection of a subpar racist added little to the snowballing relevance of the nominee's political ideology in Senate confirmation proceedings, Nixon refused to let the episode be so dismissed. In a speech to the nation, Nixon criticized the "vicious assaults" on Haynesworth and Carswell and concluded that "when all the hypocrisy is stripped away, the real issue was their philosophy of strict construction of the Constitution—a philosophy I share."[126]

Robert Bork.   Almost twenty years later, Ronald Reagan went out of his way to emphasize Robert Bork's conservative ideology as the justification for his nomination to the Supreme Court in 1987, and a confirmation battle ensued over whether Bork was too conservative to be acceptable.[127] The Bork confirmation fight may fairly be characterized as a watershed, not because it signaled a major departure from past practice, but because it served as the culmination of developments that were very nearly a century in the making. Interest groups had come to play an increasingly significant role in the Senate's rejections of Parker, Haynesworth, and Carswell, a role that in Bork's case would arguably be decisive in turning the tide of public opinion against the nominee.[128] Senate and public interest in the appointments process had likewise increased over time, as confirmation hearings and the nominee's participation in those hearings gradually became an expected part of the process, leading to televised gavel-to-gavel coverage of Bork's testimony before the Senate Judiciary Committee.[129] Finally, the nominee's ideology and its relevance to his acceptability as a justice had become a more prominent issue over the course of the four previous Senate rejections of Supreme Court nominees and was all the more salient in Bork's case because his confirmation proceedings were uncluttered by other issues.

As with the Parker nomination, Bork defenders argued that conditioning a Supreme Court nominee's confirmation on whether his or her future decisions would be ideologically compatible with the political views of the Senate majority compromised judicial independence. Senator Orrin Hatch alluded to "the precedents of the Senate" and bemoaned those Supreme Court nominations that had been "chopped off by a dull political axe." In those instances, Hatch opined, "it was the Court that was left bleeding. It was the Court that suffered a loss of independence, integrity and institutional individuality."[130] Clearly, however, Hatch was fighting an uphill battle, given the adverse precedent that he himself was obliged to concede. Bork's nomination was defeated by a vote of forty-two to fifty-eight. Following Bork's rejection, President Reagan quickly nominated Douglas Ginsburg in his stead—too quickly, as it turned out, when the nominee was forced to withdraw after admitting that he smoked marijuana while on the faculty at Harvard.

The Lessons of Bork.   After his defeat, Robert Bork predicted that "the tendency . . . will be to nominate and confirm persons whose performance once on the bench cannot be accurately, or perhaps even roughly, predicted by the President or by the Senate."[131] So it was with David Souter, who President George H. W. Bush nominated in 1990. An obscure New Hampshire judge, so little was known about Souter that he was widely characterized as a "stealth candidate."[132] The approach worked: Souter was confirmed without serious incident. Then came Clarence Thomas.

In 1991, Thurgood Marshall—the first African American appointed to the Supreme Court—resigned, creating a vacancy that President George H. W. Bush proposed to fill with another African American: Clarence Thomas, a federal circuit court judge and former chairman of the Equal Employment Opportunity Commission. Proceedings in the Senate Judiciary Committee unfolded in two distinct phases.[133] In the first, Democrats (who controlled the Senate at the time) challenged Thomas as a nominee whose political ideology was too conservative and who was insufficiently forthcoming with the Judiciary Committee about his views on a range of issues. The Senate Judiciary Committee vote on Thomas split seven to seven, and the nomination was poised to go to the Senate floor for final action, when a Judiciary Committee source leaked information that Anita Hill, a former EEOC employee, had claimed that Thomas sexually harassed her on the job. The Judiciary Committee reconvened. Thomas denied the charges, decried the Committee's inquiry as a "high-tech lynching for uppity blacks," and the second phase of the confirmation proceedings quickly degenerated into highly partisan acrimony.[134] Thomas was ultimately confirmed by a vote of fifty two to forty-eight, but Democratic opposition to the Bork and Thomas nominations deeply angered Senate Republicans, who would later respond in kind by derailing the confirmation of President Clinton's nominees to the lower courts, as discussed in the next section of this chapter.

The Bork and Thomas confirmation fights led by Senate Democrats and leftward leaning interest groups left Senate Republicans deeply resentful, and it was widely anticipated that "payback" would be forthcoming when two vacancies arose on the Supreme Court during Democratic president Bill Clinton's tenure.[135] Unlike his Republican predecessors, however, Clinton displayed little interest in spending scarce political capital on controversial Supreme Court nominees, and went out of his way to consult with Senate leaders from both sides of the political aisle before nominating Ruth Bader Ginsburg in 1993 and Stephen Breyer in 1994. Unlike Souter, Ginsburg and Breyer were well known, but as consensus nominees provoked no significant opposition.[136]

It would be another eleven years before the next vacancy on the Supreme Court, and again, a confrontation was expected. President George W. Bush was on record as saying that he supported the appointment of justices like Clarence Thomas and Antonin Scalia[137]—two of the Court's most predictable conservatives—and interest groups on the left and right amassed sizable war chests to support or oppose the president's first nominee, sight unseen.[138]

Initially at least, President Bush did not follow through as expected: He nominated D.C. Circuit Judge John Roberts to replace Sandra Day O'Connor as associate justice, and when Chief Justice Rehnquist died on the eve of Roberts's confirmation hearings, the president redesignated Roberts to fill Rehnquist's seat. Roberts had not taken public positions on politically divisive issues of the day—most notably, on abortion rights (although, by virtue of his prior executive branch experience, he may have been seen as an ally of the president in cases testing the limits of executive power in the ongoing "War on Terror").[139] It was generally assumed that Roberts was conservative, but the extremity of his ideological bent was not widely known. During his confirmation hearings, Senate Democrats sought Roberts's views on a range of constitutional questions, but were systematically rebuffed on the grounds that answering questions on issues that could come before the Court would compromise his impartiality as a justice—a strategy that nominees had employed with increasing frequency since the Bork nomination. Although some Democrats opposed Roberts either because he had not answered questions to their satisfaction or because they suspected him of being too conservative, he was confirmed with relative ease by a vote of 78-22.

To fill the O'Connor vacancy, Bush nominated his White House Counsel, Harriet Miers, who, like Roberts, was unencumbered by a paper trail elaborating her views on ideological issues that Senate Democrats might use against her. Miers, however, did not have Roberts's credentials or experience, which gave rise to rumblings of cronyism among liberals, and almost explosive opposition from conservatives, who regarded the less qualified Miers as a squandered opportunity for President Bush to name an established ideological conservative to the Court. Bush ultimately withdrew the nomination.

In Roberts and Miers, President Bush had found nominees whose political ideologies remained sufficiently obscure to stymie Senate Democrats. The net effect was to continue a "mini-trend," first tested by President George H. W. Bush with the Souter nomination, and adopted by President Clinton, in which the president selected nominees with an eye toward avoiding or foiling confrontations over ideology in the Senate.[140] It was, however, not to last. In opposing Harriet Miers, the message from the president's conservative supporters was loud and clear: they had elected the president to pack the Court with prominent ideological conservatives and welcomed a fight with Senate Democrats to make that happen. While the Miers nomination was pending, commentator James Buchanan vented the conservatives' complaint:

> You've got Luttig, you've got Priscilla Owen, Janice Rogers Brown, Alito, countless others we've been preparing . . . who are as certain in their judicial philosophy as Robert Bork was, and then we are handed a . . . blank slate whose commendation, according to White House briefers, is she's never taken a stand. This White House has ducked the fight. . . . The President has recoiled from greatness. He has retreated . . . into the old politics of compromise and consensus on what for us was the greatest issue of his second term.[141]

After the Miers withdrawal, President Bush placated his conservative critics by nominating Samuel Alito, a judge with the United States Court of Appeals for the Third Circuit, whose character, credentials, and experience were above reproach, and whose name appeared high on the wish list of those clamoring for the appointment of a staunch conservative. Liberals railed, conservatives rejoiced, and Republican senator Orrin Hatch predicted "Armageddon." Following a brief truce, the president and Senate had returned with a vengeance to a state of war over nominee ideology.

In sum, the tradition of congressional restraint in most areas of court governance has coincided with a different trend in the Supreme Court appointments arena, where Senate partisans have actively sought to manipulate the Court's composition—and so its decision making—by evaluating judicial nominees with reference to their ideological bent and rejecting those whose decisions are likely to be politically unacceptable. The Senate's fixation on the decision-making ideology of Supreme Court nominees began in earnest over a century ago, on the eve of the Populist, Progressive, and New Deal eras, which, as discussed in chapter 2, featured the first of the great anticourt movements to yield no significant, externally imposed curbs on the federal judiciary. Coincidence? Perhaps not.

The rise of customary judicial independence has been accompanied by a corresponding decline in judicial accountability, which has resulted from the gradual rejection of various means of congressional control over judicial decision making—such as impeachment, court packing and unpacking, and jurisdictional manipulation. The appointments process, by virtue of its highly partisan tradition, its unique interbranch dynamic, and the relative ease with which partisan, ideologically motivated rejections can be accomplished, has evolved separately, unencumbered by the same judicial independence norms. As more draconian methods for controlling the courts and their decisions fell into disrepute, the confirmation process became the last best hope for legislators seeking to preserve some measure of judicial accountability.

Moreover, as the movement toward holding judges prospectively accountable for their decisions by means of the confirmation process took root, it may have diminished further still the perceived need to hold judges accountable in other ways. To the extent that the appointments process is calculated to select mainstream justices who think, more or less, like those who appoint them (and to reject outliers who do not), the occasions in which the decisions of those justices will so alienate the political branches and their constituencies as to prompt retaliation may be fewer.[142] And regardless of the extent to which presidents and senators can in fact reduce the future incidence of unacceptable decisions via the appointments process, the emerging perception that they can do so has meant that when unacceptable decisions occur, the political response of first resort is increasingly to address the problem with new appointments rather than by other, discredited means of court control.

Appointment of Lower Court Judges ∾

Like the selection of Supreme Court justices, the business of nominating and confirming lower court judges has always been an intensely partisan one. And like the selection of Supreme Court justices, presidents have long taken an interest in the decision-making ideologies of their nominees, while the Senate has begun to do so much more recently.[143]

The Emergence and Maturation of Senatorial Courtesy

Until the 1970s, the story of the Senate's participation in the appointment of lower court judges was largely one of patronage and gamesmanship embodied in "senatorial courtesy." At the roots of senatorial courtesy lie the vestiges of a substantive concern that animated the founders' desire for Senate participation in the appointments process: by virtue of being geographically dispersed, senators may be better positioned than presidents to identify the best-qualified nominees from their respective states. In practice, however, senatorial courtesy encompasses two related and nakedly political rules: first, if a senator objects to the president's nomination of a judge from the senator's home state, the Senate will (ordinarily) block the nomination out of deference or "courtesy" to the objecting senator; second, because a lower court nominee will not be confirmed if the nominee's home-state senators object, such senators (ordinarily) have the power to profoundly influence, if not dictate, who the president's nominees will be. Senatorial courtesy has exerted a profound influence on the selection of lower court judges generally and district judges in particular—with presidents enjoying greater latitude when it comes to naming circuit judges.[144]

Senatorial courtesy was first invoked during the Washington administration, when the Senate voted to postpone the confirmation of the president's nominee to serve as the naval officer for the Port of Savannah, following objections from Georgia's senators. The practice did not gain a stronghold in the appointments process, however, until the mid-nineteenth century. Joseph Harris noted, "Washington and other early presidents consulted members of the House as well as the Senate about local appointments in their states, and also consulted other prominent citizens; they did not feel obligated to nominate the choice of the senators from the state in which the office was situated."[145] In his study of lower court nominations between 1829 and 1861, Kermit Hall likewise found that in selecting nominees, presidents often relied heavily on personal, family, or professional relationships; on state or local political ties; or on their own political agendas. He found that home-state senators did not gain control of the process until the mid-nineteenth century, when the political party structure began to mature.

> The systematic involvement of senators of a president's party in the selection of district judges in their home states . . . [was an] attribute of a modern, party-directed selection process [that] developed slowly and incompletely. Not until the Pierce administration could senators from the President's party dictate judicial nominations. Nor was the practice fully established even then. . . . In its most complete sense, senatorial courtesy was a post–Civil War phenomenon.[146]

Thereafter, however, senatorial courtesy became so entrenched that by 1944, one author would conclude that "with respect to District Court judges . . . the Senate has expropriated the President's power of nomination so far as concerns appointments of interest to senators of the party in power."[147] In 1953, another would echo that "the custom of senatorial courtesy . . . has in effect transferred from the president to the senators of his party the selection of district judges in their own state."[148] This is not to imply that presidents ceased to take an interest in lower court confirmations; to the contrary, any number of presidents exhibited a desire to improve the quality or to shape the ideological bent of the inferior courts. And, as Harold Chase found, "when a president chooses to inject himself into the appointment of district judges, he can at times do so effectively."[149] Thus, for example, a number of presidents have circumvented senatorial courtesy by means of the Constitution's so-called recess appointments clause, to put their preferred candidates on the bench, if only temporarily.[150] Theodore Roosevelt succeeded in talking senators down from blocking nominations in which he had substituted his preferences for theirs.[151] Woodrow Wilson did the same.[152]

And in 1952, Dwight Eisenhower institutionalized the practice of consulting the American Bar Association before making nominations.[153] Chase nevertheless concedes that "there are precious few cases in our history where a senator of the president's party has lost a pitched battle to reject a nomination to a federal office *in his own state*."[154] Moreover, for a "good part of our history," he notes, a senator could block a district court nomination unencumbered by the need to explain his objection: "It was only necessary for the senator to state that the nominee was 'personally obnoxious' to him to invoke the courtesy."[155]

In the twentieth century, the practice of senatorial courtesy became streamlined with the advent of the blue slip. In evidence as early as 1917 and a part of the Senate Judiciary Committee's standard operating procedure by the 1950s, the blue slip was literally a blue slip of paper sent to senators, on which they could object to nominations from their home states.[156] As originally conceived, withholding a blue slip would signify acquiescence to a nomination, but in practice, as a Senate staff memorandum explained, "[n]o hearing has been scheduled on a nominee in the absence of a returned blue-slip," which rendered the failure to submit a blue slip "an automatic and mechanical one-member veto over nominees."[157] As a practical matter, senators employed the blue slip to block nominations only rarely. A study conducted in 1980 revealed that 88 percent of senators responding had never used the blue slip to object to a nomination, and even then, with only two aberrational exceptions, its use had been for the purpose of temporarily delaying, rather than killing, nominations. The study's author explained, "Problems with home state senators presumably will be dealt with *before* the need for withholding a blue-slip arises."[158]

Criticism of senatorial courtesy intensified at midcentury. A number of senators openly questioned the practice.[159] One commentator, complaining that "contrary to Hamilton's assertion, the senators of the president's own party can and do themselves 'choose' appointees to the federal bench," argued that "some method should be devised whereby the President could be timely and impartially apprised concerning the highly qualified persons available for appointments to the federal judiciary."[160] In a like vein, another, charging that the Senate had "abdicated its function" to home-state senators, urged the president to create merit selection commissions akin to those used by a number of state governors to assist them with judicial selection.[161] A third worried that delegating judicial selection to local senators and their state party networks, with no meaningful check on their power, had led to the appointment of sycophants who lacked the requisite independence.

> [T]he fact that inferior judgeships are treated as "party pie" is not the worst of it. Worse is the fact that these judgeships have become local "party pie." . . . Every vacancy results in a wild scramble and pulling of political wires which is only less hurtful to judicial independence and disinterestedness than is a popular primary or election.[162]

The Decline of Courtesy and the Ascent of Ideology

Gradually, senatorial courtesy began to weaken, if only slightly. In 1934, Senator Huey Long could declare that there was no "duty to be imposed upon any member of the Senate to justify his reasons for stating that a nomination was personally obnoxious to him" and that "no Senator would have to present anything except his own objection, and his own proposal that a nomination should not be confirmed by the Senate."[163] But by the early 1970s, the situation had changed. The clerk of the Senate Judiciary Committee explained: "[a senator] just can't incant a few magic words like 'personally obnoxious' and get away with it. He must be prepared to fight, giving his reasons for opposing the nominee."[164]

Apart from inviting judicial dependence on local politicians, appointing judges by means of an "old boy" network all but excluded women and minorities from the candidate pool. This was the concern that led President Jimmy Carter to deliver the first significant body blow to senatorial courtesy in 1976, when he requested that senators establish nominating commissions in their states for the explicit purpose of appointing more women and people of color. Nominating commissions had been used by an increasing number of states since Missouri instituted the first "merit selection" system in 1917, and, as noted earlier, proposals for the president to make comparable use of like bodies had been advocated at least since the 1950s. Although

Carter's proposal met with initial resistance, nominating commissions were in place in thirty-one states by 1980.[165]

The influence of individual senators on judicial selection in their respective states remained considerable during the Carter administration, but the interposition of nominating commissions loosened their grip and gave the president the leverage needed to further his goal of nominating more judges from underrepresented segments of the public. For his part, Senate Judiciary Committee chair Edward Kennedy tried to weaken senatorial courtesy still further by announcing that he would not stop the committee's investigation of nominees simply because a senator objected via a blue slip; rather, Kennedy would let the committee decide whether to proceed in any given case. As a practical matter, however, Kennedy's efforts culminated in little, as the committee opted in favor of respecting the traditional blue-slip process.[166]

Ronald Reagan, like many presidents before him (most recently, Richard Nixon), expressed an interest in selecting judges whose views of the Constitution mirrored his own. And like many presidents before him, Reagan appreciated what political science research has confirmed: that the general concordance that exists between the views of a president and those reflected in the decisions of the judges he appoints is diminished by the influence of home-state senators from the president's party on the selection process.[167] Reagan, however, went further than his predecessors to wrest control of lower court appointments from home state senators, by making the president's agenda to appoint politically conservative judges a priority, by insisting that senators furnish the White House with a list of prospective nominees rather than forcing the president's hand with a single name, and by thoroughly vetting the judicial philosophy of prospective nominees.[168]

Prior to the Reagan administration, confrontations between the president and the Senate over lower court appointments were common enough. But they were typically confrontations in which the Senate sought to punish a president for disregarding the spoils system by nominating a judge that a home-state senator found objectionable. It may well be that those confrontations were sometimes predicated on philosophical differences between presidents and the home-state senators over the political ideology of the nominees at issue, but until the latter part of the twentieth century, that would have been beside the point as far as the Senate was concerned—a home-state senator could invoke the courtesy without bothering to explain why. The net effect of delegating lower court selection to local senators had been to obviate the need for the Senate to engage in meaningful, collective deliberation of the nominees' merits; whereas the impact of the nominee's political ideology on his or her future decision making had been a prominent issue in Supreme Court confirmation proceedings since the 1880s, it had been largely absent from the lower court confirmation process.[169]

That changed during the Reagan administration. As the president pushed to appoint ideological conservatives, Senate Democrats and liberal interest groups pushed back. While the most visible battles occurred at the Supreme Court level, they were not so confined. In 1986, Beauregard Sessions III withdrew his nomination to an Alabama district court after the Senate Judiciary Committee voted against confirmation, in light of concern over the nominee's views on race and other issues.[170] In that same year, the vice president broke a tie vote in the Senate to confirm the nomination of Daniel Manion to the U.S. Court of Appeals for the Seventh Circuit, over objections based in significant measure on the nominee's ideology.[171] Then came the Bork hearings, the impact of which, as one commentator observed, "quickly seeped down to the lower courts. . . . Areas once regarded as inappropriate for Senate scrutiny—especially nominees' views on specific issues—became the central topics at many confirmation hearings."[172]

"[T]he evidence is equally compelling," writes a preeminent scholar of lower court appointments, "that the Bush Sr. administration scrutinized potential judicial nominees in terms of their ideology and judicial philosophy."[173] Like Ronald Reagan, George H. W. Bush had a number of appointments confrontations with the Senate over the decision-making ideology of his nominees. Beyond the Clarence Thomas spectacle, concern over a nominee's judicial philosophy drove the Senate Judiciary Committee to kill the nomination of Judge Kenneth Ryskamp to the Eleventh Circuit in 1990 and generated significant opposition to the ultimately successful appointment of Edward Carnes to that same court two years later.[174]

Most accounts of President Bill Clinton's appointments indicate that Clinton's priorities, like President Carter's, lay with diversity and not ideological purity.[175] Unlike Carter, however, Clinton took office at a time when Senate Republicans were red and sore from years of chafing by Democrats intent on disrupting the efforts of Republican presidents to change the ideological complexion of the federal courts. Clinton avoided confrontations over his Supreme Court nominees by making choices that were consciously calculated to avoid opposition.[176] Circuit court appointments, however, were another matter. It bears emphasis that while district court confirmations were sometimes contested during the Reagan and George H. W. Bush administrations, lower court appointments battles gradually came to focus almost exclusively on the circuit courts—which had become the courts of last resort for the vast majority of federal litigants.

In 1996, Republican presidential candidate and senator Bob Dole made a campaign issue of the "liberal activists" Clinton had appointed to the federal bench. Dole described the judicial decisions of various Clinton-appointed judges and inducted their authors into a "hall of shame."[177] Republican-controlled House and Senate Judiciary Committees held hearings on judicial activism, and conservative interest groups lobbied the Senate to block the nomination of activist judges generally.[178]

Although the Senate succeeded in voting down the district court nomination of Missouri justice Ronnie White, the primary weapon in the arsenal of Senate Republicans intent on thwarting the appointment of Clinton nominees was the stall, which encompassed a range of tactics: failing to schedule committee hearings on nominees, delaying committee action on nominees who received hearings, and postponing floor action on nominees reported out of Committee—by, for example, placing holds on objectionable nominations.[179] It had long been customary for the confirmation process to slow down during presidential election years, as senators from the party opposing the president sought to preserve as many nominations as possible for his successor. For example, in the Ninety-sixth Congress, which ended with the election of Ronald Reagan in 1980, 97.9 percent of President

Carter's circuit court nominees received Senate hearings, and an average of ninety-one days separated nomination from final Senate action; in the immediately preceding Congress, 100 percent received hearings, and final Senate action followed nomination by an average of only thirty-two days. Similarly, in the Ninety-eighth Congress, which culminated in the reelection of Ronald Reagan in 1984, 93.3 percent of the president's circuit court nominees received hearings, and an average of fifty-two days passed between nomination and final Senate action; in the Ninety-seventh Congress, 100 percent received hearings, in a process that took an average of only thirty-three days to run its course.

Then came the Bork hearings, in 1987. The percentage of circuit court nominees to receive hearings during Congresses ending in presidential election years dropped from more than 90 percent four years previously to just above 70 percent in 1987–88, where it hovered during Congresses ending in the 1992 and 1996 elections, before plummeting again to 46.9 percent in 1999–2000. Likewise, the time separating nomination from final Senate action on circuit court nominees spiked from an average of just over fifty days in 1983–84 to more than 170 days in Congresses ending in 1988 and 1992, before rising to 194 days in 1996—the end of Clinton's first term.

Escalating confirmation delays during the Clinton administration were at least as stark in Congresses that ended in the middle of the president's term. Circuit court nominees of Presidents Carter and Reagan had been processed in an average of no more than fifty days in Congresses that ended in 1978, 1982, and 1986. The time increased to eighty-two days for president George H. W. Bush in 1990 and to 103 days in the middle of Clinton's first term, in 1994. It then ballooned to 258 days in the middle of Clinton's second term, in 1998. The percentage of circuit court nominees to receive a hearing during Congresses ending in the middle of a presidential term, which had stayed above 90 percent between 1978 and 1994, dipped to 78 percent in 1998. Indeed, by 1998, the pace of Senate confirmations for lower court nominees slowed to such a point that the issue became a central cause for concern in Chief Justice Rehnquist's annual address on the state of the judiciary.[180]

The Senate's delay tactics during the Clinton administration did more than simply postpone the confirmation of objectionable nominees. "The data reveal the strategic value of foot-dragging: The longer the Senate delays a nomination, the less likely the nominee will be confirmed," concluded a study of senatorial delay between 1947 and 1998. The authors explain: "[T]here are no quick rejections; judicial nominations are defeated by Senate inaction rather than action."[181] When President Clinton left office, forty-two nominees remained unconfirmed; most of them had not been given hearings.[182]

During the presidency of George W. Bush, the lower court appointments process underwent a series of radical changes. Senate Democrats and Republicans were evenly divided at the start of Bush's presidency. Then, after Republican senator James Jeffords announced his departure from the party, the Democrats gained the upper hand until the midterm elections, when the Republicans regained a narrow majority. During the brief time they were in control, Senate Democrats succeeded in defeating the nominations of Charles Pickering and Priscilla Owen by voting them down in the Judiciary Committee and declining to report the nominations to the Senate floor.[183] The Democrats' primary strategy, however, was to borrow the tactic employed by their Republican counterparts during the Clinton administration: delay. In the 107th Congress, only 61.3 percent of the president's circuit court nominees were given a hearing—a record low in modern times for a Congress ending in the middle of a presidential term.[184] The percentage of a president's judicial nominations confirmed during the first year of his term continued its downward slide, from 93 percent in Reagan's first term, 90 percent in his second, 61 percent for George H. W. Bush, 57 percent in Clinton's first term, and 46 percent in his second, to 44 percent in the first year of George W. Bush's presidency.

When the Republicans controlled the Senate, Judiciary Committee chair Orrin Hatch changed the rules governing the blue-slip process: henceforth, not just one but both of a state's senators would need to object before a nomination could be blocked. Whereas the blue slip had once been used only as a means to delay a nomination temporarily, it had more recently become a means to defeat nominations altogether, an abuse Chairman Hatch was willing to tolerate when President Clinton was in power, but not now.[185] He later proceeded to hold confirmation hearings in the teeth of objections from one and sometimes both of a nominee's home-state senators.[186] The net effect was to diminish the minority's access to traditional weaponry in confirmation battles, which led furious Democrats to look elsewhere.

They found refuge in the hold and the filibuster. The hold was a device of long-standing but uncertain origin, whereby any senator could privately prevail on their party leader to delay floor action on a matter.[187] Michigan's Democratic senators succeeded in placing holds on three nominations to the Sixth Circuit, in retaliation for holds their Republican counterparts had placed on President Clinton's nominations.[188] Republicans responded by proposing to do away with the hold altogether.[189]

The filibuster had first been used to block a judicial nomination in 1968, when Senate Republicans blocked President Johnson's nomination of Justice Abe Fortas to be chief justice of the Supreme Court. Records reflect that cloture—a vote to end debate—was sought in seventeen judicial nominations between 1968 and 2002, which implies seventeen attempts to end a filibuster.[190] In none of those cases except that of Fortas, however, did the nominee ultimately fail to win confirmation.[191] In the 108th Congress, however, Senate Democrats successfully employed the filibuster to block ten nominations.[192] Moreover, there were some indications that the Democrats' objectives went beyond a generalized desire to block the appointment of judges they regarded as too conservative, to include the more specific objective of preventing the president from filling vacancies on particular courts where important cases were impending.[193]

Republicans responded by threatening to change Senate rules to prohibit filibusters in confirmation proceedings, on the grounds that the supermajority vote needed to end a filibuster was inconsistent with the Constitution, which provided that a president's nominee was to be confirmed by a simple majority of the Senate.[194] Among the options actively under consideration were a formal change to Senate rules and the so-called nuclear option, in which Republican vice president Dick Cheney, in his capacity as president of the Senate, would be asked to rule that the cloture rule did not apply to confirmation proceedings and that debate could thus be ended on a majority vote.

In the spring of 2005, the dispute came to a head, as Senate Majority leader Bill Frist threatened to exercise the nuclear option to prevent Democrats from filibustering five pending circuit court nominations and Democrats threatening to retaliate by obstructing other Senate business. A potential crisis was averted by a bipartisan compromise among Senate moderates, wherein three nominations would proceed, while two would remain subject to a filibuster.

The rules of the Senate Judiciary Committee include a corollary to the filibuster and cloture. As of 1979, there were no limits on debate within the committee. It was then that Chairman Edward Kennedy proposed altering the committee's rules to permit the chair to call a matter to a vote whenever he and a majority of the committee concluded that sufficient time for debate had occurred.[195] Senator Orrin Hatch objected, arguing that one of the "rights" a senator has is to "talk as long as he wants to as long as he can stand" and that "these rights are far superior to the right of this Committee to rubber stamp legislation out on the floor." As a compromise, the committee approved Rule IV, which provided that "the chairman shall entertain a non-debatable motion to bring a matter before the Committee to a vote" and that "if there is objection to bringing the matter to a vote without further debate," the debate can be ended only on a motion that garners "ten votes in the affirmative, one of which must be cast by the minority." During the Clinton administration, Chairman Orrin Hatch acknowledged that Rule IV "effectively establish[ed] committee filibuster rights." In 2003, Senate Democrats invoked Rule IV to block committee votes on three of President Bush's circuit court nominees; Chairman Hatch, however, overruled their objection and forced a vote. As to his earlier statements, Hatch declared that "he was wrong to say they could filibuster." He now contended that Rule IV was intended only to serve "as a tool by which a determined majority of the Committee could force a recalcitrant chairman to bring a matter to vote," and he queried, "if the rule were intended to prevent votes, why doesn't it say so?"[196]

For his part, President George W. Bush made it clear that he shared his recent Republican predecessors' commitment to appointing ideological conservatives. As if to punctuate the point, upon assuming office, he ended the fifty-year tradition of consulting the

American Bar Association before making nominations; the practice had fallen out of favor with conservatives after it gave Bork a mixed (though favorable) rating. In the ABA's stead, Bush substituted the conservative Federalist Society as an informal advisor.[197] In response to the Democrats' delay tactics, he declared that the nation faced "a vacancy crisis in the federal courts, made worse by senators who block votes on qualified nominees."[198] He responded to the Judiciary Committee's rejection of Charles Pickering and Priscilla Owen in the 107th Congress by renominating them in the 108th Congress. And when Pickering's second nomination was defeated by a filibuster, the president took the unprecedented step of appointing him and Bill Pryor (whose nomination had likewise fallen victim to a filibuster) to the Fifth and Eleventh Circuits, respectively, during a one-week recess in the middle of a congressional term—prior to then, recess appointments had been made only during lengthy breaks, typically at the end of a Congress or annual session.[199]

Those who have criticized the conflagration over judicial ideology that enveloped the lower court appointments process during the Clinton and George W. Bush administrations have often decried its adverse impact on judicial independence. Republican senator John Cornyn complained that "abusive filibusters . . . uniquely threaten both presidential power and judicial independence."[200] Democratic senator Patrick Leahy worried that "if we don't have consensus nominees . . . we ultimately are going to diminish the independence of the judiciary."[201] Supreme Court justice Anthony Kennedy warned that it was a danger to judicial independence for the Senate to insist on nominees with specific views.[202] Liberal activist Nan Aron contended that President Bush's commitment to appointing only strict constructionists posed a dire threat to the judiciary's independence.[203]

The prevalence and strength that customary independence holds in other contexts makes it understandable that Republicans and Democrats alike would invoke its talismanic powers in the service of their respective causes in the appointments process. But concern for judicial independence has never played a significant role in the appointment of lower court judges. For almost two hundred years, the Senate's interest in lower court appointments was largely a function of its members' desire to dole out patronage to local lawyers—a desire that was, if anything, at odds with the subsequent independence of the lawyers appointed. Given the absence of customary independence from the culture of judicial appointments, it is understandable that independence norms would not suddenly emerge to constrain the Senate's conduct when, in the 1980s, it began to hold district and circuit judges prospectively accountable for their future decision making, by weeding out ideological extremists.

As with the Supreme Court confirmation process, the Senate's recently acquired interest in the political ideology of lower court nominees may have been an inevitability, given Congress's increasing inability to control judicial decision making by other means in arenas where customary independence has held sway. And by virtue of its forward-looking nature, the appointments process is an especially attractive means by which a highly polarized Senate can influence judicial decision making— relative to more problematic, backward-looking efforts to punish judges for decisions previously made.[204] There is, however, cause for concern that the lower court appointments process is on the cusp of destabilization. Norms that have governed the appointments process for decades and sometimes centuries have been jettisoned to further partisan causes in an ideological holy war over the future of the federal judiciary. Gone are the traditions of the president consulting the American Bar Association before making a nomination; of the Senate Judiciary Committee routinely scheduling hearings on nominees; of the Senate acting promptly on pending nominations; of senators limiting their resort to using the hold or the blue slip to delay, rather than defeat, nominations; of respecting the prerogatives of home-state senators to invoke senatorial courtesy; of senators resisting the impulse to defeat judicial nominations by means of the filibuster; of respecting the rights of senators to debate until stopped by a vote of cloture; of adhering to the Senate Judiciary Committee's rules that restrict the chair's authority to end debate on a nomination; and of the president making recess appointments only at the end of a congressional term or session.

My purpose here is not to bemoan the loss of any specific norm in the appointments process; rather, it is merely to emphasize that the web of norms that has long governed the appointments process has begun to unravel. The implications of this development for the future of the appointments process itself are troubling enough. Even more troubling, perhaps, is the possibility that the ongoing partisan jihad over judicial politics could overrun the borders of the appointments process and destabilize neighboring areas of court governance, where customary independence has kept the peace for generations. This possibility is explored in chapter 6.

CHAPTER FIVE

The Role of the Courts in Preserving Customary Independence ∾

THE INSTITUTIONAL NORMS elaborated on in preceding chapters are not excerpted from a protracted congressional soliloquy. Rather, they are the product of a centuries-old conversation with the courts. The courts' half of that conversation (as reflected in the decisions they make) has been much more widely studied, for which reason I have spent less time with what the courts have said directly or indirectly to Congress than with what Congress has said to and about the courts. Nevertheless, if the conversation is to be fully understood, both sides need to be heard. This chapter begins by reviewing the ways in which the judiciary has helped perpetuate independence norms through a tradition of restraint. I will then turn to more recent developments in which the courts have taken a more confrontational stance in their relationship with Congress.

The Tradition of Restraint ∾

The restraint that Congress has traditionally exhibited toward the judiciary in most contexts has been reciprocated by the courts in three ways. First, the courts have developed myriad conflict-avoidance doctrines to sidestep controversies that could provoke congressional retaliation. Second, the courts have sometimes averted crises by acquiescing to congressional will in key cases when cycles of court-directed hostility have reached their peak. Third, the courts have traditionally exercised their powers of self-government in ways deferential to and solicitous of the desires of Congress.

If one looks only at the ways in which the third branch of government has acquiesced to the first, it suggests the possibility that the courts are not so much independent decision makers paying their respects to a coequal as they are victims paying tribute to an extortionist—an implication belied by studies revealing that courts do not routinely kowtow to congressional preferences.[1] When, however, the judiciary's occasional genuflections to the legislature are reexamined in tandem with the evolution of independence norms in Congress, a more nuanced explanation emerges, in which the courts' occasional, short-term displays of deference, offered in a spirit of comity, have promoted long-term congressional acceptance of customary independence.

Conflict Avoidance Devices: The "Passive Virtues"

There is an extensive literature addressing the ways in which a motivated court can avoid deciding controversial cases that could provoke congressional ire. Professors John Ferejohn and Larry Kramer link that literature to the study of judicial dependence and independence. They set out to "chart the major lines of institutionalized judicial self-restraint," in support of their hypothesis that "if Congress and the executive have seldom exercised their power to impair the judiciary, . . . this may be because the judiciary has acted in such a way that Congress and the executive have seldom felt the need to do so."[2] Courts have at their disposal a range of conflict-avoidance mechanisms that enable them to retreat from deciding cases that may be too contentious for their comfort. As described shortly, justiciability doctrines allow courts to dodge questions that are too abstract, that are asked too soon or too late, or that are simply too "political"; rules of constitutional construction minimize the need for courts to reach constitutional questions that might require them to invalidate congressional enactments or executive branch actions; federalism-promoting doctrines ostensibly aimed at reducing federal court interference with state prerogatives also permit courts to avoid decisions that could prompt an angry response from a Congress solicitous of states' rights;[3] and the Supreme Court may simply manipulate its case agenda by denying petitions for certiorari that seek review of cases the Court regards as too volatile.

Justiciability Doctrines

The nation was less than five years old when the Supreme Court declined an overture from President Washington to render an advisory opinion on the interpretation of treaties with England and France.[4] The precedent stuck. In the twentieth century, the general rule against advisory opinions has been subdivided into a handful of doctrines aimed at ensuring that issues presented to a federal court are suitable for adjudication, or "justiciable." Courts have long acknowledged that justiciability doctrines have both a constitutional and a prudential dimension. As to the constitutional dimension, the text of Article III limits the courts' exercise of judicial power to the specific context of "cases" or "controversies."[5] In order for there to be a live case or controversy, the party bringing suit must claim an actual injury, or else the action will be dismissed for lack of standing; the injury complained of must have already materialized, or else the action will be dismissed for want of ripeness; and the injury must not have already been redressed, or else the action will be dismissed on grounds of mootness. As a separate, but related, matter, the text of the Constitution arguably delegates to the political branches alone the task of interpreting some constitutional questions; if the party bringing suit asks a court to answer such questions, the action will be dismissed as presenting a nonjusticiable "political question."[6]

If justiciability doctrines began and ended with the requirements of Article III, their relationship to interbranch conflict avoidance would be more attenuated. To be sure, the requirements for live cases or controversies alone could prevent the courts both from becoming embroiled in potentially explosive interbranch altercations over matters that remained speculative or premature and from rekindling the ashes of old conflagrations that had already been doused. But whenever the constitutional threshold for justiciability was technically met, courts asked to decide incendiary issues would have no choice but to light the interbranch powder keg.

The prudential dimension to justiciability, in contrast, is better tailored to suit the purpose of giving the courts added flexibility (over and above that furnished by the open textual weave of Article III and ambiguous interpretive precedent) to avoid political maelstroms, even when constitutional requirements are satisfied. Judge Robert Bork made this point nicely, in a passage that would later be quoted with approval by the Supreme Court.

> All of the doctrines that cluster about Article III—not only standing but mootness, ripeness, political question, and the like—relate in part, and in different though overlapping ways, to an idea, which is more than an intuition but less than a rigorous and explicit theory, about the constitutional and prudential limits to the powers of an unelected, unrepresentative judiciary in our kind of government.[7]

Justice Felix Frankfurter made a similar observation a generation earlier (relying on the views of Justice Brandeis, offered a generation before that).

> The restriction of our jurisdiction to cases and controversies within the meaning of Article III of the Constitution is not the sole limitation on the exercise of our appellate powers, especially in cases raising constitutional questions. The policy reflected in numerous cases and over a long period was thus summarized in the oft-quoted statement of Mr. Justice Brandeis: "The Court [has] developed, for its own governance in the cases confessedly within its jurisdiction, a series of rules under which it has avoided passing upon a large part of all the constitutional questions pressed upon it for decision."[8]

Frankfurter explained that such rules derived from considerations of "the fundamental federal and tripartite character of our National Government and from the role—restricted by its very responsibility—of the federal courts . . . within that structure," concerns that "press with special urgency in cases challenging legislative action."[9] Brandeis likewise attributed the Court's reluctance to reach the merits of constitutional questions to "the 'great gravity and delicacy' of [the Court's] function in passing upon the validity of an act of Congress."[10]

The conceptual utility of the dichotomy between constitutional and prudential considerations breaks down in practice. The Supreme Court has hopelessly blurred the distinction, openly conceding that it "has not always been clear" which of the two it has relied on in dismissing cases as nonjusticiable.[11] Suffice it to say that the justiciability doctrines are replete with crisp dichotomies, enumerated factors, and essential elements captured in pithy phrases that create a veneer of precision, beneath which lies a muddle of prudential and constitutional analyses. Of the standing requirement, Professors Charles Alan Wright, Arthur Miller, and Edward Cooper have written that "at any single moment there are almost unlimited opportunities to disagree in applying the currently fashionable phrases," leading "exasperated courts and commentators" to conclude that it is "no more than a convenient tool to avoid uncomfortable issues."[12]

Rules of Constitutional Construction

The earlier quoted concurrence of Justice Brandeis in *Ashwander v. Tennessee Valley Authority* alluded to subconstitutional, prudential rules that courts followed to avoid unnecessary confrontations with Congress. Some of those rules emanated from the justiciability doctrines just discussed. Others, however, are better characterized as rules of constitutional construction. Thus, for example, Brandeis's list included the following: "[t]he Court will not 'anticipate a question of constitutional law in advance of the necessity of deciding it'"; "[t]he Court will not pass upon a constitutional question although properly presented by the record, if there is also present some other ground upon which the case may be disposed of"; and "[w]hen the validity of an act of the Congress is drawn in question, . . . it is a cardinal principle that this Court will first ascertain whether a construction of the statute is fairly possible by which the question may be avoided."[13]

Frederick Schauer has noted that "[a]lthough the strategy of construing a statute so as to avoid having to make a constitutional decision did not originate with Brandeis's *Ashwander* opinion, it was *Ashwander* that gave the principle so much of its enduring importance."[14] For Brandeis, the raison d'être for these rules was to minimize the extent to which courts must rule on the constitutionality of a statute, given the "gravity and delicacy" of that task. Schauer recasts the point in cost-benefit terms: for Brandeis, the benefits of routine judicial review are outweighed by "the costs . . . of judicial review itself, especially the costs of ignoring the 'fundamental rule of judicial restraint' and thus allowing an unelected judiciary unnecessarily to exercise the power to invalidate the acts of coordinate branches of the federal government." "The rationale of *Ashwander*," reports Schauer, "is that 'the Court should avoid constitutional confrontations with Congress.'"[15]

In addition to the canons of constitutional construction outlined in *Ashwander,* the courts have created tiers of scrutiny that enable them to defer to the political branches on a wide range of constitutional questions. Thus, for example, in a host of contexts, courts will uphold political branch action in the teeth of a constitutional challenge as long as the action at issue is supported by a "rational basis." Ferejohn and Kramer admonish:

> Remember, judicial forbearance need not take the form of holding some matter formally nonjusticiable. . . . [I]t is far more typical for the Court to exercise jurisdiction while applying substantive legal tests that leave political actors free to choose their course of action without any realistic threat of judicial intercession.[16]

Federalism-Promoting Doctrines

The U.S. federal system calls for the coexistence of two sovereign governments, one at the state level and the other at the national level. The inevitable tension that federalism creates between state and national governments has shaped the federal judiciary from its inception. As discussed in chapter 1, the framers of the U.S. Constitution declined to establish inferior federal courts outright, for fear that they might usurp their state counterparts and opted instead to defer the issue for congressional resolution.

The fledgling federal courts quickly learned the importance of deference to state sovereignty. In the 1793 decision of *Chisolm v. Georgia,* the Supreme Court held that states were subject to federal suits for actions to recover war debts. The state of Georgia reacted with fury, enacting legislation declaring that anyone who enforced the Court's decision "shall suffer death, without the benefit of clergy, by being hanged," and within a matter of weeks, Congress moved to placate the states by adopting the Eleventh Amendment, overturning the decision.[17] The fallout from the *Chisolm* episode left little doubt that state sovereignty was a matter of acute interest, not just to the states but to Congress, which was prepared to act swiftly and decisively when federal courts displayed insufficient sensitivity to state autonomy. To this day, members of Congress often reserve their most vituperative criticism of the federal courts for decisions that, in their view, unduly limit the prerogatives of state and local governments to regulate such matters as abortion, school prayer, prison overcrowding, school busing, local elections, and so on.

Over time, the Supreme Court has developed a body of doctrine that has reduced the need for federal courts to embroil themselves in state affairs, thereby promoting a spirit of comity between the state and federal systems and reducing the frequency of confrontations with a Congress that is, at least from time to time, quite protective of state rights. It is an area of law that is widely studied and should be familiar to any law student who has taken a class in federal jurisdiction. In lieu of bootstrapping a three-credit course to this chapter, I offer the following summary of some federalism-promoting doctrines, to the end of conveying a general sense of their nature and scope.

Doctrinal limits on diversity of citizenship jurisdiction. The diversity jurisdiction statute authorizes federal courts to decide issues of state law in cases arising "between . . . citizens of different states."[18] One straightforward reading of that statute would permit the federal courts to decide cases in which any one plaintiff and any one defendant are from different states: for example, a Wisconsin plaintiff could file a diversity claim against Illinois and Wisconsin defendants, asking the federal courts to resolve a dispute of state tort, property, or contract law. But the Supreme Court has confined diversity jurisdiction to cases where diversity of citizenship is "complete," that is, where there is no plaintiff who shares citizenship with any defendant.[19] In an age when multiparty litigation is increasingly the norm, the "complete diversity" requirement has diminished dramatically the number of state law cases in which the federal courts are enabled to entwine themselves. Moreover, even when diversity of citizenship is complete, the federal courts have excluded all domestic relations disputes from their jurisdictional bailiwick, on the grounds that such matters are of a distinctly local character[20]—notwithstanding that the diversity jurisdiction statute, by its terms, excludes no substantive issues of state law from its scope.

Doctrinal limits on federal question jurisdiction. Federal courts are authorized by statute to hear cases "arising under" federal law.[21] One could easily read that language to empower the federal courts to decide any case that calls on them to resolve an issue of federal law. But the Supreme Court has limited federal question jurisdiction to cases in which the federal issue is raised in a well-pleaded complaint.[22] This limitation excludes from the federal trial courts a host of state law cases in which a federal question is raised by a defendant or other party—as, for example, when a defendant newspaper publisher asserts that the First Amendment protects the publisher from liability for state common-law defamation.

Doctrinal limits on federal court authority to develop the common law. The *Erie* doctrine requires federal courts to follow state judge-made common law (rather than general common law of their own making) when deciding cases within the scope of their diversity jurisdiction.[23] The Rules of Decision Act, in place since 1789, requires the federal courts to follow state law in diversity cases, but prior to the *Erie* decision, the term *law* had meant, in this context, statutory and constitutional law only.[24] By reinterpreting the Rules of Decision Act to require federal court adherence to state common law as well, the *Erie* doctrine effectively ceded development of the common law to the states, thereby diminishing the opportunities for conflict between state and federal systems.

Doctrinal expansion of the Eleventh Amendment. The Eleventh Amendment to the U.S. Constitution deprives the federal courts of jurisdiction to hear suits filed against a state "by citizens of another state." Read literally, the amendment does not bar federal question claims brought against a state by its own citizens, but the Supreme Court has ruled otherwise.[25] In effect, the Court has read the Eleventh Amendment so broadly as to create general state sovereign immunity from suit in the federal courts, thus excluding from the federal system an entire class of politically sensitive cases.[26]

Abstention doctrines. Over time, the Supreme Court has developed a cluster of doctrines calling on the federal courts to abstain from deciding cases within their jurisdiction that would entangle the federal courts in politically sensitive state issues. Thus, for example, the *Younger* abstention doctrine authorizes the federal courts to withdraw from cases implicating important state interests when the same matter is being litigated in the state courts.[27] *Pullman* abstention requires the federal courts to delay the exercise of jurisdiction to give the state courts an opportunity to clarify unresolved questions of state law that could obviate the need for the federal courts to decide the case on constitutional grounds.[28] *Thibodaux* abstention, in turn, enables the federal courts to postpone decisions in diversity jurisdiction cases pending state court resolution of unresolved state law issues, if the issues are of unique interest to the state government.[29] And *Burford* abstention compels the federal courts to cede jurisdiction when there are state administrative procedures in place to resolve an issue of special significance to the state.[30]

It bears emphasis that the various federalism-promoting devices just summarized are self-imposed by the courts rather then imposed on them by Congress. In some instances, these devices are ostensibly derived from judicial interpretations of congressional enactments or constitutional amendments, but even then, it is the federal courts that have elected to fill gaps in statutory or constitutional text with a body of doctrine that diminishes their authority to intrude on state affairs. Some applaud these federalism-promoting doctrines as good government in action, while others condemn them as unduly timid abdications of judicial power. In either case, however, they provide the federal courts with the tools they need to avoid confrontations—not just with the states, but with Congress, which disgruntled state citizens can be expected to petition for redress if the federal courts are perceived to undermine important state powers or rights.

Agenda Setting

There are very few cases that the Supreme Court is required by law to hear. In the vast majority of cases, the Supreme Court picks and chooses from among thousands of petitions for writs of certiorari and agrees to hear only those matters it wants to hear.[31] As various scholars have argued, this gives the Court the discretion to set its agenda by selecting cases that will further the justices' personal political goals, meet the Court's institutional responsibilities to settle conflicts among the lower courts, and respond to external forces (e.g., the legal profession, interest groups, and the Department of Justice) that mobilize to pursue their causes in the courts.[32] It likewise provides the Court with the discretion to decide what will not be on its agenda— such as cases that could provoke unwanted fights with Congress.

Demonstrating that the Court denies petitions for writs of certiorari to sidestep confrontations with the political branches is difficult. On the one hand, the five or more justices who decline to hear a case offer no explanation for their decisions; the perceived need to avoid confrontations will arise infrequently, and even then it may sometimes be overridden by other priorities. On the other hand, dissents from denial of petitions for writ of certiorari occasionally point to the Court's desire to avoid untimely controversy as the reason for the denial. Thus, for example, in *Ratchford v. Gay Lib,* Justice William Rehnquist (joined by Justice Harry Blackmun) began his dissent from the Court's denial of a cert petition by observing: "There is a natural tendency on the part of any conscientious court to avoid embroiling itself in a controversial area of social policy unless absolutely required to do so. I therefore completely understand, if I do not agree with, the Court's decision to deny certiorari in this case."[33] Chief Justice Warren Burger's dissent was less understanding but more direct.

> Unlike the District Court and the Court of Appeals, Congress has accorded to us through the Judiciary Act of 1925, . . . the discretion to decline to hear a case such as this on the merits without explaining our reasons for doing so. But the existence of such discretion does not imply that it should be used as a sort of judicial storm cellar to which we may flee from controversial or sensitive cases.[34]

Alexander Bickel referred to these various mechanisms at courts' disposal for declining to address issues that could tread on the toes of a political branch as "passive virtues."[35] As described earlier, such mechanisms often quite openly make law of politics, by fusing "prudential" considerations to legal doctrines that empower courts to decide cases or not, with implicit and sometimes explicit reference to the political temperature of the issue before them. Critics have characterized these "passive virtues" as "subtle vices"[36] that enable courts to abdicate their constitutional duties in unprincipled ways, and Bickel himself conceded:

> techniques and allied devices for staying the Court's hand . . . cannot themselves be principled in the sense in which we have a right to expect adjudications on the merits to be principled. They mark the point at which the Court gives the electoral institutions their head and itself stays out of politics, and there is nothing paradoxical in finding that here the Court is most a political animal.[37]

If the "passive virtues" are evaluated in the limited context of the cases in which they are exercised, they would seem to institutionalize a form of judicial dependence on the political branches, by authorizing and encouraging the courts to defer to the will of Congress or the president when "prudence," rather than the Constitution, dictates. But it would be a mistake to take so narrow a view. Instead, the "passive virtues" should be evaluated in the broader context of the customary independence story that has been told here. To the extent that the courts' occasional short-term acquiescence to the will of a political branch is traded for the preservation of long-term independence norms, it is a trade that is both principled and independence-enhancing. Dean Anthony Kronman's synthesis of Bickel's philosophy makes a similar point.

> [I]f the Court always found some reason to postpone troublesome decisions—those that are likely to infuriate or offend—one might legitimately question whether the path of principle had not in fact been abandoned after all. From time to time, however, the Supreme Court does render decisions that it knows will be unpopular, and these stand as a kind of warrant for the Court's continuing commitment to principle. Indeed, in Bickel's view, the Court is more likely to keep this commitment if it has the freedom to avoid decision. The requirement to decide every constitutional question in a principled fashion must inevitably force many more conflicts between principle and opinion than the Court can tolerate, and thus gives it a powerful incentive to conform its principles to public sentiment—a tendency that in the long run is certain to deaden the Court's appreciation of its educative responsibilities.

> The passive virtues are therefore not only consistent with a continuing commitment to principle, they actually help to sustain this commitment by reducing some of the pressures that might otherwise make it impossible to maintain.[38]

Kronman and Bickel's focus was on the extent to which the Court's occasional resort to the passive virtues protects its long-term capacity to uphold the law from the diffuse vagaries of "opinion" and "pressure." Their point gains focus and strength if it is appreciated that the courts are doing more than seeking to avoid pressure; they are seeking to preserve a structure of constitutional norms that have been centuries in the making.

The institutional norms that I have explicated in preceding chapters are so integrated into the American constitutional landscape as to be taken for granted by some scholars who study the courts' conflict-avoidance doctrines. Schauer, for example, dismisses the need for deferential rules of constitutional construction to avoid confrontations between the courts and Congress: "there is little to suggest that Congress can or would do anything in response to a Supreme Court decision that would rise to the level of what we might call 'disobedience.'"[39] Outright defiance is indeed unlikely, as are impeachment of the offending justices, cuts to the Supreme Court's budget, and sudden alteration of the Court's size. Earlier chapters demonstrate that the reasons such reactions are unlikely have a lot to do with customary independence as it has matured under congressional care. This chapter, in turn, suggests that the courts assist in the care and feeding of institutional independence norms through the strategic use of judicial restraint. If the judiciary's use of conflict-avoidance doctrines is appreciated as a means to the long-term ends of perpetuating independence norms, rather than to the short-term ends of avoiding a congressional backlash in a given case, then the courts' resort to such doctrines—even when the immediate threat of retaliation from a political branch is nil—begins to make sense.

In a similar vein, political science research reports little systematic evidence to support the proposition that the Supreme Court defers to congressional preferences when deciding cases.[40] Indeed, independence norms are sufficiently entrenched to render systematic deference unnecessary. Occasional and strategic deference, however, calculated to preserve independence norms, is another matter.

Finally, Ferejohn and Kramer comment on "the remarkable fact" of "how reluctant the federal judiciary has historically been to take an expansive view of its jurisdiction or its authority[, e]ven when the political branches might want courts to take a more active role in guiding social change."[41] Once again, however, this fact becomes less remarkable if conflict-avoidance mechanisms are understood as a means to preserve the judiciary's independence over the long term. By exercising restraint much of the time—even when Congress would be content to see the courts play a more active role—the courts perpetuate an atmosphere of goodwill that enables them to weather periods of criticism without jeopardy to their long-standing autonomy.

Key Cases in Which the Courts Have Retreated from Conflict

When spikes of court-directed criticism have reached their peak, the beginning of the downward slope has often been marked by a pivotal case—or string of cases—in which a court or judge has retreated from confrontation-provoking results. A few examples should suffice.

In 1803, the Jeffersonians were in power and on the warpath against the courts, as detailed in chapter 2. Congress, with the support of the president, had just enacted legislation stripping sixteen Federalist judges of their tenure by obliterating the judgeships they occupied, thereby effectively removing judges entitled to tenure during good behavior without resort to the impeachment process. The constitutionality of the act was challenged, briefed, and argued. Less than a month earlier, Chief Justice Marshall had declared in *Marbury v. Madison* that the Court possessed the power to invalidate unconstitutional acts of Congress.[42] And yet, in *Stuart v. Laird*,[43] the Court issued a terse opinion upholding the statute that repealed the federal judgeships, in language betraying no awareness that the constitutionality of the repeal was even at issue.

The Jeffersonians then turned their attention to the impeachment process and tried unsuccessfully to remove the strident Federalist Samuel Chase from office, as described in chapter 3. The widely reported legacy of this case was to establish a precedent against the impeachment and removal of federal judges on account of their decisions. Often lost in the fray, however, is that Justice Chase became a mere shadow of his former self in his decade on the bench after his acquittal in the Senate.[44] Whether he was chastened or merely unwell is disputed; in either case, however, the episode was a sobering one for his fellow Federalists on the bench. Leon Friedman and Fred Israel observed: "Jefferson's Party was not without gains in the controversy over Chase. Thereafter, judges generally were more careful in what they did and how they spoke."[45] This retreat of Chase and his colleagues undoubtedly contributed to the gradual cessation of court-directed hostilities.

During the Andrew Jackson administration, the death of John Marshall is generally credited as ending a period of heightened interbranch friction in the 1830s. It bears emphasis, however, that the reason Marshall's death facilitated the end to this cycle of anti-Court sentiment is in no small part because Marshall's successor, Roger Taney, retreated from his predecessor's controversial posture in cases relating to state versus federal power.[46] This may have had more to do with President Jackson's strategic appointment of a more politically compatible chief justice than with the Court rethinking its views in an effort to restore equilibrium, but the relationship between a change in the Court's decision making and the end of a period of disaffection with the Supreme Court is nonetheless clear.

During Reconstruction, the Radical Republican Congress made it quite clear that it would not tolerate judicial interference with the Reconstruction agenda. As elaborated in chapter 2, when the constitutionality of a pivotal piece of Reconstruction legislation was appealed to the Supreme Court and when Congress signaled its interest in passing legislation to withdraw the Court's jurisdiction to hear the pending appeal, the Supreme Court dutifully delayed deciding the case, to give Congress time first to enact the legislation and then to override a presidential veto.[47] When the anticipated measure finally became law, the Court obligingly dismissed the case for want of jurisdiction, in *Ex parte McCardle*.[48] It is virtually indisputable that the Court bent over backwards to avoid deciding a case that could have infuriated Congress, and there is ample room to argue that its decision to dismiss would have been different if Congress had not been waving a gun in the general direction of the Court's head. In any event, the Court's decision in *McCardle* contributed to a gradual de-escalation of interbranch friction that had pervaded the relationship between the branches for the previous fifteen years.

Then, there is the famous "switch in time that saved nine"[49]—Justice Owen Roberts's change of heart that shifted the five-to-four balance on the Supreme Court in favor of upholding FDR's New Deal legislation. Disagreement persists as to whether Roberts's switch was motivated by the fear that FDR would make good on his court-packing plan or by the results of the 1936 election, which may have convinced him that the Court's views had fallen too far out of step with the public's. In either case, Roberts's change of vote obviated the need for Roosevelt to persist in his plan to control the courts.

Attacks on the Warren Court were ultimately hushed with the appointment of Chief Justice Warren Burger, who with only occasional exception led the Court in a less controversial direction. Although the transformation was brought about by new Court appointments, rather than changes of view by Court veterans, the point nonetheless remains that changes in Court decision making contributed to the restoration of normal relations.

The import of the foregoing cases should not be misunderstood or overstated. In no case can one prove that a judge disregarded his view of the law and reached the wrong result simply to relieve political pressure, although available evidence sometimes suggests that possibility. But that is not really the point. The point is that perpetuation of institutional norms leading Congress to preserve the judiciary's autonomy—even when disaffection with the courts runs high—has, from time to time, been aided by the courts themselves, whose retreat at critical moments has banked the fires of court-curbing movements.

Deferential Self-Government

A third way in which the courts have contributed to interbranch equilibrium and the perpetuation of independence norms is through self-government that is consciously deferential to congressional preferences. As elaborated on shortly, the emergence of the judiciary as a self-regulating branch traveled in tandem with extrajudicial communications—from courts to Congress—that until recently tended to be quite mindful of the need to preserve interbranch comity. That, in turn, helped to minimize confrontations that could lead to court curbing.

For as long as Congress has regulated the courts, judges have employed extrajudicial means to communicate their wants, needs, and fears to Congress. During the first decade of the Republic, for example, individual Supreme Court justices proposed legislation, assisted congressional committees in developing amendments to the Judiciary Act of 1789, and lobbied for a variety of other legislative reforms.[50] The movement toward greater judicial self-administration that, as described in chapter 2, redefined the relationship between Congress and the courts in the twentieth century was paralleled by a gradual increase in the flow of formal and informal interbranch communication on the subject of legislation regulating the courts. The connection between these two developments is obvious enough: as the judiciary became an independent, self-regulating branch of government, the expectation increased commensurately that it, like its counterpart in the executive branch, would defend its budget requests, recommend legislation it favored, and lobby against legislation it opposed. Thus, the two pieces of legislation central to establishing the judiciary as a self-governing branch—one establishing the Conference of Senior Circuit Judges (later renamed the Judicial Conference of the United States) and the other creating the Administrative Office of the United States Courts—imposed new obligations on and created new opportunities for representatives of the third branch of government to communicate with the first.

Legislation authorizing the creation of the Judicial Conference of the United States provides that the "Chief Justice shall submit to Congress an annual report of the proceedings of the Judicial Conference and its recommendations for legislation,"[51] and since its inception in 1922, the conference has included legislative proposals in its annual report. Moreover, proposals advocated in the annual report are first considered by one or more Judicial Conference committees that act on issues called to their attention by (among others) legislators.[52] Legislators solicit comments and testimony from conference committee members on pending bills that the committee has reviewed both before and after the conference as a whole has voted on them. Once the conference has taken a position, conference committee chairs will write, telephone, or visit key legislators to clarify or urge adoption of the conference's position.[53]

The Administrative Office Act of 1939 further expanded the points of interaction between courts and Congress, in three ways. First (as discussed in chapter 2), the Administrative Office of the United States Courts replaced the Department of Justice as the source of the judiciary's administrative support, which meant that the judiciary would henceforth communicate directly with Congress (rather than through the executive branch) on its budget and related matters. Second, the act required the director of the administrative office to submit to Congress annual reports concerning the business of the courts.[54] Third and perhaps most important, the act instructed the director to "[p]erform such other duties as may be assigned to him by the Supreme Court or the Judicial Conference of the United States."[55] These "other duties" have included testifying at congressional hearings, providing members of Congress with draft legislation to implement proposals approved by the Judicial Conference, and directing particular judges or staff to lobby Congress in support of conference positions.

This movement toward greater judicial branch involvement in legislative affairs accelerated dramatically in the last quarter of the twentieth century, amid calls for even more interbranch communication. Some argued that judges need to sensitize legislators to the impact of legislation on an overburdened judiciary. Others emphasized the special expertise that judges can lend legislators on the complexities of court improvements legislation. Still others have suggested that the judiciary would be aided in its efforts to make headway in Congress if judges had a greater appreciation for the constraints within which Congress operates in the arena of judicial reform.

Further enhancing interbranch communication were a series of court-reform commissions created by Congress in the latter third of the twentieth century. Comprised of judges and legislators (among others), these commissions convened meetings to address issues of mutual interest, such as the operation of the federal courts, judicial discipline and impeachment, and criminal sentencing. In that same time, the judiciary established the Office of Legislative Affairs and the

Office of Judicial Impact Assessment (which assesses the impact of proposed legislation on the courts) within the Administrative Office of the United States Courts, while several hundred judges formed the Federal Judges Association, to lobby Congress on matters of judicial salaries, budgets, and administration. Finally, for years, the Brookings Institution sponsored a series of annual conferences—for federal judges and legislators—explicitly designed to improve interbranch communications.

As the judiciary came into its own as an independent institution, it remained acutely aware that its emerging institutional autonomy resulted from congressional delegations of power that could be undone. Thus, it tended to be quite deferential to Congress in its communications. Chief Justice Rehnquist reflected this awareness as recently as in his 1996 year-end report on the federal judiciary.

> I am struck by the paradox of judicial independence in the United States: we have as independent a judiciary as I know of in any democracy, and yet the judges are very much dependent on the Legislative and Executive branches for the enactment of laws to enable the judges to do a better job of administering justice.[56]

The judiciary's traditional deference is displayed in a variety of ways. First (and perhaps most noticeably), judges manifest a keen awareness that when they appear as witnesses in congressional hearings, they do not call the shots but are cast in the unfamiliar role of supplicants. For those who have not attended hearings at which judicial branch witnesses testify, transcripts fail to capture the atmospherics of the deference of the third branch to the first. Suffice it to say that, with rare exception, representatives of the judicial branch exhibit an array of deferential behaviors, ranging from smiles and idle chat preceding the hearing, to introductory remarks that credit the chair for her support and leadership, to the respectful tone with which questions—even accusatory ones—are answered.

Second, the Judicial Conference has a long-standing policy of not speaking to Congress unless spoken to. In 1980, Judge Elmo Hunter explained to the Senate Subcommittee on Improvements in Judicial Machinery:

We do not ask you or tell you or advise you how to pass on bills unless you invite our comments. We are very careful. My committee simply will not respond concerning legislation unless the invitation originates with one or the other of the bodies of the Congress.[57]

This is a policy that is often honored in the manipulation, if not the breach. When the judiciary's interest in a piece of legislation is keen, it has sometimes solicited invitations to comment and at other times relied on informal remarks of legislators as standing invitations to comment on any matter of interest to the courts.[58] The point nevertheless remains that the underlying policy is born of the judiciary's deference to congressional prerogatives on matters of legislation regulating the courts.

Third, rather than oppose unwelcome legislative proposals outright, the Judicial Conference has frequently sought to blunt their impetus by proposing intrajudicial remedies to address the perceived problem. The net effect is to reinforce the perception that the judiciary will administer itself in ways responsive to congressional concerns, even when it is not prepared to support a given piece of legislation. In 1990, for example, Senate Judiciary Committee chair Joseph Biden had become increasingly concerned by reports of excessive expense and delay in civil litigation and introduced legislation that would impose on all district judges plans for managing civil cases. Many federal judges reacted with near apoplexy to what they perceived as legislative micromanagement. Rather than simply oppose the legislation, however, the Judicial Conference countered with what its representative characterized as "a 14-point program to address the problems of cost/delay as a response to the first Biden bill."[59] Although Senator Biden rejected the conference's proposal and pressed ahead with the Civil Justice Reform Act, the essential point is that the conference's opening gambit was to derail the legislation through deferential self-administration.

A similar strategy has worked well for the Judicial Conference in its efforts to deflect legislative proposals to allow cameras in federal courtrooms. Although virtually every state system permits cameras of one kind or another in their courts, federal courts have long resisted such proposals. In 1988, in the face of mounting pressure from the media, the Judicial Conference appointed an ad hoc committee to study proposals that would allow cameras in the courtroom. Two years later, the conference had taken no further action. In September 1990, Robert Kastenmeier, the chair of the House Judiciary Committee's Subcommittee on Courts, wrote a letter to the Judicial Conference, implying that legislation opening the federal courts to cameras would be inevitable if the Judicial Conference did not lift the ban on its own.[60] In that same month, the Judicial Conference established a pilot project authorizing limited use of cameras in courtrooms, on an experimental basis.

More recently, many judges were angered by a Senate bill, introduced in 2002, that would limit the ability of federal judges to attend all-expense-paid judicial education seminars underwritten by organizations interested in cases that attendees would later decide as judges. The Judicial Conference opposed the legislation, but again, its representatives employed appeasement tactics. The Senate Judiciary Committee was considering a bill to increase judicial salaries. Senator Russell Feingold—who had sponsored the proposal to regulate judicial seminar attendance—indicated that he had planned to attach his bill as an amendment to the legislation on the pay raise, but would not do so because he had been given "assurances that the Judicial Conference will again take a look at this problem and try to address it internally."[61]

Finally, the judiciary likewise employs appeasement tactics to avoid congressional interference in the arena of procedural rule making. Although Congress clearly possesses the constitutional power to enact procedural rules for federal courts and has built into the Rules Enabling Act an opportunity for it to suspend rules promulgated by the Judicial Conference before such rules become effective, the judiciary has come to regard its rule-making authority as a defining feature of its institutional autonomy. The judiciary is thus quite openly territorial on the subject of rules revision and characterizes it as "troubling" when "bills are introduced in the Congress to amend federal rules directly by statute, bypassing the orderly and objective process established by the Rules Enabling Act."[62]

To reduce the frequency of congressional intrusion into the rule-making process, the judiciary has been quite attentive to congressional preferences. In the past thirty years, intrajudicial rule making has become more politicized by interest groups that have sought to influence the Judicial Conference to amend procedural rules governing such issues as discovery, class actions, and litigation misconduct. As much as the judiciary might prefer to close its doors to the politics of interest groups, it understands that if it ignores those groups, their next stop will be Congress. Thus, in 1988, the Judicial Conference supported legislation codifying the practice—which it had already implemented—of opening its rule-making proceedings to the public, which, asserted Chief Judge Jack Weinstein, "should reduce the necessity of congressional intervention through legislation."[63] A decade later, the conference's Civil Rules Advisory Committee reported on its former chairman's views that "it is very important that the Advisory Committee continue the openness policy that it has been following, and that it continue to engage the hard issues," adding that "Congress will be deferential to the process as long as the Committee continues to engage the important issues openly, thoughtfully, and rationally."[64] The message is clear: to retain its rule-making autonomy, the judiciary accommodates Congress.

The New, More Confrontational Judiciary ∾

Taken together, the varied devices discussed to this point in this chapter have enabled the courts to preserve the interbranch equilibrium that has fostered the maintenance of independence norms. However, some evidence suggests that the judiciary may be turning a new page in its relationship with Congress—one that is considerably less deferential to the legislature's prerogatives and that could test the strength of that relationship.

Supreme Court–Imposed Limits on Congressional Power

In the last decade of the twentieth century, the Supreme Court began to limit congressional power in ways not seen since the New Deal, by reducing the scope of congressional authority to regulate commerce, implement the Fourteenth Amendment, and promote state compliance with federal law.[65] Liberals have excoriated the Court's decisions as a usurpation of power that subjugates Congress and the will of the people, while conservatives have applauded those same decisions as supplying a long-overdue check on runaway congressional power. Numerous law school symposia have been devoted to analyzing the significance of these decisions, and little purpose would be served here by rehashing the articles those symposia have generated. Suffice it to say that the Rehnquist Court's reinterpretation of the constitutional limits on congressional power across a growing line of cases represents a dramatic departure from the more generous and deferential approach that the Supreme Court had taken in the preceding six decades. To that extent, the Court's recent decision-making tangent may fairly be characterized as a departure from the tradition of restraint described in this chapter. Such a departure acquires added significance when it is appreciated that these are the handful of cases the Court has opted to decide from among the thousands of petitions for certiorari filed. While the agenda-setting process enables the Court to exhibit restraint by declining to hear confrontation-provoking cases, the Court's decision to seek such cases out sends a very different message.

This does not necessarily imply that the Court is putting its customary independence from Congress in jeopardy. First, it must be remembered that the tradition of restraint serves to establish a reservoir of goodwill that preserves independence norms and thereby enables the Court to uphold the law by making the occasional, countermajoritarian decision without fear of retaliation. While some would quarrel with whether the Court is upholding the law in these recent cases, the point remains that departures from the tradition of restraint are what justify the tradition in the first place. Second, although the Court's recent decisions restricting congressional power have angered liberal and Democratic academics, policy wonks, and a handful of legislators, it is far from clear that the minds who matter most—namely, those of the more conservative Republican congressional majority—regard those decisions as either countermajoritarian or inconsistent with the tradition of judicial restraint. Barry Friedman and Anna Harvey have argued, "the seeming tension between Congress and the Court rests on a misconception, to wit: Because the Court is striking down congressional statutes, Congress disagrees with what the Court is doing."[66] Rather, they posit that a conservative Congress is unlikely to be angered by a conservative Court invalidating liberal legislation enacted years before by a predecessor Congress. Even if the Court's abrupt turn to the political right does manifest activism or lack of restraint, it is not of a sort that is likely to cost the Court political capital with Congress, at least in the short run.

In other words, the Supreme Court's recent decisions may have taken Congress to task in ways not witnessed for over half a century, but the immediate impact on the Court's customary independence is likely to be negligible. The longer-term impact, however, may be another story. Liberals have long regarded the federal courts as countermajoritarian champions for the rights and liberties of the politically frail. That view is seemingly contradicted by the Rehnquist Court's recent campaign that has overturned legislation protecting the rights of groups that liberals hold dear. Insofar as those decisions disillusion an independent judiciary's most reliable defenders by convincing them that the Court is less interested in following the law (as embodied in sixty years of precedent) than in implementing a conservative political agenda, the long-term prospects for customary independence become uncertain. Granted, conservatives may come to the defense of the courts, as liberals have in the past. But many conservatives have long been suspicious of "activist" judges who "legislate from the bench" and may therefore be more likely to defend independence norms as fair-weather friends than as true believers—the implications of which are explored further in chapter 6.

Recent Developments in the Judiciary's Lobbying Tactics

The caseload of the federal courts increased at a rate in excess of population growth throughout the latter half of the twentieth century, for many and varied reasons. Some observers attributed the development to a "litigation explosion" sparked by trial lawyers. Others attributed it to the public's "delusion" that courts can cure all social ills. Still others attributed the increase to a "law explosion" precipitated by innumerable pieces of legislation creating new causes of action in the federal courts.[67]

When a new bill proposes to add cases to the federal courts' dockets, the Judicial Conference could limit its role to advising Congress on how many more judges and dollars would be required to process the influx of cases. Toward the end of the twentieth century, however, the judiciary became increasingly concerned about uncontrolled expansion of its ranks. Apart from their general aversion to diluting the prestige of federal judicial office, judges were concerned that unrestricted expansion would gradually undermine the strength and integrity of the branch by making it difficult to ensure an adequate supply of highly qualified judges and by exceeding the number of judges that a single system could administer effectively.[68]

An obvious alternative to increasing the supply of judges was to reduce the demand for judicial services by cutting back on—or at least limiting the expansion of—federal jurisdiction. As the judiciary became increasingly desirous of limiting its growth, its willingness to take a corporate position on the wisdom of legislative proposals adding to the federal court's caseload slowly changed, from never to sometimes to usually.[69] And as described in its Long Range Plan (I discuss the *proposed* plan later), the circumstances under which the Judicial Conference will concede the desirability of adding to the federal courts' jurisdiction has become quite limited.[70]

As early as the 1950s, the conference began taking occasional positions on proposals relating to its subject-matter jurisdiction.[71] For our purposes here, however, the story begins in 1977, when the Judicial Conference urged Congress to abolish or retrench the federal courts' jurisdiction to hear cases between citizens of different states on matters of state law. It defended its proposal to end so-called diversity jurisdiction, not only as a way to reduce federal court caseload, but also as a means to address what might fairly be characterized as a federalism concern.[72] Eliminating the federal courts' authority to hear diversity cases would, in the words of Chief Justice Warren Burger, "return to the state courts . . . what must reasonably be recognized as state court jurisdiction by any twentieth century standard."[73] Burger's federalism concern was clearly grounded in public policy, not constitutional law. The Constitution expressly authorizes Congress to equip with diversity jurisdiction whatever lower courts it establishes.[74] The Judicial Conference's position was simply that disputes of state law are better resolved in state courts and that because we no longer need to worry about state courts favoring their citizens at the expense of outsiders, there is no further need to provide a federal forum for cases between citizens of different states.

The plot began to thicken in 1991, when Chief Justice Rehnquist sent a letter to the chair of the House Judiciary Committee to "convey the opposition of the Judicial Conference to proposed legislation that would provide for federal jurisdiction over offenses traditionally reserved for state prosecution."[75] The attached memorandum argued that pending legislation that would make violent felonies involving firearms a federal crime "would be inconsistent with long-accepted concepts of federalism, and would ignore the boundaries between appropriate State and Federal action."[76] In 1992, the chief justice wrote a newspaper editorial in which he observed that the "federal courts were always intended to complement state court systems, not supplant them," and he characterized this proposition as an "important historical limitation[] . . . circumscrib[ing] the scope of federal judicial power."[77] In his view, "[t]o shift large numbers of cases presently being decided in the state courts for reasons that are largely symbolic would be a disservice to . . . the whole concept of federalism."

Rehnquist took issue with the pending Violence Against Women Act, which would create a federal cause of action for women who had been victimized by certain forms of violent crime. "The bill's new private right of action is so sweeping," the chief justice cautioned, "that it could involve the courts in a host of domestic-relations disputes." Although the Judicial Conference ultimately decided to withdraw its formal opposition to the Violence Against Women Act, Judge Richard Arnold, who served as chair of the Judicial Conference's Budget Committee at the time, later acknowledged that the decision was tactical. As he explained, "What the Judicial Conference initially said was, 'We don't think this is an appropriate place to federalize; let the states handle this.'" Senator Joseph Biden, the chair of the Senate Judiciary Committee and the principal sponsor of the legislation, reacted so negatively to the conference's position that, in Arnold's words, "[b]y the time he got through with us, you would have thought we were in favor of rape." Arnold explained the consequence: "the Conference retreated and decided, 'Okay, we will not take any position on the Act.' It was counterproductive politically for us to attempt it."[78]

In 1994, a Judicial Conference committee issued its *Proposed Long Range Plan for the Federal Courts.*[79] There, it observed that "[a]s Congress continues to 'federalize' crimes previously prosecuted in the state courts, and to create civil causes of action over matters previously resolved in the state courts, the continued viability of judicial federalism is unquestionably at risk." Accordingly, the plan recommended that "[i]n principle, criminal activity should be prosecuted in federal court only in those instances in which state court prosecution is not appropriate" and that "Congress should assign civil jurisdiction to the federal courts only to further clearly defined and justified federal interests, and it should not create new rights of action concerning matters traditionally cognizable by state courts."

Given the Judicial Conference's long-standing support for ending diversity jurisdiction out of respect for the primacy of state court jurisdiction, its subsequent opposition to legislation creating new federal rights of action on the grounds that they, too, were best reserved for state court resolution seemed at first to be more of the same. As with the federalism concern animating its position on diversity jurisdiction, the conference's objections to federalizing various civil and criminal actions appeared—at the time they were raised—to present issues of public policy and not constitutional law. After all, for nearly two-thirds of a century, the Supreme Court had consistently taken a highly deferential view of congressional power to regulate commerce and implement the equal protection clause of the Fourteenth Amendment.[80] Given the Court's expansive interpretations of congressional power, the possibility seemed remote that the conference's policy-based objections to legislation creating new causes of action in the federal courts would morph into constitutional imperatives.

Then, in 1995, the Supreme Court pulled the trigger. In that year, the Court decided *United States v. Lopez,*[81] the first in a line of cases (discussed generally in the preceding subsection of this chapter) that diminished the scope of congressional power. Writing for the majority in a five-to-four decision, Chief Justice Rehnquist declared that Congress lacked constitutional authority under the commerce clause to federalize the crime of possessing a gun within a school zone. As noted earlier, it was the first time in nearly sixty years that the Court had invalidated a congressional enactment on such grounds.[82] Five years later, in *United States v. Morrison,* the Supreme Court ruled—in another five-to-four decision, with the majority opinion again written by the chief justice—that Congress lacked constitutional power to enact a critical component of the Violence Against Women Act.[83]

To put as fine a point on it as possible, federal judges first walked the halls of Congress as lobbyists, doing their best to kill legislation federalizing cases traditionally tried in the state courts, and then, when that effort failed, they headed back to their courthouses, donned judicial robes, and declared the legislation unconstitutional. That characterization is a little unfair, insofar as the "judiciary" doing the lobbying was the Judicial Conference, comprised almost entirely of circuit and district judges, while the "judiciary" ultimately declaring the legislation unconstitutional was the Supreme Court, comprised almost entirely of justices who are unaffiliated with the Judicial Conference. However, the chief justice of the United States heads both the Judicial Conference and the Supreme Court, and it was the chief justice who spearheaded the Judicial Conference's lobbying effort to thwart the legislation and who—as author of the Supreme Court's majority opinions—declared that legislation unconstitutional.

This one-two punch of opposing proposed legislation and then declaring it unconstitutional if it becomes law is one the judiciary appears ready and willing to use again. In 2000, the Judicial Conference announced its opposition to legislation that would allow cameras in federal courtrooms, on the grounds that it could "seriously jeopardize the rights of citizens to receive a constitutionally guaranteed right to a fair trial."[84] In that same year, it opposed legislation that would restrict judges' ability to attend educational seminars paid for by private groups interested in the outcomes of cases the judges decided, in part because it "raises potential constitutional issues, such as imposing an undue burden on speech."[85] When the branch of government ultimately responsible for reviewing the constitutionality of congressional enactments announces its opposition to proposed legislation on constitutional grounds, the implications for Congress are clear: either drop the bill, or suffer the consequences.

This approach is troubling in two specific respects. First, it jeopardizes the appearance of judicial impartiality. By taking positions that question the constitutional validity of pending legislation, the Judicial Conference has come dangerously close to reconstituting itself as a council of revision that offers advisory opinions on the constitutionality of legislation before it is enacted. When, during the Constitutional Convention, James Madison proposed the creation of a council of revision comprised in part of federal judges, the proposal was rejected. Rufus King objected to establishing such a council for reasons shared by a majority of the delegates: "[T]he Judges ought to be able to expound the law as it should come from them, free from the bias of having participated in its formation."[86] King's concern applies with equal, if not greater, force today. A judiciary that collectively opposes enactment of a statute on constitutional grounds is ill suited to offer an unbiased assessment of its constitutionality later. Moreover, today's corporate judiciary is offering constitutional advice on pending legislation as a lobbyist seeking to advance its institutional self-interest, which further complicates the ability of its individual judges to appear impartial when they later invalidate legislation on grounds consistent with the Judicial Conference's self-serving position.

Second, this tactic all but invites retaliation in kind by Congress. The preceding chapters in this book have been dedicated to demonstrating that our conception of an independent judiciary derives less from the text of the Constitution or from judicial divinations of that text than from institutional norms that have emerged over the course of the relationship between the courts and Congress and that are now an entrenched part of our constitutional culture. One of the core norms cutting across most areas of court governance is that Congress should not use its legislative and other powers to manipulate the federal courts' exercise of judicial power. In other words, Congress should not and historically has not disestablished courts, held the judiciary's budget hostage, or threatened judges with impeachment as means to control judicial decision making. The courts, in contrast, have begun to brandish their judicial power as a means to manipulate Congress in its exercise of legislative power. If the courts persist in this strategy, it may be only a matter of time before Congress rethinks its reluctance to do unto the judiciary what the judiciary seems quite willing to do unto Congress.

It would be premature, however, to predict a congressional backlash. To date, the legislation that the Supreme Court has invalidated has not been especially near or dear to the congressional majority, and the bills that the Judicial Conference has questioned have been too low in their political profile to provoke retaliatory strikes. It bears emphasis, however, that the conflict-avoidance strategies cataloged in this chapter provide the courts with a means to create the reservoir of goodwill that enables them to make highly unpopular decisions from time to time without jeopardizing long-standing independence norms. By embarking on a conflict-seeking strategy of challenging the constitutionality of pending legislation as lobbyists and then invalidating the legislation as judges, the judiciary may risk depleting that reservoir in ways that wear congressional patience thin and threaten the spirit of comity that has long defined the interbranch relationship.

CHAPTER SIX

The Dynamic Equilibrium ∾

THE RELATIONSHIP BETWEEN judicial independence, judicial accountability, and congressional oversight of the federal courts may fairly be characterized as one of "dynamic equilibrium." This is not a phrase I lay claim to coining; to the contrary, it has found a home in such diverse fields as economics, botany, mathematics, chemistry, art, and medicine. Its meaning, however, is surprisingly stable across disciplines, which adds to the appeal of its import here. A chemistry dictionary, for example, defines "dynamic equilibrium" as "the condition of balance between varying, shifting and opposing forces which is characteristic of living processes." Abstract artist Piet Mondrian used "dynamic equilibrium" to describe a "universal balance achieved by forces in motion." A botanical glossary defines it as "a system that retains much the same condition because of the action of opposing forces which proceed at more or less equal rates."

The dynamic or opposing forces chronicled in this monograph have been several. First is the interplay between the institutions of Congress and the courts. Second is the conceptual tension between judicial independence and judicial accountability. Third is the collision between the practically immovable object of constitutional text and the unstoppable force of shifting social, political, and economic priorities. Fourth is the clash between the two dominant political parties and the issues that divide them.

Equilibrium, or balance between these dynamic and opposing

forces, has likewise been facilitated through several means. First are the institutional and constitutional norms, customs, or conventions that have fostered systemic stability and flexibility as well as respect for an independent judiciary. Second is the related notion of interbranch comity that is animated by the deference one department of government regards as due its coordinate departments and by concern for the consequences if such deference is not shown. Third is the constitutional structure itself, with its checks (which facilitate interbranch dynamism) and balances (which lead to interbranch equilibrium).

Dynamic Equilibrium as an Explanatory Device ∾

Dynamic equilibrium is, in one respect, an explanatory device. In the context of chapter 2 of this book, dynamic equilibrium explains the stability and growth of the judiciary's independence from Congress over time, despite cyclical calls for the first branch of government to put the third branch in its place by manipulating court size, structure, jurisdiction, and budgets. Judicial independence norms and a pervasive spirit of comity combined to preserve equilibrium between the dynamic forces of a sometimes exasperating judiciary and a sometimes angry Congress and likewise helped to maintain a balance between independence and accountability, a balance that favored independence despite an alignment of raw constitutional power that would seem to tip the scales heavily toward greater accountability. In the context of chapter 3, dynamic equilibrium clarifies how and why federal judges have survived the recurrent efforts of congressional factions to impeach and remove judges for making bad decisions and have ultimately emerged triumphant. Congress's evolving appreciation for the judiciary's decisional independence produced a norm against removing judges on account of their decisions, and that norm combined with the natural unwieldiness of the impeachment mechanism to preserve balance between courts and Congress during periods of intense and often partisan antipathy toward judges and the judiciary.

One could fairly argue that the developments described in chapters 2 and 3 did not foster interbranch equilibrium so much as disequilibrium that tipped the independence-accountability balance sharply in favor of independence. Without relinquishing the point that independence norms have helped to dissuade Congress from overwhelming the courts as it has periodically threatened to do, thereby preserving interbranch stability or "equilibrium," there is something to the argument that in the arenas of court governance and judicial impeachments, independence norms have done better than resist episodic assaults by congressional factions—they have gained ground over time. To the extent that these developments have created disequilibrium in the independence-accountability balance, chapter 4 rationalizes the Senate's increasingly aggressive stance in the confirmation process as an accountability-enhancing measure that restores systemic equilibrium between courts and Congress, independence and accountability.

Read in isolation, chapters 2–4 could create the misimpression that the dynamism giving rise to a state of relative equilibrium between the courts and Congress has been entirely intracongressional. Chapter 5 inventories the carrots and sticks that the judiciary has employed to protect and promote its independence from Congress. Scholars and judges have long argued that doctrinal and ad hoc displays of judicial deference to popular and legislative will have enabled the judiciary to avoid confrontations with Congress. In the larger context of this work, however, such displays of judicial deference suggest that more is at work than "Pavlovian justice" in which the courts salivate or cringe at the feet of the congressional master. The likelihood that Congress would punish individual judges or the judiciary for any given decision— however outrageous—seems remote, given the entrenchment of judicial independence norms within the first branch. Rather, the judiciary's traditional decision-making deference to congressional prerogatives can be better understood as a dynamic means to preserve the equilibrium that nurtures and protects independence norms over the long term.

Dynamic Equilibrium as an Instrumental Value ∾

Dynamic equilibrium is thus an explanatory device that helps to describe how congressional oversight of the federal courts works. But it is more than that. In a representative democracy grounded in a written constitution that separates interdependent powers of government and delegates the task of interpreting the law to an independent judicial branch, dynamic equilibrium describes how congressional oversight of the federal courts *should* work. The dynamic equilibrium between the first and third branches of government furthers three core values inherent in our constitutional structure: the value of constitutional stability and change, the value of limited governmental power, and the value of an independent judiciary.

The Value of Constitutional Stability and Change

A written constitution ensures a measure of stability that simple, direct democracy does not. It formalizes the will of the people in an organic text that supersedes other popularly enacted laws. At the same time, in order for constitutions to embody the will of the people over time, stability must be counterbalanced by mechanisms for constitutional change to accommodate enduring shifts in political priorities.[1]

The dual values of stability and change—equilibrium and dynamism—are reflected in Article V of the U.S. Constitution, which subjects the Constitution to amendment but only through a process requiring supermajority approval by state and federal governments. This requirement functionally forecloses change (and thereby promotes stability) except where the political resolve for amendment is strong and widespread.[2] In practice, however, the Article V barriers to changing the Constitution have been very nearly impenetrable, thwarting all but seventeen of more than eleven thousand amendments proposed since 1791.[3]

The amendment process, however, has proved not to be the only vehicle for constitutional change. The brevity of the Constitution and the openness of its textual weave have invited additional dynamism through the process of constitutional interpretation by the courts. An enormous volume of scholarship has been devoted to the study of evolving constitutional doctrine (or "living constitutionalism") and the countervailing impulse for stability that is served by the judiciary's respect for its own precedent, for the "original intent" of the Constitution's drafters, and for the "plain meaning" of the Constitution itself.[4]

As this book has been dedicated to demonstrating, Congress likewise has a role to play in promoting constitutional change and stability. Congress constrains (or does not constrain) both the courts' independence to interpret the Constitution as they see fit and Congress's own interpretation of the Constitution in the context of resolving political questions about court oversight with reference to its own precedent. If we accept the inherent importance of stability and the capacity for change in a constitutional democracy, the dynamic equilibrium described here, in which Congress adheres to stable yet gradually evolving constitutional norms in its management of judicial independence and accountability, is intrinsically desirable.

The Value of Limited Governmental Power

Limited governmental power is a core value underlying a constitutional structure in which the departments of government are separated and interdependent. Separation of the government into legislative, executive, and judicial branches is calculated to avoid overconcentration of political power in a single place, while interdependence created by a system of checks and balances enables each branch to protect itself from encroachments on its powers by the others. Peter Shane thus derives two general constitutional norms from separation and interdependence: first, "[n]o branch of government should use its autonomous powers to usurp the core powers of a coordinate branch or to undermine a coordinate branch's capacity to exercise its core powers at all"; and second, "[n]o branch of government should seek to eliminate longstanding forms of interdependency between the branches."[5]

In expressing these norms in terms of what the branches *should* do, Shane implicitly recognizes that they do not necessarily reflect what the branches *must* do. Separated powers and checks and balances notwithstanding, it is clear that Congress possesses the means both to undermine the judiciary's power to say what the law is and to compromise the judiciary's capacity to hold Congress in check through the exercise of judicial review: Congress has the power to remove uncooperative judges via the impeachment process, disestablish unpopular courts, cut court budgets, gut court jurisdiction, and so on. The equilibrium preserved by specific institutional norms that regularize and constrain the exercise of congressional control over the courts thus furthers the goals of limited governmental power reflected in the broader constitutional norms that Shane articulates. Moreover, the Senate's increasingly aggressive posture in the appointments process diminishes the countervailing concern that Congress has gone too far and ceded so much independence to the courts as to eliminate its check on judicial power. In his study of constitutional "conventions" (a term borrowed from Great Britain), James Wilson does a nice job of cataloging the various ways in which the political branches' adherence to their own norms or conventions limits governmental power.

> Conventions prevent tyranny, constrain discretion, distribute power, enhance efficiency and accountability, strengthen separation of powers, and generate internal morality. The written text initially allocates many broad constitutional powers to different groups of political leaders, but the exercise of such powers is often not amenable to effective judicial review. Only conventions can control the implementation of many constitutional powers.[6]

The Value of an Independent Judiciary

The framers of the U.S. Constitution clearly contemplated the creation of an independent judiciary, as reflected in the text of Article III, James Madison's notes of the Constitutional Convention, and the Federalist Papers. When "we the people" commit ourselves to be governed by a constitution, we commit ourselves to the rule of law. And when the structure of that constitution delegates to a separate judicial branch the task of upholding the rule of law and keeping the political branches in check through the exercise of judicial review—as our federal and state constitutions do—it suggests the need for a judiciary that is independent of those other branches. Tenure and salary protections are thus merely the U.S. Constitution's chosen means to protect an independent judiciary, the necessity for which exists independently, inherent in our system of government. Shane therefore identifies judicial independence as a core constitutional value and requisite across federal and state governments, irrespective of how judges are selected, retained, or compensated.

It is not an exaggeration to say that a republican system of government, defined in the American tradition, depends upon the judicial capacity to enforce constitutional limits on legislative and
executive power. Independence sufficient to render judicial review
meaningful is a corollary requirement of republican constitutional
order.[7]

Tenure and salary protections notwithstanding, the delegates to
the U.S. Constitutional Convention unwittingly put the judiciary's
independence at risk (as discussed in chapter 1) by giving Congress
the discretionary power to establish inferior courts—or not. The
move was intended simply to postpone debate over whether to create
federal trial courts, thereby sidestepping the opposition of those who
feared that such courts would usurp the role played by state trial
courts. Giving Congress the power to create lower courts had nothing
to do with rendering the third branch of government more accountable to (and hence more dependent on) the first. But that was its practical effect, as demonstrated shortly thereafter by the 1802 repeal of
the Midnight Judges Act, which extinguished sixteen judicial offices
and ousted their unpopular occupants. When Congress's powers to
impeach, adjust Supreme Court jurisdiction, and appropriate funds
for the judiciary's budget and salary increases were combined with
other powers implicitly sanctioned by its overarching authority to
establish inferior courts (including the powers to control lower court
size, structure, jurisdiction, rule making and administration), it created the potential for a nearly total eclipse of the judiciary's independence from Congress.

Yet no such eclipse has occurred. The burden of this book has been
to demonstrate that the judiciary's independence has remained unob-
scured, in no small part because entrenched congressional respect for
judicial independence has counterbalanced cyclical calls to curb the
courts and has given rise to a state of dynamic equilibrium that the
judiciary has helped to preserve through its own tradition of self-
restraint. The net effect has been for institutional norms to preserve
core judicial independence values when constitutional structure alone
could not.

Dynamic Equilibrium and the Future of Courts-Congress Relations ∾

The independence norms described and defended in this chapter have been over two hundred years in the making. Every cycle of court-directed hostility since the founding of the United States has elicited hand-wringing from court defenders that judicial independence is at risk of being eaten whole by congressional carnivores. Yet recent cycles have passed with little more than a bit of nibbling. New reports of wolves in the hills are thus understandably greeted with a measure of skepticism. But the parable of the boy who cried wolf cuts both ways. On the one hand, it tells us that alarmists do the public a disservice; on the other hand, it tells us that alarmists are sometimes right.

Alarmists do no disservice, however, if the dire consequences they predict never materialize because the community is put on alert to a bona fide threat and takes preemptive action. Every cycle of court-directed hostility has featured serious and substantial congressional factions intent on curbing the courts in significant ways. It would be a mistake to assume that independence norms have been so deeply entrenched as to render either these episodic challenges inconsequential or the vigilant defense of those norms unnecessary to their preservation.

With respect to the current cycle of disaffection with the courts, there is no reason to believe that collapse of the dynamic equilibrium is imminent. The likelihood that Congress will, at any time soon, begin radically retaliating against courts that make outrageous decisions—by impeaching the errant judges, disestablishing the offending courts, doubling their size to alter their decision-making majority, or diminishing their budget—is still quite low.

Developments that have been generations in the making, however, threaten to destabilize the dynamic equilibrium and the independence norms that it has nurtured for over two centuries. Judicial independence is defensible only insofar as independent judges follow the law. The system immunizes judges from the electorate and their representatives, on the assumption that if judges are protected from political pressure, they will decide cases according to the facts as they find them and according to the law as they conclude it is written. If, in deciding cases, independent judges do not follow the law but merely satiate their own political appetites, then the justification for insulating them from the public and their elected representatives largely disappears.

Legal Realism, Postrealism, and Their Impact on Public Perception

In the bygone age of formalism, defending judicial independence was easy. The law was determinate, determinable, and there to be discovered and expounded by wise judges, as long as their independent judgment remained unpolluted by extraneous threats or other influences. The legal realism movement changed all that, with the insight that law is not the embodiment of eternal truth but a malleable, human invention. Jerome Frank made the point powerfully in 1930.

> Myth-making and fatherly lies must be abandoned—the Santa Claus story of complete legal certainty; the fairy tale of a pot of golden law which is already in existence and which the good lawyer can find, if only he is sufficiently diligent; the phantasy of an aesthetically satisfactory system and harmony, consistent and uniform, which will spring up when we find the magic wand of rationalizing principle. We must stop telling stork fibs about how a law is born and cease even hinting that perhaps there is still some truth in Peter Pan legends of a juristic happy hunting ground in a land of legal absolutes.[8]

The implication that this myth-busting exercise held for the judicial function was obvious: if law is not absolute, then judges have choices to make. In discussing how a judge makes those choices, Benjamin Cardozo opined that in cases where the law is unclear, the judge must assess "the comparative importance or value of the social interests that will be thereby promoted or impaired"; and that in making such value assessments, the judge "must get his knowledge just as the legislator gets it, from experience and study and reflection; in brief, from life itself." Cardozo concluded that the judge and the legislator each is "legislating within the limits of his competence,"

although the "limits for the judge are narrower" because "[h]e legis-
lates only between gaps. He fills the open spaces in the law. How far
he may go without traveling beyond the walls of the interstices cannot
be staked out for him upon a chart."[9]

Legal realists generally remained comfortable with this new reality,
because they assumed that the value choices judges made would typically mirror those of society. In 1925, Max Radin explained:

> Judges, we know, are people. I know a great many. Some were my
> schoolmates. . . . They eat the same foods, seem moved by the
> same emotions, and laugh at the same jokes. Apparently they are a
> good deal like ourselves. If, therefore, in a controversy in which we
> are engaged, we could rid ourselves of the personal interest in it,
> we might shrewdly guess that a great many judges would like to
> see the same person win who appeals to us.[10]

The critical legal studies (CLS) movement in the last quarter of the
twentieth century, however, exposed a more problematic side to legal
realism. For CLS proponents, judges are not necessarily "a good deal
like" the public they purport to serve. Rather, they are elites who go
to school with the likes of Max Radin, who laugh at jokes that people
of privilege find funny, and whose value choices are shared by fellow
white, male elites, not by society as a whole. Thus, they perpetuate a
way of thinking about the law that is calculated, consciously or not, to
preserve the political domination of the elites whose values they share.

During this same period, political scientists added focus to the
lessons of legal realism, with studies revealing that among the various
factors that influence judicial decision making, the judge's personal
political views or attitudes were the most important.[11] It was the academic intelligentsia that led the journey from formalism and "legal
absolutes," through legal realism and its benign discovery of non-law-
related influences on judicial decision making, to a darker, postrealist
world in which judicial elites subjugate the underclass or disregard the
law and impose their private political preferences. But the general
public has not been immune to these developments. It has been steeping in this emerging culture of realism and postrealism long enough
to lead one legal theorist to declare that "we are all legal realists
now."[12]

If so, the implications for judicial independence are clear and potentially dire. Insofar as judges abuse their independence by implementing their political or class agendas instead of adhering to the law, it would seem that the time has come to rethink, in a fundamental way, the need for their independence. Alan Tarr points to the public perception that "judicial decisions are not regularly determined based on their legal merits" as evidence that "the American public has learned—perhaps all too well—the lessons of legal realism." Tarr argues that such a perception "weakens considerably the rule-of-law arguments for judicial independence."[13] The more that the public and their representatives think that judges generally—not just a particular judge or panel of judges in isolated cases—follow their political leanings instead of the law, the more likely it becomes that long-established independence norms will be challenged with increasing intensity and will ultimately yield to calls for greater judicial accountability to Congress.

A report of the American Bar Association issued in 2003 identifies the "emergence of a skeptical and conflicted public" as a recent trend contributing to politicization of the courts. The report points to a public opinion poll conducted in 2001 in which 76 percent of respondents thought that the word "political" described judges well or very well—which corroborates the view that the public has internalized some postrealist thinking. At the same time, 79 percent thought that judges were also "dedicated to facts and law," and 58 percent thought judges "make decisions based more on facts and law" than "on politics and pressure from special interests."[14] Seventy-seven percent expressed some or a great deal of confidence in their judges, 76 percent responded that the term "fair" described judges well or very well, and 63 percent said the same of the term "impartial."[15]

More recent data suggests that the public has become increasingly critical of the courts. An Associated Press poll conducted in April 2005 found that 43 percent thought that "judges rely mostly on personal feelings and political views," while just over half thought that "judges make decisions mostly on their interpretation of the law."[16] Five months later, a poll conducted for the *A.B.A. Journal* found that 56 percent agreed with the statement that "judicial activisim . . . seems to have reached a crisis" because "judges routinely overrule the will of the people, invent new rights, and ignore traditional morality." In that same poll, 56 percent believed that court opinions should be in line with voters' values and judges who repeatedly ignore those values should be impeached, while 46 percent believed that judges were "arrogant, out of control, and unaccountable," as compared to only 38 percent who disagreed.[17] Against that backdrop, the recent round of attacks on "judicial activism" and "legislating from the bench" may signify more than just another cycle of court-directed animus.

The Postrealist Impact on Judicial Appointments

The war between the Senate, the president, and the political parties for control of the power to appoint Supreme Court justices has been waged for more than two hundred years. Battles of the past century have shifted fronts to focus more on the political acceptability of the nominee's future decision making. More recently, battles have been fought on the assumption that a judge's political philosophy exerts an impact on how she will decide cases that is as, if not more, important than the law itself. The ascendancy of that postrealist assumption at a time when the Senate is closely divided and sharply polarized has had the unprecedented effect of sucking the lower courts into the vortex of the political branch struggle for control of the appointments process as never before. Moreover, such partisan contests fuel the argument of those who complain that life tenure merely enables presidents and senators to entrench their political preferences in the judicial branch, the judges of which will dictate the course of American law long after those who appointed them have gone.[18]

The future implications of the current appointments struggle remain uncertain. There is every reason to believe that Supreme Court confirmation proceedings will remain highly politicized affairs focused on the political acceptability of nominees' future decision making. As argued in chapter 4, this is not necessarily a bad thing, to the extent that its focus on the future decision making of judicial nominees enables the Senate to counterbalance the judiciary's long-term independence gains in other areas of court governance with a measure of prospective accountability in the appointments process.

With respect to the lower courts, there is no obvious end in sight to the recent upsurge of political interest in the appointment of district and circuit court judges. Again, one may argue that this is for the better: district and circuit judges play too important a role in American government to be selected on the basis of backroom deals dominated by considerations of political patronage and senatorial courtesy, and it is about time that the president and Senate take judicial appointments and the political philosophies of judicial decision makers seriously. Yet the brinksmanship of appointments politics has escalated so rapidly as to become potentially destabilizing.

As detailed in chapter 4, the controversial lower court nominee—a virtual oxymoron just a generation ago—has become commonplace, as each of the major political parties has forsworn its rival's competing vision of the judicial role and threatened to impose its will by confirming or defeating the divisive nominee of the day. Independence norms have never played a significant role in the judicial appointments process, as argued in chapter 4. However, other norms governing the manner in which judicial appointments are made have regularized selection procedures, delineated permissible practices, and settled expectations for senators, presidents, and nominees alike. Those processes have recently been disrupted by political actors whose determination to confirm or reject specific nominees for ideological or partisan reasons has overridden their commitment to abide by established rules and conventions, thereby jeopardizing the stability of the appointments process.

On the one hand, it is possible that after a brief period of turmoil, the lower court appointments process will be supplanted by other political priorities and return to quiet obscurity. The process could be restabilized by a future president who—like Clinton, Carter, Johnson, or Eisenhower—has no particular interest in spending scarce political capital to reshape the ideological face of the lower courts in his image. President Clinton, for example, achieved bipartisan consensus on the appointment of two Supreme Court justices in the aftermath of the Bork and Thomas imbroglios, by negotiating agreements with Republican and Democratic Senate leaders before nominations were made. If a future president viewed lower court appointments battles as an unwelcome distraction and wanted to normalize the process, he or she might well achieve positive results through resort to similar tactics. In that vein, President George W. Bush succeeded in breaking an appointments deadlock in the waning months of his first term by negotiating a deal with Senate Democrats in which he agreed not to make additional recess appointments in exchange for Democrats' assurance that they would not block the confirmation of twenty-five noncontroversial nominations then pending.[19]

On the other hand, the postrealist views animating political interest in judicial appointments have been generations in the making and show no signs of abating. President Bush's controversial nomination of conservative judge Samuel Alito to the Supreme Court (at the time this book went to press) signified the president's renewed willingness to go to war with Senate Democrats to secure the appointment of a judge whose ideological bent mirrored that of his conservative base. The integrity of the appointments process has been the first victim of an ends-justifies-means strategy recently employed by presidents and senators, but it may not be the last. If the president and Senate are prepared to jettison long-respected conventions in the service of appointing judges who will decide cases to their liking, they may also be willing to rethink the independence norms that have long obstructed their control of judges and the judiciary in other areas of court governance.

The Postrealist Impact on Jurisdiction Reform

One place where independence norms would appear to be undergoing recent reevaluation is in the area of federal court jurisdiction. After Congress withdrew the Supreme Court's jurisdiction to hear McCardle's appeal in the immediate aftermath of the Civil War, efforts to deprive federal courts of subject-matter jurisdiction over particular kinds of cases, as a means to forestall unpopular decisions, have (with the heavily qualified exception of the Norris-LaGuardia Act) been almost universally unsuccessful. In the latest cycle of anti-court sentiment, however, Congress has traded the blunt instrument of court stripping for more precise surgical tools that have succeeded in cutting away at judicial decision-making discretion, despite objections that they curb the courts in similar ways:

> In the Illegal Immigration Reform and Immigrant Responsibility Act of 1996 (IIRIRA), Congress restricted judicial review of administrative actions relating to immigrants.[20]

In the Prison Litigation Reform Act of 1996 (PLRA), Congress imposed significant limits on prisoner litigation of civil claims in the federal courts.[21]

In the Antiterrorism and Effective Death Penalty Act (AEDPA) of 1996, Congress imposed stringent limits on habeas actions filed by state prisoners in federal courts.[22]

With respect to these enactments, postrealist thinking clearly drove proponents of the legislation to look for ways to limit the decision-making independence of federal judges. As to the IIRIRA, the need for the legislation was explained in terms of "too much legislating from the bench in which advocates for immigrants go around shopping for a judge and finding some pretext to overturn the will of Congress."[23] The PLRA was defended as necessary to "restrain liberal federal judges who see violations of constitutional rights in every prisoner complaint."[24] And the AEDPA was designed, in the words of Senate sponsor Orrin Hatch, to thwart "loony judges in the Federal courts who basically will grant a habeas corpus petition for any reason at all."[25]

Given the chronic failure of jurisdiction-stripping legislation to gain traction in Congress, these recent enactments would seem to signal a dramatic departure from established independence norms. But the situation is more complicated than that. First, recent enactments limit jurisdiction in far subtler ways than the ill-fated, ham-handed jurisdiction-stripping proposals that preceded them, suggesting that they may have flown "under the radar" of established independence norms. Second, although these legislative initiatives do appear to constrain the decision making of liberal-leaning lower courts, commentators have noted that they simultaneously reinforce and codify the direction taken by the more conservative Supreme Court and, to that extent, do not curb the Court as much as they support it.[26] Third, with respect to the lower courts, it bears emphasis that the Judicial Conference—which represents the inferior courts alone and not the Supreme Court—opposed none of these enactments and, in the case of the AEDPA, assisted in its development. Perhaps the conference's silence, if not complicity, is attributable to the influence of Chief Justice Rehnquist, who headed both the Supreme Court and the Judicial Conference; or perhaps its inclination to resist encroachments on its decision-making autonomy was offset by a desire to diminish the judiciary's workload. In recent years, the judiciary has rushed to the aid of its own independence when Congress has threatened to impeach errant judges, delay cost of living adjustments, include the judiciary in government shutdowns amid budget battles with the president, and delay the confirmation of needed judges. And it has not hesitated to oppose jurisdiction reform proposals that it has regarded as contrary to the judiciary's institutional best interests. Its failure to object here thus sent a powerful message to Congress: the judiciary did not regard these jurisdiction-curbing proposals as a threat to its autonomy—long-standing independence norms to the contrary notwithstanding.

In short, the congressional Visigoths did not storm the gates of a theretofore impregnable judicial castle and plunder its independence; rather, the judiciary lowered the drawbridge and invited Congress into the parlor. Now that they are within the walls, whether the Visigoths will take advantage and begin ransacking or leave quietly, content with the memory of a lovely evening shared, remains to be seen. The signs, however, are not encouraging. In 2004, the House of Representatives passed bills stripping the federal courts of jurisdiction to hear cases relating to the Defense of Marriage Act and the Pledge of Allegiance, and Senate Judiciary Committee chair Orrin Hatch expressed his intention to support the passage of those bills in the Senate, describing them as "part of a piecemeal solution . . . to solve what social conservatives have long been viewing as the problem of activist judges, particularly on the federal bench."[27] And in 2005, legislation imposing significant new curbs on federal court authority to hear state habeas actions passed the Senate.

The Postrealist Impact on Criminal Sentencing

Beginning in the 1980s, criminal sentencing came under increased criticism amid political branch wars against crime and drugs. The perceived problem was multifaceted. First, there was bipartisan concern that criminal defendants were receiving radically disparate sentences for comparable crimes: liberals worried about some defendants being sentenced too harshly, and conservatives worried about other defendants not being sentenced harshly enough.[28] Second, there was political interest in getting tough on crime in general and on drug crime in particular.[29] Again, the concern was bipartisan, but on this point, the issue was of primary consequence to conservatives, with liberals wishing to avoid being left behind. As district judge Stanley Sporkin described it at a law school conference, "[t]he conservatives thought the so-called 'activist' judges were too soft on crime and the liberals did not want to be outgunned in the war on crime."[30] Clearly on the minds of conservatives, then, was the postrealist concern that unless prevented from doing so, liberal federal judges would manipulate their sentencing discretion to mollycoddle criminals.

To address these problems, Congress established a framework for the creation of sentencing guidelines (to cabin judicial discretion) and proliferated mandatory minimum sentences for specified crimes (to thwart leniency)—despite objections from many federal judges that they needed sentencing discretion to administer justice fairly.[31] Clearly enough, these actions diminished the decision-making independence of federal judges, but a qualification is in order. Congress has always had a role to play in controlling judicial sentencing discretion, by establishing maximum sentences for specified crimes, permissible sentence ranges, and, occasionally, mandatory minimums.[32] Although one can quarrel with whether unduly rigid sentencing guidelines and mandatory minimum sentences micromanage judges in ways detrimental to the administration of justice, it is hard to claim that they run afoul of some long-standing independence norm against congressional interference with judicial sentencing discretion. Thus, while some have argued that mandatory minimum sentences threaten the judiciary's independence in fundamental ways,[33] judges have tended not to play the judicial independence card directly, objecting instead on the grounds that unduly rigid limits on their discretion compromises the fairness of the sentencing function.[34]

That much said, more recent developments in the sentencing arena have combined with those relating to judicial appointments and jurisdiction reform to create an atmosphere in which Congress appears increasingly doubtful whether judges and the judiciary can be trusted to follow the law without greater political branch control of their decision making. In 2002, Minnesota district judge (and Reagan appointee) James Rosenbaum testified before the House Judiciary

Committee in opposition to sentencing guidelines that he regarded as unduly restrictive, based in part on his own experience as a sentencing judge. In response to Rosenbaum's testimony, Congress launched an investigation into Judge Rosenbaum's sentencing practices, sought to subpoena his files, issued a twenty-two-page report accusing him of offering misleading testimony, and swiftly enacted legislation further limiting the authority of judges to depart from the sentencing guidelines and requiring that future departures be reported to Congress.[35]

This new legislation, which Representative Tom Feeney added as an amendment to an essentially unrelated (but enormously popular) piece of legislation, was attacked by Chief Justice Rehnquist as an "unwarranted and ill-considered effort to intimidate individual judges in the performance of their judicial duties" that threatened the judiciary's independence.[36] Feeney was unfazed. "Some judges simply refuse to follow the law," he declared. He cited Rosenbaum as an example, before continuing:

> Such extreme conduct may require action beyond the modest and long overdue reforms made by the Feeney amendment, but they are an important start to the affirmation of a simple precept— judges should follow, not make the laws. However, if insisting on that precept "intimidates" federal judges, then perhaps that is a good thing.[37]

Federal judges responded with anger, defiance, and action. "They can have their blacklists," declared one district judge, "[b]ut we have life tenure."[38] Said another, "If Congress wants to make a deck of cards for the judges like they did for the bad guys in Iraq, make me the ace of spades."[39] A third resigned.[40] A fourth defied the statute's reporting requirement by placing all relevant court documents under seal.[41] A fifth declared the law unconstitutional on the grounds of separation of powers, explaining,

> For too long, the judicial branch has remained silent in the face of repeated encroachments by the other two branches; like frogs in a simmering pot, we adjust to the new temperature and complain among ourselves that it seems a tad warm, but then accept the new order of things to repeat the process anew after the next encroachment.[42]

A sixth was resigned that "Congress and the Attorney General have instituted policies designed to intimidate and threaten judges into refusing to depart downward" and that "those policies are working."[43]

More recently, the Supreme Court invalidated mandatory application of the sentencing guidelines altogether, effectively gutting the Feeney amendment.[44] Feeney characterized the decision as "an egregious overreach into Congress' constitutional power," adding that "[i]f the courts throw out the sentencing wholesale, we will have a really big battle"[45]—foreshadowing another acrimonious round of finger-pointing and belly-bumping.

Postrealism and the Political Awakening of Evangelical Conservatives

In the latest cycle of court-directed hostility, Congress has reserved its most virulent criticism for judicial decisions that protect behavior which conservative Christians regard as sinful, or impede behavior that conservative Christians deem spiritually redemptive—for example, cases that uphold the right to abortion; authorize gay marriage; ban prayer in public schools; enjoin public displays of the Ten Commandments; and prohibit schools from requiring students to pledge their allegiance to "one nation, under God." This is no coincidence: Political mobilization of Christian conservatives in the last quarter of the twentieth century has clearly contributed to postrealist erosion of congressional confidence in judicial independence and the rule of law.

For this new breed of Christian conservative, natural law trumps all, and judges who are serious about the rule of law should interpret and apply constitutional, statutory, and common law in a manner consistent with the higher teachings of God. President George W. Bush appealed directly to such sentiments with the observation that "We need common sense judges who understand that our rights are derived from God." If judges with "common sense" recognize that all rights are "derived from God," then judges who protect rights that God does not approve, or who fail to protect rights that God does approve, presumably lack common sense, and have—in the words of the Traditional Values Coalition—"hijacked America's courts to impose an extremist anti-God agenda on America."[46] Accordingly, conservative Christian organizations have mobilized to support President Bush's nominees and thwart Democratic opposition.

Impressing religious fervor into the service of political movements is not a modern development. James Morone chronicles "the politics of sin in American history" across chapters on the Puritans, Abolition, Prohibition, and the "social gospel" of the New Deal and the Sixties.[47] Against this backdrop, Morone is not overly troubled by the recent political reawakening of the evangelical right in which "the Puritans roar again":

> Whatever lies ahead, the past offers one final lesson. When the established faiths—political, social, religious—begin to grow stale, there is always another hot American revival in the wings.[48]

American political, social, and religious life may well be as resilient as Morone posits, but it remains to be seen whether the rule of law is comparably durable. If conservative Christian efforts to control the courts are ultimately overtaken by a movement to restore respect for judicial independence and the rule of law, there is room for optimism. If, however, the political influence of Christian conservatives persists, or gives way to a new school of thought equally committed to bludgeoning the courts into submission to its views of the law, the postrealist free-fall will continue to accelerate.

The sad and peculiar case of Theresa Schiavo tested the limits of the evangelical right's political influence in Congress, and brought the uncertain future of judicial independence and the rule of law into bold relief. Years after an incident in which Ms. Schiavo collapsed, leaving her in what most doctors called "a persistent vegetative state," Ms. Schiavo's husband asked a Florida state court for permission to withdraw her feeding tube. After additional years of litigation the court agreed, over the objection of Ms. Schiavo's parents.[49] Angry Christian conservatives lobbied the Republican-controlled Congress to pass emergency legislation giving the federal courts the authority to hear the Schiavo case anew. Congress quickly obliged, and for the first time in his presidency, President George W. Bush cut a vacation short and raced back to Washington to sign the legislation.

The federal courts came to the same conclusion as their state counterparts, the feeding tube was not reinserted, and Ms. Schiavo passed away shortly thereafter. Legislation sponsors were furious: Senator Rick Santorum called the courts' action "unconscionable."[50] "That kind of judge needs to be worried about what kind of role Congress will play in his future," warned Representative Steve King.[51] The courts had "thumbed their nose at Congress and the president," fumed House Majority Leader Tom DeLay, adding that "the time will come for the men responsible for this to answer for their behavior."[52] Christian conservative leaders echoed those sentiments, characterizing the courts' decisions as "a gross abuse of judicial power," and "very dramatic proof of what we are saying: that the judiciary is out of control," adding that the episode represented "the opening shot in a Supreme Court nomination battle that we expect sooner rather than later."[53]

In short, Congress and the evangelical conservatives whose concerns it shared, disapproved of a state court's decision in a right-to-die case, created federal court jurisdiction for the explicit purpose of changing the case's outcome by handing it to a new judge, and reacted with threats and outrage when the new judge did not reach the desired result. One possible conclusion to draw from this episode is that politically energized Christian conservatives have gained the upper hand and are leading Congress to abandon the customary independence it has traditionally afforded the courts. Consistent with that possibility, conservative Republican legislators have used Schiavo as the rallying cry for imposing new controls on renegade courts: "We set up the courts. We can unset the courts. We have the power of the purse," declared DeLay, who called for a congressional investigation into judicial activism in the Schiavo case and beyond;[54] "When their budget starts to dry up, we'll get their attention," added King.[55] As a means to hold judges more accountable, House Judiciary Committee Chair James Sensenbrenner proposed to establish an office of inspector general for the federal judiciary.[56] A former aide to moderate Republican senator John McCain viewed the congressional response to Schiavo as an ominous development, noting that the Republican Party's focus "used to be on the rule of law," but "[a]ll that's been tossed out the window because of the demands of the religious right."[57]

There is, however, another possibility: Schiavo may simply be an aberration in which the constraints of time led Congress to take precipitous and ill-advised action—a mistake it may be loath to repeat. Eighty-two percent of Americans polled disapproved of congressional intervention in the Schiavo matter, and a majority agreed with the decision of the federal courts. Conservative scholar Douglas Kmiec expressed confidence that "as greater distance is put between Terri Schiavo's death and today, cooler heads will prevail," adding that otherwise "the Republican Party will be doing itself serious long-term damage."[58] Indeed, moderate Republicans acknowledged that those who criticize judges for legislating from the bench might likewise question legislators for adjudicating from the congressional floor,[59] and both President Bush and Vice President Richard Cheney expressed their support for an independent judiciary and took pains to distance themselves from the post-Schiavo calls of congressional conservatives to curb the courts. Ironically, then, an alternative lesson of the Schiavo affair could ultimately be that Congress micromanages judicial decision making at its political peril (at least in the context of private family matters), which may ultimately do more to restore than disrupt the imperiled dynamic equilibrium.

To no small extent, the post-Schiavo hullabaloo was a prequel to a much noisier row anticipated when the next in a series of vacancies occurred on the Supreme Court (as of 2005, only one member of the Court was under 65 years old). Of particular interest was whether the political pull of the evangelical right would be sufficient to dissuade the president and Senate Republicans from relenting to Senate Democrats over the future of the filibuster in confirmation debates. Republican Senate Majority Leader Bill Frist went out of his way to align himself with Christian conservatives in a special appearance at a massive, televised event headlined "Justice Sunday: Stopping the Filibuster Against People of Faith," where he berated Democrats for exploiting the filibuster and urged its abolition in confirmation proceedings.[60] Democratic Senate Minority Leader Harry Reid threatened to obstruct Senate operations at every turn if Frist and his fellow Republicans did not back down.[61] The issue came to a head in May 2005, in the context of Senate floor votes on five controversial circuit court nominations that Democrats opposed. A bipartisan group of Senate moderates ultimately brokered a temporary truce, wherein the

Democrats agreed not to filibuster the confirmation of three pending nominees in exchange for Republican assurances that the Democrats would not be barred from blocking the remaining two.

The truce merely postponed a final resolution of the filibuster's fate, but it did signal a measure of institutional reluctance to sacrifice settled practices and procedures in the service of short-term political gain. The evangelical right, however, remains an important force with which to reckon. By recasting the controversial questions judges resolve as moral absolutes that Congress must defend against judicial usurpation, Christian conservatives have rigidified the already polarized political environment on Capitol Hill and complicated the task of those intent on achieving a more enduring compromise that could perpetuate equilibrium.

These recent trends in which Congress has begun to assert greater control over judicial decision making by means of manipulating judicial appointments, subject-matter jurisdiction, and criminal sentencing—while an energized Christian right has flexed its political muscle in an effort to persuade Congress to do even more—contribute collectively to the suspicion that we may be amid more than just another cycle of antipathy toward the courts. Rather, we may be in the early stages of a postrealist movement that is giving rise to a sustained and more deeply skeptical view of the courts and of the appropriate limits of their independence from Congress.

The Contribution of the Federal Courts to the Uncertain Future of the Dynamic Equilibrium

Thus far, the discussion of recent events contributing to the potential for future destabilization of the dynamic equilibrium has focused on the extent to which Congress has internalized postrealist attitudes and reoriented its oversight—of court appointments, jurisdiction, and decision making (in criminal sentencing)—to place greater emphasis on judicial accountability to the political branches. But judges and the judiciary have also played a part in disrupting the delicate balance in the relationship between courts and Congress.

Beginning with the New Deal, when the Supreme Court started looking far less skeptically at governmental interference with economic relationships and far more skeptically at governmental interference with civil and political rights, political liberals and moderates joined the ranks of the judiciary's staunchest allies. As long as the rights they held dear received continued Supreme Court protection against encroachments from the state (and occasionally federal) governments, the political left and center could be counted on to defend an independent judiciary from threats to control judicial decision making. Meanwhile, the political right, frustrated by generations of adverse decisions on subjects ranging from desegregation and criminal procedure to school prayer and abortion, became a breeding ground for the postrealist suspicion that liberal judges were disregarding the law and "legislating from the bench."

At the end of the twentieth century, however, the Rehnquist Court turned the tables. A series of decisions curtailed Congress's power (under the commerce clause) to regulate such issues as handguns in school zones and violence against women, diminished Congress's authority to require state compliance with federal antidiscrimination laws, and resolved the 2000 presidential election in favor of George W. Bush. Prominent liberal critics decried the Court's "activist" decision making and began calling for greater political controls on the Court. If the Court under the leadership of Chief Justice John Roberts persists in alienating the political left, it is possible that the roles will simply reverse and that the political right will become the new guardian of an independent judiciary and of the rule of law. If so, conservatives are likely to be mercenary guardians, jaundiced by a generation of suspicion that liberal judges abused their independence by ignoring the law and implementing their own political predilections. Meanwhile, for liberals who had long been true believers in an independent judiciary, the Supreme Court's recent decisions have rocked their faith and threatened to make postrealists of the judiciary's most stalwart defenders.

Ironically, one of the most immediate threats to the public's continued faith in the courts may come from the Supreme Court itself, in the form of dissenting opinions issued by Associate Justice Antonin Scalia that appear calculated to debunk the notion that the Supreme Court is committed to the rule of law. Scalia's dissents are notoriously blunt and colorful, which ensures that they are widely quoted in daily papers and on the evening news. He is savagely disparaging of his colleagues' views—as "nothing short of ludicrous," "beyond absurd," "nothing short of preposterous," and "ridiculous"—and argues that they "cannot be taken seriously" and do not "pass the most gullible scrutiny."[62]

Commentators disagree as to whether such name-calling is refreshing and iconoclastic or uncivil and boorish—an issue of less relevance here than one raised by a discrete subset of Justice Scalia's dissents that implicitly challenges the legitimacy of the Court's decisions. Among the accusations Scalia has leveled at one or another of the majority's opinions is that it follows the "homosexual agenda,"[63] casts the Court in the role of "Robin Hood,"[64] "vandalizes . . . our people's traditions,"[65] has "no foundation in American law and barely pretends to,"[66] and is grounded in "nothing but philosophical predilection and moral intuition."[67] The message seems clear enough: according to Scalia, the Court is behaving like vandals and thieves, implementing its preferred political agendas and predilections, and disregarding the law and barely pretending to do otherwise.

Given that Justice Scalia's colleagues have sworn to uphold the Constitution and laws of the United States, one might suppose that they would feel a bit put out by one of their brethren accusing them of violating their oaths of office on a regular basis. But apparently this is not so. "[T]he Court is a model of civility," Justice Clarence Thomas remarked in 1998, adding, "I have yet to hear the first unkind words exchanged among my colleagues."[68] Clearly, words in writing do not count. At around the same time, Justice Ruth Ginsburg, when asked about Justice Scalia's latest attack on a majority opinion written by Justice Stephen Breyer, noted that Breyer "is not easily offended and enjoys [Scalia's] sparkling wit, as I do."[69]

One suspects that Justice Scalia's colleagues know him well enough off the bench not to take his dyspeptic screeds literally or personally. But as one commentator has observed of Scalia's diatribes, "[e]ven though it appears the justices are professionals willing to take sharp criticism in stride, a fundamental and unresolved question is with what stride laypersons may view such attacks."[70] In other words, the public is being fed a steady diet of messages, from a member of the Court, that judges abuse their independence by imposing their political will rather than interpreting the law—messages that the public may begin to take seriously, even if the remainder of the Court does not. To the extent that people do take such postrealist messages seriously, it further weakens arguments for their elected representatives to preserve long-standing independence norms in Congress.

For its part, the Judicial Conference of the United States seems strangely oblivious to developments that have rendered the judiciary's continued independence from Congress increasingly precarious. As described in chapter 5, federal judges have recently invalidated legislation enacted over their opposition as a Judicial Conference. In other instances, the conference has raised constitutional objections to pending legislation, creating the distinct impression that its judges stand ready to employ their judicial power to implement the conference's lobbying agenda. Such developments can only fuel mounting suspicions that judges manipulate the law to implement their political agendas. Moreover, employing judicial power to limit legislative power as a means for the judiciary to achieve its legislative goals seems calculated to anger a Congress that could easily adopt a reciprocal strategy of employing its legislative and other powers to curb judicial power. Independence norms have long deflected the efforts of congressional factions to implement such a reciprocal strategy, but now is hardly an auspicious time for the judiciary to test the continuing strength of those norms, if it is desirous of conserving its independence gains and preserving the dynamic equilibrium.

I do not mean to imply, as others have recommended, that judges should exercise greater decision-making restraint to diminish congressional anger and protect their independence (although the Judicial Conference would be well advised to reconsider its current lobbying strategy). As described in chapter 5, the courts appear to have employed such an approach from time to time, but the success of that strategy has depended on such restraint appeasing the congressional faction intent on controlling the courts, which is unlikely to work under the present circumstances. Today, a restrained judicial response to a problematic state statutory restriction on, for example, homosexual rights will delight conservatives and enrage liberals, while a restrained judicial response to a problematic exercise of congressional power to implement the Fourteenth Amendment at the expense of the states and for the benefit of some disadvantaged group will please liberals and infuriate conservatives. Postrealist anger animates conservative and liberal camps alike within today's closely divided Congress, and "restraint" is all in the eye of the beholder. Thus, the prospect that deferential decision making could defuse the latest cycle of court-directed hostility seems remote.

Revisiting the Role of Law in Judicial Decision Making

Judicial independence is indeed "at a crossroads," as Professors Stephen Burbank and Barry Friedman have written. This chapter has defended the dynamic equilibrium as a means to protect the value of an independent judiciary but not as an end in itself. Rather, judicial independence is an instrumental value intended to preserve the rule of law. If, as postrealists insist, independent judges ignore the rule of law and implement their own policy predilections, judicial independence loses its raison d'être and simply liberates unelected judicial elites to trump the majority's political preferences with their own. In a postrealist world, then, judicial independence is worse than an empty slogan—it is toxic to core values in a representative democracy.

Despite the apocalyptic tone of the foregoing paragraph, the legal community as a whole has not taken postrealist claims all that seriously. Judges begin their legal careers with three years of acculturation in law school, where they are trained to "think like lawyers"—to divine the law from judicial decisions, statutes, administrative rules, and the policies that underlie them; to capitalize on the law's indeterminacy for the benefit of clients, by learning to argue both sides of disputable legal questions; and to defend their arguments with reference to the law, not to their feelings or personal beliefs. In that process, students become well aware that the language of the law is inherently imprecise and that liberal and conservative judges will clarify those imprecisions in different and often predictable ways. Many—perhaps most—students accept that the law's tent is big enough to accommodate competing interpretations. Some do not and challenge what they regard as politically motivated deviations from the "right" result. Even then, however, the rule of law values that law school inculcates are reinforced by criticism marginalizing judicial decisions that can only be defended in extralegal terms.

After graduation, many of the best students begin their legal careers with judicial clerkships, where they are expected to cull applicable law from the briefs of the parties and independent research, to the end of drafting opinions for judges whose commitment to resolving disputes with reference to applicable law is simply a given. The legal reasoning and writing skills acquired in these judicial apprenticeships are highly prized by lawyers in the public and private sectors, who hire former judicial clerks as litigators. In their position as litigators, they become adept at assessing when the facts and law are so clear that settlement is advisable or summary judgment is likely, when ambiguities in the law or its application can be exploited on a client's behalf, and how a given judge is likely to resolve those ambiguities given her past decisions and political philosophy. Judicial nominees are typically drawn from this pool of experienced litigators, who have been immersed in the legal culture for decades, who tell the Senate Judiciary Committee—under oath—that they will follow the law, and who swear on a Bible to uphold the Constitution and laws of the United States. The notion that they leave all of that behind the moment they don their robes— that they then promptly begin to satiate their political appetites with- out regard to their views of applicable law—strikes most judges and lawyers as too preposterous to be taken seriously.

It may, however, be dangerous for the legal profession to persist in what Judge Patricia Wald has characterized as a "ho-hum" reaction to postrealist assertions that the law does not matter to judges. The dom- inant school of thought within the political science world posits that judges decide cases based primarily on their political attitudes and demonstrates quite convincingly that in the Supreme Court, at least, the influence of a justice's political philosophy on her judicial deci- sion making is profound. That view is echoed by shrill conservatives (including Justice Scalia) and liberals, who routinely condemn as ille- gitimate or "activist" the controversial judicial decisions they disfavor, even as they quietly praise as principled applications of the law the decisions they like. Over time, it is reasonable to anticipate that these postrealist critiques of judicial decision making will be internalized by the public and ultimately acted on by their elected representatives, to the detriment of the judiciary's independence, unless a competing vision of the relationship between law and politics emerges.

As noted earlier, compared to political scientists, most judges and lawyers possess a very different understanding of the way law works, born of experience in the classroom, the office, and the courtroom. Their understanding is anecdotal but pervasive in scope, and it cumulatively yields a powerful narrative that is in tension with the conclusions many political scientists draw from attitudinal studies.[71] Political scientists can rightly accuse judges and lawyers of paying too little attention to the implications of data generated by such studies, but lawyers and judges can just as rightly claim that many political scientists give short shrift to the legal community's narratives when evaluating the nature of the relationship between politics, law, and judicial decision making.[72]

The time has come to revisit the nature and relevance of law in a more sustained way. The stakes are high. If we ultimately conclude that judges employ law as a shill to conceal nakedly political decision making of a sort best reserved for Congress or the people, then insulating such decision making from the influence of Congress or the people becomes largely indefensible, except to the limited extent necessary to promote efficient operation of the courts. If, however, we conclude that judges continue to play an important role in preserving the rule of law, then judicial independence retains its status as a vital instrumental value, and the constitutional norms that have protected the judiciary's independence for over two centuries deserve continuing support.

I am, of course, not indifferent to the outcome of this exercise. As a current law professor and a former law student, judicial clerk, litigator, House Judiciary Committee staffer, and judicial branch "lobbyist," my biases are on my résumé, if not on my sleeve. But those of us whose experiences lead us to believe that independent judges typically do try to follow the law can no longer expect others to accept that conclusion as an article of faith when it is challenged by a significant segment of a sister discipline and by the intuitions of a growing percentage of the American public, who will ultimately have a lot to say about whether judicial independence stays or goes. Rather, we must commit ourselves to reexamining the nature of law and its continuing relevance to judicial decision making, to the end of supplementing, qualifying, and, in some instances, contradicting the postrealist conception of judicial decision making.

In such an undertaking, there is considerable room for lawyers and political scientists to work cooperatively. After all, political scientists who study the courts are less concerned with whether judges should follow the law than with whether they do follow the law (or something else); the aim of these scholars is to understand how judicial decision making works. Indeed, such political scientists as Cornell Clayton, Howard Gillman, and Keith Wittington have already gone a long way toward integrating the law and other institutional influences into a more nuanced and encompassing theory of judicial decision making. Lawyers, judges, and law professors have a meaningful contribution to make to such efforts, by exploring and explaining the extent to which the law and its interpretation can be influenced by political values without losing its essential character as law. The time to make that contribution is now.

Notes ∾

INTRODUCTION

1. Joan Biskupic, *Bork, Uncorked: The Judge Holds Supreme Court in Contempt,* WASHINGTON POST, Mar. 16, 1997, at C01.

2. Vincent Bugliosi, *None Dare Call It Treason,* THE NATION, Feb. 5, 2001, *available at* http://www.thenation.com/doc.mhtml?i=20010205&s=bugliosi.

3. Ralph Z. Hallow, *Republicans out to Impeach "Activist" Jurists,* WASHINGTON TIMES, Mar. 12, 1997, at A1.

4. Sean Hannity & Alan Colmes, *Hannity & Colmes* (Fox News television broadcast, July 9, 2003).

5. *Oregon Moves to Impeach Justices; Democrats Seek a Query Into High Court's Recount Ruling,* WASHINGTON POST, July 24, 2001, at A07.

6. Stephan Dinan, *DeLay Threatens to Curb Courts' Jurisdiction; Vents Ire Over Pledge of Allegiance,* WASHINGTON TIMES, Mar. 6, 2003, at A04. These developments are discussed further in chapter 6.

7. Megan Garvey, *The Recall Campaign; 9th Circuit Fires Up Conservatives Again; the Ruling on the Recall Election May Provide More Ammunition for Republican Efforts in Congress to Split Up the Appeals Court,* LOS ANGELES TIMES, Sept. 17, 2003, at A22.

8. Stephen Dinan, *House Targets Judicial 'Errors' with a New Strategy; Votes to Stop Enforcement of Rulings on Pledge, Posting,* WASHINGTON TIMES, July 29, 2003, at 1.

9. Todd Gillman, *GOP Group Plans to Turn Up Scrutiny on Federal Judges,* DALLAS MORNING NEWS, July 27, 2003.

10. Larry D. Kramer, *The Supreme Court v. Balance of Powers,* NEW YORK TIMES, Mar. 3, 2001, at A13.

11. LARRY D. KRAMER, THE PEOPLE THEMSELVES: POPULAR CONSTITUTIONALISM AND JUDICIAL REVIEW (2004).

12. Larry D. Kramer, *The Arrogance of the Court*, WASHINGTON POST, May 23, 2000, at A29.

13. Kramer, *supra* note 10.

14. Dinan, *supra* note 6.

15. Hallow, *supra* note 3.

16. *See* Charles Gardner Geyh, *The Elastic Nature of Judicial Independence and Judicial Accountability, in* THE IMPROVEMENT OF THE ADMINISTRATION OF JUSTICE 167 (7th ed. 2001).

17. Terri Jennings Peretti, *Does Judicial Independence Exist? The Lessons of Social Science Research, in* JUDICIAL INDEPENDENCE AT THE CROSSROADS: AN INTERDISCIPLINARY APPROACH 103 (2002).

18. U.S. CONST. art. III, § 1.

19. See *infra* chapter 1.

20. Stephen Burbank, *The Architecture of Judicial Independence*, 72 S. CAL. L. REV. 315, 339 (1999).

21. William H. Rehnquist, Keynote Address, 46 AM. U. L. REV. 267, 274 (1996).

22. Calvin R. Massey, *Rule of Law and the Age of Aquarius*, 41 HASTINGS L.J. 757, 760 (1990) (quoting Geoffrey de Q. Walker for the proposition that "an independent judiciary is an indispensable requirement of the rule of law"); L. Ralph Mecham, *Introduction to Mercer Law Review Symposium on Federal Judicial Independence*, 46 MERCER L. REV. 637, 638 (1995) (judicial independence is a "cornerstone of a free society and the rule of law"); William C. Whitford, *The Rule of Law*, 2000 WIS. L. REV. 723, 728 (judicial independence is "widely seen as critically necessary to the effective implementation" of a rule of law); Frances Kahn Zemans, *The Accountable Judge: Guardian of Judicial Independence*, 72 S. CAL. L. REV. 625, 631 (1999) ("an independent judiciary" is a "necessity" for the rule of law).

23. *Public Hearing of the Commission on the Separation of Powers and Judicial Independence*, American Bar Association 171–72, Dec. 13, 1996 (testimony of Prof. Daniel Meador), *available at* http://www.abanet.org/govaffairs/judiciary.

24. Charles Gardner Geyh & Emily Field Van Tassel, *The Independence of the Judicial Branch in the New Republic*, 74 CHI.-KENT L. REV. 31, 32–33 (1998).

25. John Ferejohn & Larry Kramer, *Independent Judges, Dependant Judiciary: Institutionalizing Judicial Restraint*, 77 N.Y.U. L. REV. 962 (2002).

26. Satoshi Kanazawa & Mary Still, *The Emergence of Marriage Norms: An Evolutionary Psychological Perspective, in* SOCIAL NORMS 274, 278 (Michael Hechter & Karl-Dieter Opp eds., 2001).

27. MICHAEL J. GERHARDT, THE FEDERAL APPOINTMENTS PROCESS: A CONSTITUTIONAL AND HISTORICAL ANALYSIS 255 (2000).

28. H. L. A. Hart conceptualized law in terms of "primary rules of obligation" that distinguish acceptable from unacceptable behaviors and "secondary rules" that "specify the ways in which the primary rules may be conclusively ascertained, introduced, eliminated, varied and the fact of their violation conclusively determined." In the context of the relationship between courts and Congress, the first set of norms, distinguishing acceptable from unacceptable judicial behavior, establishes primary rules

of judicial obligation (even though, in a broader context, these rules could be characterized as secondary insofar as they regulate the means by which courts uphold "primary" civil and criminal laws). In contrast, norms or rules that specify how Congress ascertains and modifies the primary rules of judicial obligation clearly qualify as "secondary" rules in Hart's analytical framework (H.L.A. HART, THE CONCEPT OF LAW 79–99 (2d ed. 1994)).

29. EDNA ULLMANN-MARGALIT, THE EMERGENCE OF NORMS 8 (1977).

30. Michael J. Glennon, *The Use of Custom in Resolving Separation of Powers Disputes*, 64 B.U. L. REV. 109, 128–33, 147 (1984).

31. *Id.* at 133.

32. James G. Wilson, *American Constitutional Conventions: The Judicially Unenforceable Rules That Combine with Judicial Doctrine and Public Opinion to Regulate Political Behavior*, 40 BUFF. L. REV. 645 (1992).

33. At least one scholar, however, has underscored the importance of the undertaking. *See* Charles Cameron *in* JUDICIAL INDEPENDENCE AT THE CROSSROADS, *supra* note 17, at 134.

34. An important exception is reflected in the work of then professor and now judge Robert A. Katzmann. *See* JUDGES AND LEGISLATORS: TOWARD INSTITUTIONAL COMITY (Robert A. Katzmann ed., 1989); ROBERT A. KATZMANN, COURTS AND CONGRESS (1997).

35. JEFFREY SEGAL & HAROLD SPAETH, THE SUPREME COURT AND THE ATTITUDINAL MODEL (1993). Segal and Spaeth, in turn, credit the work of Glendon Schubert. *See* GLENDON SCHUBERT, THE JUDICIAL MIND: THE ATTITUDES AND IDEOLOGIES OF SUPREME COURT JUSTICES, 1946–1963 (1965).

36. *Id.* at 73.

37. *Id.* at 69 ("Members of the Supreme Court further their policy goals because they lack electoral or political accountability, ambition for higher office, and comprise a court of last resort that controls its own jurisdiction").

38. *See* Jeffrey A. Segal, *Supreme Court Deference to Congress: An Examination of the Marksist Model, in* SUPREME COURT DECISION-MAKING: NEW INSTITUTIONAL APPROACHES 234 (Cornell Clayton & Howard Gillman eds., 1999).

39. LEE EPSTEIN & JACK KNIGHT, THE CHOICES JUSTICES MAKE xiii (1998); Lee Epstein, Jack Knight, & Andrew D. Martin, *The Supreme Court as a Strategic National Policy Maker,* 50 EMORY L.J. 583 (2001). *See also* FORREST MALTZMAN, JAMES F. SPRIGGS II, & PAUL J. WAHLBECK, CRAFTING LAW ON THE SUPREME COURT: THE COLLEGIAL GAME (2000); WALTER F. MURPHY, ELEMENTS OF JUDICIAL STRATEGY (1964).

40. Howard Gillman & Cornell Clayton, *Beyond Judicial Attitudes: Institutional Approaches to Supreme Court Decision-Making, in* SUPREME COURT DECISION-MAKING: NEW INSTITUTIONAL APPROACHES 6–7 (Cornell Clayton & Howard Gillman eds., 1999). *See generally* Rogers Smith, *Political Jurisprudence, the "New Institutionalism," and the Future of Public Law,* 82 AM. POL. SCI. REV. 89 (1988); THE SUPREME COURT IN AMERICAN POLITICS: NEW INSTITUTIONALIST APPROACHES (Howard Gillman & Cornell Clayton eds., 1999); Howard Gillman, *The Court as an Idea, Not a Building (or a Game): Interpretive Institutionalism and the*

Analysis of Supreme Court Decision-Making, in SUPREME COURT DECISION-MAKING: NEW INSTITUTIONAL APPROACHES 6–7 (Cornell Clayton & Howard Gillman eds., 1999).

41. Howard Gillman & Cornell Clayton, *Beyond Judicial Attitudes: Institutional Approaches to Supreme Court Decision-Making, in* SUPREME COURT DECISION-MAKING: NEW INSTITUTIONAL APPROACHES 6–7 (Cornell Clayton & Howard Gillman eds., 1999).

42. *Id.* at 7.

43. Symposia abound. *See, e.g., Introduction* to Symposium, *Federal Judicial Independence,* 46 MERCER L. REV. 637 (1995); Symposium, *Perspectives on Judicial Independence* 64 OHIO ST. L.J. (2003); Symposium, *Independence of the Judiciary* 38 U. RICH. L. REV. 565 (2003); Symposium, *Judicial Independence,* 25 HOFSTRA L. REV. 703 (1997); Symposium, *Judicial Independence,* 29 FORDHAM URB. L.J. 791 (2002); Symposium, *Judicial Independence* 14 GA. ST. U. L. REV. 737 (1998); Symposium, *Judicial Independence and Accountability,* 72 S. CAL. L. REV. 311 (1999).

44. A number of significant works by academic lawyers explore related subjects by looking beyond conventional conceptions of law, but their relationship to judicial independence is largely tangential. *See, e.g.,* MICHAEL GERHARDT, THE IMPEACHMENT PROCESS: A CONSTITUTIONAL AND HISTORICAL ANALYSIS (2d ed. 2000); MICHAEL GERHARDT, THE APPOINTMENTS PROCESS: A CONSTITUTIONAL AND HISTORICAL ANALYSIS (2003); BRUCE ACKERMAN, WE THE PEOPLE (1991).

45. *See, e.g.,* Michael J. Gerhardt, *Rediscovering Nonjusticiability: Judicial Review of Impeachments after Nixon,* 44 DUKE L.J. 231 (1994) (defending nonreviewability of impeachment decisions as political questions); Mark Tushnet, *Principles, Politics, and Constitutional Law,* 88 MICH. L. REV. 49 (1989) (arguing that appointments are best characterized as giving rise to political questions).

46. *Public Hearing of the Commission on the Separation of Powers and Judicial Independence,* American Bar Association 6–7, Feb. 21, 1997 (testimony of acting professor of law John Yoo), *available at* http://www.abanet.org/govaffairs/judiciary.

47. Willy v. Coastal Corp., 503 U.S. 131, 137 (1992) ("Article I, §8, cl. 9 authorizes Congress to establish the lower federal courts. From almost the founding of the country it has been firmly established that Congress acting pursuant to its authority to make all laws necessary and proper to their establishment may also enact laws regulating the conduct of those courts").

48. See *infra* chapter 5.

49. See *infra* chapter 6.

50. *Id.*

CHAPTER 1

1. *See* Peter M. Shane, *Who May Discipline or Remove Federal Judges? A Constitutional Analysis,* 142 U. PA. L. REV. 209, 216 (1993).

2. *See* RICHARD E. ELLIS, THE JEFFERSONIAN CRISIS: COURTS AND POL-

ITICS IN THE YOUNG REPUBLIC 6 (1971); *see also* Joseph H. Smith, *An Independent Judiciary: The Colonial Background*, 124 U. PA. L. REV. 1104, 1112–13 (1976).

3. *See* EDWARD DUMBAULD, THE DECLARATION OF INDEPENDENCE AND WHAT IT MEANS TODAY 115 (1950).

4. THE DECLARATION OF INDEPENDENCE para. 11 (U.S. 1776).

5. *See* DUMBAULD, *supra* note 3, at 108–12.

6. *See id.*

7. THE DECLARATION OF INDEPENDENCE para. 10.

8. JOHN ADAMS, THOUGHTS ON GOVERNMENT (1776), *reprinted in* 4 THE WORKS OF JOHN ADAMS, SECOND PRESIDENT OF THE UNITED STATES 189, 198 (Charles Francis Adams ed., Charles C. Little & James Brown 1851).

9. GORDON S. WOOD, THE CREATION OF THE AMERICAN REPUBLIC, 1776–1787, at 161 (1969).

10. *See id.; see also* Smith, *supra* note 2, at 1153–55.

11. WOOD, *supra* note 9, at 161.

12. JULIUS GOEBEL, JR., 1 HISTORY OF THE SUPREME COURT OF THE UNITED STATES: ANTECEDENTS AND BEGINNINGS TO 1801, at 97 (1971).

13. *Id.* at 98.

14. *See id.* at 133–37.

15. *See id.* at 137–41.

16. James Wilson, Debate in Pennsylvania Ratifying Convention (Dec. 11, 1787), *in* 4 THE FOUNDERS' CONSTITUTION 139, 139 (Philip B. Kurland & Ralph Lerner eds., 1987).

17. Thomas Jefferson, Notes on the State of Virginia, Query 13, 120–21 (1784), *in* 1 *id.* at 319–20.

18. Cases of the Judges of the Court of Appeals, 8 Va. (4 Call) 135, 138 (1788).

19. *Id.* at 143.

20. *Id.*

21. *Id.* at 145.

22. *Id.*

23. *Id.* at 145–46.

24. *Id.* at 142.

25. *See* GOEBEL, *supra* note 12, at 129 n.120.

26. Patrick Henry, Statement at the Virginia Ratification Convention (June 12, 1788), *in* 3 THE DEBATES IN THE SEVERAL STATE CONVENTIONS ON THE ADOPTION OF THE FEDERAL CONSTITUTION 313, 325 (Jonathan Elliot ed., J.B. Lippincott & Co. 1863) [hereinafter Elliot's DEBATES].

27. 5 U.S. (1 Cranch) 137 (1803).

28. Ninth Virginia Resolution, *in* WILLIAM M. MEIGS, THE GROWTH OF THE CONSTITUTION IN THE FEDERAL CONVENTION OF 1787, at 234–35 (1900).

29. James Madison, Notes (Aug. 27, 1787), *in* 2 THE RECORDS OF THE FEDERAL CONVENTION OF 1787, at 426, 428 (Max Farrand ed., 1911) [hereinafter FARRAND].

30. *See* WOOD, *supra* note 9, at 160–61.

31. James Madison, Notes (Aug. 27, 1787), *in* 2 FARRAND, *supra* note 29, at 428.

32. *Id.* at 429.

33. *Id.*

34. James Madison, Notes (July 18, 1787), *in id.* at 40, 44–45.

35. *Id.* at 45.

36. *Id.*

37. James Madison, Notes (Aug. 27, 1787), *in id.* at 429.

38. *Id.* at 430.

39. U.S. CONST. art. III, § 1.

40. *See* Willy v. Coastal Corp., 503 U.S. 131, 136 (1992).

41. *See* Ninth Virginia Resolution, *supra* note 28, at 234–35.

42. James Madison, Notes (June 4, 1787), *in* 1 FARRAND, *supra* note 29, at 96, 104–5.

43. *See* James Madison, Notes (June 5, 1787), *in id.* at 119, 119 ("The words, 'one or more' were struck out before 'inferior tribunals' as an amendment to the last clause of Resoln. 9ᵗʰ").

44. *See* Robert Yates, Notes (June 5, 1787), *in id.* at 126, 126.

45. James Madison, Notes (June 5, 1787), *in id.* at 29, at 124.

46. *Id.*

47. Among the opponents, Pierce Butler "could see no necessity for such tribunals." He argued, "The State Tribunals might do the business," and Luther Martin agreed, arguing that the federal courts "will create jealousies & oppositions in the State tribunals, with the jurisdiction of which they will interfere" (James Madison, Notes (July 18, 1787), *in* 2 FARRAND, *supra* note 29, at 45–46).

48. Such proponents as Nathaniel Gorham argued that "[i]nferior tribunals are essential to render the authority of the Natl. Legislature effectual," while Randolph "observed that the Courts of the States can not be trusted with the administration of the National laws" (*id.* at 46).

49. *Id.*

50. For instance, in the early years of the Republic, there were no federal jails; the federal government paid jail fees to local jails. Court was held not in federal buildings but in rented facilities, such as taverns or local officials' homes.

51. James Madison, Notes (June 4, 1787), *in* 1 FARRAND, *supra* note 29, at 97.

52. James Madison, Notes (July 19, 1787), *in* 2 *id.* at 51, 56; *see also* James Madison, Notes (June 2, 1787), *in* 1 *id.* at 79, 86 (reporting John Dickinson's observation that "the Legislative, Executive, & Judiciary departments ought to be made as independ[en]t as possible"); James Madison, Notes (June 4, 1787), *in id.* at 96, 98 (reporting James Wilson's statement that "the Legislative Exe[cutive] and Judiciary ought to be distinct & independent"); James Madison, Notes (June 6, 1787), *in id.* at 132, 138 (reporting James Madison's statement that "the Judiciary Departm[en]t ought to be separate & distinct from the other great Departments").

53. Rufus King thought the "the Judges ought to be able to expound the law as it should come before them, free from the bias of having participated in its formation" (James Madison, Notes (June 4, 1787), *in* 1 *id.* at 96, 98). John Dickinson believed that "a junction of the Judiciary to [the Council of Revision], involved an improper mix-

ture of powers" (James Madison, Notes (June 6, 1787), *in id.* at 132, 140). Caleb Strong opined that "the power of making ought to be kept distinct from that of expounding, the laws" (James Madison, Notes (July 21, 1787), *in* 2 *id.* at 73, 75). Luther Martin noted if the council of revision were adopted, judges would be obliged to invalidate "popular measures of the Legislature" not only in the course of judicial review but also as members of the Council, which could cause the Court to lose "the confidence of the people" (*id.* at 77).

54. *See* Ninth Virginia Resolution, *supra* note 28, at 239–40.

55. GOEBEL, *supra* note 12, at 206.

56. *See, e.g.,* Martin H. Redish, *Federal Judicial Independence: Constitutional and Political Perspectives,* 46 MERCER L. REV. 697, 703 (1995).

57. *See, e.g.,* James Madison, Notes (Aug. 20, 1787), *in* 2 FARRAND, *supra* note 29, at 344 (motion of Elbridge Gerry requesting that "the Committee be instructed to report . . . a mode of trying [the Supreme] Judges [in cases of] impeachment"); *id.* at 524 (statement of Gouverneur Morris alluding to the Senate's power to try the impeachment of judges in earlier and later drafts).

58. James Madison, Notes (July 20, 1787), *in id.* at 66–67.

59. James Madison, Notes (Aug. 20, 1787), *in id.* at 344.

60. James Madison, Notes (July 20, 1787), *in id.* at 64.

61. James Madison, Notes (July 20, 1787), *in id.* at 67.

62. James Madison, Notes (July 20, 1787), *in id.* at 69.

63. James Madison, Notes (June 1, 1787), *in* 1 *id.* at 69.

64. *See* Journal (Sept. 4, 1787), *in* 2 *id.* at 493, 493. This debate took place in the context of executive impeachment, but the clause the delegates were crafting was to apply to all civil officers of the United States.

65. *See* James Madison, Notes (Sept. 8, 1787), *in id.* at 547, 550.

66. *Id.*

67. *Id.*

68. MICHAEL GERHARDT, THE FEDERAL IMPEACHMENT PROCESS: A CONSTITUTIONAL AND HISTORICAL ANALYSIS 10 (2d ed. 2000).

69. *Id.* at 103–4.

70. *See* James Madison, Notes (Sept. 14, 1787), *in* 2 FARRAND, *supra* note 29, at 612, 612.

71. THE FEDERALIST NO. 78, at 469 (Alexander Hamilton) (Clinton Rossiter ed., 1961).

72. THE FEDERALIST NO. 79, at 472 (Alexander Hamilton) (Clinton Rossiter ed., 1961).

73. Federalist Alexander Hamilton argued in favor of tenure during good behavior in THE FEDERALIST NO. 78 (*supra* note 71). Brutus and other anti-Federalists likewise professed to support tenure during good behavior. *See, e.g.,* BRUTUS, THE POWER OF THE JUDICIARY (pt. 1) (Mar. 20, 1788), *reprinted in* THE ANTIFEDERAL-IST PAPERS 222, 223 (Morton Borden ed., 1965) ("I do not object to the judges holding their commissions during good behavior. I suppose it a proper provision provided they were made properly responsible"); THE FEDERAL FARMER, LETTER XV (Jan. 18, 1788), *reprinted in* LETTERS FROM THE FEDERAL FARMER TO THE REPUBLICAN

97, 99 (Walter Hartwell Bennett ed., 1978) ("[I]t is well provided, that the judges shall hold their offices during good behaviour").

74. BRUTUS, *supra* note 73, at 223–24.

75. *Id.* at 224.

76. *Id.*

77. THE FEDERALIST NO. 78, *supra* note 71, at 466.

78. THE FEDERALIST NO. 81, at 484–85 (Alexander Hamilton) (Clinton Rossiter ed., 1961).

79. In THE FEDERALIST NO. 65, at 396 (Alexander Hamilton) (Clinton Rossiter ed., 1961), Hamilton reiterates this point: "A well-constituted court for the trial of impeachments" would have as "[t]he subjects of its jurisdiction . . . those offenses which proceed from the misconduct of public men, or, in other words, from the abuse or violation of some public trust." He concludes, "They are of a nature which may with peculiar propriety be denominated POLITICAL, as they relate chiefly to injuries done immediately to the society itself."

80. James Wilson went so far as to say that Congress would not dare to impeach and remove judges who did their duty by invalidating unconstitutional legislative enactments:

> It is said that, if [judges] are to decide against the law, one house will impeach them, and the other will convict them. I hope gentlemen will show how this can happen; for bare supposition ought not to be admitted as proof. The judges are to be impeached, because they decide an act null and void, that was made in defiance of the Constitution! What House of Representatives would dare to impeach, or Senate to [convict], judges for the performance of their duty? (James Wilson, Statement at the Pennsylvania Ratification Convention (Dec. 4, 1787), *in* 2 Elliot's DEBATES, *supra* note 26, at 453, 478)

81. *See, e.g.,* A NATIVE OF VIRGINIA, OBSERVATIONS UPON THE PROPOSED PLAN OF FEDERAL GOVERNMENT (MAY 17, 1788), *reprinted in* 9 THE DOCU-MENTARY HISTORY OF THE RATIFICATION OF THE CONSTITUTION 655, 686–87 (John P. Kaminski & Gaspare J. Saladino eds., 1990) ("To have entered minutely into the subject, to have filled in all its parts, would have employed almost as much time as framing the Constitution itself, and would have spun out the work to a tedious length. In that case the Convention must have ascertained the number of inferior courts necessary, the number of judges and other offices, with their salaries, the times of holding the federal courts, . . . the introduction of which in a system of government would have made a strange appearance. They therefore properly left to Congress the power of organizing by law the Federal Court"); Edmund Pendleton, Statement at the Virginia Ratification Convention (June 18, 1788), *in* 3 Elliot's DEBATES, *supra* note 26, at 517, 517 ("The first clause contains an arrangement of the courts—one supreme, and such inferior as Congress may ordain and establish. This seems to me to be proper. Congress must be the judges, and may find reasons to change and vary them as experience shall dictate. It is, therefore, not only improper, but exceedingly inconvenient, to fix the arrangement in the Constitution itself, and not leave it to laws which may be changed according to circumstances").

82. THE FEDERAL FARMER, *supra* note 73, at 99. The Federal Farmer elaborated:

> [T]he legislature does not appear to be limited to improper rules or principles in instituting judicial courts: indeed the legislature will have full power to form and arrange judicial courts in the federal cases enumerated, at pleasure, with these eight exceptions only. 1. There can be but one supreme federal judicial court. 2. This must have jurisdiction as to law and fact in the appellate causes. 3. Original jurisdiction, when foreign ministers and the states are concerned. 4. The judges of the judicial courts must continue in office during good behavior—and, 5. Their salaries cannot be diminished while in office. 6. There must be a jury trial in criminal causes. 7. The trial of crimes must be in the state where committed—and, 8. There must be two witnesses to convict of treason.
>
> In all other respects Congress may organize the judicial department according to their discretion. (*id.* at 99–100)

83. JAMES MONROE, SOME OBSERVATIONS ON THE CONSTITUTION (ca. May 25, 1788), *reprinted in* 9 THE DOCUMENTARY HISTORY OF THE RATIFICATION OF THE CONSTITUTION, *supra* note 81, at 844, 872.

84. *See, e.g.,* WILLIAM H. REHNQUIST, 1996 YEAR-END REPORT ON THE FEDERAL JUDICIARY 1 (Jan. 1, 1997), *available at* http://www.uscourts.gov/cj96.htm ("I am struck by the paradox of judicial independence in the United States: we have as independent a judiciary as I know of in any democracy, and yet the judges are very much dependent on the Legislative and Executive branches for the enactment of laws to enable the judges to do a better job of administering justice").

85. Pendleton, *supra* note 81, at 517.

86. Letter from Samuel Osgood (Feb. 20, 1789), *in* 4 THE DOCUMENTARY HISTORY OF THE SUPREME COURT OF THE UNITED STATES, 1789–1800, at 364, 364 (Maeva Marcus ed., 1992) [hereinafter DOCUMENTARY HISTORY OF THE SUPREME COURT].

87. *See* Representative William Smith, Debate in the House of Representatives (Aug. 29, 1789), *in* 11 DOCUMENTARY HISTORY OF THE FIRST FEDERAL CONGRESS OF THE UNITED STATES OF AMERICA, MARCH 4, 1789–MARCH 3, 1791, at 1348, 1348 (Charlene Bangs Bickford et al. eds., 1992) [hereinafter DOCUMENTARY HISTORY OF THE FIRST CONGRESS]; *see also* Representative Egbert Benson, Debate in the House of Representatives (Aug. 29, 1789), *in id.* at 1368, 1368 ("It is not left to the election of the legislature of the United States whether to adopt or not, a judicial system like the one before us; the words in the constitution are plain and full, and must be carried into operation"); Representative Elbridge Gerry, Debate in the House of Representatives (Aug. 31, 1789), *in id.* at 1385, 1386 ("We are to administer this constitution, and therefore we are bound to establish these courts, let what will be the consequence").

88. Representative Aedanus Burke, Debate in the House of Representatives (Aug. 29, 1789), *in id.* at 1374, 1374.

89. *See* Michael G. Collins, *Article III Cases, State Court Duties, and the Madisonian Compromise,* 1995 WIS. L. REV. 39, 43.

90. *See id.* at 105–19.

91. *See, e.g.,* Representative Michael Stone, Debate in the House of Representatives (Aug. 31, 1789), *in* 11 DOCUMENTARY HISTORY OF THE FIRST CONGRESS, *supra* note 87, at 1380, 1385 (arguing that the Congress has the discretion not to establish inferior courts, and arguing against them: "this system cannot in its nature be agreeable to the state governments, or to the people. I do not think this, then, the proper time to establish these courts").

92. *See* James Madison, Debate in the House of Representatives (Aug. 31, 1789), *in id.* at 1359, 1359 ("It will not be doubted that some judiciary system is necessary to accomplish the objects of the government; and that it ought to be commensurate with the other branches of government. . . . The legislative power is made effective for its objects; the executive is co-extensive with the legislative, and it is equally proper that this should be the case with the judiciary").

93. Representative John Vining, Debate in the House of Representatives (Aug. 31, 1789), *in id.* at 1376, 1376–77.

94. *See* Judiciary Act of 1789, ch. 20, 1 Stat. 73.

95. *See* BRUTUS, THE POWER OF THE JUDICIARY (pt. 4) (Mar. 6, 1788), *reprinted in* THE ANTIFEDERALIST PAPERS, *supra* note 73, at 236, 237 ("No man can say where the supreme court are to hold their sessions; the presumption is, however, that it must be at the seat of the general government. In this case parties must travel many hundred miles, with their witnesses and lawyers, to prosecute or defend a suit. No man of middling fortune, can sustain the expense of such a law suit"); THE FEDERAL FARMER, LETTER III (Oct. 10, 1787), *reprinted in* LETTERS FROM THE FEDERAL FARMER TO THE REPUBLICAN, *supra* note 73, at 13, 23 ("I do not, in any point of view, see the need of opening a new jurisdiction to these causes . . . of suffering foreigners, and citizens of different states, to drag each other many hundred miles into the federal courts"); Letter from Edmund Pendleton to James Madison (July 3, 1789), *in* 4 DOCUMENTARY HISTORY OF THE SUPREME COURT, *supra* note 86, at 444, 444 ("This [judicial] department is the Sore part of the Constitution & requires the lenient touch of Congress. To quiet the fears of the Citizens of being drag'd from large distances from home, to defend a suit for a small sum, which they had better pay however unjust, than defend with success, is . . . worthy of attention").

96. *See* GOEBEL, *supra* note 12, at 473 ("[T]he localization of the federal inferior courts revealed an intention to quiet the alarums raised regarding the threatened inconvenience of the federal system").

97. Letter from David Sewall to George Thatcher (Apr. 11, 1789), *in* 4 DOCUMENTARY HISTORY OF THE SUPREME COURT, *supra* note 86, at 374, 374.

98. Letter from Nathaniel Peaslea Sargeant to John Adams (Apr. 25, 1789), *in id.* at 380, 380.

99. *See* GOEBEL, *supra* note 12, at 472.

100. *See id.* at 472 n.40.

101. SIR MATTHEW HALE, THE HISTORY OF THE COMMON LAW OF ENGLAND 162 (Charles M. Gray ed., University of Chicago Press photo. reprint 1971) (3d ed. 1739).

102. *See, e.g.,* WILFRED J. RITZ, REWRITING THE HISTORY OF THE JUDI-

CIARY ACT OF 1789, at 3 (1990) (noting that the so-called Judiciary Act of 1789 was in fact titled an act providing for the establishment of "courts," and arguing that the concept of the courts *qua* "judiciary" is a modern development).

103. Letter from Fisher Ames to William Tudor (July 12, 1789), *in* 4 DOCUMENTARY HISTORY OF THE SUPREME COURT, *supra* note 86, at 461, 461.

104. Letter from Edward Shippen to Robert Morris (July 13, 1789), *in id.* at 464, 465; *see also* Letter from Robert Livingston to Oliver Ellsworth (June 24, 1789), *in id.* at 420, 420 ("I am not clear that more than one circuit in a year will be necessary, & whether the number of Judges you assign will be sufficient to ride two circuits & execute the other duties of their departments with due deliberation"); Letter from Edmund Pendleton to James Madison (July 3, 1789), *in id.* at 444 (discussing "[t]he fatigue of the Circuits & other accidents" that would inevitably diminish the participation of Supreme Court justices on the circuit courts).

105. Letter from James Madison to Samuel Johnson (July 31, 1789), *in id.* at 491, 491.

106. Letter from Thomas FitzSimons to Benjamin Rush (June 2, 1789), *in id.* at 400, 400.

107. Letter from Edmund Randolph to James Madison (June 30, 1789), *in id.* at 432, 433.

CHAPTER 2

1. Letter from William Giles to Thomas Jefferson, Mar. 16, 1801, *reprinted in* DICE ROBINS ANDERSON, WILLIAM B. GILES: A STUDY IN THE POLITICS OF VIRGINIA AND THE NATION FROM 1790 TO 1830, at 77 (1914).

2. 5 U.S. (1 Cranch) 137 (1803).

3. The Court's constitutional analysis (such as it was) in *Stuart v. Laird* (5 U.S. (1 Cranch) 299 (1803)) was confined to upholding the section of the 1802 act that reinstated circuit riding; arguments attacking the validity of the repeal generally, a summary of which preceded the Court's opinion in the published report of the case (*id.* at 303), were ignored by the Court.

4. *Quoted in* MARY VOLCANSEK & JACQUELINE LUCIENNE LAFON, JUDICIAL SELECTION: THE CROSS-EVOLUTION OF FRENCH AND AMERICAN PRACTICES 90 (1988).

5. *Quoted in* Barry Friedman, *The History of the Countermajoritarian Difficulty* (pt. 1), 73 N.Y.U. L. REV. 333, 396 (1998).

6. *Id.* at 401.

7. *Id.* at 399.

8. *Id.* at 399–404.

9. 17 ANNALS OF CONG. 114 (1808) (statement of William Giles).

10. FELIX FRANKFURTER & JAMES M. LANDIS, THE BUSINESS OF THE SUPREME COURT 32 (1927).

11. Charles Gardner Geyh & Emily Field Van Tassel, *The Independence of the Judicial Branch in the New Republic*, 74 CHI.-KENT L. REV. 31, 57–58 (1998).

12. ERWIN C. SURRENCY, HISTORY OF THE FEDERAL COURTS 36 (1987).

13. *Id.*

14. Act of Mar. 2, 1792, ch. 22, § 1, Stat. 333; FRANKFURTER & LANDIS, *supra* note 10, at 22.

15. Act of Apr. 29, 1802, ch. 31, § 4, Stat. 158.

16. 40 ANNALS OF CONG. 1173 (1823).

17. *Id.*

18. *Id.*

19. Act of Mar. 3, 1837, ch. 34, 5 Stat. 176.

20. 2 REG. DEB. 502 (1826).

21. *Id.* at 873.

22. 6 REG. DEB. 571 (1830).

23. 2 REG. DEB. 916–17 (1826).

24. *Id.* at 475.

25. *Id.* at 506–7.

26. In 1823, Representative Plumer effectively rejected the alternative of a circuit court system in the same breath as he presented it, observing "that a similar system having been once adopted, and subsequently abandoned, its re-enactment would probably be opposed" (40 ANNALS OF CONG. 117 (1823)). Senator Holmes was equally dismissive in 1826: "Another proposition was to restore the old system of 1801. To that there were many objections which it is not necessary to mention; the Senate would not now be disposed to restore that system" (2 REG. DEB. 487 (1826)). *See also* EDWIN SURRENCY, HISTORY OF THE FEDERAL COURTS 24 (1987) ("One of the unfortunate results of the repeal of the Act of 1801 was the creation of a precedent against similar reform").

27. 2 REG. DEB. 414 (1826).

28. *Id.* at 877–79.

29. *Id.* at 469.

30. *Id.* at 2518.

31. 6 REG. DEB. 543 (1830). Senator Woodbury made a similar point four years earlier:

> This bill is to be passed mainly for the removal of local evils, now existing in the West. . . . Why not then remove those evils . . . without touching the Supreme Court? . . . [A]s a cure for a mere local disease, why should you begin to tamper with parts of the system not disordered? (2 REG. DEB. 465 (1826)).

32. 2 REG. DEB. 497–98 (1826).

33. *Id.* at 526.

34. *Id.* at 2579 (reporting Senate amendment in House).

35. *Id.* at 2581 (statement of James Johnson).

36. *Id.* at 671.

37. The bill passed as Act of Mar. 3, 1837, ch. 34, 5 Stat. 176. For a discussion of Jackson's efforts to win passage for a bill to expand the system, see FRANKFURTER & LANDIS, *supra* note 10, at 47.

38. Frankfurter and Landis preface their discussion of congressional efforts to cope with westward expansion by observing that "[c]ongressional preoccupation with

judicial organization is extremely tenuous all through our history" (FRANKFURTER & LANDIS, *supra* note 10, at 36). They conclude the section by noting that "the need for judicial reorganization was recognized by all parties and its fulfillment was indefinitely postponed" because "[l]egislation affecting judicial structure, unless it calls for whole-sale appointments, is without the driving force of a powerful, concentrated economic, political, or social interest" (*id.* at 42).

39. Paul Finkelman, *The* Dred Scott *Case, Slavery, and the Politics of Law,* 20 HAMLINE L. REV. 1, 9–10 (1996).

40. Scott v. Sandford, 60 U.S. 393, 406, 450–51 (1856).

41. N.Y. DAILY TRIB., Mar. 10, 1857, at 6.

42. N.Y. DAILY TRIB., Mar. 7, 1857, at 4.

43. *Id.* at 5.

44. CONG. GLOBE, 39th Cong., 2d Sess. 501–2 (1867).

45. David P. Currie, *The Constitution in the Supreme Court: Civil War and Reconstruction, 1865–73,* 51 U. CHI. L. REV. 131, 144 (1984).

46. See *infra* notes 47–55 and accompanying text, for a discussion of court packing and unpacking during Reconstruction.

47. *Quoted in* William W. Van Alstyne, *A Critical Guide to* Ex parte McCardle, 15 ARIZ. L. REV. 229 (1973).

48. *Ex parte* McCardle, 74 U.S. (7 Wall.) 506 (1868).

49. ERWIN CHEMERINSKY, FEDERAL JURISDICTION 181 (3d ed. 1999) (summarizing the arguments in favor of jurisdiction stripping).

50. Barry Friedman, *The History of the Countermajoritarian Difficulty* (pt. 2), 91 GEO. L.J. 1 (2002).

51. CHEMERINSKY, *supra* note 49, at 177.

52. Act of Mar. 3, 1863, ch. 100, § 1, 12 Stat. 794.

53. FRANKFURTER & LANDIS, *supra* note 10, at 72.

54. CHARLES FAIRMAN, HISTORY OF THE SUPREME COURT OF THE UNITED STATES: RECONSTRUCTION AND REUNION, 1864–88 (pt. 1), at 167–68 (Paul A. Freund ed., 1971).

55. CONG. GLOBE, 39th Cong., 1st Sess. 3698 (1866).

56. *Id.*

57. FAIRMAN, *supra* note 54, at 169.

58. James H. Chadbourn & A. Leo Levin, *Original Jurisdiction of Federal Questions,* 90 U. PA. L. REV. 639, 642–43 (1942) (characterizing the 1875 act as "sneak" legislation).

59. *Quoted in* 2 CHARLES WARREN, THE SUPREME COURT IN UNITED STATES HISTORY 423 n.1 (1937).

60. Act of Apr. 10, 1869, ch. 22, § 1, 16 Stat. 44.

61. FRANKFURTER & LANDIS, *supra* note 10, at 60.

62. *Id.* at 70–71.

63. CONG. GLOBE, 40th Cong., 3d Sess. 1366 (1869).

64. *Id.* at 414.

65. *Id.* at 813.

66. FRANKFURTER & LANDIS, *supra* note 10, at 74.

67. CONG. GLOBE, 41st Cong., 1st Sess. 208 (1869).

68. *Id.*, 40th Cong., 3d Sess. 1486 (1869) (statement of Senator Stewart: "[I]f we give to the South a judiciary who can perform the duties devolving upon them it will do more to settle that country, do more to establish law, order, and peace, than anything else"); *id.*, 41st Cong., 1st Sess. 208 (1869) (statement of Senator Trumbull: "It was important also . . . that we should have circuit courts held throughout the reconstructed [s]tates of the South and those still unreconstructed by a circuit judge, who should go from [s]tate to [s]tate . . . administering and enforcing the laws of the United States").

69. *Id.*, 41st Cong., 3d Sess. 208 (1870).

70. *Id.*

71. *Id.*, 40th Cong., 3d Sess. 1486 (1869).

72. *Id.*, 41st Cong., 1st Sess. 213 (1869).

73. *Id.*

74. *Id.* at 341.

75. Senator Buckalew, for example, noted: "There is force in the observation . . . that after these judges are once appointed you cannot reduce the number. Their tenure of office is during good behavior—substantially a life tenure—and you cannot reduce the number and thus retrace the step which you have taken. Therefore an increase in the number of these judges ought to be made upon great deliberation" (*id.*, 40th Cong., 3d Sess. 1487 (1869)).

76. *Id.*, 41st Cong., 1st Sess. 216 (1869) (statement of Senator Edmunds).

77. *Id.*

78. *Id.* at 208.

79. *Id.* at 211.

80. *Id.* at 214.

81. *Id.* at 208.

82. Edmunds conceded that the bill perpetuated circuit riding, but he maintained, "that is a mere formal matter" (*id.* at 209). Buckalew agreed that "the practical effect of this measure will be . . . to separate the judges of the Supreme Court altogether from circuit court duty" (*id.*, 40th Cong., 3d Sess. 1487 (1869)).

83. *Id.*, 41st Cong., 1st Sess. 214 (1869). Buckalew likewise favored the justices "traveling into different sections of the country and becoming, to some extent, acquainted with local facts, the character of [the] people, and the various interests in different parts of the country, all of which is of great service even to a dignified judge of the Supreme Court when he comes to perform the duties of his office" (*id.*, 40th Cong., 3d Sess. 1487 (1869)).

84. *Id.*, 40th Cong., 3d Sess. 1487 (1869).

85. *Id.*, 41st Cong., 1st Sess. 209 (1869).

86. *Id.* at 214 (statement of Senator Edmunds).

87. Senator Trumbull stated: "The Senator from Vermont regards it as a great desideratum to have the justices of the highest court in the country hold circuit courts and become familiar with the practice in the different parts of the country; and so the Senator from Missouri thinks, and I agree. . . . [T]he trouble is that the country is so large and the business has so increased that it is impossible that the justices of the

Supreme Court should be able to perform the necessary circuit duties throughout the different [s]tates. . . . Still it was desirable to connect them as far as practically it could be done with the circuit system; and hence the bill . . . requires the justices of the Supreme Court at least once in two years to go into each district in their respective circuits" (*id.,* 40th Cong., 3d Sess. 1484 (1869)).

88. *Id.,* 41st Cong., 1st Sess. 211 (1869).

89. *Id.*

90. *Id.* at 212–14 (statement of Senator Williams).

91. *Id.* at 215.

92. *Id.* at 214.

93. 198 U.S. 45 (1905).

94. Peter G. Fish, The Politics of Federal Judicial Administration 18 (1973).

95. *Id.* (footnotes omitted).

96. William S. Carpenter, Judicial Tenure in the United States 81 (1918).

97. George Dix, *Death of the Commerce Court: A Study in Institutional Weakness,* 8 Am. J. Legal Hist. 238, 251–52 (1964).

98. *Id.* at 248.

99. *Id.* at 244–45 ("Faced with the inevitability of restrictions of some sort, the roads seemed to have accepted regulation by the Commission as preferable to regulation by the individual states or the federal judiciary").

100. 50 Cong. Rec. 4206 (1913) (statement of Representative Murdock quoting President Taft).

101. Frankfurter & Landis, *supra* note 10, at 172–73.

102. *See id.* at 173.

103. For an exhaustive discussion of the events leading up to the court-packing plan, including those summarized in the present discussion, see Stephen O. Kline, *Revisiting FDR's Court-Packing Plan: Are the Current Attacks on Judicial Independence So Bad?* 30 McGeorge L. Rev. 863 (1999).

104. William G. Ross, A Muted Fury: Populists, Progressives, and Labor Unions Confront the Courts, 1890–1937 (1994).

105. Frankfurter & Landis, *supra* note 10, at 159.

106. 50 Cong. Rec. 4541 (1913).

107. 50 Cong. Rec. 4208 (1913).

108. *Id.* at 4208–9.

109. *Id.* at 4208.

110. *Id.* at 2147.

111. 25 I.C.C. 59 (1911).

112. Dix, *supra* note 97, at 254–58.

113. 50 Cong. Rec. 4540 (1913).

114. *Id.* at 4541.

115. *Id.* at 5410.

116. *Id.* at 5411–12.

117. *Id.* at 5414.

118. *Id.* at 5410. Senator Williams concurred with Smith to the extent of adding that Chief Justice Marshall himself conceded the validity of the repeal in private conversations (*id.*). Williams was more cautious than Smith, however, noting that Congress's authority to abolish judgeships derived from its power to abolish the court to which the judges were appointed; in this case, the judges had technically been appointed as circuit judges, not Commerce Court judges per se, which led Williams to doubt whether Congress could eliminate a circuit judgeship without abolishing the circuit court (*id.*).

119. *Id.* at 5415.

120. *Id.*

121. EDWIN WITTE, THE GOVERNMENT IN LABOR DISPUTES 84 (1932).

122. 38 Stat 731 (1914).

123. Duplex Printing Press Co. v. Deering, 254 U.S. 443, 470 (1921).

124. Witte, *supra* note 121 at 84.

125. *See also* Ross, *supra* note 104 at 290–91.

126. *Id.* at 302.

127. *See id.* at 309.

128. *Id.* at 302 (footnotes omitted).

129. *Reorganization of the Fed. Judiciary: Hearings on S. 1392 before the Senate Comm. on the Judiciary,* 75th Cong. 760, 763 (1937).

130. *Id.* at 539, 546.

131. John A. Ferejohn & Larry D. Kramer, *Independent Judges, Dependent Judiciary: Institutionalizing Judicial Restraint,* 77 N.Y.U. L. Rev. 962, 981 (2002). For a careful study of the relationship between partisanship, patronage, and judicial expansion, see DEBORAH J. BARROW, GARY ZUK, & GERARD S. GRYSKI, THE FEDERAL JUDICIARY AND INSTITUTIONAL CHANGE (1996).

132. John M. De Figueiredo & Emerson H. Tiller, *Congressional Control of the Courts: A Theoretical and Empirical Analysis of Expansion of the Federal Judiciary,* 39 J.L. & ECON. 435, 459–60 (1996).

133. Administrative Office of the U.S. Courts, History of Federal Judgeships, Table A: Summary of Judicial Conference Recommendations on U.S. Courts of Appeals Judgeships and Resulting Congressional Action (2003).

134. BARROW, ZUK, & GRYSKI, *supra* note 131, at 93–94.

135. Ann Pelham, *Circuit Conference: At Work and Play,* LEGAL TIMES, May 28, 1990, at 7. Senate Judiciary Committee chair Joseph Biden reacted testily to Mecham's remarks, suggesting that the judiciary also employed a patronage system when determining judgeship needs. He noted that the Judicial Conference had invariably requested as many new judgeships as the individual circuits had asked for, a "whatever you want you get" approach that smacked of "playing politics and doling out patronage" and that justified the Senate in second-guessing some conference recommendations (*The Civil Justice Reform Act of 1990 and the Judicial Improvements Act of 1990: Hearings on S. 2027 and S. 2648 before the Senate Comm. on the Judiciary,* 101st Cong. 2d Sess. 308 (1990)).

136. *See supra* note 84 and accompanying text.

137. 13 CONG. REC. 3464 (1882).

138. *See generally* FRANKFURTER & LANDIS, *supra* note 10.

139. *Id.* at 93–102.

140. 13 CONG. REC. 3504 (1882).

141. *Id.*

142. *Id.*

143. *Id.* at 3598.

144. *Id.*

145. *Id.* at 3597–98.

146. *Id.* at 3604.

147. *Id.* at 3697.

148. 21 CONG. REC. 10,224 (1890).

149. *Id.*

150. 13 CONG. REC. 3546 (1882).

151. *Id.*

152. *Id.*

153. 13 CONG. REC. 3605 (1882).

154. 21 CONG. REC. 10,305 (1890).

155. *Id.*

156. *Id.* at 10,223.

157. *Id.* at 10,223–24 (emphasis in original).

158. 13 CONG. REC. 3788 (1882).

159. *Id.*

160. *Id.*

161. 21 CONG. REC. 10,231 (1890).

162. *Id.*

163. *See* M.A. MUSMANNO, PROPOSED AMENDMENTS TO THE CONSTITUTION 82 (1929).

164. *See id.* at 86.

165. 13 CONG. REC. 3830 (1882).

166. *See* FRANKFURTER & LANDIS, *supra* note 10, at 61–65 & 64 n.28.

167. *See id.* at 64.

168. 96 U.S. 369 (1877).

169. *See* Removal Act of 1875, ch. 137, 18 Stat. 470.

170. James Chadbourn & A. Leo Levin, *Original Jurisdiction of Federal Questions,* 90 U. PA. L. REV. 639, 642–43 (1942) (quotation marks omitted).

171. One notable exception is legislation passed in 1887 that withdrew the federal courts' diversity of citizenship jurisdiction over litigation involving national banks by declaring such banks to be citizens of every state in which they were located. *See* Ferejohn & Kramer, *supra* note 131.

172. 10 CONG. REC. 850 (1880).

173. *See generally* FRANKFURTER & LANDIS, *supra* note 10, at 98–102.

174. 13 CONG. REC. 3546 (1882).

175. *Id.*

176. *Id.* at 3867.

177. *Id.*

178. *Id.* at 3868.

179. *Id.*

180. *Id.*

181. 21 CONG. REC. 3404 (1890).

182. JURISDICTION OF THE COURTS OF THE UNITED STATES, H.R. REP. NO. 50-942, at 3–4 (1888).

183. *See* FRANKFURTER & LANDIS, *supra* note 10, at 99–100.

184. *Id.* at 100.

185. *Id.*

186. 21 CONG. REC. 3403–4 (1890).

187. *Id.* at 10,306.

188. Roscoe Pound, *The Causes of Popular Dissatisfaction with the Administration of Justice* (1906), *reprinted in* 46 J. AM. JUDICATURE SOC'Y 55, 55 (Aug. 1962).

189. *Id.* at 56.

190. *Id.* at 66.

191. *Id.* at 56.

192. *See id.* at 55–66.

193. 62 CONG. REC. 200 (1921).

194. *Id.*

195. *Id.* at 201.

196. *Id.*

197. *Id.*

198. *Id.* at 202.

199. *Id.*

200. *Id.*

201. *Id.*

202. *Id.*

203. 62 CONG. REC. 4863 (1922).

204. *Id.*

205. *Additional Judges, United States Dist. Courts: Hearings on S. 2432, S. 2433, and S. 2523 before the Senate Comm. on the Judiciary,* 67th Cong. 14 (1921).

206. 62 CONG. REC. 4863 (1922).

207. *Id.* at 4864.

208. *Additional Judges, United States Dist. Courts: Hearings on S. 2432, S. 2433, and S. 2523 before the Senate Comm. on the Judiciary,* 67th Cong. 14 (1921).

209. 62 CONG. REC. 4853 (1922).

210. *Id.*

211. *Id.*

212. S. REP. NO. 70-440, pt. 2, at 9 (1928) (minority views).

213. Stephen Yeazell, *The Misunderstood Consequences of Modern Civil Process,* 1994 WIS. L. REV. 631.

214. *Admin. Office of the United States Courts: Hearings on S. 3212 before the Senate Comm. on the Judiciary,* 75th Cong., 3d Sess. 8 (1938).

215. *Id.* at 10–11.

216. 84 Cong. Rec. 9807 (1939).

217. *Id.* at 9309.

218. *Admin. Office of the United States Courts: Hearings on S. 3212, supra* n. 214, at 11.

219. 84 Cong. Rec. 9310 (1939).

220. Bernard Schwartz, Super Chief 280 (1983).

221. *Id.* at 280–81.

222. 116 Cong. Rec. 11,913 (1970), *reprinted in* Emily Field Van Tassel & Paul Finkelman, Impeachable Offenses 91–96 (1999).

223. Paul Brest, *Congress as Constitutional Decisionmaker and Its Power to Counter Judicial Doctrine,* 21 Ga. L. Rev. 57, 79 (1986).

224. *See* Clifford Lytle, The Warren Court and Its Critics 24 (1961).

225. 28 U.S.C. §§ 620, 623 (2000); *see also* Russel Wheeler, *Empirical Research and the Politics of Judicial Administration: Creating the Federal Judicial Center,* 51 Law & Contemp. Probs. 31, 41–43 (1988).

226. *Id.* at 33.

227. 28 U.S.C. § 372 (2000 & Supp. 2002).

228. *See* Irving R. Kaufman, *The Essence of Judicial Independence,* 80 Colum. L. Rev. 671, 699–700 (1980).

229. For a definitive history of the act and the reasons for its passage, see Stephen Burbank, *Procedural Rulemaking under the Judicial Councils Reform and Judicial Conduct and Disability Act of 1980,* 131 U. Pa. L. Rev. 283 (1982). *See also* The National Commission Report on Judicial Discipline and Removal 14 (1993) ("The Commission believes that a power in the judiciary to deal with certain kinds of misconduct furthers both the smooth functioning of the judicial branch and the broad goal of judicial independence").

230. Jack Harrison Pollack, Earl Warren: The Judge Who Changed America 289 (1979) (discussing "Nixon's campaign fulminations over the need to replace 'Warrenite' justices with 'law-and-order' appointees").

CHAPTER 3

1. Michael Gerhardt, The Federal Impeachment Process: A Constitutional and Historical Analysis 109–10 (2d ed. 2000).

2. *See* Asher C. Hinds, Hinds' Precedents of the House of Representatives (1907); Clarence Cannon, Cannon's Precedents of the House of Representatives (1935); Lewis Deschler, Deschler's Precedents of the House of Representatives (1979).

3. With respect to each impeachment inquiry, accusations of wrongdoing were recorded by type, without accounting for multiple allegations against a specific judge in a single category. Thus, a judge accused of favoritism in three instances and usurpation of power in a fourth, was "credited" with two types of accusation—one for favoritism and the other for abuse of power— notwithstanding that there was a total of four accusations.

4. Emily Field Van Tassel & Paul Finkelman, Impeachable Offenses: A Documentary History From 1787 to the Present 93–95 (1999) (reproducing the text of the articles of impeachment against Pickering).

5. *Quoted in* Eleanore Bushnell, Crimes, Follies, and Misfortunes: The Federal Impeachment Trials 59 (1992).

6. Letter from Roger Griswold to John Rutledge (Dec. 14, 1801), *quoted in* Richard E. Ellis, The Jeffersonian Crisis: Courts and Politics in the Young Republic 43 (1971).

7. Annals of Cong., 7th Cong., 2d Sess. 460 (1803).

8. Lynn Turner, *The Impeachment of John Pickering,* 54 Am. Hist. Rev. 485, 489 (1949).

9. *Id.* at 505.

10. *Id.* at 505–6.

11. *Id.*

12. Bushnell, *supra* note 5, at 45.

13. Annals of Cong., 7th Cong., 2d Sess. 642 (1803).

14. *Id.*

15. S5360, U.S. President, *Message from the President of the United States, Enclosing Sundry Documents, Relative to John Pickering* (Feb. 18, 1803).

16. Annals of Cong., 8th Cong., 1st Sess. 341 (1804).

17. 2 Stat. 97 (1801).

18. Annals of Cong., 8th Cong., 1st Sess. 342 (1804).

19. Report of the Committee to whom were referred on the 4th Instant, a Message from the President of the United States, Enclosing Sundry Documents Relative to John Pickering, District Judge of the District of New Hampshire 10–18 (Feb. 18, 1803).

20. Annals of Cong., *supra* note 18, at 328–29.

21. *Id.*

22. *Id.* at 360.

23. *Id.* at 361.

24. *Id.* at 363–64.

25. *Id.* at 365.

26. *Id.*

27. Van Tassel & Finkelman, *supra* note 4, at 92.

28. 3 Albert Beveridge, The Life of John Marshall 160 (1919).

29. George Lee Haskins, Foundations of Power: John Marshall, 1801–1805, at 91 (1981).

30. 4 Dumas Malone, Jefferson the President: First Term, 1801–1805, at 465 (1970).

31. *Quoted in* 1 Charles Warren, The Supreme Court in United States History 156 (1923).

32. William H. Rehnquist, Grand Inquests 60–61 (1992).

33. Annals of Cong., 8th Cong., 1st Sess. 806 (1804).

34. *Id.* at 807.

35. *Id.* at 809.

36. HINDS, *supra* note 2, at § 2342.

37. ANNALS OF CONG., 8th Cong., 1st Sess. 1171 (1804).

38. *Id.*

39. *Id.* at 1177.

40. *Id.* at 1177–78.

41. *Id.* at 1178.

42. ANNALS OF CONG., 8th Cong., 1st Sess. 680, 728 (1804).

43. Letter from John Marshall to Samuel Chase (Jan. 23, 1805), *in* JOHN MARSHALL, 6 THE PAPERS OF JOHN MARSHALL 347 (1990).

44. 2 TRIAL OF SAMUEL CHASE 9 (1805) (statement of Mr. Hopkinson).

45. *Id.* at 13–14.

46. *Id.* at 335–36.

47. *Id.* at 336.

48. *Id.* at 340.

49. *See* James Madison, Notes (Sept. 8, 1787), in 2 FARRAND, *supra* chapter 1, note 29, at 550.

50. 1 TRIAL OF SAMUEL CHASE at 102 (statement of Justice Chase).

51. *Id.*

52. *Id.* at 109.

53. *Id.* at 343.

54. *Id.* at 383.

55. 2 *id.* at 17.

56. *Id.* at 81.

57. *Id.* at 125.

58. *See, e.g.,* BUSHNELL, *supra* note 5, at 53 ("he did not shed his Federalist raiment when sitting on the bench nor hide his partisanship to ensure the appearance of a fair trial"); WARREN, *supra* note 29, at 273 (referring to Chase's "unnecessarily strenuous support of the Sedition Law," his "prejudicial and passionate conduct of trials," and his "arbitrary and unusual rulings").

59. BUSHNELL, *supra* note 5, at 85.

60. 2 TRIAL OF SAMUEL CHASE 18–19 (1805).

61. REHNQUIST, *supra* note 32, at 134.

62. BUSHNELL, *supra* note 5, at 92–96.

63. *Id.*

64. REG. DEB., Apr. 21, 22, & 24, 1830, at 810, 814, & 818.

65. *Id.* at 814.

66. *Id.* at 815.

67. BUSHNELL, *supra* note 5, at 98.

68. *Reprinted in* VAN TASSEL & FINKELMAN, *supra* note 4, at 110–14.

69. ARTHUR STANSBURY, REPORT OF THE TRIAL OF JAMES H. PECK 290 (1833).

70. *Id.* at 189.

71. *Id.* at 304 (statement of Ambrose Spencer).

72. *Id.* at 428.

73. *Id.* at 489 (argument of William Wirt).

74. *Id.* at 473.

75. *Id.* at 573.

76. VAN TASSEL & FINKELMAN, *supra* note 4, at 116.

77. 39 CONG. REC. 219 (1904) (statement of Henry Palmer).

78. *Id.* at 221.

79. *Id.* at 244.

80. HINDS, *supra* note 2, at § 2474.

81. 39 CONG. REC. 245 (1904) (statement of Congressman Charles Littlefield).

82. PROCEEDINGS IN THE SENATE OF THE UNITED STATES IN THE MAT-TER OF THE IMPEACHMENT OF CHARLES SWAYNE 394 (1905).

83. *Id.* at 42 (answer of Judge Swayne).

84. *Id.* at 76 (statement of Congressman Henry Palmer).

85. *Id.* at 683 (statement of John Thurston).

86. Van Tassel and Finkelman have published tables summarizing the Senate votes. See VAN TASSEL & FINKELMAN, *supra* note 4, at 92, 102, 108, 124. Pickering had at least nominally been deemed "guilty as charged" of making an ill-motivated and erroneous ruling, on a vote of nineteen to one (with several abstentions). After that, Chase narrowly escaped a similar fate, on a Senate vote to convict that ran as high, on one count, as nineteen in favor to fifteen against; Peck was acquitted, with twenty-one votes for conviction and twenty-two against; and Swayne was acquitted by a margin of thirty-one for to fifty-one against in four of the five articles pertaining to his contempt orders, with thirty-five for and forty-seven against in the fifth.

87. VAN TASSEL & FINKELMAN, *supra* note 4, at 146.

88. *Id.* at 165.

89. H.R. MISC. DOC. NO. 12–300 (1811).

90. HINDS, *supra* note 2, at § 2489.

91. *Id.* at § 2488.

92. *Id.* at § 2489.

93. HINDS, *supra* note 2, at § 2496; *see also* CONG. GLOBE, 35th Cong., 2d Sess. 59 (1858) (statement of Mr. Taylor).

94. CONG. GLOBE, 35th Cong., 2d Sess. 60 (1858) (statement of Mr. Taylor).

95. *Id.* at 66.

96. *Id.*

97. *Id.* at 60.

98. H.R. REP. NO. 45–142, at 17.

99. *Id.* at 18.

100. *Id.* at 20.

101. *Id.* at 19.

102. 77 CONG. REC. 2417 (1933).

103. 78 CONG. REC. 7061 (1934).

104. *Id.*

105. This trend may be confined to the relatively less partisan political realm of judicial impeachments. In the impeachment inquiry of President Clinton, the House appeared to have reverted to a probable cause standard, which was met by predictable applause from those who favored impeachment and by catcalls from those who did

not. *See* David Kendell, *John Field Simms Memorial Lecture Series: Constitutional Vandalism,* 30 N.M. L. REV. 155, 167–69 (article by President Clinton's lawyer, opposing the use of a probable cause standard); Jonathan Turley, *Congress as Grand Jury: The Role of the House of Representatives in the Impeachment of an American President,* 67 GEO. WASH. L. REV. 735–90 (article by an outspoken supporter of Clinton impeachment, favoring the use of a probable cause standard).

106. HINDS, *supra* note 2, at § 2026.

107. STANSBURY, *supra* note 69, at 476.

108. HINDS, *supra* note 2, at § 2496.

109. *Id.*

110. *Id.* at § 2497.

111. *Id.*

112. *Id.* at § 2498.

113. CONG. GLOBE, 35th Cong., 2d Sess. 37 (1858).

114. *Id.* at 38.

115. HINDS, *supra* note 2, at § 2498.

116. CONG. GLOBE, 35th Cong., 2d Sess. 85 (1858).

117. HINDS, *supra* note 2, at § 2498.

118. *Id.* at § 2519.

119. CANNON, *supra* note 2, at § 525.

120. *Conduct of Emory Speer: Hearings before a Subcommittee of the House Committee on the Judiciary,* 63rd Cong. 11 (1914).

121. CANNON, *supra* note 2, at § 527.

122. *Id.*

123. HINDS, *supra* note 2, at § 2489.

124. CONG. GLOBE, 35th Cong., 2d Sess. 66 (1858) (statement of Mr. Taylor).

125. 77 CONG. REC. 2419 (1933).

126. *Id.* at 2420.

127. *Id.*

128. *Id.*

129. *Id.* at 2421.

130. Warren Grimes, *The Role of the U.S. House of Representatives in Proceedings to Impeach and Remove Federal Judges, in* RESEARCH PAPERS OF THE NATIONAL COMMISSION ON JUDICIAL DISCIPLINE AND REMOVAL 39, 136 (1993).

131. *Id.* at 136–37

132. *Id.* at 68.

133. Grimes offers other "possible causes of the decline in House impeachment inquiries," two of which seem most apt here: the House has avoided "unnecessary or unwarranted investigations of judges that may have been conducted during earlier periods"; and "the House, in more recent years, has declined to act because it is preoccupied with other business or finds impeachment burdensome" (*id.* at 69–70).

134. Findings and Conclusions of Robert W. Kastenmeier on Citizen Petitions to Impeach Three Federal Judges (Sept. 25, 1986) (on file with author).

135. *Id.* at 9.

136. *Id.*

137. *Id.* at 8.

138. *Id.* at 9.

139. Letter from Peter Rodino to Charles Hatcher (Oct. 14, 1986) (on file with author).

140. Pub. L. No. 96–458, 94 Stat. 2035 (1980).

141. HINDS, *supra* note 2, at § 2506.

142. *Id.* at § 2509.

143. VAN TASSEL & FINKELMAN, *supra* note 4, at 115.

144. HINDS, *supra* note 2, at § 2513.

145. CANNON, *supra* note 2, at §§ 526–27.

146. *Official Conduct of Judge Ferdinand A. Geiger: Hearing before the House Committee on the Judiciary,* 75th Cong. 138, 140 (1938).

147. Emily Field Van Tassel, *Resignations and Removals: A History of Federal Judicial Service—and Disservice—1789–1992,* 142 U. PA. L. REV. 333 (1993).

148. AN INDEPENDENT JUDICIARY: REPORT OF THE ABA COMMISSION ON JUDICIAL INDEPENDENCE AND SEPARATION OF POWERS 19 (1997).

149. 116 CONG. REC. 11,913 (1970) (statement of Congressman Gerald Ford), *reproduced in* VAN TASSEL & FINKELMAN, *supra* note 4, at 54–60.

CHAPTER 4

1. MICROSOFT ENCARTA COLLEGE DICTIONARY 718 (2001).

2. U.S. CONST. art. VI.

3. *Quoted in* Paul Carrington & Adam Long, *The Independence and Democratic Accountability of the Supreme Court of Ohio,* 30 CAP. U. L. REV. 455, 471 (2002). The chief justice was not identified by name.

4. 1 THE RECORDS OF THE FEDERAL CONVENTION OF 1787, at 119 (Max Farrand ed., 1911) [hereinafter FARRAND].

5. *Id.* at 120.

6. *Id.*

7. 2 *id.* at 41.

8. *Id.* at 42.

9. *Id.* at 81.

10. *Id.*

11. *Id.* at 21, 66.

12. *Id.* at 119.

13. 2 *id.* at 81.

14. *Id.* at 41.

15. *Id.* at 42.

16. *Id.* at 43.

17. *Id.* at 81.

18. *Id.* at 81–82.

19. *Id.* at 44.

20. *Id.* at 44.

21. *Id.* at 41.

22. 1 *id.* at 292.

23. 2 *id.* at 44.

24. *Id.* at 81.

25. *Id.* at 82.

26. *Id.* at 83.

27. *Id.*

28. *Id.* at 539.

29. *Id.* at 538–39.

30. *Id.* at 539.

31. The Federalist No. 38 (James Madison), *available at* http://www
.yale.edu/lawweb/avalon/federal/fed38.htm.

32. The Antifederalist Nos. 76–77 (Richard Henry Lee), *available at*
http://www.wepin.com/articles/afp/afp76–77.html.

33. 2 Farrand, *supra* note 4, at 83

34. The Federalist No. 76 (Alexander Hamilton), *available at* http://www
.yale.edu/lawweb/avalon/federal/fed33.htm.

35. John C. Eastman, *The Limited Nature of the Senate's Advice and Consent Role*,
36 U.C. Davis L. Rev. 633, 647–48 (2003).

36. Terrell Carver, *Ideology: The Career of a Concept*, in Ideals and Ideologies: A Reader 4 (Terence Ball & Richard Dagger eds., 3d ed. 1999).

37. Christopher Wolfe, *The Senate's Power to Give "Advice and Consent" in Judicial Appointments*, 82 Marq. L. Rev. 355, 357 (1999).

38. See chapter 2.

39. John Rutledge (1795); Alexander Wolcott (1811); John Spencer (1844);
George Woodward (1845); Jeremiah Black (1861); Ebenezer Hoar (1870); William
Hornblower (1893); Wheeler Peckham (1894); John Parker (1930); Clement
Haynesworth (1968); Harold Carswell (1969); and Robert Bork (1987).

40. John Crittenden (1828); Roger Taney (1835); and George Badger (1853).

41. Edward Bradford (1852); William Micou (1853); Henry Stanbery (1866);
Stanly Matthews (1881); and John Read (1844).

42. Reuben Walworth (1844); Edward King (1844); George Williams (1874);
Caleb Cushing (1874); Abe Fortas (1968); and Douglas Ginsburg (1987).

43. The first president to take an obvious interest in the ideology of his nominees
was the outgoing Federalist John Adams, who, as recounted in chapter 2, packed the
court with Federalist partisans as a means to counteract the influence of the incoming
Jeffersonian Republicans. As a practical matter, the president has almost always nominated judges from the ranks of his own political party, which implicitly underscores
the priority that presidents place on appointing judges with shared political values. For
an exhaustive treatment of the factors presidents have taken into account when making supreme court nominations, see Henry Abraham, Justices and Presidents: A Political History of Appointments to the Supreme Court
(3d ed. 1992).

44. Letter from Timothy Pickering to George Washington (July 31, 1795), *in* 1
The Documentary History of the Supreme Court of the United
States, 1789–1800, at 774 (Maeva Marcus & James R. Perry eds., 1985).

45. Letter from Edmund Randolph to George Washington (July 29, 1795), *in id.* at 773.

46. Letter from Thomas Jefferson to William Giles (Dec. 31, 1795), *in id.* at 821.

47. Letter from John Adams to Abigail Adams (Dec. 16, 1795), *in id.* at 812.

48. Executive Journal—Senate, Feb. 4, 1811, at 165.

49. Abraham, *supra* note 43, at 41.

50. Connecticut Courant, Feb. 13, 1811 (emphasis in original).

51. Columbian Centinel, Feb. 20, 1811.

52. New England Palladium, Feb. 19, 1811.

53. *Id.,* Feb. 13, 1811.

54. 1 Charles Warren, The Supreme Court in United States History 798–99 (Fred B. Rothman & Co. 1987) (1926). *See also* Paul Simon, Advice and Consent: Clarence Thomas, Robert Bork, and the Intriguing History of the Supreme Court's Nomination Battles 174–75 (1992); Abraham, *supra* note 43, at 100.

55. 4 Journal of the Executive Proceedings of the Senate of the United States of America 465 (Feb. 2, 1835) ("Resolved, That it is inexpedient to appoint a judge of the Supreme Court of the United States to fill the vacancy occasioned by the resignation of Gabriel Duvale, until a new arrangement shall be made of the circuit courts by act of Congress").

56. 4 The Papers of Daniel Webster, Correspondence 100 (Charles M. Wiltse & Harold D. Moser eds., 1980).

57. Harper's Weekly, Jan. 1, 1870, at 3 ("His spotless character, his ability, his professional accomplishment and experience are unquestionable").

58. N.Y. Times, Jan. 8, 1870, at 1 ("[H]e would have been confirmed, but for the fact that he was a citizen and resident of New England, and did not intend to remove to the Southern Circuit for which the office, to which he was nominated, was created last spring").

59. See chapter 2.

60. The Nation, Feb. 10, 1870, at 81.

61. Letter from Former Senator Edwin D. Morgan to Ulysses S. Grant (Dec. 23, 1869), *in* 20 The Papers of Ulysses S. Grant 54 (John Y. Simon ed., 1995).

62. 1 George F. Hoar, Autobiography of Seventy Years 306 (1903).

63. Moorfield Storey & Edward W. Emerson, Ebenezer Rockwood Hoar 197 (1911).

64. Letter from John Marshall to Henry Clay (Nov. 28, 1828), *in* 7 The Papers of Henry Clay 550 (Robert Seager II ed., 1982).

65. United States Telegraph, Jan. 22, 1829.

66. Abraham, *supra* note 43, at 40.

67. Letter from Henry Clay to John J. Crittenden (Jan. 6, 1829), *in* 7 Henry Clay, *supra* note 64, at 590.

68. 3 Journal of the Executive Proceedings of the Senate of the United States of America 637 (Jan. 29, 1829) (Senator Chambers).

69. Resolution on Feb. 12, 1829, 3 Journal of the Executive Proceedings of the Senate of the United States of America 644 (1829).

70. Joseph P. Harris, The Advice and Consent of the Senate: A Study of the Confirmation of Appointments by the United States Senate 66–67 (1953); Abraham, *supra* note 43, at 106; Simon, *supra* note 54, at 182.

71. Letter from Henry Clay to John Crittenden (Jan. 24, 1844), *in* 10 Henry Clay, *supra* note 62, at 5 (Robert Seager II ed. 1982).

72. Letter from Thurlow Weed to John J. Crittenden (Mar. 17, 1844), *quoted in* 2 Warren, *supra* note 54, at 115.

73. Letter from Robert Tyler to John Calhoun (Nov. 8, 1844), *in* 19 The Papers of John C. Calhoun 12 (Clyde N. Wilson ed., 1990) ("Judge King is possessed of unquestioned abilities"); Letter from James Buchanan to Governor Shunk (Dec. 18, 1844), *in* 6 The Works of James Buchanan 77 (John Bassett Moore, ed. 1909) ("There are few lawyers, if any, in Philadelphia, that are [Read's] superiors"); Abraham, *supra* note 43, at 106 (Walworth described as "an able lawyer"); Harris, *supra* note 70, at 68 (Walworth characterized as "unquestionably of the highest legal ability").

74. 2 Warren, *supra* note 54, at 116 ("The heated contest which had long prevailed between the President and the Whig Senate made it unlikely that his appointments would be confirmed"). Harris, *supra* note 70, at 67 ("[T]he rejections were due to the bitter hostility of the Whigs toward Tyler").

75. N.Y. Daily Times, Feb. 16, 1853, at 4. *See also* Abraham, *supra* note 43, at 40; Simon, *supra* note 54, at 186; Harris, *supra* note 70, at 70.

76. Shelby Cullom, Fifty Years of Public Service 153 (1911).

77. Philip B. Kurland, *The Appointment and Disappointment of Supreme Court Justices,* 1972 Ariz. St. L.J. 183, 208.

78. Simon, *supra* note 54, at 192–94 (noting that rejection was likewise attributable to the nominee's views on abolition and to the withdrawal of secessionist Democrats).

79. N.Y. Tribune, Jan. 29, 1861, at 5.

80. N.Y. Times, Apr. 17, 1866, at 1.

81. Abraham, *supra* note 43, at 124–25. For a discussion of whether Congress was intent on "unpacking" the Supreme Court when it reduced the size of the Court and thereby effectively killed Stanbery's appointment, see chapter 2.

82. Letter from Francis Wharton to John C. Calhoun (Dec. 24, 1845), *in* Calhoun, *supra* note 73, at 360.

83. Letter from Benjamin Brewster to John C. Calhoun (Jan. 14, 1846), *in id.* at 441–42.

84. The Diary of James K. Polk 185 (Jan. 22, 1846) (Milo Milton Quaife ed., 1910).

85. Letter from James Buchanan to Louis McLane (Feb. 26, 1846), *in* 6 Buchanan, *supra* note 73, at 386–87 ("I have for years been anxious to obtain a seat on the bench of the Supreme Court").

86. Michael J. Gerhardt, The Federal Appointments Process: A Constitutional and Historical Analysis 145–46 (2003) (describing Woodward's rejection as illustrative of the proposition that "[m]uch more often than not, presidents have paid dearly for ignoring or failing to give adequate respect to senator-

ial courtesy"); THE DIARY OF JAMES K. POLK, *supra* note 84, at 194 (Jan. 24, 1846) (reporting on Buchanan's remark to the attorney general "that if he had been consulted at the time Mr. Woodward was nominated to the Senate . . . he would have been confirmed").

87. 28 AMER. L. REV. 274 (1894), *cited in* 2 WARREN, *supra* note 54, at 719.

88. *Id.*

89. *Id.* ("The only objection waged against his qualifications was that he was a natural advocate, and that his temperament was not judicial").

90. *Id.*

91. N.Y. TIMES, Jan. 14, 1894, at 1.

92. 2 GEORGE F. HOAR, AUTOBIOGRAPHY OF SEVENTY YEARS 172 (1903).

93. HERBERT J. BASS, "I AM A DEMOCRAT": THE POLITICAL CAREER OF DAVID BENNETT HILL 241 (1961).

94. 1 GEORGE S. BOUTWELL, REMINISCENCES OF SIXTY YEARS IN PUBLIC AFFAIRS 122 (1902). *See also* 1 HOAR, *supra* note 92, at 173 (1903); N.Y. TIMES, Jan. 14, 1874, at 1.

95. N.Y. TIMES, Jan. 11, 1874, at 1.

96. N.Y. HERALD, Jan. 13, 1874, at 3, *cited in* 2 WARREN, *supra* note 54, at 557.

97. Letter from Charles Sumner to Francis W. Bird (Jan. 15, 1874), *in* 2 THE SELECTED LETTERS OF CHARLES SUMNER 627 (Beverly Wilson Palmer ed., 1990), *quoted in* 2 WARREN, *supra* note 54, at 559.

98. See chapter 2.

99. Harold Helfman, *The Contested Confirmation of Stanley Matthews to the United States Supreme Court,* 8 BULL. OF THE HIST. & PHIL. SOC'Y OF OHIO 155, 160–61 (1950).

100. *Id.* at 162–63.

101. ABRAHAM, *supra* note 43, at 136.

102. See *supra* notes 87–93 and accompanying text.

103. HARRIS, *supra* note 70, at 106.

104. *Id.* at 100.

105. *Id.* at 113.

106. *Id.* at 117–19.

107. *Id.* at 125–27.

108. 72 CONG. REC. 7950 (1930).

109. *Hearings before the Subcommittee of the Committee of the Judiciary, U.S. Senate, on the Confirmation of John J. Parker to Be an Associate Justice of the Supreme Court of the United States,* 71st Cong., 2d Sess. 75 (1930).

110. ABRAHAM, *supra* note 43, at 42; HARRIS, *supra* note 70, at 128.

111. *Quoted in* SIMON, *supra* note 54, at 248–49.

112. 72 CONG. REC. 8192 (1930).

113. *Id.* at 7950.

114. *Id.* at 7949–50.

115. *Id.* at 7951.

116. ROBERT KATZMANN, COURTS AND CONGRESS 19–24 (1997).

117. CRS Report RL31948, *Evolution of the Senate's Role in the Nomination and Confirmation Process: A Brief History,* by Betsy Palmer 10 (June 5, 2003).

118. *Id.* at 11.

119. ABRAHAM, *supra* note 43, at 287–91; GERHARDT, *supra* note 86, at 126–27.

120. ABRAHAM, *supra* note 43, at 291; GERHARDT, *supra* note 86, at 85.

121. SHELDON GOLDMAN, PICKING FEDERAL JUDGES: LOWER COURT SELECTION FROM ROOSEVELT THROUGH REAGAN 198 (1997).

122. ABRAHAM, *supra* note 43, at 15.

123. *Id.*

124. Yale Law School dean Louis Pollak characterized Carswell's credentials as "more slender" than "any Supreme Court nominee put forth this century," while conservative professor William Van Alstyne declared that there was "nothing in the quality of the nominee's work to warrant any expectation whatever that he could serve with distinction on the Supreme Court" (*id.* at 17). That prompted Roman Hruska, one of Carswell's staunchest Senate supporters, to offer the timeless defense that "even if he is mediocre," the mediocre of the world "are entitled to a little representation," because "we can't have all Brandeises, Cardozos, and Frankfurters and stuff like that there" (116 CONG. REC. 7498 (1970)).

125. ABRAHAM, *supra* note 43, at 16–17; Simon, *supra* note 54, at 291–92.

126. ABRAHAM, *supra* note 43, at 18.

127. KATZMANN, *supra* note 116, at 28.

128. *Id.* at 34–35.

129. *Id.* at 19.

130. 133 CONG. REC. 10,884 (1987).

131. ROBERT BORK, THE TEMPTING OF AMERICA: THE POLITICAL SEDUCTION OF THE LAW 347 (1990).

132. STEPHEN CARTER, THE CONFIRMATION MESS: CLEANING UP THE FEDERAL APPOINTMENTS PROCESS 81–82 (1994).

133. For a more detailed description of the Thomas confirmation proceedings, *see* Michael J. Gerhardt, *Divided Justice: A Commentary on the Nomination and Confirmation of Clarence Thomas,* 60 G.W. L. REV. 969 (1992).

134. *The Thomas Nomination: Excerpts from Senate's Hearings on the Thomas Nomination,* N.Y. TIMES, Oct. 12, 1991, at A12.

135. Neil Lewis, *Conservatives Set for Fight on Supreme Court Nominees,* N.Y. TIMES, Nov. 13, 1992, at B16.

136. MICHAEL GERHARDT, THE FEDERAL APPOINTMENTS PROCESS 296 (2000).

137. Harriet Chang, *Election Could Shape Supreme Court for Years to Come,* SAN FRANCISCO CHRONICLE, Oct. 2, 2004, at A4.

138. Peter Baker, *Parties Gear Up for High Court Battle,* WASHINGTON POST, June 27, 2005.

139. *Bush's Choice of Miers for High Court Stuns Activists,* NEW JERSEY RECORD, Aug. 4, 2005, at A01; Joan Biskupic, Toni Locy, and Richard Willing, *Next Question on Nominee: What Does He Really Think?* USA TODAY, July 21, 2005, at 01A; Charlie

Savage, *Miers Has Backed Wide Executive Role*, BOSTON GLOBE, Oct. 5, 2005, at A22.

140. *See supra* notes 132, 135, and 136 and accompanying text.

141. *Meet the Press*, Oct. 9, 2005.

142. Barry Friedman & Anna Harvey, *Electing the Supreme Court*, 78 IND. L.J. 123, 137 (2003).

143. For a discussion of the factors presidents have taken into account when nominating lower court judges, see generally GOLDMAN, *supra* note 121; KERMIT HALL, THE POLITICS OF JUSTICE: LOWER FEDERAL JUDICIAL SELECTION AND THE SECOND PARTY SYSTEM 1829–61 (1979).

144. Stephen Burbank, *Politics, Privilege, and Power: The Senate's Role in the Appointment of Federal Judges*, 86 JUDICATURE 24, 25–26 (2002).

145. HARRIS, *supra* note 70, at 314.

146. HALL, *supra* note 143, at 171–72.

147. EVAN HAYNES, SELECTION AND TENURE OF JUDGES 23 (1944).

148. HARRIS, *supra* note 70, at 380.

149. HAROLD CHASE, FEDERAL JUDGES: THE APPOINTING PROCESS 11 (1972).

150. HARRIS, *supra* note 70, at 255–57.

151. *Id.* at 91.

152. *Id.* at 96.

153. CHASE, *supra* note 149, at 125–28.

154. *Id.* at 9.

155. *Id.* at 7.

156. Palmer, *supra* note 117, at 8; Brannon Denning, *The "Blue-slip": Enforcing the Norms of the Judicial Confirmation Process*, 10 WM & MARY BILL RTS. J. 75, 76 (2001).

157. *Quoted in* Denning, *supra* note 156, at 78.

158. Elliott Slotnick, *Reforms in Judicial Selection: Will They Affect the Senate's Role?* 64 JUDICATURE 60, 69 (1980).

159. HARRIS, *supra* note 70, at 229–31.

160. Ben Miller, *Federal Judicial Appointments: The Continuing Struggle for Good Judges*, 41 A.B.A. J. 125 (1955).

161. HARRIS, *supra* note 70, at 324.

162. Burke Shartel, *Federal Judges—Appointment, Supervision, and Removal: Some Possibilities under the Constitution*, 15 J. AM. JUD. SOC'Y 21, 22 (1931).

163. *Quoted in* Palmer, *supra* note 117, at 6.

164. *Quoted in* CHASE, *supra* note 149, at 7.

165. GOLDMAN, *supra* note 121, at 244.

166. Denning, *supra* note 156, at 83.

167. Ashlyn Kuersten & Donald Songer, *Presidential Success through Appointments to the United States Courts of Appeals*, 31 AM. POL. RES. 107 (2003).

168. GOLDMAN, *supra* note 121, at 288–89 (requiring multiple names); Sheldon

Goldman, *Unpicking Pickering in 2002: Some Thoughts on Lower Court Selection and Confirmation,* 36 U.C. DAVIS L. REV. 695, 698 (2003) (vetting prospective nominees).

169. *Id.* at 710 ("Judicial selection before the presidency of Ronald Reagan was primarily patronage or partisan as opposed to policy agenda driven").

170. HARRY P. STUMPF, AMERICAN JUDICIAL POLITICS 185 (2d ed. 1998).

171. *Id.* at 185–86.

172. G. Calvin MacKenzie, *Starting Over: The Presidential Appointments Process in 1997* (The Century Foundation, 1998).

173. Goldman, *supra* note 168, at 701.

174. STUMPF, *supra* note 170, at 186.

175. *Id.* at 189–90.

176. MARK SILVERSTEIN, JUDICIOUS CHOICES: THE NEW POLITICS OF SUPREME COURT CONFIRMATIONS 175 (1994) (Clinton "permitted the battlefield to shift from the confirmation process in the Senate to the selection process in the White House," in which he "grant[ed] powerful friends and foes alike a veto power over the nominee," which "assured Clinton the easy confirmation he sought").

177. Robert Cohen, *Dole Attacks Clinton on Judicial Appointments,* STAR LEDGER, Apr. 20, 1996.

178. *Judicial Activism: Defining the Problem and Its Impact: Hearings on S.J. Res. 26 before the Subcomm. on the Constitution, Federalism, and Property Rights of the Senate Comm. on the Judiciary,* 105th Cong., (1997); *Judicial Misconduct and Discipline: Hearings before the Subcomm. on Courts and Intellectual Property of the House Judiciary Comm.,* 105th Cong. (1997).

179. Data on scheduled hearings are derived from Goldman, *supra* note 168, at 709; data on delay are derived from *Justice Held Hostage: Politics and Selecting Federal Judges; The Report of the Citizens for Independent Courts Task Force on Federal Judicial Selection, in* UNCERTAIN JUSTICE: POLITICS AND AMERICA'S COURTS 50 (2000).

180. David Broder, *Partisan Sniping on Judicial Vacancies Gets Louder,* WASHINGTON POST, Jan. 3, 1998.

181. Sarah Binder & Forrest Maltzman, *Senatorial Delay in Confirming Federal Judges, 1947–1998,* 46 AM. J. POL. SCI. 190, 195 (2002).

182. Stephanie Seymour, *The Judicial Appointment Process: How Broken Is It?* 39 TULSA L. REV. 691, 702 (2004).

183. Michael J. Gerhardt, *Federal Judicial Selection as War* (pt. 3), 15 REGENT U. L. REV. 15, 31 (2002).

184. Goldman, *supra* note 168, at 709; Gerhardt, *supra* note 183 at 30–31.

185. Denning, *supra* note 156, at 84; Seymour, *supra* note 182, at 703.

186. Charles Hurt, *Four Judicial Nominees Get Hearings despite "Blue-slips,"* WASHINGTON TIMES, July 15, 2003; *Pink Slip for Blue-slip,* FORT WORTH STAR-TELEGRAM, Apr. 5, 2003.

187. Palmer, *supra* note 117, at 9–10.

188. John Nowacki, *Leahy Presides over Judicial Vacancy Crisis,* INSIGHT ON THE NEWS, June 3, 2002, at 46.

189. Jesse Holland, *Senators Mull Getting Rid of Secret Holds,* WASHINGTON POST, June 17, 2003.

190. Palmer, *supra* note 117, at 12–13.

191. *Id.*

192. The nominees were Janice Rogers Brown, Miguel Estrada, Richard Griffin, David McKeague, Carolyn Kuhl, William Myers, Priscilla Owen (who had been renominated), Charles Pickering (who had been renominated), Bill Pryor, and Henry Saal.

193. David Von Drehle, *Turmoil over Court Nominees,* WASHINGTON POST, Jan. 3, 2004 (discussing leaked memos, prepared by Kennedy staffers, reflecting a strategy to delay filling Sixth Circuit vacancies while an important case was pending).

194. Paul Kane, *GOP Cools to Judicial Gambit,* ROLL CALL, Sept. 13, 2004. I am indebted to Seth Frotman, whose excellent paper on filibusters in Senate Judiciary Committee proceedings was helpful to the development of the discussion here.

195. For a description of the events culminating in promulgation of Rule IV, see Statement of Senator Russell Feingold, Executive Business Meeting, Mar. 27, 2003, *available at* http://judiciary.senate.gov/print_member_statement.cfm?&wit_id=85.

196. 149 CONG. REC. S9951 (2003).

197. David Greene & Thomas Healy, *Battle Looms over Judges,* BALTIMORE SUN, May 6, 2001, at A1.

198. Darryl Fears, *Bush Urges Confirmation of Estrada; Democrats Cite Latino Nominees Blocked by GOP in Past,* WASHINGTON POST, Feb. 23, 2003.

199. Mary Orndorf, *US Claims Putting Pryor on Bench Constitutional,* BIRMINGHAM NEWS, Aug. 3, 2004.

200. John Cornyn, *The Constitution and the Judiciary,* OpinionJournal.com, May 6, 2003.

201. Joan Biskupic, *Hostile Senate Not Part of Bush Strategy,* USA TODAY, Mar. 10, 2002.

202. Dahlia Lithwick, *Confirmation Consternation,* SLATE, Apr. 14, 2003.

203. Nan Aron, *The Problem with "Strict Constructionist" Judges,* THE HILL, Apr. 17, 2002.

204. Neil Devins, *The Federalism-Rights Nexus: Explaining Why Senate Democrats Can Tolerate Rehnquist Court Decision-Making but Not the Rehnquist Court,* 73 U. COLO. L. REV. 1307, 1325 (2002).

CHAPTER 5

1. Jeffrey A. Segal, *Supreme Court Deference to Congress: An Examination of the Marksist Model, in* SUPREME COURT DECISION-MAKING: NEW INSTITUTIONALIST APPROACHES 255 (Cornell Clayton & Howard Gillman eds., 1999).

2. John A. Ferejohn & Larry D. Kramer, *Independent Judges, Dependent Judiciary: Institutionalizing Judicial Restraint,* 77 N.Y.U. L. REV. 962 (2002).

3. *Id.* at 997–1002. Ferejohn and Kramer discuss a fourth conflict-avoidance mechanism, "internal discipline," which refers both to the structure of appellate review and the formal mechanisms for disciplining judicial misbehavior. Unlike the

other mechanisms, which are court-generated doctrines, internal discipline mechanisms are creatures of Congress (they are discussed as such in chapter 2).

4. ERWIN CHEMERINSKY, FEDERAL JURISDICTION 49–50 (3d ed. 1999); *see also,* Maeva Marcus & Emily Van Tassel, *Judges and Legislators in the New Federal System,* 1789–1800, *in* JUDGES AND LEGISLATORS: TOWARD INSTITUTIONAL COMITY 31 (Robert A. Katzmann ed., 1988).

5. U.S. CONST. art. III, § 2.

6. For a more detailed discussion of the justiciability doctrines, see CHEMERINSKY, *supra* note 4, at 43–168.

7. Vander Jagt v. O'Beill, 699 F.2d 1166, 1178–79 (1983) (Bork, J., concurring), *quoted in* Allen v. Wright, 468 U.S. 737, 750 (1984).

8. Poe v. Ullman, 367 U.S. 497, 502–03 (1961) (citation omitted).

9. *Id.*

10. Ashwander v. Tennessee Valley Authority, 297 U.S. 288, 345 (1936) (Brandeis, J., concurring).

11. Valley Forge Christian College v. Americans United for Separation of Church and State, 454 U.S. 464, 471 (1982).

12. CHARLES ALAN WRIGHT, ARTHUR MILLER, & EDWARD COOPER, FEDERAL PRACTICE AND PROCEDURE: JURISDICTION § 3531 (1984) (citation omitted).

13. *Ashwander,* 297 U.S. 346–49 (1936) (Brandeis, J., concurring) (citations omitted).

14. Frederick Schauer, Ashwander *Revisited,* 1995 SUP. CT. REV. 71, 73.

15. *Id.* at 90–91 (citation omitted).

16. Ferejohn & Kramer, *supra* note 2, at 1034.

17. ERWIN CHEMERINSKY, FEDERAL JURISDICTION 395 (3d ed. 1999).

18. 28 U.S.C. § 1332 (2000).

19. Strawbridge v. Curtiss, 7 U.S. (3 Cranch) 267 (1806).

20. *Ex parte* Burrus, 136 U.S. 586 (1890).

21. 28 U.S.C. § 1331 (2000).

22. Louisville & Nashville Railroad v. Mottley, 211 U.S. 149 (1908).

23. Erie Railroad v. Tompkins, 304 U.S. 64 (1938).

24. *See, e.g.,* Swift v. Tyson, 41 U.S. (16 Pet.) 1 (1842) (interpreting the Rules of Decision Act (28 U.S.C. § 1652)).

25. Hans v. Louisiana, 134 U.S. 1 (1890).

26. Ferejohn & Kramer, *supra* note 2, at 1031.

27. Younger v. Harris, 401 U.S. 37 (1971); *see also* CHEMERINSKY, *supra* note 4, § 13.3.

28. Railroad Comm'n of Texas v. Pullman Co., 312 U.S. 496 (1941).

29. Louisiana Power & Light Company v. City of Thibodaux, 360 U.S. 25 (1959).

30. Burford v. Sun Oil, 319 U.S. 315 (1943).

31. Pub. L. No. 100–352, 102 Stat. 662 (1988).

32. *See, e.g.,* Charles R. Epp, *External Pressure and the Supreme Court's Agenda, in* SUPREME COURT DECISION-MAKING: NEW INSTITUTIONALIST APPROACHES

255 (Cornell Clayton & Howard Gillman eds., 1999) (discussing the impact of external mobilization and the Court's sense of institutional responsibility on agenda setting); JEFFREY A. SEGAL & HAROLD J. SPAETH, THE SUPREME COURT AND THE ATTITUDINAL MODEL 165–207 (1993) (focusing on the role of the justices' attitudes in agenda setting).

33. Ratchford v. Gay Lib, 434 U.S. 1080 (1978) (Rehnquist, J., dissenting), reh'g denied, 435 U.S. 981 (1978).

34. Id. at 1081 (Burger, C.J., dissenting).

35. Alexander Bickel, The Supreme Court 1960 Term Foreword: The Passive Virtues, 75 HARV. L. REV. 40 (1961).

36. Gerald Gunther, The Subtle Vices of the "Passive Virtues": A Comment on Principle and Expediency in Judicial Review, 64 COLUM. L. REV. 1, 25 (1964).

37. Bickel, supra note 35, at 51.

38. Anthony Kronman, Alexander Bickel's Philosophy of Prudence, 94 YALE L.J. 1567, 1585–86 (1985).

39. Schauer, supra note 14, at 91.

40. Segal, supra note 1, at 255 (Cornell Clayton & Howard Gillman eds., 1999).

41. Ferejohn & Kramer, supra note 2, at 1037.

42. 5 U.S. (1 Cranch) 137 (1803).

43. 5 U.S. (1 Cranch) 299 (1803).

44. MELVIN UROFSKY, THE SUPREME COURT JUSTICES: A BIOGRAPHICAL DICTIONARY 110–11 (1994).

45. LEON FRIEDMAN & FRED ISRAEL, 1 JUSTICES OF THE SUPREME COURT 197 (1969).

46. Barry Friedman, The History of the Countermajoritarian Difficulty (pt. 1), 73 N.Y.U. L. REV. 333, 413 (1998).

47. Barry Friedman, The History of the Countermajoritarian Difficulty (pt. 2), 91 GEO. L. J. 1, 30–31 (2002).

48. 74 U.S. (7 Wall.) 506 (1869).

49. No one seems to be quite sure who coined this famous expression. For a list of the possibilities, see Barry Friedman, The Countermajoritarian Difficulty (pt. 4), 148 U. PA. L. REV. 971 n.9 (2000). The court-packing plan is discussed in greater detail in chapter 2.

50. Maeva Marcus & Emily Van Tassel, Judges and Legislators in the New Federal System, in JUDGES AND LEGISLATORS: TOWARD INSTITUTIONAL COMITY (Robert A. Katzmann ed., 1988).

51. 28 U.S.C. § 331 (2000).

52. ELMO B. HUNTER, THE JUDICIAL CONFERENCE AND ITS COMMITTEE ON COURT ADMINISTRATION 6–12 (Federal Judicial Center 1986).

53. For example, the House hearing record on the Court Reform and Access to Justice Act of 1988 included six follow-up letters from Judicial Conference representatives who had testified before the House Judiciary Committee's subcommittee that was processing the legislation (Court Reform and Access to Justice Act: Hearings on H.R. 3152 before the Subcomm. on Courts, Civil Liberties, and the Administration of Justice of the House Comm. on the Judiciary, 100th Cong., 1st & 2d Sess. 901–17 (1987–88)).

54. Administrative Office Act of 1939, § 305, 53 Stat. 1223, 1224 (codified as amended at 28 U.S.C. § 601).

55. 28 U.S.C. § 604(a)(24) (2000).

56. William H. Rehnquist, 1996 Year-End Report on the Federal Judiciary (Jan. 1, 1997), *available at* http://www.uscourts.gov/cj96.htm.

57. *Judicial Conference and Councils in the Sunshine Act, S. 2045: Hearing before the Subcomm. on Improvements in Judicial Machinery of the U.S. Senate Comm. on the Judiciary,* 96th Cong., 2d Sess. 19 (1980) (statement of Hon. Elmo B. Hunter, chairman, Comm. on Court Admin., Judicial Conference of the United States).

58. Robert W. Kastenmeier & Michael J. Remington, *A Judicious Legislator's Lexicon to the Federal Judiciary, in* Judges and Legislators: Toward Institutional Comity 84 (Robert Katzmann ed., 1988) (discussing the Judicial Conference soliciting invitations to comment); *Judicial Conference and Councils in the Sunshine Act, S. 2045: Hearings before the Subcomm. on Improvements in Judicial Machinery of the U.S. Senate Comm. on the Judiciary,* 96th Cong., 2d Sess. 20 (1980) (Judge Elmo Hunter, asked why the Judicial Conference communicated its opposition to judicial discipline legislation without waiting for an invitation to do so, explained that at a recent conference hosted by the Brookings Institution, he "thought that [he] heard an invitation to advise the Congress at any time of any pressing need or problem of the judiciary").

59. *Federal Courts Study Comm. Implementation Act and Civil Justice Reform Act: Hearing on H.R. 5381 and H.R. 3898 before the Subcomm. on Courts, Intellectual Property, and the Administration of Justice of the House Comm. on the Judiciary,* 101st Cong., 2d Sess. 104 (1990) (statement of Robert F. Peckham, chair, Judicial Conference ad hoc Subcomm. on the Civil Justice Reform Act).

60. Saundra Torry, *Federal Courts to Experiment with Televised Civil Trials,* Washington Post, Sept. 13, 1990, at A2.

61. Remarks by Senator Russ Feingold on Judicial Pay Raise Bill (May 2003), *available at* http://www.communityrights.org/ExposesJudicialLobbying/Junkets/Feingold.asp.

62. Committee on Long Range Planning, Judicial Conference of the United States, Proposed Long Range Plan for the Federal Courts (1994), *quoted in* Peter G. McCabe, *Renewal of the Federal Rulemaking Process,* 44 Am. U. L. Rev. 1655, 1684 (1995).

63. Rules Enabling Act: Hearings before the Subcomm. on Courts, Civil Liberties, and the Administration of Justice of the House Comm. on the Judiciary, 98th Cong., 1st & 2d Sess. 196 (1983–84).

64. Minutes of Civil Rules Advisory Committee (Mar. 20 & 21, 1997), *available at* http://www.uscourts.gov/rules/Minutes/cv3–97.htm.

65. Dawn E. Johnsen, *Ronald Reagan and the Rehnquist Court on Federal Power: Presidential Influences on Constitutional Change,* 78 Ind. L.J. 363 (2003).

66. Barry Friedman & Anna Harvey, *Electing the Supreme Court,* 78 Ind. L.J. 123, 125 (2003); *see also,* J. Mitchell Pickerill & Cornell W. Clayton, *The Rehnquist Court and the Political Dynamics of Federalism,* 2 Perspectives on Politics 233 (2004).

67. Charles Gardner Geyh, *Why Judicial Elections Stink,* 64 Oh. St. L.J. 43 (2003) (discussing competing theories for caseload increases).

68. Report of the Federal Courts Study Committee 7 (1990).

69. Judith Resnik, *Constricting Remedies: The Rehnquist Judiciary, Congress, and Federal Power,* 78 Ind. L.J. 223 (2003).

70. Judicial Conference of the United States, Long Range Plan for the Federal Courts (1995).

71. Resnik, *supra* note 69, at 286–88.

72. *End May Be Coming for Diversity Jurisdiction,* 63 A.B.A. J. 477 (1977).

73. *Chief Justice Burger's 1977 Report to the American Bar Association,* 63 A.B.A. J. 504, 506 (1977).

74. U.S. Const. art III, § 2.

75. Resnik, *supra* note 69, at 224.

76. 140 Cong. Rec. 11177 (1994) (reproducing letter of Sept. 19, 1991, from William Rehnquist to Jack Brooks).

77. William Rehnquist, *Congress is Crippling Federal Courts: Ever-Expanding Number of "Federal" Crimes Belong in State Courts Instead,* St. Louis Post-Dispatch, Feb. 16, 1992.

78. Richard S. Arnold, *The Federal Courts: Causes of Discontent,* 56 SMU L. Rev. 767, 774 (2003).

79. Committee on long range planning of the Judicial Conference of the United States, *supra* note 62, at 20–23 (1994).

80. Johnsen, *supra* note 65.

81. United States v. Lopez, 514 U.S. 549 (1995).

82. Erwin Chemerinsky, Constitutional Law: Principles and Politics 194 (1997).

83. United States v. Morrison, 529 U.S. 598 (2000).

84. News Release of the Administrative Office of the U.S. Courts (Sept. 6, 2000), *available at* http://www.uscourts.gov/Press_Releases/press_090600.html.

85. News Release of the Administrative Office of the U.S. Courts (Sept. 19, 2000), *available at* http://www.uscourts.gov/Press_Releases/press09192000.html.

86. James Madison, Notes (June 4, 1787), *in* 1 The Records of the Federal Convention of 1787, at 96, 98 (Max Farrand ed., 1911).

CHAPTER 6

1. Vincent Blasi, *The Pathological Perspective and the First Amendment,* 85 Colum. L. Rev. 449 (1985) ("The undeniable importance of adaptation and, under some views of the objectives of constitutionalism, creative innovation at the margins of application should not lead us to ignore the significant role played in a constitutional regime by a core of relatively stable and consistently enforced central norms").

2. Tracy Thomas, *Congress' Section 5 Power and Remedial Rights,* 34 U.C. Davis L. Rev. 673, 701 (2001).

3. Richard B. Bernstein & Jerome Angel, *Amending America: If We Love the Constitution So Much, Why Do We Keep Trying to Change It?* 301–3 (1993).

4. Morton J. Horowitz, *Foreword: The Constitution of Change—Legal Fundamentality without Fundamentalism,* 107 HARV. L. REV. 30 (1993); Howard Gillman, *The Collapse of Constitutional Originalism and the Rise of the Notion of a "Living Constitution" in the Course of American State-Building,* 11 STUD. AM. POL. DEV. 191 (1997); Adam Winkler, *A Revolution Too Soon: Woman Suffragists and the "Living Constitution,"* 76 N.Y.U. L. REV. 1456, 1460–65 (2001).

5. Peter Shane, *When Interbranch Norms Break Down: Of Arms-for-Hostages, "Orderly Shutdowns," Presidential Impeachments, and Judicial "Coups,"* 12 CORNELL J.L. & PUB. POL'Y 503, 513 (2003).

6. James G. Wilson, *American Constitutional Conventions: The Judicially Unenforceable Rules That Combine with Judicial Doctrine and Public Opinion to Regulate Political Behavior,* 40 BUFF. L. REV. 645, 651–52 (1992).

7. Peter M. Shane, *Interbranch Accountability in State Government and the Constitutional Requirement of Judicial Independence,* 61 LAW & CONTEMP. PROBS. 21, 30 (1998).

8. Jerome Frank, *Law and the Modern Mind* (1930), *reprinted in* AMERICAN LEGAL REALISM 206–7 (William W. Fisher III et al. eds., 1993).

9. Benjamin Cardozo, *The Nature of the Judicial Process* (1921), in AMERICAN LEGAL REALISM, *supra* note 8, at 176–77.

10. Max Radin, *The Theory of Judicial Decision: Or How Judges Think* (1925), in AMERICAN LEGAL REALISM, *supra* note 8, at 196.

11. See the introduction to the present book.

12. Joseph William Singer, *Legal Realism Now,* 76 CAL. L. REV. 465, 467 (1988).

13. G. Alan Tarr, *Rethinking the Selection of State Supreme Court Justices,* 39 WILLAMETTE L. REV. 1445, 1460 (2003) (citing Frances Kahn Zemens, *The Accountable Judge. Guardian of Judicial Independence,* 72 S. CAL. L. REV. 625, 640 (1999)) Tarr's comments, although offered in an analysis of state courts, apply with equal force to their federal counterparts. It is relatively clear that the general public does not distinguish between state and federal courts when expressing their general views on judges and the judiciary.

14. American Bar Association, JUSTICE IN JEOPARDY: REPORT OF THE COMMISSION ON THE 21ST CENTURY JUDICIARY 17 (2003).

15. Greenberg, Quinlan, Rosner Research Inc., *Justice at Stake Frequency Questionnaire* (Nov. 7, 2001), *available at* http://faircourts.org/files/JASNationalSurvey Results.pdf.

16. Will Lester, *Poll: Most Want Assertive Senate on Judges,* ASSOCIATED PRESS, May 20, 2005.

17. Martha Neil, *Half of U.S. Sees: "Judicial Activism Crisis,"* ABA Journal E-Report, Sept. 30, 2005.

18. Jack M. Balkin & Sanford Levinson, *Understanding the Constitutional Revolution,* 87 VA. L. REV. 1045 (2001).

19. Paul Kane, *Parties Reach Agreement on Judicial Nominations,* ROLL CALL, May 19, 2004.

20. 110 Stat. 3009–546 et seq. §§ 304–6, 381, 604.

21. 110 Stat. 1321–66.

22. Pub. L. No. 104–132, 110 Stat. 1214 (1996).

23. Patrick J. McDonnell, *Panel Upholds Deadline for Amnesty Seekers,* L.A. TIMES, May 1, 1997, at A3 (statement of Ira Mehlman of the Federation for American Immigration Reform).

24. John Sullivan, *States and Cities Removing Prisons from Courts' Grip,* N.Y. TIMES, Jan. 30, 2000, at A1 (quoting "one of its chief legislative proponents").

25. 142 CONG. REC. S3352–01 (Apr. 16, 1996).

26. Vicki C. Jackson, *Introduction: Congressional Control of Jurisdiction and the Future of Federal Courts—Opposition, Agreement, and Hierarchy,* 86 GEO. L.J. 2445, 2448–53 (1998).

27. Alexander Bolton, *Courts May Be Stripped on Pledge,* THE HILL, Sept. 16, 2004, at 1.

28. David M. Zlotnick, *The War within the War on Crime: The Congressional Assault on Judicial Sentencing Discretion,* 57 SMU L. REV. 211, 215–18; David Margolick, *Judicial Dissent,* AUSTIN AMERICAN-STATESMAN, May 24, 1992, at E1.

29. Zlotnick, *supra* note 28, at 218–20.

30. *Mandatory Minimums in Drug Sentencing: A Valuable Weapon in the War on Drugs or a Handcuff on Judicial Decision,* 36 AM. CRIM. L. REV. 1279, 1298 (1999).

31. Sentencing Reform Act of 1984, 28 U.S.C. § 992; Anti-Drug Abuse Act of 1986, 21 U.S.C. § 841. For criticism of these enactments by a government commission comprised of judges, legislators, and lawyers, see REPORT OF THE FEDERAL COURTS STUDY COMMITTEE 133–36 (1990).

32. Philip Oliss, *Mandatory Minimum Sentencing: Discretion, the Safety Valve, and the Sentencing Guidelines,* 63 U. CIN. L. REV. 1851, 1851–52 (1995).

33. *See, e.g.,* Editorial, *War against Civil Liberties,* ST. LOUIS POST-DISPATCH, Oct. 31, 1992, at 2B (agreeing with the Cato Institute that mandatory minimum sentences have "compromised judicial independence").

34. *See* Margolick, *supra* note 28.

35. David Rubenstein, *Rosenbaum Inquisition,* THE NATION, Dec. 29, 2003.

36. Tony Mauro, *Rehnquist Begins New Year with Stern Words,* LEGAL INTELLIGENCER, Jan. 6, 2004, at National News 4.

37. Tom Feeney, *Rep. Feeney Defends Measure to Thwart Sentencing by Whim,* PALM BEACH DAILY BUSINESS REVIEW, Apr. 28, 2003, at A7.

38. Ian Urbina, *New York's Federal Judges Protest Sentencing Procedures,* N.Y. TIMES, Dec. 8, 2003, at B1. I thank Joel Mayers for compiling these articles in an informative seminar paper.

39. *Id.*

40. Urbina, *supra* note 38.

41. *Id.*

42. U.S. v. Detwiler, 338 F. Supp. 1166 (D. Or. 2004).

43. U.S. v. Kirsch, 287 F. Supp. 2d 1005, 1006 (D. Minn. 2003).

44. U.S. v. Booker, 125 S. Ct. 738 (2005).

45. Dan Christensen, *The Short Life of the Feeney Amendment,* 46 BROWARD DAILY BUS. REV., No. 31 (Jan. 24, 2005).

46. Reverend Louis P. Sheldon, *Our Battle Plan to Take Back the Courts,* http://www.OurBattlePlan.com.

47. James Morone, Hellfire Nation: The Politics of Sin in American History (2003).

48. *Id.* at 497.

49. For a timeline of developments in the Schiavo case, *see, The Terri Schiavo Case,* N.Y. Times, A16, April 1, 2005.

50. Bob Egelko, *Schiavo Case Widens Divide Between Congress and Courts,* San Francisco Chronicle, A3, April 2, 2005.

51. Charles Babington, *GOP Is Fracturing over Power of Judiciary,* Washington Post, April 7, 2005.

52. Carl Hulse & David Kirkpatrick, *Even Death Does Not Quiet Harsh Political Fight,* N.Y. Times, April 1, 2005, at A1.

53. Carl Hulse & David Kirkpatrick, *Casting an Angry Eye on Courts, Conservatives Prime for Bench-Clearing Brawl in Congress,* N.Y. Times, March 23, 2005, at A15.

54. Rick Klein, *DeLay Apologizes for Blaming Federal Judges in Schiavo Case but House Leader Calls for Probe of "Judicial Activism,"* Boston Globe, April 14, 2005.

55. Ruth Marcus, *Booting the Bench,* Washington Post, April 11, 2005.

56. Pamela MacLean, *Does the Judiciary Need a Watchdog?* National Law Journal, May 23, 2005.

57. Gwyneth Shaw & Gail Gibson, *For Congress, a Quiet Retreat From Schiavo Politics,* Baltimore Sun, 1A, March 27, 2005.

58. Bob Egelko, *Schiavo Case Widens Divide Between Courts and Congress,* San Francisco Chronicle, A3, April 2, 2005.

59. Shaw & Gibson, *supra* note 57.

60. Charles Babington, *Frist Urges End to Nominee Filibusters,* Washington Post, April 25, 2005.

61. Jesse Holland, *Panel Resends Blocked Bush Nominees,* Associated Press, March 18, 2005.

62. Erwin Chemerinsky, *The Jurisprudence of Justice Scalia: A Critical Appraisal,* 22 U. Haw. L. Rev. 385 (2000) (referencing Scalia's dissents).

63. Lawrence v. Texas, 123 S. Ct. 2472, 2496 (2003) (Scalia, J., dissenting).

64. Brown v. Legal Found. of Wash., 123 S. Ct. 1406, at 1428 (Scalia, J. dissenting).

65. J.E.B. v. Alabama *ex rel.* T.B., 511 U.S. 127, 163 (1994) (Scalia, J., dissenting).

66. Romer v. Evans, 517 U.S. 620, 653 (1996) (Scalia, J., dissenting).

67. Planned Parenthood of S.E. Pa. v. Casey, 505 U.S. 833, 1000 (1992) (Scalia, J., dissenting).

68. Remarks of Clarence Thomas to the National Bar Association in Memphis, TN (July 29, 1998), *printed in* Washington Times, July 31, 1998, at A21.

69. Richard Carelli, *Civility Reigns at Supreme Court,* Associated Press, June 12, 1998.

70. Kristofor J. Hammond, *Judicial Intervention in a Twenty-First Century Republic: Shuffling Deck Chairs on the Titanic?* 74 Ind. L.J. 653 (1999).

71. *See, e.g.,* Terri Jennings Peretti, *Does Judicial Independence Exist? The Lessons of Social Science Research,* in JUDICIAL INDEPENDENCE AT THE CROSSROADS: AN INTERDISCIPLINARY APPROACH 103, 111 (Stephen Burbank & Barry Friedman eds., 2002) ("The assumption that independent judges use their freedom to decide impartially according to law is contradicted by the empirical evidence").

72. One striking exception is C.K. ROLAND & ROBERT A. CARP, POLITICS AND JUDGMENT IN FEDERAL DISTRICT COURTS (1996).

Index

Page numbers in italic refer to tables.